THE REBECCA RIOTS

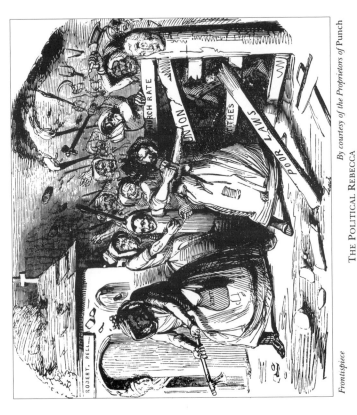

Frontispiece   *By courtesy of the Proprietors of Punch*

THE POLITICAL REBECCA

The rioting is used to illustrate national politics. The gate-keeper is Sir Robert Peel, and the gate-posts, two members of his government. The woman with an axe and a satchel inscribed 'Rint' is Daniel O'Connell

THE
REBECCA RIOTS

A Study in Agrarian Discontent

By

DAVID WILLIAMS

CARDIFF

UNIVERSITY OF WALES PRESS

1986

© Hilarie M. Williams, 1978

First published 1955
Reprinted 1971
Paperback edition 1986
Reprinted 1992
Reprinted 1998

British Library Cataloguing in Publication Data

A catalogue record for this book is available from the British Library

ISBN 0–7083-0933–X

Cover illustration courtesy of The Illustrated London News Picture Library
Cover design by Neil Angove
Printed in Wales by Dinefwr Press, Llandybïe

To

the memory of
my parents
DAVID & ANNE WILLIAMS
and their forbears
Sons and Daughters of Rebecca

And they blessed Rebekah and said unto her,
let thy seed possess the gates of those which
hate them.

Genesis, xxiv, 60

PREFACE

The Rebecca Riots in West Wales began in the summer of 1839. They ceased as suddenly as they had started, and for three and a half years the countryside was undisturbed. Then, in the winter of 1842, they broke out again with greater violence, and, this time, continued throughout the following year. They spread like a contagion, first along the borders of Carmarthenshire and Pembrokeshire, then into the Teify valley, afterwards into the Towy valley, and finally into the semi-industrialised area of south Carmarthenshire. Outside this compact geographical region there were very few incidents. Harriet Martineau described them as 'the strangest series of riots that has occurred in our time'. By day the countryside seemed quiet, but at night fantastically disguised horsemen careered along highways and through narrow lanes on their mysterious errands. They developed uncanny skill in evading the police and the infantry, and, mounted though they were on their unwieldy farm horses, they also succeeded in outwitting the dragoons. The *Annual Register* spoke of the incredulity with which news of their exploits was received, of the amusement at the discomfiture of the authorities, and of the uneasiness caused by this evidence of unsuspected social malaise. Admittedly it was a rebellion *pour rire*, but it had a sinister undertone.

A highly intelligent writer in the *Revue des deux Mondes* saw that the riots were such stuff as myths are made on. In a hundred years' time, he foretold, Rebecca would be personified in one man, the leader of a jacquerie who, like Robin Hood, administered natural justice. Rebecca has, indeed, become part of the folk-tradition of West Wales. Nothing in the history of Welsh Nonconformity is more remarkable than the attraction which this recourse to violence has had for it. The movement has usually been represented as the uprising of an oppressed peasantry, particularly against the burden of the toll-gates. Its causes were far more deep-seated than that; the gates were only tangible objects which could be destroyed. The early nineteenth century saw a breakdown in the social structure of rural Wales, with its outmoded systems of government and administration, when the pressure of a greatly increased population upon a backward economy produced disturbances. The early chapters of this book are therefore devoted to an analysis of the social structure and to an examination of the underlying factors which brought about its collapse.

I have to thank a great many correspondents for information, and I have recorded my indebtedness to them in footnotes. Their interest is, itself, a social phenomenon. It lies, however, almost exclusively in minute details of particular incidents. To have brought these into the text would have meant overloading the narrative to the point of unreadability. It is on this account that the narrative chapters have been somewhat excessively documented, so that local historians may know where to look for further information on matters of interest to them.

I also have to thank the staffs of the National Library of Wales and of the Public Record Office for much courtesy over many years, as well as Mr. J. F. Jones, the curator of the Carmarthenshire County Museum. Sir Frederick Rees has kindly read the early chapters in manuscript, and I have profited by his discernment as on many previous occasions. I have profited also from the expert cartographical skill of Dr. Margaret Davies, who very kindly prepared the sketch maps, and from the constant advice of Dr. Elwyn Davies in seeing the book through the press. My wife relieved me of much tedium in preparing the index.

The publication of this book has been aided by a generous grant from the Thomas Ellis Memorial Fund, which is here gratefully acknowledged.

DAVID WILLIAMS

UNIVERSITY COLLEGE OF WALES
ABERYSTWYTH
31 *December* 1954

CONTENTS

ILLUSTRATIONS

MAPS

Chapter I

THE GENTRY OF WEST WALES

THE land of West Wales has an individuality of its own. Rivers running to the west and south, which, with their innumerable tributaries, are its main characteristic, bind it together irrespective of county boundaries. The northern part of Cardiganshire lies outside this region; it looks towards the Dovey estuary, and, in dialect as in sentiment, has a close affinity with North Wales. The River Teify, on the other hand, which forms the boundary between Cardiganshire and Carmarthenshire for a great part of its course, is the unifying factor in the valley through which it flows, and this, to a lesser extent, is true of the Loughor which divides Carmarthenshire from Glamorgan. In no sense do these rivers mark any distinct cultural divisions, and they can have been chosen as administrative boundaries only because their definiteness precluded the possibility of dispute. Around this region there is a wide expanse of open moorland. It reaches the considerable height of two and a half thousand feet at Plynlymon in the north and the Black Mountain in the south, but is not otherwise very high. It is its width which has made of it a formidable barrier, and this was especially so in days when communication and transport were more difficult than in ours. Even today it can be impassable in winter, for it is crossed by few main routes. On a clear day the traveller may well find himself in an isolated spot where one rounded hill seems to lie behind another indefinitely. Yet, once the land begins to dip, he is soon down in a wooded valley, with farm-houses and cultivated fields. He is, nevertheless, conscious of having crossed over from one region into another. The Wye and the Usk and the Tawe, and the streams which feed them, lead to lowlands where men speak a different dialect, or even a different language, and follow a different way of life.

Within this unity there is infinite diversity of landscape.
The long coastline itself presents much variety. In Cardiganshire the narrow coastal strip is, in places, cultivated almost
to the cliff's edge, although its green fields are interspersed
by many creeks with sandy beaches where small ports have
grown to importance and then decayed. This gives way in
Pembrokeshire to rugged cliffs and stormy headlands, the
haunts of innumerable birds. Here, even the monotony of
a sea horizon is broken by several islands, ranging in size
from Ramsey, which is large enough to be inhabited, to
barren rocks like the Bishop and his Clerks. It was of the
latter that George Owen, the historian of Pembrokeshire,
remarked in the sixteenth century that they 'preached deadly
doctrine to their winter audience', although they had, he
said, the undoubted merit of being always in residence,
unlike his contemporaries, the dignitaries of the neighbouring
cathedral of St. David's. The magnificent inlet of Milford
Haven pierces deep into the shire, but beyond, again, is the
rocky coast with its beaches of golden sand. Finally, in
Carmarthenshire, there are marshy flats where man, for
generations, has striven against the ever-encroaching sea.
In some places, as at Laugharne and Kidwelly, he has
succeeded in recovering large areas, and converting them
into fertile land; in others the sea has gained the victory,
and the coastal village of Hawton lies forever buried beneath
the sand-dunes.

The backbone of West Wales is formed by a continuation
of the Plynlymon moorland, which runs between the parallel
rivers, the Teify and the Towy, and ends in the Presely hills
in Pembrokeshire. Destitute of trees in its higher reaches, it
is bleak and formidable in winter, but in summer it bursts
into colour with its stretches of gorse and of heather. It has
made of north Carmarthenshire a land which has scarcely
a mile of even ground. The river valleys on either side are
rich in pasture. Their mild climate and fertile earth have
given them a greenness of vegetation rivalled only in the
lowlands of south Pembrokeshire. These rivers are the

arteries of the land, and it is along their banks that are to be found, almost jostling one another by their proximity, the mansions of the gentry who dominated the life of this neighbourhood for a dozen generations, and who formed one of the opposing classes in the struggle which it is the purpose of this book to describe.

In broad outline, this western peninsula corresponds to the ancient kingdom of Deheubarth, which had its capital at Dinefwr, a hill-top citadel in the vale of Towy, near the town of Llandeilo. With the passing of the centuries the line of its kings and princes lost its power, and, indeed, almost vanished, though some trace of kingly descent remained in the family of Abermarlais, lords of the manor of Llansadwrn. They were entirely overshadowed in the fifteenth century by the rise of a new house, whose founder, Gruffydd ap Nicholas, leased the Dinefwr lands from the Crown. His son married the heiress of Abermarlais, so that his grandson, Rhys ap Thomas, had in his veins the blood of ancient kings. Valiant service to King Henry VII won for him the Garter and the virtual rulership of West Wales. He lived in regal estate in his castle of Carew in south Pembrokeshire, and the seventeenth-century historian, Fuller, says of him, that although 'he was never more than a knight, he was little less than a prince in his native country'. His grandson's ambition brought ruin to the house and execution for treason to himself. Never again did the family entirely regain its former eminence. In time its Carmarthenshire estates were restored, but it did not recover its lands in Pembrokeshire. Occasionally a member of the house of Dinefwr sat in parliament in the succeeding centuries, but did so with no distinction until the election in 1754 of George Rice, who represented Carmarthenshire for twenty-five years and may well be regarded as the second founder of his house. He held offices in the government of George II, but more important than this was his marriage, in 1756, to the only daughter and heiress of William, second Baron

Talbot of Hensol in Glamorgan. The first Baron Talbot, lord chancellor of England, had himself married an heiress, thereby acquiring the land which was to form 'the mineral kingdom' leased by Anthony Bacon, the founder of the great ironworks at Cyfarthfa. The second Baron Talbot secured an earldom, and moreover, since this title would lapse at his death through the lack of a male heir, succeeded in having conferred upon himself a barony, taking its name from Dinefwr, his son-in-law's estate, with special reversion to his daughter. Thereby she, in turn, became Baroness Dynevor, and, on her death, her son, George Talbot, became third baron. He lived most of his time at Barrington Park, the lord chancellor's seat near Burford, but, in 1817, he resumed his paternal name of Rice, and he served as lord-lieutenant of Carmarthenshire.

When the Rebecca Riots first seriously disturbed his peace in 1842, Lord Dynevor was an old man of seventy-seven. He therefore delegated his duties of organising resistance to the rioters to his son, George Rice, who had adopted the additional name of Trevor on inheriting an estate in Sussex. George Rice Trevor was then forty-seven years of age, and he had sat in parliament for Carmarthenshire since 1820. Not only was he by birth the 'natural leader' in West Wales; he was, in addition, widely experienced in both local and central administration. He was an active, resourceful and fair-minded man. But his life was clouded by what must have been to him a grave misfortune. He was, himself, the twelfth in direct male descent from the great Sir Rhys ap Thomas, but he had, to succeed him, only four daughters. Thus, when he died in 1869, after having become fourth baron, most of the family wealth passed to his daughters, leaving merely the Carmarthenshire estate and the title to his cousin, the fifth Baron Dynevor.

Despite the pre-eminence of the Dynevor family, its seven thousand acre estate in West Wales was dwarfed by the seventy thousand acres of its chief rivals, the Cawdors of Stackpole and of Golden Grove.[1] Here again the family fortunes had been established by a combination of real ability and fortunate circumstance. Marriage with the heiress of the Lorts of Stackpole had brought Sir Alexander Campbell of Cawdor, in Nairnshire, in the north of Scotland, down to south Pembrokeshire. He thereby obtained an estate which covered virtually the whole of seven parishes south of Milford Haven, as well as a considerable part of another three.[2] His son, John, who has been described as perhaps the ablest representative of an able race,[3] married a Pryse, of the ancient family. of Gogerddan, near Aberystwyth, and acquired lands in Cardiganshire.[4] It was their grandson, John Campbell, who was raised to the peerage as Baron Cawdor in 1796. Early in the following year he acquired considerable renown, when a French force descended upon Pembrokeshire in 'the last invasion of Britain'. The lord-lieutenant was Lord Milford of Picton Castle. Lord Cawdor was then forty-one years of age, and the lord-lieutenant was thirteen years his senior, but Cawdor, to use his own words, 'found it necessary after some conversation with Lord Milford to offer to take the whole (command) on myself',[5] and he did so with energy and complete success, although it may, perhaps, be doubted whether his intervention was entirely appreciated by Lord Milford. Seven years later, by a freak of fortune which has never been adequately explained, he succeeded to the vast estates of the Vaughans of Golden Grove, thus becoming a near neighbour to Lord Dynevor in the vale of Towy.

The Vaughans had risen to eminence through the favour of the Stuarts. John Vaughan received the title of earl of Carbery at the hands of James I, and his son, the second earl, somewhat ignominiously commanded the royalist forces in South Wales in the Civil War. The peerage lapsed with the third earl through lack of a male heir, but the estates passed to his daughter, the duchess of Bolton. Throughout this period, which covered the whole of the seventeenth century, the Vaughans of Golden Grove dominated the life of Carmarthenshire, and, with very few

2

breaks, continuously represented both the shire and borough
of Carmarthen in parliament. The duchess died without
issue, and her estates passed to a kinsman, whose grandson,
John Vaughan, bequeathed them, in 1804, not to any one
of his many relatives but to his friend, John Campbell, the
first Baron Cawdor. According to tradition the two men
had in their youth made the Grand Tour together, and, on
the continent, in order to prevent difficulties should either
of them die suddenly while abroad, had made wills
bequeathing the whole of their possessions to each other.
Vaughan's will, however, dated as late as 1786, entirely
disproves this story, although it offers no explanation for
his strange action.[6] Whatever the reason for it may have
been, the Campbells thereby became the largest landowners
in West Wales. They held in Pembrokeshire one of the
finest consolidated estates in the kingdom, all of it valuable
land, with no mountain, waste or common.[7] They now
acquired some fifty thousand acres in Carmarthenshire, and
became lords of twenty-five manors covering almost half
the county, including vast stretches of waste land. Here they
exercised manorial rights which were almost regal in nature,
for some were derived from the ancient lands of the royal
house of Lancaster. The manorial courts continued to be
held, and though their functions were declining in importance, the quit rents and court fees were still considerable.[8]
In addition there were the Cardiganshire estates, together
with rents and royalties from quarries and leadmines.[9]
Finally, the Campbells were patrons of a dozen livings
within the three shires.[10] To this great patrimony
John Frederick Campbell succeeded in 1821, when he was
thirty-one years of age, and six years later he was raised to
an earldom, as Earl Cawdor and Viscount Emlyn, the latter
title being held by his son. The earl, like his forbears, was
active in public affairs as well as in furthering his private
interests, and to him, more than to anyone else, was due the
abolition in 1830 of the Courts of Great Sessions which had

provided Wales, for three centuries, with a separate system for the administration of justice.[11]

The houses of Dinefwr and of Golden Grove were easily first in importance in West Wales, but scarcely less influential, through its many ramifications, was the clan of the Philippses. It proudly traced descent from Cadifor the Great, lord of West Wales at the time of the Norman Conquest, and derived its origin from Cil-sant, on the borders of Carmarthenshire and Pembrokeshire. The Philippses had become settled at Cwmgwili, near Carmarthen, and at Pentypark, near Haverfordwest, and, through marriage, a member of the family had acquired the Picton estate in Pembrokeshire. The greatest of their race was the 'good' Sir John Philipps of Picton Castle, who, in the opening years of the eighteenth century, had devoted much of the vast wealth which he had inherited and had acquired through marriage to objects of philanthropy. His son, the sixth baronet (also named Sir John Philipps) was, according to his cousin, Horace Walpole, 'a notorious Jacobite', and in his day the clan played an outstanding part in the tumultuous politics of the shire and borough of Carmarthen. The seventh baronet, Sir Richard Philipps, became Lord Milford in 1776, and was the lord-lieutenant at the time of the French landing at Fishguard, but he died in 1823 without issue, and the title lapsed. The Picton estate of over twenty thousand acres[12] passed to a distant cousin, Richard Grant, who assumed the name and arms of Philipps, and was, himself, created Baron Milford in 1847, after having represented Haverfordwest in parliament for nineteen years.

The chief opponents of the Picton Castle interests in Pembrokeshire were the Owens of Orielton, a mansion some three miles from Pembroke, and only a mile or two, as the crow flies, from Lord Cawdor's seat at Stackpole. The Owens came originally from Anglesey, and had obtained Orielton through marriage in Queen Elizabeth's time. But the last of the direct line died unmarried in 1809, and his vast estates in Pembrokeshire and in North Wales,

together with eight thousand acres in Tasmania, also passed
to a distant cousin, John Lord, who assumed the name of
Owen and was created a baronet by fresh patent in 1813.[13]
The new squire had had sufficient recklessness in his youth
to be married at Gretna Green, but he was an extremely
able man, and was a barrister by profession. He lived in
great splendour at Orielton, and in his day the domination
of the political life of Pembrokeshire by the Owens of Orielton
reached its highest point. He sat in parliament for fifty-one
years. His extravagant mode of life and his enormous
electioneering expenses overtaxed his resources, and Orielton was sold some years before his death in 1861. His son
succeeded to his father's title, but to very little else. He
successfully retained his father's seat in two more elections,
but, after that, the Owens of Orielton, who had sat in
seventy-six   parliaments,   were   not   seen   again   at
Westminster.[14]

In Cardiganshire the rival houses were Gogerddan and
Crosswood (Trawsgoed). Of the two, the former was of
greater antiquity, for it claimed descent from the ancient
princes of Ceredigion, and since the sixteenth century it had
been supreme in the northern part of the shire. The discovery
of lead upon the estate had brought the family considerable
wealth, but the mines soon became exhausted. Like so many
other old Welsh families, the house of Gogerddan ended, in
the late eighteenth century, in an heiress who had married
an Englishman. Their only son, Pryse Loveden, resumed
the family surname in 1798, and, as Pryse Pryse, he represented the boroughs of Cardigan in parliament for thirty
years. He owned an estate of thirty thousand acres, much
of it woodland and sheepwalks and barren open moorland.
It produced a gross rental, however, of some ten thousand
pounds a year.[15] Half-a-dozen miles across country to the
south was the rival house of Crosswood, with an estate of
forty thousand acres, about half of which, again, consisted
of rough pasture and mountain land.[16] An estimate of its
rental in the first decade of the nineteenth century placed

it, also, at ten thousand pounds a year.[17] The Vaughans of Crosswood had emerged into importance in the seventeenth century, when the family fortunes had been established by John Vaughan, who had temporised during the Civil War, but had become, after the Restoration, chief justice of the Court of Common Pleas. His grandson, who succeeded him, was a strong supporter of the Revolution of 1688, and was made Viscount Lisburne by the government of William III. The Vaughans of the early eighteenth century were, therefore, strongly Whig in sympathy, in contrast with the Pryses of Gogerddan, who were Jacobites. The Vaughans, also, acquired wealth through exploiting the mineral deposits found on the waste land of their manors. In 1776, the fourth viscount was created earl of Lisburne. The Rebecca Riots took place during the lifetime of his grandson, the fourth earl, but he did not take an active part in their suppression (the rioting, in fact, barely reached the limits of his estates). In the next decade he represented Cardiganshire in parliament for a few years.

Closely associated with Gogerddan and Crosswood were the two satellite houses of Hafod and Nanteos. Unlike every other mansion in West Wales, Hafod was situated, not on the coastal plain or in one of the fertile lowland valleys, but seven hundred feet above sea-level, in a country of steep hills and narrow ravines and waterfalls. It passed by marriage in the early eighteenth century into the possession of the Johnes, an old Carmarthenshire and Cardiganshire family, but it was in no sense noteworthy until the romantic Thomas Johnes succeeded to the estates in 1780 and decided to make Hafod his home. He made its name known throughout the length and breadth of the land, for not only did he decree that there should arise in this rocky wilderness a stately Gothic palace, girdled around by gardens and caverns and grottoes, but he improved upon nature itself by planting four million trees.[18] Fate dealt with him unkindly. His only son died in infancy; his other child, a daughter, when she was twenty-seven. In 1807 his mansion was destroyed by fire, and with it part of his collection of books and works of art; and although, with great courage, he immediately undertook to rebuild, his losses and his extravagance involved him in financial embarrassment, and he had to leave Hafod. Nevertheless for twenty years without a break he represented Cardiganshire in the house of commons as the nominee of Lord Lisburne.[19] On his death in 1816 he was succeeded as member for Cardiganshire by William Edward Powell of Nanteos. Like the earls of Lisburne, the fortunes of the Powells had been established by a judge, Sir Thomas Powell, successively baron of the Exchequer and justice of the King's Bench. But Sir Thomas owed his elevation to James II, and, unlike the Vaughans, was therefore a Tory. His son acquired Nanteos by marriage. In time the Powells obtained much of the land of Strata Florida, and, also, the abbey's most treasured possession, the Cup of Healing, said to have been made from the wood of the True Cross. The discovery of a rich vein of lead near Strata Florida in 1751 wrought great changes in the family fortunes. Disputes immediately broke out between the Crown, which claimed mineral rights on the waste lands of what it held to be ancient Crown manors, and the local landowning families, notably those of Nanteos and Crosswood, who claimed that the land was freehold. The superintendent of Crown mines in Cardiganshire was the Welsh litterateur, Lewis Morris, and he proceeded to exploit the newly discovered vein. But he soon had to contend with rioting instigated by the landowners themselves. This reached a climax in February 1753, when a mob, led by two magistrates, seized the mine by force, and conveyed Lewis Morris to Cardigan gaol. Hitherto Nanteos had been allied to Gogerddan, but the protracted litigation which followed this riot, and their common interests, brought Nanteos and Crosswood together, and in the important election of 1761 Nanteos supported Crosswood against Gogerddan,[20] although unsuccessfully. Henceforth the alliance was unbroken, and it was as the Lisburne nominee that

Thomas Edward Powell represented Cardiganshire continuously in parliament from 1816 to 1854. When he retired (two months before his death) it was to make way for the earl of Lisburne himself. Powell was also lord-lieutenant of Cardiganshire and colonel of militia. If we are to judge by his letters he found the Rebecca Riots a sore trial to his patience.

The lists of high sheriffs for the three shires of West Wales give an indication of the remarkable number of lesser gentry who lived within this area. Sometimes their estates were considerable. That of Edwinsford (Rhydodyn) on the Cothi, a tributary of the Towy, amounted to some ten thousand acres.[21] By the strange fatality which seemed to overtake Welsh houses in the late eighteenth century it passed through an heiress to an Englishman, James Hamlyn, whose son added the family name of Williams to his own. In addition there were many estates of over a thousand acres, but others amounted to only a few hundreds, and very frequently these were mortgaged to the extreme limit. However meagre they were in rents, they were, nevertheless, rich in prestige or, at least, in pretentiousness. Their owners were often distantly related to the great magnates, as well they might be, for these were nothing if not prolific. The great Sir Rhys ap Thomas, for example, in addition to his legitimate offspring, acknowledged fourteen bastards, ten by his favourite concubine, the sister of the abbot of Talley, and four by other ladies.[22] Many families in West Wales must therefore have been united in blood to the house of Dinefwr. Others were the last vestiges of what may have been still older Welsh and Norman stocks. Moreover, this class, which lived by the rents and profits of land, merged imperceptibly into another class of owners who lived by farming themselves. Many of these, also, were encumbered with mortgages, and were unable to withstand the economic crisis of the early nineteenth century.

Notice has already been taken of the surprising number
of Englishmen who succeeded to Welsh estates by marrying
their heiresses. Others bought estates when they came on
the market. Frequently the new owners had made fortunes
in trade, and wished to invest their wealth in land, which
was still the chief source of social prestige and of political
influence. The most notable example in West Wales,
Sir William Paxton, was a London banker who had amassed
a great fortune in India. With this he bought an estate in
the vale of Towy and built an elegant mansion at Middleton
Hall. His political aspirations will be noticed later, and his
association with Carmarthenshire proved temporary, but
he has left a permanent mark on the landscape in Paxton's
Tower, a surprising triangular edifice surmounted by
a turret which he raised in honour of Nelson and which can
be seen for miles around.[23]

The advent of other newcomers was in more obscure
circumstances, and two instances must be noticed here,
since the individuals concerned are important dramatis
personæ in the narrative which is to follow. Of these,
William Chambers, senior, came to Llanelly House in 1825,
from Bicknor in Kent, as life-tenant of the Stepney estate.
The Stepneys themselves had come to Pembrokeshire in the
sixteenth century, when union with England had opened up
Wales to the English gentry, and Alban Stepneth had established himself at Prendergast by Haverfordwest, building up
a great fortune by marrying two heiresses.[24] The family
acquired a consolidated estate in Carmarthenshire when
three successive Stepneys married the heiresses of Llanelly,
Llangennech, and Derwydd. Sir John Stepney, the eighth
baronet, a son of the last marriage, was minister at the courts
of Dresden and Berlin. He died unmarried in 1811, and the
baronetcy passed to his brother, Sir Thomas Stepney,
a groom of the bedchamber to the duke of York. He was an
eccentric character, described by a contemporary as one of
the 'loungers of the old school, who at the meridian hour
daily saunter on the steps of Brooks's, and its neighbouring

pavement', and his person was said to be 'as well-known in St. James's Street as the golden cross on the top of St. Paul's Cathedral'.[25] Sir Thomas did not, however, succeed to the estates. According to family tradition Sir John Stepney had quarrelled with his relatives, and wished to spite them by tying up his property in his will and leaving it to strangers. Certainly his will is so extraordinary as to be almost incredible, and still more extraordinary is the fact that one legatee after another died without heirs until the estate passed in 1825 to William Chambers. Meanwhile, Llanelly House had been deserted by the family for sixty years.[26]

William Chambers, senior, was then fifty-one years of age, and his son, William Chambers, junior, was sixteen. They decided to make the mansion in Llanelly their home. The town was on the eve of a period of great economic expansion, and for thirty years a leading part in its development was played by both father and son. In 1828, the father became high sheriff of Carmarthenshire.[27] The son, who was educated at St. John's College, Cambridge,[28] was a man of markedly liberal opinions. He soon joined his father on the bench of magistrates; in fact, at the time of the Rebecca Riots, they were the only resident magistrates in Llanelly.[29] He was one of the founders, in 1839, of the Llanelly Reform Society. It was in the following year that he made his greatest contribution to the industrial development of the town, when he established the South Wales Pottery at an outlay of ten thousand pounds. His part in the Rebecca Riots was much misunderstood, for his liberal sympathies led him to accept an invitation to be chairman at one of the most important of Rebecca's demonstrations by day, while as a magistrate he vigorously suppressed her activities by night. On this account he was not entirely trusted by the authorities, while, on the other hand, his property was set on fire by the rioters. Nevertheless he continued to live in Llanelly. He served as chairman of its Board of Guardians, and when, in 1850, the corrupt oligarchy of burgesses which administered the town's estates was replaced by a local

Board of Health, he became its first chairman. His father died in 1855, and the Llanelly estate then reverted (although only after a long and expensive law suit) to the Stepney family. William Chambers thereupon purchased Hafod, which had changed hands more than once since the days of Thomas Johnes. He, in turn, had surrendered it before he died in 1882.[30]

Even more radical, and enigmatic, was the conduct of Edward Crompton Lloyd Hall, the heir to the Cilgwyn estate. This small property of some sixteen hundred acres[31] was situated on the Cardiganshire side of the Teify, near Newcastle Emlyn. The Lloyds of Cilgwyn had dominated Adpar, the part of Newcastle Emlyn which lies across the river and which was one of the boroughs of Cardiganshire,[32] but the family came to an end with the death of Thomas Lloyd in 1801. He had been a captain in the Royal Navy, and was also an agriculturist of some repute. He was, in fact, part-author of the survey of Cardiganshire published by the unofficial Board of Agriculture in 1794.[33] But he had been forced to mortgage his estate,[34] and by his will be left it (in unexplained circumstances)[35] to be divided, one-third to go to his cousin, Thomas Lloyd of Coedmor, and the remainder to Richard Braithwaite, rear-admiral of the White in the Royal Navy.[36] The admiral's daughter was married to Benjamin Edward Hall of Paddington, who assumed possession of Cilgwyn, but the division was not made until after his son, Edward Crompton Lloyd Hall, had come of age in 1828.[37] This young man was educated in the new University College, London,[38] and was called to the Bar by the Inner Temple.[39] He proceeded to practise on the South Wales Circuit, which had replaced the old Courts of Great Sessions, and, as early as 1830, at the age of twenty-three, he deputised for his father (who was ill) as high sheriff of Cardiganshire.[40] Six years later, the Carmarthen Liberals (including the mayor and town clerk) memorialised the home secretary, Lord John Russell, to have him appointed their recorder,[41] but in this they were unsuccessful. On more

than one occasion he represented his friend, William
Chambers, junior, in actions which the latter brought before
quarter sessions.[42] His practice was evidently considerable.
He also took an interest in agriculture, and, as a tenant of
his father's at Emlyn Cottage, won prizes given by the
Tivyside Agricultural Association for the best rams.[43] But
his neighbours do not seem to have been enamoured of him.
He antagonised the Welsh people by repeatedly advocating
the abandonment of their language;[44] indeed, when the
notorious education commissioners visited Wales in 1846,
it was he who supplied them with the notion, which they
readily accepted, that the Welsh language distorted the
truth, favoured fraud and abetted perjury, because it had
been 'the language of slavery'.[45] The gentry also were
suspicious of him, as we shall see. Nevertheless he was at
pains to stress his gentility, and, even before his father's
death in 1849, he had adopted the name of FitzWilliams,
owing to his belief that this had been the old family name in
Yorkshire, the plebeian Hall having intruded itself only in
Tudor times.[46] He was not alone in this stylishness, for this
was exactly the time when the Wilkinses of Brecon became
De Wintons,[47] and the Joneses of Llanarth became
Herberts,[48] leading the head of the great border family of
Herberts to fear that, if the process continued, he might have
to change his own surname to Jones.

When the Rebecca Riots became serious, in the winter of
1842, Lloyd Hall was thirty-five years of age. He was known
as an ultra-radical in politics. At the height of the disturbances he addressed meetings to advocate the vote by ballot,
and he repeatedly gave advice to the rioters by broadsheets
and letters to the press. Yet at the same time he was sending
to the Home Office, almost daily at one period, lengthy
reports on the situation, in his meticulous handwriting.
These are of the utmost value to the historian, but the Home
Office did not acknowledge receipt of the great majority of
them, for it was, even then, making secret enquiries into
Lloyd Hall's own opinions and activities. The country

magistrates, to whose ignorance he was constantly drawing attention, had cause to fear him, for he repeatedly pointed out infractions of the turnpike laws committed by them, and urged people to bring actions against them in the courts. They, on their part, attributed his demagogy to his vanity, his unbounded confidence in his legal talents and his craving for notoriety, and thought that he wished to play the part of the 'O'Connell of Wales'.[49]

Finally among the newcomers to West Wales were the great industrialists who developed the coalfield on the eastern border of our area. Lewis Weston Dillwyn, a Quaker who came to Swansea to manage the Cambrian Pottery Works which his father had bought in 1801, made a name for himself as a scientist (he became Fellow of the Royal Society at the age of twenty-five), and made the beautiful Swansea china celebrated throughout the land. In 1818 he entered into a parliamentary contest in Glamorgan (one of the first of the new monied men to do so in Wales) but thought it wise to withdraw before the poll. After the Reform Act of 1832, however, he sat for Glamorgan in two parliaments. In the meantime he had married the heiress of John Llewellyn of Penlle'r-gaer. His two sons, named respectively John Dillwyn Llewelyn and Lewis Llewelyn Dillwyn, had the distinction of capturing the first Rebecca leader, and the attorney-general, Sir Frederick Pollock, urged that a baronetcy be bestowed on the elder brother as a reward, though nothing came of it.[50] Further west, at Llanelly, the greatest industrialist of the early nineteenth century was Richard Janion Nevill. His father and he were the pioneers of copper smelting in the Llanelly district, an industry which flourished for over half a century. The son, who lived at Llangennech Park, served as high sheriff of Carmarthenshire in 1836, and, as a magistrate, was active in suppressing the riots.

It is not easy to estimate the feelings of the older families towards these newcomers. Their celebrated contemporary, Lady Charlotte Guest, has a poignant passage in her diary describing a conversation with Mrs. Waddington (mother of the future Lady Llanover) in which both ladies ruefully discussed the slights and indignities which they had to suffer because they were 'connected with Trade', even though 'Trade' in their cases meant such stupendous undertakings as the Dowlais Works.[51] The Industrial Revolution, and the Napoleonic War which coincided with it in time, had led to inflated fortunes, the owners of which bought up not merely isolated holdings but also some of the smaller estates in their entirety. The lesser gentry thus found themselves displaced by middle class shop-keepers, lawyers and business men. If anything, this served only to increase the sense of superiority which they derived from their descent, and which was none the less pronounced because it was based neither on their own ability nor on any services to the community. Yet their great pride in their ancestry had not led them to retain the language of their forbears, for they were rapidly becoming anglicised, thus adding a difference in language between them and their tenants to the already existing difference in class. Anglicisation was often associated with non-residence, especially on the part of those who sought greater refinement than their old-fashioned country houses afforded them.[52] This had important social and economic consequences. The well-known traveller, Benjamin Heath Malkin, was struck by the number of mansions in north Cardiganshire, and deplored the fact that few of them were tenanted. There were proprietors in this area, he said, who collectively drew out of the country twenty-five thousand pounds annually 'without ever seeing the spot from whence they derived their wealth'. The country's resources were thereby drained away and the tradesmen and labouring classes impoverished.[53] The community, also, lost the leadership and the steadying influence which an educated gentry could have supplied, and this was the more serious in view of the new problems which the nineteenth century brought with it. Non-residence was less frequent in English-speaking south Pembrokeshire than in the Welsh parts.[54]

Class differences were undoubtedly far more pronounced in the early nineteenth century than they were later on, and the pretentiousness of the gentry was matched by the servility of the peasantry. Most of the travellers who described their tours in Wales at this time drew attention to this.[55] To the gentry this servility was but 'respect for the old families', and when it grew less, for reasons which will be discussed later, they felt that honesty and other virtues departed with it.[56] But the gentry as a class were themselves in a state of decay, and this was especially true of squireens who resided on their estates. Inadequately educated, they spent their useless lives in the preservation of game and its wholesale slaughter. They were arrogant, extravagant and shiftless, and a countryman living near the mansion would know that his year's rent, gathered with immense toil, might be spent on an evening's entertainment.[57] But their estates were mortgaged, and they were facing ruin even before the final debacle of the country banks.[58] The parallel with Ireland was clear to Sir James Graham, the home secretary in Peel's administration. He was a landowner himself, and his condemnation of the Welsh gentry is the more noteworthy on that account. 'I grieve to say', he wrote to the prime minister, 'that South Wales bids fair to rival Ireland. Poverty and the misconduct of landlords are at the root of crime and of discontent in both countries.' He added that 'this is a truth not the less dangerous because it cannot be openly declared'.[59]

The consequence of this decay was serious, since the gentry constituted the 'landed interest' which alone, in so far as West Wales was concerned, was represented in parliament. For it had never hitherto been envisaged that parliament should represent the majority of the nation; it was intended to represent the 'interests' within the state, and in West Wales there was but one 'interest'. This has to be borne in mind in considering the opposition to parliamentary reform, for this change involved an entirely different way of political thinking and was not merely an extension of the franchise. Naturally the landed interest was dominant in the countryside. The three shires of West Wales had each been granted one seat in parliament by the Act of 1536 which had united England and Wales. The franchise, at the same time, had been restricted (as in England) to free-holders with land of an annual value of forty shillings. They were relatively few, but their number had considerably increased through the fall in the value of money in the intervening centuries. In particular it must be remembered that holders of leases for an indefinite term, that is, for one or more lives, ranked as freeholders in this respect. This gave the landowners a means of increasing the number of their supporters before an election by granting fictitious leases. Such leases were, in fact, frequently given for the life not of a tenant but of a third party, generally an old man, and they were seldom put into writing. But the landed interest also controlled the boroughs of West Wales in the absence of any large industrial or commercial undertakings. Frequently the local landowner owned several burgages within a borough, and, even if he did not, he generally had a strong body of supporters there. The borough franchise might differ from one borough to another, but in general, in Wales, it was vested in the freemen. A person might, however, become a freeman, and therefore a voter, not merely through birth, or marriage to a freeman's daughter, or apprentice-ship to a freeman, but by gift of the corporation, and these honorary freemen, again, could be created in expectation of a contested election.

A system of contributory boroughs, entirely peculiar to Wales, had been created in the sixteenth century. The act of 1536 had given the right to elect a member solely to the shire town, but had enjoined that all other ancient boroughs within the shire should contribute towards the payment of his wages. The obvious injustice of this was rectified seven years later when the right of election was extended to all these contributory boroughs.[60] Carmarthen, however, had none. There the right to vote was vested in its burgesses only, and an attempt to extend it even to those living within the town who paid scot and lot (that is to say, rateable contributions towards local and national taxes) was defeated in 1727.[61] But the creation of honorary freemen was particularly notorious in Carmarthen.[62] Pembroke had as its contributory boroughs not only Tenby but also the rural parish of Wiston, near Haverfordwest. The Owen family controlled both Pembroke and Tenby, which were in the immediate neighbourhood of Orielton, and sought to disfranchise Wiston, which was outside their influence. Their attempt culminated in the election of 1710. This contest showed that they had some justification for their attitude, for on that occasion no less than 239 freemen of this tiny borough arrived at Pembroke to register their votes. They met with a hot reception. The fire bell was rung and a tumult ensued. The Owen supporters put a guard on the town hall, and threatened to knock on the head any Wiston men who attempted to vote. These were driven to take refuge in various houses, but, nevertheless, they later succeeded in assembling on the castle green, and solidly declared their intention of voting against Orielton. The returning officer disregarded this, but the house of commons disagreed with him, and resolved that the freemen of Wiston, whether resident or not, had the right to vote.[63]

The position of Haverfordwest was peculiar, for it was itself a county borough with a member of its own. This unique privilege had been granted to it by Henry VIII, at the instance, it is said, of Mary Berkeley, the widow of Thomas Perrot of Haroldston, a mansion outside the town. Tradition has always credited her with having been the king's mistress, and her famous son, Sir John Perrot, certainly believed that Henry VIII was his father. But if the respectable inhabitants of Haverfordwest obtained their exclusive privileges only through the gratification of a king's amorous desires, they retained them for three and a half centuries, until 1885. Haverfordwest, however, differed from most other Welsh boroughs through the exercise of the franchise by those who paid scot and lot, and the house of commons ruled also, in 1715, that freemen could be created in Haverfordwest only by the consent of the majority of the common council of the borough,[64] thus limiting the abuse of creating honorary freemen for political purposes.

The affairs of the Cardigan boroughs were still more chaotic. In addition to Cardigan, these were Aberystwyth, Lampeter, Adpar, and Tregaron. There were grave doubts, however, whether Tregaron was in any sense a borough, although its burgesses had exercised the right to vote on several occasions. The lords of the manor of Tregaron were the Powells of Nanteos, and in preparation for the election of 1729 Thomas Powell secured the creation of no less than eight hundred burgesses of Tregaron, although the whole town had scarcely more than forty houses altogether. The ensuing election at Cardigan led to a riot in which one man was killed. Thomas Powell accused the mayor of Cardigan of partiality. One of his adherents admitted that he had offered the mayor £500 'for his interest', but claimed that he had done so only as a stratagem to find out the position of the other side, and maintained that the mayor's answer was that he had already been promised more by them. The election was scandalous enough to be drawn to the attention of parliament, and the house of commons ruled that the burgesses of Tregaron had no right to vote. It ruled, however, in respect of the other boroughs that the right was vested in the burgesses at large, and that residence was not a necessary qualification.[65] The belief that Adpar, also, was disfranchised by parliament is entirely unfounded.[66] There the borough simply fell into decay when the portreeve was ousted from his office in 1741, and subsequently no corporate act was done.[67] It is on this account that the Reform Act of 1832, while it disregarded Tregaron, renewed the status of Adpar as a borough. Nothing, however, could better illustrate the deterioration of parliamentary representation before 1832 than the fact that such boroughs as Wiston and

Adpar, or even Haverfordwest, had privileges which the
town of Merthyr Tydfil did not have.

The parliamentary system, like so many other aspects of
society in the early decades of the nineteenth century, was
becoming obsolete. Not only was it being subjected to
pressure by new forces; it had, itself, become outworn. For
the representation of an area such as West Wales was not
based on any political principle; it depended solely upon the
rivalry of the local families. Scarcely ever is it possible to say
with certainty whether a particular member was a Whig or
a Tory, at least until support or opposition to the Reform
Act provided a criterion. For reasons of prestige, these
families were prepared to fight contested elections at
enormous expense, and, when successful, they reimbursed
themselves through the spoils system, which was at its worst
in the last years of the unreformed parliament. The Owens
of Orielton and the Vaughans of Crosswood were insatiable
in their demands for favours.[68] And the attitude of their
supporters, as an acute observer remarked later on in the
century, 'was less that of citizens contending for their rights
than of clansmen vehemently battling for their respective
chieftains'.[69]

The alignment of these families has already been briefly
indicated. In Carmarthenshire the division was between the
Red party which supported Dynevor, and the Blue party of
their opponents, and this division affected all aspects of
public life. There were Red and Blue packs of hounds, and,
as we shall see later, there were even Red and Blue turnpike
trusts. But there were frequent regroupings which make the
fortunes of the two parties very difficult to follow. The Blues
were predominant in the borough of Carmarthen throughout
the latter part of the eighteenth century, in the heyday of
Griffith Philipps of Cwmgwili and his son, John George
Philipps. Besides, the Whig interest in both borough and
shire was strengthened, and complicated, by the meteoric
intervention of the nabob, William Paxton. His contest for

the shire in 1802 has become famous because the details of his expenditure on entertainment (amounting to £15,690 4s. 2d.) have been preserved.[70] He had the support of Golden Grove and of Cawdor, as well as of Lord Milford and the Philipps clan, and of Sir John Stepney, but his opponent, (Sir) James Hamlyn Williams of Edwinsford, had the still more powerful support of Dynevor. The poll was kept open for the maximum period, that is fifteen days, and resulted in Paxton's defeat by 1,267 votes to 1,222.[71] This was greeted with rioting in Blue Carmarthen. Not only did Paxton appeal against the result; so also did an elector who had presented himself as a candidate but had withdrawn (on the payment of £5,000 to him by Paxton, according to Williams). He accused both Paxton and Williams of wholesale bribery. Paxton complained of partiality by the returning officer in rejecting votes tendered for him and receiving those in favour of his opponent. A thousand or more witnesses were brought up to London from Carmarthenshire,[72] and Paxton gave up the struggle only because it would be impossible to go through the whole list of voters and bring them all to London.[73] But a few months later (December 1803), John George Philipps surrendered the representation of Carmarthen borough, and was succeeded by Paxton. It may well be that the Cwmgwili resources had been severely taxed by the continuous electioneering activities of father and son over a period of half a century (the election of 1796, alone, had cost the family £64,000),[74] and that Paxton had made it possible for John George Philipps to recoup himself; it is at least certain that Philipps's acceptance of the Chiltern Hundreds virtually marked the eclipse of Cwmgwili. Paxton, however, transferred to the shire in 1806, for a shire seat still carried far more prestige than that of a borough, but he held it for only five months. In 1821 he once more contested the borough, but was defeated by John Jones of Ystrad, and with that his costly intervention in the political life of Carmarthenshire came to an end.

With the eclipse of Cwmgwili, the Whig borough of Carmarthen fell more and more under the influence of Cawdor. To begin with he was ably supported by John Jones of Ystrad, who was, in many ways, the most interesting figure in the public life of West Wales until his death in 1842. He was born in the town of Carmarthen in 1777, of an old family in the borough, and was educated at Eton. He inherited wealth from several relatives, and established a very successful practice as a barrister in South Wales. If one is to judge by the four thousand volumes of his library he was a man of considerable culture. There is no doubt about his personal charm and popularity. Besides, he held various public offices as chairman of quarter sessions and recorder of Kidwelly, and he did a great deal of legal work for his fellow citizens gratuitously. On the other hand, the expenses of his numerous elections were borne by public subscription. In early life he was a disciple of Charles James Fox, and supported the Whig interest in the borough of Carmarthen. But he broke with Cawdor, according to his own account 'to prevent Carmarthen becoming a Family borough', and he unsuccessfully contested the borough against Lord Cawdor's brother in 1812. Even so, it is difficult to call him a Tory, for his politics were largely personal. The opponents of Cawdor in the Pembroke boroughs found him a seat from 1815 to 1818, when he again contested Carmarthen without success. As we have seen, he defeated Sir William Paxton in 1821, and he retained his seat until the Reform Act. He led the opposition in parliament to the abolition of the Courts of Great Sessions, an action probably not unconnected with his own vested interests as a barrister and with his opposition to Lord Cawdor, who was the chief supporter of the measure. This has made him something of a hero to later nationalists, despite the fact that (although he had a perfect knowledge of Welsh himself) he strongly deplored the continuance of the Welsh language.[75]

The politics of Cardiganshire and Pembrokeshire, and their respective boroughs, were inextricably intertwined

with those of Carmarthenshire, if only because the Cawdor
interests bestrode all three shires. The first Baron Cawdor
himself had represented the Cardigan boroughs until he was
raised to the peerage in 1796, when he was succeeded by
a member of the allied house of Crosswood, the future third
earl of Lisburne. But the latter was displaced in 1818 by
Pryse Pryse of Gogerddan, who had adopted his mother's
family name, and who, despite the Tory affiliations of
Gogerddan, was liberal in his politics. In the shire, on the
other hand, it was the Lisburne nominee, Thomas Edward
Powell of Nanteos, who had undisputed possession of the
seat for thirty-eight years. Thus the shire and the boroughs
were represented for many years by two men drawn from
the opposing sides but differing little in class or in principle.
In Pembrokeshire, the house of Orielton had to contend
against both Picton Castle and the Cawdors, but, on the
whole, did so successfully, and for the greater part of the
time, held the boroughs seat as well.

It was clear that the system had ceased to be tolerable, and
West Wales was caught up in the movement for parliamentary reform. The advocates of reform, it is true, found
much difficulty in breaking down the apathy of people who
voted in accordance with the traditional attachment of their
families,[76] while their opponents accused them of 'wicked
and atrocious attempts' directed towards 'the subversion of
our laws and government, and the annihilation of all
distinctions of rank and the sacred right of property'.[77]
Feelings became more intense when Lord John Russell
introduced his Reform Bill in 1831. All members for West
Wales either supported the bill or temporised, with the
notable exceptions of George Rice Trevor and John Jones,
who voted against it.[78] On the dissolution of parliament in
April, George Rice Trevor decided not to stand, as he
realised that his opinions were opposed to those of his
constituents, an action which won the respect of the Nonconformists.[79] In the circumstances the election in the borough
almost inevitably led to rioting. John Jones had lost much of

his popularity, and Cwmgwili, in the person of the son of the member in 1803, made a last attempt to regain the seat. There was so much uproar in the town that the returning officer reported that he was unable to execute his writ, and the election was suspended. But this did not stop the rioting. Jones was accused by Lord Cawdor of distributing liquor to his supporters; the Philipps faction, on the other hand, paraded their candidate through the streets. Special constables had to be sworn in; troops of the 93rd Regiment were brought from Brecon, and fourteen reformers were placed in gaol. A second election was held in August, and Jones was successful, but rioting broke out afresh. Two of the company of metropolitan police who had been sent down were injured, and the successful candidate, as he was being carried through the Dark Gate, was struck on the head with a stone and stunned.[80] There was, in the town of Carmarthen, a heritage of violence to which these elections had greatly contributed, violence conducted under very respectable patronage, and the great Rebecca riot of 19 June 1843 in Carmarthen can be properly understood only against this background.

The Pembrokeshire election of the same year was the most bitterly contested in the whole kingdom, and it is of great significance because, held as it was on the very eve of the Reform Act, it so clearly illustrates the break-down of the old system of parliamentary representation. Sir John Owen of Orielton had held the seat without a contest in the four previous elections. He temporised over the Reform Bill, declaring himself an advocate of reform but not of a bill which falsely assumed that character. This did not satisfy the reformers, and they found a champion in Robert Fulke Greville. He was the nephew of Charles Francis Greville, whose uncle, Sir William Hamilton (husband of Lord Nelson's Lady Hamilton) had acquired an estate in Pembrokeshire by his first marriage. On this land Charles Greville had founded, under a private act of 1790, a new town of Milford (now known as Milford Haven), by inviting

Quakers from Nantucket Island to settle there with the intention of making it a centre of South Sea whaling, and by inducing the government to build a number of frigates in its dockyard. Milford was a considerable town of two thousand people in 1831, and Greville could be assured of its support in his contest for the shire. He also had the backing of Lord Cawdor, of Sir Richard Philipps of Picton, of Lord Lisburne, and of Lord Kensington, a landowner in Pembrokeshire, whose son, the Honourable Captain William Edwardes, R.N., was the chairman of his election committee. The confidence of the people generally (and of publicans, in particular) was strengthened by a rumour that the sum of £30,000 had been deposited with Messrs. Morris, the Carmarthen bankers, to meet the expenses of the election.

Intensive preparations were made on both sides. A supporter of Orielton had, some eighteen months before the dissolution, already induced twenty of his tenants to take leases on part of their farms. The agreements were verbal only, and involved no change in the rent they paid. Moreover, all the leases were for the life of an old man of about eighty years of age, one John White. Some three weeks before the election, these leases were put into writing, but the documents were still kept by the landlord. Later on, when called upon to defend his action, he asserted: 'I chose to dispose of my property in any way I pleased for the purpose of furthering my political views'.

The election was conducted in the town of Haverfordwest, to which voters had to be brought from all parts of Pembrokeshire, however remote. There were seven polling booths, one for each hundred in the shire, and, at each, the candidates were represented by their agents and sub-agents. Nearly all the professional men in Pembrokeshire had been retained by Orielton, so that Greville had to get his from the neighbouring shires, and among them was the Carmarthen attorney, Hugh Williams, who will figure so prominently in a later chapter. In the first few days voting was brisk, but from about the sixth day the Orielton agents adopted delaying tactics in the hope of making it impossible for Greville's supporters to stay on in Haverfordwest. Stolid Pembrokeshire farmers were asked such questions as: 'Are you the Pope of Rome?'; 'Are you one of the Cardinals?'; 'Are you a peer of the realm?'; 'Do you hold office under the Crown?'; 'Are you a lunatic?'; 'Are you the prime minister?' All these questions and the answers to them were put into writing, and a voter was seldom allowed to poll in less than an hour. Debates at the booths became more and more acrimonious. When Greville protested, he was told that the practice had been started by his own agents at the Castlemartin booth (where Sir John Owen's supporters were in a great majority). Voters were minutely questioned as to their leases, and every effort was made to debar leaseholders from voting for Greville. Then, without giving a reason, the Orielton agent would object to a voter, and his case had to be referred to the assessor. This meant further delay. There were several hundred Greville voters still 'cased' when the poll was declared closed at 3 p.m. on the fifteenth day, 26 May (in accordance with 25 George III, c. 84), and nothing would induce the sheriff to extend the time.

Conditions in Haverfordwest had meanwhile become riotous. Greville had 'opened' nearly every inn in the town for his supporters. To begin with, a ticket system was employed; those who had voted for Greville were given a ticket which entitled them to refreshment. But this system soon broke down, and all who claimed to be Greville supporters were entertained (as well, no doubt, as many who were not) whether or not they had already voted, and despite the 'Treating Act' (7 and 8 William III, c. 4) which forbade the practice. The publicans kept elaborate accounts of dinners, suppers and breakfasts, of barrels of ale and bottles of spirits, of beds for voters and stabling for their horses, of pipes and tobacco. The Mariners Inn presented a bill for £1,878 10s. 7d.; the Black Horse for £750 4s.; the Wellington for £513 19s.; the Swan for £467 7s. 6d.; the Bridge End Inn for £335 4s. 3d.; as well as others whose accounts have not been preserved. Inns further afield presented bills for entertaining voters as they set out on their journey or on their return. A Solva innkeeper claimed £75 18s. 2d. for such entertainment, mainly for breakfasts, most of which included a shilling's worth of rum, no inconsiderable quantity in those days. The only Orielton bill known to the writer was for £115 1s. 7d., but this sum included the strange item of £2 5s. 4d. for shaving, and dressing and cropping the heads of forty-two of Sir John's freeholders.[81] To add to the confusion Sir John's colliers had entered the town in force, and many heads were broken.[82]

The sheriff declared Sir John Owen returned, but Greville immediately appealed. His petition was considered by a select committee in September, and numerous witnesses were examined. This committee declared the election void. It passed the severest strictures upon the culpable neglect and partiality of the sheriff and the incompetence of the assessor.[83] Yet the new election held in October did not change the result, for Sir John Owen was again returned.

The election had several repercussions. John Jones had gone to Haverfordwest to support Orielton. There he was spat upon and insulted by one of the Carmarthen reformers who had been arrested for his share in the riot in his home town and who now was prosecuted and fined £5.[84] Furthermore, John Jones had an encounter with Greville, and, in his turn, insulted him. Greville thereupon challenged him to a duel and the two men met on 22 October at Tavernspite (on the border between their respective shires), where, according to the *Cambrian* newspaper, 'Mr. Jones received Mr. Greville's shot, and, refusing to apologise, fired his pistol in the air'.[85] More serious still, one of Greville's keenest supporters, an old man in his seventies, Major Samuel Harries of Trevacoon near Fishguard, used his position as a magistrate to have one of Sir John Owen's voters arrested on various charges, notably for poaching, and refused him bail. The irascible old man had acted without reckoning with his political opponents, who had a charge brought against him in the Court of King's Bench. After dragging on, and involving the defendant in enormous expense, the case had to be removed from Pembrokeshire because of the intensity of feeling there, and was tried at the Brecknock Assizes in August 1832, when Samuel Harries was fined £500 and removed from the commission of the peace.[86] To add a final touch of the ludicrous, Greville left the country without paying the innkeepers, who brought actions against him and his agents, thereby preserving for us, in immense detail, the items of their expenditure.[87]

The Reform Act of 1832 gave Carmarthenshire a second member. It joined Llanelly to the borough of Carmarthen, Milford to the Pembroke boroughs, and Narberth and Fishguard to Haverfordwest. The uniform £10 household franchise, established in the boroughs, made a marked difference to the nature of their electorate, and introduced the thin wedge of democracy. But in the shires there was little change, for there were few copyholders in West Wales, and the enfranchisement of the £50 tenant farmers tended to strengthen the hold of the large landowners over these constituencies rather than to diminish it. The effect of the Reform Act was so slow in making itself felt that it almost appeared as if no change had been made at all. The landed interests were unimpaired. In the first elections held under the new franchise, there was not even a contest in Cardiganshire or the Cardigan boroughs, in Pembrokeshire or the Pembroke boroughs, or in Haverfordwest. George Rice Trevor was again returned at the head of the poll for Carmarthenshire, and Sir James Hamlyn Williams of Edwinsford who had displaced him in 1831 (and who was a Whig although he was the son of Paxton's opponent in 1802) was ousted. In the Carmarthen boroughs only did a Whig secure a seat by defeating John Jones.

One effect the 'revolution of 1832' did have; it led the landowners to close their ranks, and, to that extent, produced a clearer alignment on a class basis. Hitherto Cawdor had opposed Dynevor, but the reform agitation had raised doubts in his mind. He was naturally opposed to the ballot and to universal suffrage, but he also feared the growing threat to the established church. As late as 1835 he gave his support to Sir James Hamlyn Williams, but the latter voted in parliament for the expulsion of bishops from the house of lords, and his agent opposed the levying of a church rate in Llansawel, so that when an election came again in 1837 Cawdor transferred his support to George Rice Trevor. Cawdor's agent thereupon wrote a letter to his tenants in these terms:

> 'I shall depend upon you to plump for Colonel Trevor at the coming election, who is the only candidate supported by your noble landlord, and I have no doubt that you will do so.
> Your well-wisher, R. B. Williams.'

The agent, moreover, instructed a sub-agent to interview four tenants who were suspected of supporting the other side and who were in arrear with their rents, on the first day of the poll at Llandeilo, and to explain to them that as they were 'so independent and so very ungrateful for the indulgence and favour shown to them by their landlord', he would expect to receive their rents immediately, and would then see 'what further is to be done in the matter'.

The storm which this produced took Cawdor by surprise. He was 'traduced' in the local press.[88] Nonconformists advocated, satirically, either that all tenant farmers should be disfranchised or that their votes should be transferred *en bloc* to their landlords.[89] More immediately important was the submission to parliament of a petition drawing attention to this interference by a peer in the election of a commoner, and it must have infuriated Cawdor to learn that of the two petitioners one was the whipper-snapper Edward Crompton Lloyd Hall. The house of commons thought the matter of sufficient interest to devote to it the whole sitting of 12 June 1838. But Cawdor found an able apologist in Sir James Graham, now member for the Pembroke boroughs. Graham had served in the Whig cabinet which had prepared the first Reform Bill, but he, also, had had second thoughts and had abandoned his colleagues to throw in his lot with Sir Robert Peel. This lost him the election of 1837 in Cumberland. But he and Lord Cawdor were 'very old and intimate friends', and Cawdor's 'former hostility to Sir John Owen was now', in Graham's words, 'converted into cordial co-operation',[90] so Sir John Owen's son was persuaded to resign the Pembroke boroughs in his favour, and Graham was elected 'without a dissentient voice'.[91] It would be naïve to assume that this did not involve a subvention to the dwindling fortunes of Orielton, and Graham wrote to Peel: 'My wish to sit beside you in the House of Commons has been stronger perhaps than my strict sense of right'.[92] But he represented Pembroke for only three years. He was to become Peel's chief lieutenant, and was home secretary in his great ministry from 1841 to 1846. This was a post for which Graham was scarcely suited, for he was rigid and unconciliatory in his manner and in his attitude towards social problems, but it was to him that it fell to deal with the Rebecca Riots. In the debate on the action of Lord Cawdor's agent he argued strongly 'that landlords might appropriately guide the judgment of their tenants'. Lord John Russell made great play of Cawdor's change of front, and of his tenants 'wandering about in search of information as to which way their landlord was going to vote', but expressed himself satisfied that attention had been drawn to 'the universality of the practice'.[93]

The representation of West Wales, therefore, continued virtually unaltered. In the Carmarthen boroughs, it is true, the banker, David Morris, had been returned in 1837 and continued to hold his seat for over a quarter of a century. He lived among his constituents, and received the support of the Nonconformists, so that he differed in outlook from the landed gentry. But his conduct in parliament was utterly undistinguished; even during the Rebecca Riots, which had their focus in Carmarthen, he remained silent.[94]

Elsewhere the gentry arranged matters among themselves. When Viscount Emlyn, the son of the earl of Cawdor, came of age, Sir John Owen obligingly surrendered the Pembrokeshire seat to him, and transferred himself to the boroughs, an action which his opponents could only explain as having been done 'for a consideration'.[95] The 'Holy Alliance' between Cawdor and Dynevor, also, was now complete, and when John Jones died in 1842, after again representing Carmarthenshire for five years, they were able to arrange for the return of a Tory member without a contest. The growing forces of democracy had little opportunity to express themselves. The framework of government had not been altered to correspond to changes in the social structure, and the sense of frustration caused by this contributed much to the uneasiness which prevailed in the countryside.

Chapter II

LOCAL GOVERNMENT AND ADMINISTRATION

T HE authority which the gentry exercised over the countryside, and which was scarcely diminished, as we have seen,
by the reform of parliament, was all the more secure since
it continued unchanged in the administration of justice and
in local government. Both these functions were the business
of quarter sessions and of the lesser courts. It was natural
that the gentry should retain their power on these bodies, if
only because they alone could afford the time to sit upon
them. Besides, the squire, through the inbred respect felt for
him by his tenants and through his superior wealth, education and experience, should have been the natural leader of
his people. But very frequently he was not, and it was one
of the main causes of the unhealthy social life which prevailed in West Wales in the early nineteenth century that
a gulf had been formed between the gentry and the
peasantry because of non-residence, and because the
difference in class between them had become intensified by
a difference in language and a rapidly increasing difference
in religious persuasion. Thereby justice and local government had come to be administered by persons who were, to
a great extent, alien to the people whom they ruled.

The system was essentially oligarchic, if not aristocratic.
A seat on the bench of magistrates was to the lesser gentry
what a seat in parliament was to their superiors; it was
a hall-mark of pre-eminence in their own localities. That
they were prepared to go to considerable lengths to safe-
guard this distinction is shown by the 'strike' of the
magistrates in the Bala district of Merioneth in the summer
of 1838. These justices were gravely offended at Easter in
that year when the home secretary had, without consulting
them, remitted a sentence of fourteen years' transportation
on two women convicted of receiving stolen goods of trifling

value. But the real reason for their action was that 'a person had been put into the commission of the peace contrary to their wishes'. This individual was a tradesman and a Calvinistic Methodist. The lord-lieutenant of Merioneth had argued that the man could not very well be refused a seat on the bench as he had already been high sheriff. The magistrates retorted that it was bad enough to have a plebeian sheriff, but this was an office held for only one year; to have him as a magistrate for life was far worse. It was not so much on account of the religious difference, they said; this might possibly be overlooked. It was because his origin, education, connections, early habits, occupation and station in life were not such as could entitle him to be the familiar associate of gentlemen. A government investigator into the unreformed boroughs, who reported this episode, thoroughly approved of the stand taken by them. 'The refusal of the county magistrates', he stated, 'to act with a man who has been a grocer, and is a Methodist, is the dictate of genuine patriotism; the spirit of aristocracy in the county magistracy is the salt which alone preserves the whole mass from inevitable corruption.' He could not deny that wealth had its claims as well as birth, but persons who rapidly acquired wealth should rest content with the thought that their grandsons might hope to attain to the bench and to other honours; this should suffice to enable them 'still to rejoice in their riches'.[1]

There is no reason to suppose that the snobbery of the Bala magistrates was not equalled among their colleagues in West Wales, and the differences which arose between magistrates within the boroughs were frequently due to the fact that some of them, almost of necessity, were tradesmen. Besides, it has been estimated that about a quarter of the justices in the whole country were clergymen,[2] and these, in most cases, were clergymen of gentle birth. They would, also, be among the more active magistrates, as they were more easily available than their lay neighbours. But there had always been a feeling that the passing of sentences in quarter sessions was not quite consonant with the functions of a priest, and, with the growth of Nonconformity in Wales, which was more marked in the second quarter of the nineteenth century than at any period before or since, the antagonism to clerical magistrates became very pronounced.[3] It was at the root of the demand, constantly reiterated by the Rebecca rioters, that a stipendiary magistracy should be established. Moreover, the class distinction between the magistrates and the peasantry was still further accentuated by the nature of the offences which were dealt with at quarter sessions. The records of these bodies abound, above all else, with instances of petty theft; but petty thieving was not a crime which the gentry themselves would be likely to commit. Drunkenness was certainly as prevalent among them as among more ordinary people, but their roistering did not often bring them before the courts. Criminal justice, therefore, was to them a matter which concerned the lower classes; their whole attitude towards it was coloured by the fact that they did not regard themselves as likely to be subject to its jurisdiction.

As the office of magistrate was considered to be one of so much dignity, the number of those who coveted it was naturally very large. The printed list for 1838 for Pembrokeshire alone contains no less than 253 names, and those for subsequent years do not differ from it to any great extent.[4] But the list was largely fictitious. It included all the titled gentry of the shire, few of whom had qualified to act as magistrates or had any intention of doing so. Of those who had qualified, some neglected their duties and attended quarter sessions only when there were jobs to be filled. Many were non-resident, while some, who were not, still lived at a considerable distance from the centres of population in the petty sessional divisions in which they were expected to serve. Some were too old to act, or too ill, especially when it became necessary for them to accompany troops during the Rebecca rioting. In fact there were large stretches of country with no resident magistrates at all.[5]

I. DYNEVOR CASTLE 1822

Engraving by C. Askey after J. P. Neale

II. A Cardiganshire Cottage in the Late Nineteenth Century

Thus, despite the lengthy list for each shire, in practice it was only a few who were active, and the countryside suffered from a dearth of magistrates. This became a matter of concern both to the government and to the magistrates themselves, especially when the country became disturbed.[6] The former was apt to be critical of 'the want of energy displayed by the magistrates'; the latter bitterly resented such strictures, and drew attention to the difficulty which they encountered in attempting to cope with disturbances which had occurred fifteen miles and more away from their residences.[7] In consequence, when the Rebecca rioting was at its height, the Home Office wrote identical letters to the lords-lieutenant of the three shires asking them, without delay, to supply a list of all magistrates and of their places of residence, and urging them, if the numbers were insufficient, to take immediate action in recommending names to the lord chancellor.[8] But it was not a simple matter. George Rice Trevor feared that there was no one fit to be named in the semi-industrialised area of Pontyberem and Llan-non, which had become a focus of disturbance,[9] while in other districts it was not found possible to appoint magistrates 'without descending to a grade of persons who have not usually been included in the commission of the peace'.[10] Once more the rigidity of class distinction was seen to be militating against the health of the social life of a rapidly changing community.

The preservation of law and order was, moreover, only one aspect of the work performed by the magistrates; they also administered the expenditure of a considerable amount of public money. The assessment of the county rate, or 'county stock', was rough and ready. As late as 1832 the various hundreds of Cardiganshire were assessed on the basis of an apportionment made in 1748, and those of Carmarthenshire on an apportionment made 'thirty years since', while the position in Pembrokeshire was even more obscure.[11] There the clerk of the peace, himself, 'could not find out upon what valuation the county rate was based'.[12]

4

The Poor Law Amendment Act of 1834 made it necessary for this to be changed, but, even so, the new valuation for Pembrokeshire was determined by a committee of magistrates who went around the shire questioning the parish officers and 'making inquiries of the most intelligent people of the parishes', and there is no reason to believe that the work was done more scientifically in the other shires.[13] There was, indeed, the added difficulty that the county and poor rates were now collected together, and could not easily be separated in the minds of the ratepayers.

But it was not the collection as much as the expenditure of the county rate which caused misgiving at this time. The treasurer's accounts were printed each quarter in the local newspapers, and the justices of assize kept a watchful eye on the activities of magistrates in quarter sessions, but it still remained true that the expenditure of public money was vested, not in persons popularly elected, but in men, nominated by the Crown on the recommendation of the lord-lieutenant, who held office for life and were drawn from one social class. The system was the reverse of democratic. Admittedly, much of this expenditure was on items which could not be controversial, such as the enormously high cost of prosecutions, the conveyance of prisoners to the gaols, and the maintenance of these gaols and houses of correction, as well as of the shire hall and the judge's lodgings. But there were also numerous salaried offices which gave scope for considerable patronage by the magistrates. Much more important was the fact, which could scarcely have been foreseen, that the highest expenditure recorded in virtually every quarterly account had come to be on county bridges, for, unlike the roads, the provision and maintenance of bridges was the concern of the shires. There were constant accusations that bridges were built, and, indeed, hills cut down, to suit the convenience of local magnates and not for the public advantage. Sir James Hamlyn Williams of Edwinsford, at the Carmarthenshire quarter sessions in October 1843, in urging that a strict enquiry should be made into the expenditure of the county stock for the last twenty-nine years, presented no less than fourteen addresses from different parishes on this particular subject.[14]

The magistrates, either singly or in pairs in petty sessions, or in full quarter sessions, decided a host of other questions. The petty sessions met regularly in each division every fortnight or every month.[15] They examined the accounts of the overseers of the poor, and of the surveyors of the highways. They swore in the constables for the hundred, and disposed of a great deal of business relating to the parishes. The magistrates often proceeded by means of indictment even in non-legal matters. For example, a stretch of road which badly needed repair would be attended to by indicting the parish in quarter sessions, and the fine imposed on the parishioners was in the nature of a rate levied to meet the expense of the repair. Much of their jurisdiction was summary, and whether it was efficient or bungling, tyrannical or paternal, depended to a great extent on individual magistrates. They were not expected to have expert knowledge of the law; they acted in the light of common sense. But they were frequently called upon to decide on matters where their own interests were involved, and, as they were drawn from the same class as those who made the laws, this served to underline the class bias of the legislation of the period.

Discontent with magistrates was fairly widespread; 'justices' justice', it was said, 'was proverbial'.[16] It is important to consider whether conditions were worse in West Wales than elsewhere. Difference in language certainly hindered the administration of justice in Wales. Cases were tried in a language which defendants barely understood, and this made the elaborate paraphernalia of the law appear to a bewildered peasantry to be a species of trickery, of chicanery, intended to deprive them of justice. It also emphasised the fact that the legal system was, in reality, an alien one, imposed upon a conquered people, and not arising indigenously out of their own social life. The provision of an interpreter was haphazard. For example, in a case arising out of the earliest Rebecca Riots in 1839, the only interpreter was the surveyor of roads who had made the original application to the magistrates;[17] in other words, it was the prosecutor who acted as interpreter. Even if justice was done in such circumstances, it was difficult to preserve the appearance that it was being done.

When the rioting was at its height, the *Times* sent a young reporter, Thomas Campbell Foster, to West Wales, and he described the situation in a remarkable series of articles, which were reproduced in the local newspapers. His activities and opinions will be discussed at length in a later chapter, but it should be mentioned here that the predominant themes in his dispatches are the inadequacy of the magistrates, their ignorance, their tyranny and their injustice. He roundly accused them of jobbery in connection with the turnpike trusts. He pointed out that the magistrates were both trustees and tally-holders of these trusts. They diverted roads to suit their convenience, he alleged, and had bridges built near their residences. He reported the people as saying that they were treated by the magistrates 'as if they were beasts and not human beings'. His accusations were stoutly denied, but he persisted in repeating them, and urged the appointment of stipendiaries.[18]

Other writers were equally insistent. Edward Crompton Lloyd Hall referred to this subject in the very first of the series of lengthy reports which he submitted to the Home Office,[19] and he constantly recurred to it. As a Londoner who had settled in Wales he was equally astonished at the ignorance of his bucolic neighbours, the squireens of the Teify valley, and at the arrogance of their pretensions. They behaved like petty potentates towards their tenantry, and treated 'like dogs' those unfortunate enough to appear before the bench.[20] The person sent by the Home Office in August 1843 to conduct a preliminary investigation in the disturbed area reported that the people had lost all confidence in the magistrates, and thought it useless to apply to them for redress.[21] Naturally this opinion was voiced in the evidence submitted to the commission of enquiry which was later established, and this was done not only by radicals such as Lloyd Hall and William Chambers, junior, but also by more conservative witnesses.[22] The commissioners themselves, while not agreeing with the demand for the appointment of stipendiaries, expressed their dissatisfaction with the magistrates. They condemned their imperfect knowledge of Welsh, their dissensions among themselves, and their neglect of duty. It appeared that within the previous three years petty sessions at Llandeilo had been adjourned no less than thirty times on account of the failure of magistrates to attend.[23] Even more serious was the accusation that magistrates adjudicated in cases relating to themselves.[24] Strange to say, the witness who made this statement to the commissioners, and who was himself a magistrate, figured in just such a case some four months later, when he and a fellow-justice were sued at the Pembrokeshire Lent Assizes of 1844 for wrongful imprisonment. A third Pembrokeshire magistrate had brought a case of breach of contract before the Narberth bench. The two justices there allowed the plaintiff to sit with them, and committed the defendant to Haverfordwest gaol for fourteen days. They seem to have realised that they had done wrong, for they offered the defendant £15 as compensation. This sum he considered inadequate, and the trial at the assizes was to determine the amount which should be paid to him. It is indicative of the uncertainty of opinion and behaviour at the time that all three magistrates (one of them being William Richards of Tenby, of whom more later) were liberal, if not even radical, in their politics.[25]

A lesser grievance, but one which figured very prominently in the agitation of the time, was the ignorance of magistrates' clerks and the exorbitant nature of their fees. A magistrate might appoint a publican, possibly one of his own tenants, as clerk,[26] and the commissioners themselves deplored the influence which such persons might acquire

over the bench.[27] There was little evidence that the fees
exacted were larger than those to which they were legally
entitled, but these were so numerous (for example, for the
complaint, for the summons, for administering the oath and
for the conviction) that the total was excessive. Practices
had varied from place to place, but, in 1836, an attempt
had been made to introduce uniformity. It still remained
true, however, that the fees frequently exceeded the penalty.
Thus a boy might be fined a shilling for a trifling offence,
but the fees would amount to the sum of nine shillings, which
might be more than a farm labourer's weekly wage. The
Rebecca commissioners advocated that magistrates' clerks
should be paid fixed salaries in lieu of fees.[28]

The tyrannical conduct of the magistrates was nowhere
more evident than in game prosecutions, for, in this matter,
their personal interests coincided with the ethos of their
class. The killing of game was still, in the early nineteenth
century, a class privilege; a whole body of legislation
restricted it to persons qualified by birth or estate. The
cruder forms of deterrents, such as man-traps and spring-
guns, now became illegal, but an act of 1828 made poaching
by night punishable by transportation on the third offence.
An act of 1832 abolished all class qualifications for sporting,
but imposed new penalties, by fine and imprisonment, for
poaching by day. Harsh punishment was not, however,
effective. As Cobbett had said, it was impossible 'to make
men believe that any particular set of individuals should
have a permanent property in wild creatures',[29] and Welsh
writers maintained that men who would not dream of
stealing became poachers because of their belief that wild
game was created for the common use of all.[30] Besides, both
birds and rabbits destroyed the farmers' crops, cultivated
as these were with such unremitting toil, and the arbitrary
conduct of gamekeepers caused much irritation. The gamekeeper, indeed, was often a more important person than the
estate agent.[31] It is probable that poaching increased in the
early nineteenth century because of the prevailing poverty,

for a craving for meat, which the peasantry so seldom tasted, made it an almost irresistible temptation. Yet it is most difficult to determine its place in the welter of contemporary opinion. The poacher caught the imagination of a later generation, and his person became imbued with much romance, to which an asperity was added by the bitter hatred of landlords on the part of militant Nonconformity later in the century. There is ample evidence of prosecutions in the earlier period. A farm servant was fined £5 at Llandovery in 1822 (a sum which, no doubt, represented his wages for about three months) for selling one pheasant to the landlord of the Nag's Head in that town,³² and the records of each succeeding quarter sessions contain case after case of the imposition of the maximum fine (under the act of 1832) for trespassing in pursuit of game, and of the much heavier penalty for actually killing a hare.³³ Nevertheless, the four hundred closely printed folio pages which contain the outpourings of peasant grievances before the Rebecca commission have few references to the game laws. One witness complained that he might be fined £5 for killing a hare worth 1s. 6d. Another spoke of the severity with which the laws were applied. 'The magistrates', he said, 'are very sharp and rather revengeful if there is anything about poaching.'³⁴ It is probable that the peasantry still regarded these laws as an inevitable part of the natural order of things; certainly they did not form one of the causes of the Rebecca Riots.

Administration was as moribund in the small boroughs of West Wales as it was in the shires.³⁵ Whatever their origin, and whether they were independent boroughs with full municipal corporations, such as Carmarthen and Haverfordwest, or were nominally independent, like Aberystwyth, or manorial boroughs administered by a court leet, as were some of the largest among them, such as Llanelly, all were under the domination of the neighbouring gentry. The small oligarchies which governed them were, in effect, the nominees of the neighbouring squire. Aberystwyth, for example, was dominated by the Pryses of Gogerddan, and Haverfordwest by the Philippses of Picton Castle. Their corporations did not regard themselves primarily as organs of local government. They resembled a bench of magistrates more than they did their modern counterparts. Besides, in many instances, they exercised a criminal and civil jurisdiction of their own, and the mayor's primary function was often that of chief magistrate.

Several of the towns concerned were, economically, in a state of decay, so that their corporations might have disappeared had it not been for rights of parliamentary representation or the possession of considerable property. The 'contributory' boroughs, as we have seen, were torn by contending political factions, and the creation of burgesses for party purposes had reduced their civic life to chaos. Even the possession of the highly-esteemed privilege of the franchise had not prevented the borough of Adpar from ceasing to function through sheer decrepitude, and the office of mayor was used in the 'contributory' borough of Wiston solely as a means of conferring relief on some old man who would thereby receive the tolls of the annual fair.[36] The creation of a uniform borough franchise by the Reform Act of 1832 removed the main source of corrupt political power in these 'contributory' boroughs. Moreover the reform of the central government was accompanied, as an almost inevitable corollary, by an enquiry into local government, and the Municipal Corporations Act of 1835, which swept away a whole mass of obsolete and unrepresentative institutions, replacing them by town councils elected by the ratepayers, was possibly more revolutionary even than the Act of 1832.

The new act established municipal corporations in the boroughs of Aberystwyth, Cardigan, Carmarthen, Haverfordwest, Llandovery, Pembroke and Tenby. Yet, even in these towns, the act did not create a new spirit overnight; nor did it deprive of power the men who had hitherto exercised it. This can be illustrated by the affairs of the borough of Tenby, which also serve to demonstrate the climate of opinion in West Wales at the time of the Rebecca Riots. The neighbouring boroughs of Tenby and Pembroke had always been closely linked together, the same persons being the leading members of both corporations.[37] They were dominated by the great house of Orielton, especially in the days of Sir John Owen, and his henchman was the all-powerful Jacob Richards. This remarkable man was a native of Swansea who had made a fortune in India and had settled in Tenby in 1810.[38] He was the founder of modern Tenby, which, in the words of a contemporary, 'he found a paltry fishing town and left a delightful watering-place'.[39] In twenty years he acquired a complete monopoly of power in Tenby.[40] He served as mayor five times, and also as deputy mayor five times. He appointed his son, William Richards, as town clerk, and, in practice, nominated the burgesses, the common council, the mayors and every officer of the corporation. He died in 1834, just before the passing of the Municipal Corporations Act. Yet, despite this reform, the mayor of Tenby for four successive years after the act was his son, William Richards. The son, indeed, served as mayor no less than twelve times, and his son, after him, eight times. Father, son, and grandson, between them, were mayors of Tenby twenty-five times, and it is surely a striking indication of the mutability of human affairs that, half a century after the grandson's death, the family is scarcely even remembered in the town which they did so much to create.

The example of William Richards not only illustrates the continuity of power from the old to the new regime; it shows also how dissensions among magistrates brought the whole system of justice into disrepute. The Municipal Corporations Act deprived the mayor and aldermen of their judicial authority, so that county magistrates now exercised juris-diction within the borough. Unlike his father, William

Richards was an opponent of Sir John Owen, and the antipathy between his supporters and the local gentry was such
that plaintiffs from the town of Tenby brought their cases
all the way to Narberth petty sessions, for fear of partiality.
It was obviously a grievance for anyone to have to bring his
witnesses ten miles in a trifling case which might well be
adjourned three times, and this was strongly deplored by the
Rebecca commissioners.[41] Moreover, this dissension led to
a spectacular incident. At the Tenby petty sessions of
30 March 1839 (although after the business of the court had
been completed, so the mayor explained in his exculpatory
letter to the Home Office), Richards called his chief
opponent on the bench 'a calumniator and a liar'. He was
immediately challenged to a duel. The two men, with their
seconds, met at the foot of Gumfreston Hill in the early
morning of All Fools' Day. There Richards, according to
his own account, fired into the air, but his opponent took
deliberate aim and shot the mayor in the groin, seriously
imperilling his life. It was possibly the last duel to be fought
in Wales; that it should be fought by two magistrates
sufficiently indicates the debasement of the system of
justice.[42]

A number of the boroughs of West Wales, namely Cilgerran, Kidwelly, Laugharne, Llanelly, Loughor, Newport
(Pembrokeshire) and St. Clears,[43] were excluded from the
provisions of the Municipal Corporations Act. That their
corporations still continued to function was due, in every
case, to the possession of considerable property. But their
continuance as organs of local government, well into the
nineteenth century, only provides yet another illustration
of the inadequacy of the old institutions to meet the needs
of a rapidly changing society. This was particularly serious
in places like Llanelly, where there was a large accumulation
of industrial population. The town was in the lordship of
Kidwelly. The lord of the manor was the earl of Cawdor,
and his agent was William Chambers, senior, who was
admitted as freeman at the court leet of 30 May 1831 and

then appointed portreeve for the ensuing year.[44] The property of the borough amounted to some six hundred acres. This was enclosed by an act of 1807, and handed over to a body of trustees. The profits were to be applied, in the first place, to the improvement of the town and port of Llanelly, the remainder being divided annually among the burgesses on Christmas Day. But while there were 156 burgesses in 1807, the number had been allowed to drop to 34 in 1835, for a very obvious reason, and their average age was over seventy. By 1848, the number was 25, and they shared the best part of £500 annually between them. By this time the population had grown to over 7,000, but the burgesses entirely ignored demands for an adequate water system and other amenities. Under threat of an action in Chancery for abuse of trust, they eventually surrendered all their rents and profits, which were handed over in 1850 to a local Board of Public Health.[45]

In Cilgerran, the corporation owned about a hundred acres, together with some quarries. This property was let out to the burgesses at almost nominal rent, and this was the sole reason for which the borough existed. In 1835, neither the portreeve, a farmer, nor the town clerk, a weaver, spoke English.[46] The inhabitants of the neighbouring town of Newport were inordinately proud of their charter. They believed, and their descendants still profess to believe, that their barony of Kemes remained a marcher lordship after 1536, the only one in Wales, a bit of false history for which they were indebted to the desire of their fellow-townsman, George Owen of Henllys, to glorify his own family.[47] It was George Owen's descendant, as lord of the manor, who selected the mayor from names presented to him by the court leet, but the other functions of the corporation had almost entirely decayed.[48] The tiny borough of St. Clears was also in decay. Its common lands had been appropriated, and such revenues as there were went for food and drink in two annual dinners. The officers in 1835 were 'farmers, artificers and labouring men, ignorant of business and imperfectly acquainted with the English language', although this was not true of the portreeve in 1852 (who later became recorder), for he was none other than Hugh Williams, the Chartist.[49] The borough of Loughor lay beyond the borders of Carmarthenshire, though within the area affected by the rioting. The lord of the manor there was the duke of Beaufort, and it was his agent who acted as steward of the court leet. Its six hundred acres of land were enclosed by an act of 1833 which allocated a one-fourteenth share to the lord of the manor, but the expense of obtaining the act and of enclosing was so great that only one hundred and sixty-eight acres remained for the use of the burgesses, and these, in time, they managed to obtain for themselves, at nominal rents, on leases of ninety-nine years.[50] In Laugharne, only, did the corporation property remain reasonably intact. The town itself was in decay 'almost like one of the old Belgian towns',[51] but it retained three hundred and thirty acres of land. This was divided into seventy-six shares of unequal size among that number of senior burgesses. A burgess retained his share, large or small, for life, and when he died it passed to the next in seniority of the landless burgesses. As the shares varied so much in size, a very careful watch was kept on the next in succession when a good share seemed likely to become available, to see that he complied with the residence qualifications. This system has persisted until the present day, and must surely be unique in the British Isles.[52]

Finally, there was the borough of Kidwelly, which deserves a paragraph to itself. The report of 1835 did not reveal that there was anything seriously wrong. The governing body was the common council of twenty-four members, chosen for life from among the burgesses. The corporation owned some fifty acres of enclosed land, and no less than seven hundred and thirty acres of common. The sole right of the ordinary burgess was to graze five head of cattle and thirty head of sheep on this land, but it was, in fact, monopolised by a dozen or so of the more substantial farmers. The report noted that no accounts were kept, and it was proved later in the century that about a hundred acres of common were 'lost' in the five years between 1835 and 1840. In 1843 the common council decided to let the whole of the corporation lands to such of the burgesses as were entitled to a share, and this they did on leases of ninety-nine years at a nominal rent, the main beneficiaries being themselves. What makes Kidwelly notable is the immensely detailed knowledge which is available of the day-to-day working of this corrupt borough. For this we are indebted to the presence in the little town during these years of Hugh Williams, who has already been mentioned and who will play a major part in the events described in the following narrative. He submitted to the Home Office in 1847 an enormously long statement on the corporation of Kidwelly, and the correspondence which ensued grew into a stupendous dossier which has lain, for a century, buried among the unused papers of that department. Even allowing for some exaggeration on his part, this correspondence gives the historian a unique picture of the personalities involved, and of their incredible activities, and enables him to see beneath the surface of the 1835 report.

Williams was particularly concerned with the administration of justice. The civil Court of Record of Kidwelly had become disused, but the mayor and senior alderman were magistrates, having exclusive criminal jurisdiction within the borough. Yet, not only did they border on being illiterate, they were also dissipated. On one occasion in 1846 both magistrates, sitting in petty sessions, were intoxicated, and the administration of justice had become 'a solemn farce'. Disorderly conduct was continually taking place in the streets and no one interfered. Drunkenness was prevalent, not least among the common councillors. Between 1838 and 1845, the council had spent nearly £300 on ale and tobacco. It settled its affairs in the Pelican Inn before meeting formally in 'hall', and then frequently 'finished the day in drunkenness and uproarious jollity'. When the council met in January 1845 to authorise the mayor to attend the funeral

of the Carmarthen general, Sir William Nott, the hero of
the march on Kabul, its members 'got vociferously drunk'
and ended their meeting with three cheers for the deceased.[53]

A word should be said of such vestiges of manorial jurisdiction as still remained in West Wales. The court baron and
the court leet had tended to merge into one another, as the
same persons served on both. Nominally, the former met
once a month, and it could act as a court for the recovery
of small debts. But its functions were primarily economic, in
so far as they related to the administration of the manor.
It regulated the use of the wastes and commons, and, in
particular, enquired into the payment (or non-payment) of
all dues to the lord, the chief rents, mortuaries, payments on
alienation of land, and the like. More intrinsically important
was the court leet, which met twice a year, normally at
Easter and Michaelmas. Its jurisdiction was wide, for it
could enquire into all offences from trespass to treason. It
punished forestallers, who bought commodities on their
way to market; regrators, who bought to sell again in the
same market or within a distance of nine miles; and
ingrossers, who bought great stocks in order to send up
prices. More particularly it dealt with barretors, the stirrers
up of strife, with common scolds, nightwalkers and vagabonds, as well as with unlicensed or disorderly alehouses,
fraudulent bakers and users of false weights and measures.
It is certain that these duties were actually performed by
courts leet in the late eighteenth century, for example in
the manors of Emlyn and of Elfed, but by the mid-nineteenth
century they had almost ceased to do so. What made the
court leet so important was the fact that it appointed the
constable for the year, and that it was this unwilling, unpaid,
and inefficient officer who was the sole guardian of the peace
in many a township in West Wales.[54]

The decline in the system of justice and the breakdown in
authority were all the more serious in view of the prevalence

of disorder in this period both in the small towns and in the countryside. The respectability of rural Wales was of later growth, an effect of the spread of Nonconformity; the background to the Rebecca Riots can only be appreciated if one bears in mind the number of crimes committed at the time which were accompanied by violence, the lack of respect for human life which was prevalent, and the constant fear of revenge.[55] The rapid growth in population had aggravated the problem, especially in the towns. In Carmarthen there was a tradition of turbulence, to which, as we have seen, the bitterly contested political elections had contributed. Open rioting had occurred there sporadically, in 1801, for example,[56] and in 1818,[57] in times of scarcity. By the forties the town's population had greatly increased, and many of the inhabitants lived in extreme poverty in its crowded back-alleys and along the riverside, often as many as four families living in a house of four rooms. Some 1,500 of them derived their living from the fisheries of the river, and, as their work was seasonal, they were frequently destitute on that account, as well as because of their improvidence.[58] The most spectacular incident in the Rebecca Riots owed much to their presence in the town.

The crimes perpetrated in the countryside were typical of those of any rural community. Yet it should be noted that an active magistrate, of considerable experience in England as well as in Wales, was of the opinion that they 'vastly exceeded the average in a similar amount of population in the English counties'.[59] The assize and quarter sessions records give details of all-too-frequent murders, of an occasional highway robbery,[60] of numerous excise convictions, and of an incredible number of thefts. With these it is not necessary to deal. It is, however, important to consider certain other types of violence which were prevalent, notably those associated with sheep stealing, especially from the commons and waste lands. The fringes of the commons, even near the towns, as for example at Kidwelly, were the habitations of 'turbulent and violent persons',[61] who erected unauthorised shacks on the common land. Along the open moorlands, conditions were even worse. As we shall see later, objection was taken to enclosure, but the pre-enclosed mountain sides were by no means the abodes of peace and contentment. A few unscrupulous persons monopolised the best grazing lands. They hired shepherds for their prowess as bullies. These harried and 'coursed' the sheep of their poorer neighbours, driving them miles away from the sheepwalks, and often mutilating or killing them. It is strange that the shepherd (whose name is synonymous with that of thief in the folklore of most countries) should have been so greatly idealised in Welsh literature. Sometimes these bullies were indicted in petty sessions, but usually they were too greatly feared for this to happen.[62] Isolated upland farms, also, were the scenes of furtive and sinister deeds. When Charlotte Williams of the parish of Llanddeusant, adjoining the Black Mountain, and her three sons were transported for sheepstealing in 1831, the remains of no less than thirty-six sheep were found buried around the homestead.[63] The daughters of Rebecca were certainly not unused to violence.

A particularly disgraceful form of crime which was prevalent along the Welsh coast was the looting of wrecked vessels driven on to the shore. There was a long tradition of this. A master mariner of Poole, in Dorsetshire, who was blown ashore in 1690 at Newgale near St. David's, complained bitterly that he was 'almost totally robbed and deprived of what the merciless waves had reduced him unto, by the more unmerciful people of that neighbourhood'.[64] The lords of various manors claimed a right to all wrecks, as, for example, in the lordship of Laugharne,[65] but they seldom had an opportunity to assert their claim for no sooner was a wreck reported than the country people from miles around assembled with their carts and carried everything away. So bent were they on this that it was dangerous to resist them. Cefn Sidan sands, near Kidwelly, were especially treacherous, and in 1828 the Carmarthen militia was called out to protect a wreck at this spot.[66] But the authorities were generally too late in arriving. A local magistrate reported three wrecks there in a week in the winter of 1833. The goods had been driven ashore, and carts had come from a distance of twenty miles. Ironmongers from the town of Carmarthen had actually hired carts to carry away bales of cotton, and the people of Kidwelly had broken up the vessels themselves for timber before they could be stopped.[67] The same magistrate reported other wrecks on Cefn Sidan in 1840 'plundered in a barefaced manner by the country people'.[68] A government report of the previous year, on the establishment of a police force, even asserted that there were, along the coast, men 'calling themselves fishermen', who had their living by plundering wrecks. They intermarried among themselves and were nearly all related to one another. They were, says the report, 'a most determined set of villains; it matters not what comes in their way, they will have it'.[69]

The same report draws attention to the increasing frequency of the outbreak of disorders associated with the practice of employing the *ceffyl pren* (the wooden horse),[70] and it is particularly important to notice that these disorders occurred in precisely the area which saw the beginning of the Rebecca Riots a few years later. The practice of holding someone up to derision by carrying him, in person or in effigy, on a wooden pole or ladder is common to the folk-custom of many lands.[71] It may have been derived from the riding of the hobby horse in ancient revelry and in Christmas games, and the phallic significance of this posture may have retained for it a suggestion of obscenity which made it particularly appropriate, to rural minds, as a punishment for marital infidelity. Edward Crompton Lloyd Hall professed to believe that it was sanctioned as a punishment for this by the laws of Hywel Dda.[72] But its application was far wider than that. The practice varied from land to land, and even from place to place, yet the incidents almost invariably bore certain characteristics. They always happened at night; the mob nearly always blackened their faces, and frequently the men dressed themselves in women's clothes; they generally acted a sort of pantomime or mock trial of the person concerned, and the whole proceedings were accompanied by a great deal of noise, such as the beating of drums or the firing of guns. These, as we shall see, were also the characteristics of the Rebecca Riots.

The first incidents brought to the attention of the authorities occurred in March 1837. The country around Cardigan was much disturbed, and no less than four parishes were involved. The mayor of Cardigan reported that six men were arrested in the parish of Cilrhedyn for taking part and were conveyed to Carmarthen gaol, and that fifteen more were wounded 'with the shot fired into the mob'. A week later there was a procession in Cardigan itself, when the mayor and two magistrates, who attempted to stop it, were assaulted, and a prisoner taken by them was rescued. Public notice of these meetings was given beforehand, and, in view of a threat of another to take place the following week, the mayor wrote to the commanding officer at Brecon to ask for assistance, but was able to countermand his request when the troops had proceeded a whole day's march towards Cardigan.[73] There is nothing in the records to indicate the reason for this outbreak; a serious incident at Cilgerran at the beginning of May of the same year was due to the vengeance of the mob on a man who had given evidence in a prosecution for cutting timber. The magistrates memorialised the Home Office, giving a very detailed account of the practice of the *ceffyl pren*, but were only told to swear in special constables who were quite ineffective. They did, however, commit one man for trial at the Cardiganshire Assizes.[74] In October 1838, a farmer was burnt in effigy in his farmyard in the parish of Llangoedmor, thereby gravely endangering his haggard, in order to intimidate him from taking on another farm as well as his own,[75] and in the same month there were several outrages in the parish of Tre-lech.[76]

Just before the destruction of the gate at Efail-wen in 1839, which was the first incident in the Rebecca Riots, the magistrates near Cardigan were begging the Home Office to send down officers of the metropolitan police to deal with the instigators of these processions,[77] and two months later the *ceffyl pren* was again carried in the neighbouring parish of Bridell.[78] Apart from this hilly area, where the three shires all meet, the only other scene of the exploits of the *ceffyl pren* noted in the records is the town of Carmarthen itself. It was paraded through the streets in May 1835, accompanied by exhibitions 'which would have disgraced the rites of Hindooism'.[79] When the proprietor of the *Welshman* was placed in gaol for a libel on one of the town's councillors, the prisoner's release, in November 1837, was celebrated by the carrying of his opponent's effigy on the *ceffyl pren*, apparently with the connivance of the mayor.[80] Yet once more, in September 1839, the peace of Carmarthen was disturbed by another procession.[81]

The subject should not be left without referring to the similar practice in these parts of holding persons up to ridicule by selling them in mock auctions. These took place frequently. For example, in June 1843, a tithe collector at Llangrannog (again in south Cardiganshire) was sold by auction. Someone impersonated the leading auctioneer in West Wales, and took bids in regular form, eventually announcing that the purchaser was the devil, and that the security had been given in the name of the clergyman of the parish.[82]

The connection between the *ceffyl pren* and the Rebecca Riots is evident. This ancient practice had flared up in the late thirties to an extent sufficient to attract the attention of the authorities, and this had happened in the area which was to witness the outbreak of rioting in the summer of 1839. The *modus operandi* was virtually the same in both episodes. But the connection was even more intimate than this. When the rioting was over, the people of St. Clears sought to revenge themselves on a person who had given evidence at the assizes by carrying him on a *ceffyl pren*. On two occasions they were stopped by the police, but the authorities were much perturbed by a threat that the attempt would be repeated on the night of the St. Clears fair, and by the statement that Hugh Williams was reported to have said that there was no law against such processions. A request was made for military assistance, but no demonstration took place on that occasion. The deputy-lieutenant, George Rice Trevor, was quite aware that 'these *ceffyl pren* processions were the root of Rebeccaism', and this had also not escaped that acute observer of social phenomena, Edwin Chadwick.[83] It can, indeed, be said with complete certainty that the Rebecca Riots were an extension of the practice of the *ceffyl pren*.

When rioting did occur on a considerable scale in the winter of 1842–3, it showed the complete breakdown of a system of justice in which the magistrates were appointed for social considerations and not because of their suitability for the office. Their letters to the home secretary reflect the panic and exasperation into which they were thrown. They were uncertain of the extent of their powers. They went in fear of violence to their own persons. Threatening letters, said a well-placed observer, 'appeared to paralyse the exertions of the gentry and clergy'.[84] Their immediate and invariable reaction was to ask for troops. In justification of them it should be said that the means at their disposal to preserve the peace were very limited. This, indeed, largely accounted for the severity of the penal code itself (at the opening of the century there were still over two hundred offences punishable by death), and of the manner in which they administered it. For if the prevention of crime was so difficult, the penalties must be made sufficiently severe to act as a deterrent. The constable, whether appointed by the court leet of the manor or by the parish vestry, was useless, and often non-existent. Industrious farmers avoided serving altogether, and where this was not possible engaged substitutes. These were usually both illiterate and indolent, men who preferred 'to earn a shilling or two by serving a warrant, rather than by attending to their work'.[85] The magistrates therefore had to fall back on the enrolment of special constables. But these were usually drawn from the same class as the rioters themselves, if they were not even in league with them. When nearly two hundred men were summoned to Carmarthen in August 1843, only six appeared, and of these three refused to be sworn.[86] Their excuse was always that their houses and property would be destroyed by the rioters. They rendered themselves liable to heavy fines, but the Home Office did not think it prudent to enforce them,[87] and the deputy-lieutenant felt that such fines could only be levied by compulsion, which would increase the excitement.[88] Baron Rolfe, who presided at the Pembrokeshire Assizes in July 1843, accurately described the situation when he asserted that the refusal to serve as special constables, or to perform their duties when sworn, marked the breaking-up of society.[89]

Failing special constables, the magistrates could resort to pensioners, the yeomanry or the regular troops. Pensioners, however, were generally aged and of little use. The yeomanry —inadequately trained and insufficiently disciplined— were apt to become panic-stricken and act foolishly. Besides, in the riot at Merthyr in 1831, they had suffered a major defeat and had been disarmed by the mob. The use of units of the regular army in civil disturbances was, in the nature of things, undesirable. Nor were they very effective. Rioters could always disperse at the approach of troops, and in West Wales they showed an uncanny skill in doing so. Large detachments were therefore useless, but they could not risk dividing themselves into small groups, for these could so easily be overwhelmed.

The inadequacy of police protection had led to a certain degree of private enterprise in this unexpected sphere. This had taken two forms. In various localities the inhabitants entered into associations in self-defence. Such was the 'Society for preventing felony' instituted at Llanddewibrefi in December 1785.[90] The society, which limited its membership to twenty, each paying an annual subscription of five shillings, had for its purpose the apprehending and prosecuting of felons, and the reimbursing of its members for any expenses incurred by them in so doing. Only seven joined in the first year, and possibly on this account the subscription was reduced to half-a-crown, so that the list for 1786 had twenty-four signatures (two of them by mark). It is clear that the main reason for the existence of the society was sheep stealing on the extensive common lands in the neighbourhood. The records of the society refer to the indictment of constables who had allowed a felon to escape, and to various payments in respect of prosecutions. In 1797 there was the sum of £20 in the hands of the treasurer, but the society, possibly unwisely, decided to use £10 'to buy a share or shares in the present English lottery'. At any rate, in 1801 there was only £15 available, although the expenses in connection with one prosecution for sheep stealing in that year amounted to £15 19s. 8d., and this was spent in vain, for the grand jury did not find a true bill. This seems to have altered the nature of the society, for henceforth there was no annual subscription. The members now agreed to enter into a bond to support each other in prosecutions for felonies, stipulating in the case of drovers who lost their beasts outside the neighbourhood that the maximum compensation would be £20. But the society does not seem to have flourished in its new form, for the records cease with the meeting of 15 March 1805.[91] The other type of private enterprise was for individuals to subscribe towards the salary of a police officer. An instance of this was the employment by a number of persons at Newtown of a private policeman when the vestry refused to pay him.[92] He was, in fact, none other than Blinkhorn, whose activities contributed so considerably to the outbreak of the Chartist riot at Llanidloes in April 1839.[93]

The outcome of the struggle between authority and disorder was, therefore, still by no means entirely certain in the early years of the nineteenth century. The menace had, in fact, increased with the deterioration of the old system and the unprecedented growth in the population. Evidently a new system had to be devised, and a start was made in 1829 with the establishment of the metropolitan police force. This proved to be so efficient that requests for its services were soon pouring into the Home Office from all parts of the country. For example, a dozen metropolitan policemen under the command of George Martin (who was soon to be in charge of the detachment in West Wales) were sent to Huddersfield to keep order in the election of 1837, and greatly distinguished themselves in baton charges on the crowd.[94] It was the success of the London police which led the government to consider the establishment of similar bodies elsewhere. A royal commission (of which Edwin Chadwick was the most important member) was set up in 1836, leading eventually to the act of 1839. But this act was only permissive. The home secretary, Lord John Russell, thereupon wrote to the quarter sessions of every shire in England and Wales urging the establishment of a rural police under the terms of the act. His proposal met with stubborn resistance. Nothing, indeed, could exceed the active hostility of the general public towards the idea of a police force at this time. Partly this may have been due to a fear that it would mean a sacrifice of liberty, but, in West Wales, the constant protests and petitions make it abundantly clear that the objection was on grounds of expense. The home secretary's letter was considered by the Pembrokeshire magistrates at their midsummer sessions on 2 July 1839. Although the first incidents in the Rebecca Riots had occurred only a few weeks previously, a mile or so across the Carmarthenshire border, the magistrates resolved that it would be inadvisable to adopt the proposal, as the county contained 'a well-conducted and peaceable population'. The existing constabulary, they said, was 'perfectly efficient for all the purposes of preserving the peace'. Besides, they thought, 'that it would be a dereliction of their duty to impose upon the yeomanry, already feeling the pressure of local taxation, the additional burden of supporting a rural police'.[95] In Glamorgan, alone of the Welsh shires, was the proposal adopted without undue delay. There a rural police was established in the summer of 1841, and Captain Charles Napier was appointed the first chief constable.[96] He was soon to be engaged in a struggle with Rebecca which brought him some personal injury, considerable ridicule and a substantial pecuniary reward.

A last attempt was made to galvanise the parish constable by an act of 1842, which made every rate-payer between the ages of twenty-five and fifty-five liable to serve. Some feeble efforts were made to implement this in various parishes,[97] but it remained inoperative. The outbreak of serious rioting in the winter of 1842–3 made some action or other imperative. Frantic appeals for the assistance of the metropolitan police were sent to the Home Office from the three shires, and these cost Carmarthenshire alone £130 a week (the penny rate realised only £5,000 a year),[98] in addition to the considerable expense of employing special constables and regular troops. Resolutions were therefore submitted to quarter sessions in favour of a rural police. These were met by counter resolutions and by meetings of protest in various parishes, while other parishes begged for exemption on the grounds that they were themselves peaceable. It should be noted that the lead was taken by the Tory, George Rice Trevor, and that the opposition was led by the Liberal, Sir James Hamlyn Williams of Edwinsford. Eventually the proposal was carried on 25 July 1843. Carmarthenshire thereby acquired a force of one chief constable (Captain Scott), who was paid £450 a year, six assistants (£150 a year), ten sergeants (22s. a week), ten constables (20s. a week), and another ten constables (18s. a week), at a total expense of some £5,000 a year.[99]

The struggle in Cardiganshire was more protracted. Here again the opposition was led by a Liberal, Pryse Pryse of Gogerddan. The situation was complicated by the fact that his area of north Cardiganshire had remained entirely undisturbed. There were protest meetings and resolutions, and the Home Office repeatedly threatened to withdraw the metropolitan police and the troops, leaving the magistrates to their own devices. Eventually, on 2 January 1844, the proposal to establish a rural police was carried by a bare majority of two. As might be expected, the force was very badly paid. The chief constable (Captain Freeman) received only £250 a year, and his one assistant £65 a year. There were, in addition, two sergeants (20s. a week) and fourteen constables (18s. a week), the total cost of the force being about £1,300 a year.[100] Pembrokeshire alone of the three shires remained adamant. Threats of the withdrawal of the metropolitan police had no effect on its magistrates. As late as 9 April 1844, the proposal was negatived by the large majority of twenty-eight votes to three.[101] By this time the disturbances were over, and the magistrates no doubt congratulated themselves that, unlike their neighbours, they had not been panic-stricken into burdening themselves with this additional expense. The risk of disorder was less intolerable to them than the disagreeable certainty of an increase in the rates.

Chapter III

THE ECONOMIC BACKGROUND

THE social structure of West Wales, which has been outlined in the preceding chapters, was based almost entirely on the ownership and cultivation of land. Its stability, therefore, depended to a marked degree on the prosperity of agriculture, and a period of depression inevitably produced agrarian unrest. The great landed estates have already been enumerated, and notice has also been taken of the lesser gentry. The class of yeomen was considerably larger, if this term is taken to include freeholders, copyholders and the holders of leases for a number of lives, but how many of these there were it is by no means easy to determine. In strict law it is probable that few tenures were purely freehold, and of those which existed many had arisen merely from a neglect to assert his claim by the lord of the manor, and particularly from a similar neglect on the part of the Crown.[1] It is noticeable that freeholds were more frequent in West Wales than in other parts of the country,[2] and especially that they were most frequent of all in the upland regions of Cardiganshire,[3] where they had originated either from the sale of Crown lands,[4] or just simply from the appropriation of parcels of common land by individuals before the period of enclosure by act of parliament. In many cases, customary freeholders, or copyholders, tended by the same process of neglect, and by the decay of the manorial courts, to become indistinguishable from freeholders. The copyhold manor of Talley, in Carmarthenshire, in parts of which descent was still, in the nineteenth century, by 'borough English', that is, to the youngest son, and where land was held by the payment of a fine, or comortha, every three years, was entirely exceptional.[5]

Respectable though the social standing of the freeholder may have been, it should, however, be borne in mind that his economic condition was generally very poor. Often his farm was small, possibly not more than twenty acres, and when he died his estate usually had to be divided between his children, so that individual holdings became smaller still. When this had happened two or three times the freehold became valueless and disappeared. The freeholder then surrendered his right to the use of common land, if he had not already lost it through enclosures, and sank to the status of a peasant. He had often been dependent for a livelihood upon obtaining additional work as a labourer; the scarcity of such employment in the countryside in the early nineteenth century therefore aggravated his condition. In many instances his property was mortgaged until it eventually passed into other hands. It was remarked that the small freeholders were the worst farmers in nineteenth-century Wales, because of their insufficient capital, their lack of agricultural education and their want of enterprise.[6] Indeed they lived a harder life than did the tenants, or even the labourers, on estates where there was reasonable security of tenure. Many abandoned their own holdings to take such tenancies. It was stated in evidence before the Land Commission of 1893 that 'the old race of hereditary yeomen had by no means died out in Radnorshire',[7] but by that time this was exceptional even in upland regions. The old freeholders had not been able to survive the economic depression of the years after Waterloo. A great proportion of such freeholders as there were in Wales at the time of the Land Commission had bought their farms only within the previous twenty years; very few of their holdings had been inherited for more than one generation.[8]

Customary tenures, where they had not become freehold, had also been undermined by the growth of leasehold. It may well be that the granting of renewable leases had arisen, at an earlier time, as a compromise, out of the confusion between the conflicting claims of the lords of the manor on the one hand and the occupiers of the soil on the other.[9] Such renewable leases were represented in the late eighteenth century by leases for lives. The unofficial Board of Agriculture, which was founded in 1793 as a voluntary body (although it received a grant from the government), initiated a series of reports on all the shires of England and Wales which throw much light on this and similar matters. The three reports on Cardiganshire, Carmarthenshire and Pembrokeshire appeared in the following year.[10] They convey the impression that most of the land in West Wales was held on lease, and generally this took the form of a lease for three lives (to which was sometimes added 'the life of the survivor', that is whether landlord or tenant[11]).

These leases varied greatly, but, usually, they involved the rendering of certain duties and services in addition to the payment of rent. A lease granted on the Bronwydd estate in 1784[12] on the lives of the farmer, his wife and his son, carried a rent of £25 a year. The landowner reserved to himself all rights to minerals, slate quarries and timber, and the leaseholder bound himself to grind all his corn at the landowner's mill. In addition the tenant must keep a sporting dog for the owner, and render to him six hens and sixty eggs at Christmas. On a Cardiganshire farm which belonged to one of the Philipps clan,[13] a lease dated as late as 1833 was granted on the life of the tenant's mother only. The rent was £30 a year, and the owner reserved to himself all mineral rights. The tenant was responsible for all repairs. He must provide a man for one day in the year to cut turf, and a team for a day to carry the turf to the neighbouring mansion (or pay ten shillings in lieu of this). He must cart annually thirty teals of lime for the owner, must keep a sporting dog for him, and deliver three hens and thirty eggs at Shrovetide, three chickens at Whitsun and one goose at the feast of All Saints. Such food renders may not have been onerous, but they could cause hardship if a farmer did not himself rear the geese or produce the other 'comestibles' enumerated. They have long remained in popular memory through a well-known Welsh ballad which takes the form of a dialogue between an old countrywoman and the local squire (of Alltyrodyn, near Llandysul). She had come begging for a lease for three everlasting lives. The squire told her that a lease for one everlasting life would do just as well. But she persisted that she must have one for three everlasting lives, and offered him a rent of £20 together with two hens at Shrovetide, two fat geese and a cartload of coal.

> Full twenty pounds to you I'll pay,
> And two fat geese in pig troughs fed,
> Two Shrovetide hens with combs all red,
> And load of coal for winter's day.[14]

A lease for lives gave the holder reasonable security, and ensured that he should reap the benefit of any improvements which he might carry out, either on the farm land or, especially, on its buildings. This benefit would not be passed on to his successor when the lease eventually fell in, for, almost invariably, this brought an increase in rent because of the enhanced value of the farm. There thus arose the persistent complaint of Welsh farmers that they were forced to pay higher rents because of the industry of their parents, and sometimes leaseholders would abstain from making improvements for this reason.[15] In particular, buildings were neglected, for neither landowners nor leaseholders would accept responsibility for them,[16] and this partly accounted for the deplorable state of farm-houses in Wales. The lease on the Bronwydd estate, which has already been mentioned, lapsed in 1832, and the rent of the last holder's son was increased from £25 to £76 a year. A lease taken on a south Pembrokeshire farm in 1756 at £58 a year fell in in 1818, when the rent was raised (for the holder's son) to £143 10s., although ten acres of land were taken from the farm.[17] (On the other hand, a lease for lives on the neighbouring farm lasted for no less than ninety-one years, from 1785 to 1876.[18]) The hardship suffered on this account by pioneers in upland regions may be illustrated from an instance on the Crosswood estate.[19] A farm carved out of the hillside was let on lease in 1797 at £8 a year. It then had no fields fenced in. Ploughing had hitherto been done by a wooden plough carried on the shoulder from one place to another, and the farm-house was a one-roomed mud cottage with no windows at all. The lease-holder improved the farm: he was, for example, the first to plough the land with horses. As a result the rent was raised in 1826 to £21. Where leases lapsed and were renewed during the war years, as in several instances on the Edwinsford estate,[20] the holders were particularly unfortunate, because the inflationary prices of the time led to the fixing of rents which proved an intolerable burden in the years of depression after the war.

Generally speaking, however, life leases which fell in during the war were not renewed. The report on South Wales issued by the Board of Agriculture in 1814, under the name of Walter Davies, which summarised and brought up to date the shire reports of 1794, shows the preoccupation with this subject in the intervening twenty years. The compiler confessed himself predisposed in favour of leases, but held that the facts were against him.[21] He admitted that no one would improve without security of tenure, but he held that leases for three lives were most objectionable since they gave so much security that the holders did not trouble to improve at all.[22] No doubt he was influenced by the many landowners with whom he had discussed the subject, for the greatly increased value of land in the war years, and the enormous rise in prices, made leases operate solely in favour of the holder. It was in the interest of the landowner that rents could be changed at frequent intervals. Within twenty years of the end of the war, the Reform Act of 1832 removed entirely the main attraction of indeterminate leases for the larger proprietors, that is the acquiring of an influence in the return of members of parliament for the shires.[23] Thus, by the time of the Rebecca Riots there were few leases for lives in West Wales;[24] none, for example, on the Dynevor estate, where they had formerly been the general mode of tenure.[25]

It would seem that the granting of life-leases was followed by an intermediary period when leases for a term of years were usual. An examination of the Cilgwyn estate papers would seem to show that leases for lives were granted until about 1800, followed by leases for years (generally twenty-one) until about the eighteen-twenties.[26] These, also, came in for much criticism, mainly on the grounds that, in the last years of the lease, the tenant got all he could out of the land,[27] leaving it in 'a state of exhaustion, dilapidation and waste'.[28] By mid-century, however, leases, whether for lives or for years, had given way as a rule to yearly tenancies. It is true that a bewildering variety of small differences in tenure still remained, in some instances resembling those prevailing in Ireland. Walter Davies noted, in 1814, a farm in mid-Cardiganshire where the owner supplied all the stock (mostly sheep), and the tenant, in return for his labour, had his house rent-free together with the keep of a number of sheep and the milk of four cows.[29] In north Carmarthenshire there were, throughout the century, farms where the owner supplied all implements and utensils, and hired cattle to the tenant at so much per head.[30] But these were exceptional. In particular, the vicious middleman system, the bane of Irish rural life, by which middle class speculators (among them Daniel O'Connell, himself) took a dozen farms and sub-let them to small tenants at twice or three times the rent, does not seem to have existed in Wales, nor the equally pernicious Irish system by which land was held by two or three tenants in partnership, thereby making the best partner suffer through the incompetence or improvidence of the worst.[31]

The ultimate social consequences in Wales of this change in land tenure, from leasehold to yearly tenancy, were momentous. Above all else it contributed to the sense of insecurity which proved to be the main solvent of the old social order. The plea of the old countrywoman for a lease for three everlasting lives came from the heart, and arose from the pitiful anxiety of a peasantry, living on the verge of destitution, lest their condition should become even worse. The enormous price fluctuations during and immediately after the war were unsettling to the life of the rural community. At the same time the growing anglicisation and absenteeism of the landowners, and the introduction of stewards and land agents from England and Scotland, was breaking down the old feudal attachment of the peasantry for the gentry. It may be that in actual numbers the displacement of the tenantry was not large. It was not one of the grievances aired by the Rebecca rioters, and it does not figure in the report of the commissioners who investigated the riots. Nothing, indeed, was more remarkable, in the later nineteenth century, than the persistence of a farm in the same family from one generation to another. It was claimed in 1894 that there were thirty-five families which had held the same farms on the Crosswood estate for nearly two centuries.[32] But the possibility of eviction was always there, especially as few tenant farmers had written agreements with their landlords. There were, for example, no written agreements on the Cawdor, Dynevor, Edwinsford or Stepney estates, or on the considerable property of the Bowens of Llwyn-gwair in north Pembrokeshire.[33] Neither were the tenants protected by any well-defined local customs. As the century progressed, the social history of rural Wales resolved itself almost exclusively into a struggle between the landowners and their tenants. The first stage in the process which precipitated this struggle was, undoubtedly, the change in the system of land tenure.

The change was the more serious since it was not offset by any marked improvement in agricultural prosperity or in the methods of farming. The latter had, indeed, been modified but little in the course of a century. This continued backwardness was due partly to the nature of the countryside and partly to difficulties of transport. Much of the land of West Wales was above the 1,000-foot contour, and was bleak and wet. In places it provided upland pasture, but it was not suitable for cultivation. Between 500 and 1,000 feet there was much woodland and rough grazing. Oats and

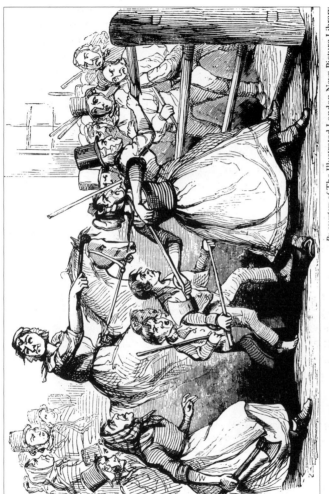

III. THE REBECCA RIOTERS

The artist was probably W. J. Linton, the friend of Hugh Williams

IV. REBECCA

A contemporary print, entitled 'Rebecca and her Daughters assembling to destroy a Turnpike Gate'

barley could be grown at this level, but the main occupation was the rearing of livestock. Generally speaking it was only the land below 500 feet which was suitable for wheat growing, and here, also, the cattle and sheep of the uplands had to be brought to be fattened for market. Such land was confined to the valleys of the Teify and the Towy, and to regions along the coast.[34] (Access to the sea was, in fact, of vital importance, since the sea provided the easiest means of transport between the isolated peninsula of West Wales and any large centres of population.) The climate was wet, especially in spring and autumn, and this, together with the uneven surface of the land, was the reason why so little corn was grown even in the lowlands, but the continual moisture and mild winters were favourable to the growing of grass and root crops.

Numerous travellers, as well as the compilers of topographical works, have left descriptions of the countryside in the late eighteenth and early nineteenth centuries. They differed greatly in their interests and in the extent of their knowledge, and they often contradict one another, but all seem to agree on the fertility of the vale of Towy. A writer of the mid-eighteenth century speaks of it as abounding with corn, grass, cattle, salmon, and woodlands.[35] A traveller of the war years considered it 'fertile to a degree which he had not yet witnessed in Wales',[36] while a major topographical work which appeared in the year of Waterloo was critical of those who still followed the authority of Camden in declaring it unsuitable for corn instead of using their own eyes.[37] Even in the lean years after the war it could be described as the fairest valley in Wales, so rich in corn, hay and pasture that it was scarcely excelled by any part of the Isle of Britain, but, in this case, some allowance must be made for the local patriotism of the writer.[38] The frequent and swift flooding of the river in rainy seasons could, however, wreak havoc on the husbandry of the vale.[39]

The agricultural revolution in contemporary England was the work of 'spirited landowners', and it was the misfortune

6

of Wales that, through non-residence or financial difficulties or lack of initiative, it was deprived of the aid of
such men. In one respect, it is true, Wales was a pioneer.
The revolution was introduced through the media of county
agricultural societies, and the first of these was in Wales.
A Dublin Society had been established in 1731 and the
(London) Society for the Encouragement of Arts, Manufactures and Commerce (now the Royal Society of Arts) in
1754. It was in imitation of the latter that an enlightened
Brecknockshire landowner, Charles Powell of Castell Madoc,
induced his neighbours to convert their hunting club into
the Brecknock Agricultural Society in the March of the
following year, the first county society in Britain.[40] It sought
to introduce improvements in husbandry and in manufactures by offering premiums. The Cardiganshire Society,
founded thirty years later,[41] was the 'favourite child'[42] of
the greatest of all Welsh reforming landowners, Thomas
Johnes of Hafod. On his own estate he introduced new crops,
improved the breeds of cattle and sheep, and, above all,
planted trees, thereby winning the gold medal of the Royal
Society of Arts three years in succession. He sought to teach
his tenants both by his own example and by precept, for he
published, in 1799, *A Cardiganshire Landlord's Advice to his
Tenants*, which discusses all aspects of agriculture.[43] He was
the Agricultural Society's first president. It offered premiums
for the best crops of turnips and potatoes, for planting
woods and reclaiming waste lands, and, later on, for
ploughing. The Pembrokeshire 'Society for the Encouragement of Agriculture, Manufactures and Industry' dates from
the same year as that of Cardiganshire (1784),[44] but it lapsed
after six or seven years. It was revived in 1806, with Charles
Hassall, the author of the Board of Agriculture's reports on
Carmarthenshire and Pembrokeshire, as its secretary. The
leading agricultural reformer in Pembrokeshire was John
Mirehouse of Brownslade, who was a near neighbour of
Lord Cawdor's at Stackpole and of Sir John Owen of
Orielton, and who, also, won the gold medal of the Royal

Society of Arts, for draining marshland in Castlemartin. Meanwhile, in 1787, a Carmarthenshire society had been formed, mainly under the patronage of John Vaughan of Golden Grove, and in 1790 had distributed premiums to the total value of over £300.[45] There were, in addition, lesser societies, such as those of Narberth and of Dewsland in Pembrokeshire, of Llandovery and of Derllys in Carmarthenshire, and the Tivyside Agricultural Association in Cardiganshire. Some, however, were shortlived, and the activities of all were spasmodic. The results, also, were disappointing, for the tenantry seldom responded to the encouragement given to them even when this was forthcoming.

The traditional agriculture of West Wales was a system of mixed farming. Where the land permitted, crops were grown until it was exhausted, and it was then restored by a combination of fallow and cattle. The fertile tract along the coast of mid-Cardiganshire was said, in 1794, to have produced crops of barley annually for sixty years without intermission,[46] and it is strange that it continued to yield anything at all. When Arthur Young visited West Wales in 1776 he noticed the usual rotation to be wheat, barley, oats, followed by some five to seven years of grass. It was only in some places that clover was sown, and it was only in a field at Dynevor that he saw turnips. He wondered how, with such a rotation, the peasantry were able to pay such high rents.[47] The reports of 1794 are unanimous in their condemnation of the practice of extracting one crop after another until the yield was hardly greater than the seed. 'The people', said Hassall, speaking of Carmarthenshire, 'have impoverished the soil, and the soil, in its turn, has impoverished them.'[48] Edward Williams (Iolo Morganwg), who was both competent to judge and predisposed in their favour, said of the inhabitants of Carmarthenshire that they were 'intelligent in all things but husbandry'.[49] As the war years dragged on, and one bad harvest followed another, the government became anxious about food supplies, and the Home Office, in 1801, circulated a request to all incumbents to provide information on the acreage of crops in their parishes.[50] These acreage returns are neither complete nor too reliable,[51] but they show the great preponderance of barley and oats over wheat even in the lowland parishes of the three shires. The total quantity of turnips and potatoes was surprisingly small. The report of 1814 outlined a great variety of rotations, approximating the Norfolk system of turnips (with manure), barley, clover (with lime) and wheat, then fallow, but this was usually on the land of persons of property. Ordinary farmers were by no means as progressive in their practices.[52] This is confirmed by a topographical dictionary published in 1833, which still speaks of constant successions of corn crops 'until the land is totally exhausted, and the last crop is scarcely equal to the seed which was sown to produce it'.[53] An unusually well-informed writer in 1849, when the Rebecca Riots were already over, discusses the improvements which had been introduced since the report of 1814.[54] Tillage had then increased with the growth of a home market in the industrial areas, and turnips now formed part of every rotation in the lowlands. But there were few good crops of corn, and fewer of turnips, in the hills. No two farmers farmed alike, but in the uplands, as a rule, crop followed crop of barley or oats without much alternation. Agricultural progress therefore continued to be slow in West Wales, even in comparison with the neighbouring shire of Brecknock.[55]

The introduction of potatoes and turnips as field crops is of more than usual importance to this study, in view of certain social consequences which will be discussed later. Writing towards the end of the sixteenth century, George Owen advised Pembrokeshire farmers to allocate their land in the proportion of thirty-seven acres to pasture, four acres to wheat, four to barley, fifteen to oats, and two to 'pease, pulse, turnepes, etc'.[56] Turnips were being grown in rotation with corn in south-eastern England as early as 1635,[57] and John Aubrey, usually well-informed, writes in 1685: 'it is certain that all the turnips that were brought to Bristol eighty years since were from Wales'.[58] If this is true, and Aubrey does not imply that the turnips were used to feed cattle, the quantities must have been very small. It was in the mid-eighteenth century that the extensive cultivation of turnips for winter feeding revolutionised farming in England. They were already, at this time, subject to tithe in Pembrokeshire,[59] but, in 1794, were still very little grown in the three shires.[60] One incumbent, who was himself both an extensive farmer and a chairman of quarter sessions, suggests an interesting explanation why the acreage for turnips was so small in 1801. He claimed that it was because, in law, the stealing of root crops was not petty larceny, so that a considerable proportion of his own crop of turnips was lost through theft, and other farmers would not undertake their cultivation on this account.[61] By 1814 turnips were very generally grown, both by the gentry and the 'common farmers'. The criticism, now, was not the neglect of this crop but the incompetent way in which it was cultivated,[62] and this, also, probably accounts for the poor crops noted in 1849.[63]

Potatoes became a staple article of diet at a later date than turnips. Men living in 1814 still remembered when they were rare enough to be sent from house to house as presents.[64] By 1794 they had become, with barley bread, the chief sustenance of the poor.[65] The acreage returns for 1801, while considerably larger than for turnips, are still an underestimate, for potatoes were grown in gardens and on headlands and odd patches of ground as well as in open fields, but it was only the latter which were taken into account. The distress of the late eighteenth and early nineteenth centuries made potatoes the chief substitute for bread,[66] and the excessive reliance on one cheap article of diet had important social consequences. It should be noted, however, that the disastrous potato disease, which made its first appearance not only in these islands but on the continent of Europe in 1844 and 1845,[67] came after the Rebecca Riots had run their course.

One reason for the backwardness of agriculture in West Wales, as well as an indication of it, was the antiquated nature of the implements used. Sledges were a common means of transport in the eighteenth century. Within the memory of a person living in 1794, there were only two carts in the parish of Penbryn, near Cardigan,[68] and it was stated in evidence in 1844 that in the 'upper parts' of mid-Wales the farmers still had scarcely any waggons at all.[69] There was, said Hassall, 'perhaps no more awkward, unmeaning tool to be found in any civilised country' than the Welsh plough, which was in common use in 1794,[70] and much space was given in the report of 1814 to suggested alternatives.[71] These were still uncommon in the 'upper districts' in 1849.[72] Later innovations, such as the threshing machine, although known in South Wales, were slow in making their appearance.[73] Threshing was still generally done by the flail on barn planks, and it provided farm labourers with their chief occupation in the late autumn and winter. This is, in fact, a matter of some significance. The only agrarian disturbances in the early nineteenth century which at all rivalled the Rebecca Riots in extent were those which broke out in the corn-growing area of south-east England in the autumn of 1830. These took the form of the destruction of the threshing machines which were depriving farm labourers of their winter work. As with the destruction of toll gates by the Rebecca rioters, the causes of discontent lay deeper than its outward manifestation, and they were, in some degree, common to both movements. But the destruction of machinery played no part in the disturbances in West Wales, for one reason because this machinery had not been extensively introduced. A far more important reason, however, lies in the class nature of the struggle. The revolt of 1830–1 was a farm labourers' revolt against their employers, although some of the smaller farmers sympathised with them. The Rebecca Riots, as will be seen, were in no sense at all a revolt of farm labourers, although they participated in the work of destruction. The riots were entirely an affair of the small farmers, and they owned such implements as they used.

Another reason for the backwardness of agriculture was the excessive, almost exclusive,[74] use of lime as a fertiliser. But lime was to prove the pith and marrow of the Rebecca problem. Two factors helped to bring this about. One was the very real need for lime, both as a plant food and to counteract the acidity of the soil. This need was greatest in the upland regions of West Wales where the soil was mainly derived from non-calcareous rocks, and where the heavy rainfall washed the calcium out of the hillsides. The second factor was the presence of abundant limestone in the southern part of the area, in a narrow band along the rim of the coal bed. When lime became generally used as a fertiliser it is difficult to say. George Owen seems to imply that it was in his lifetime,[75] but it would appear that the farmers then burnt their own lime. Permanent limekilns were only erected in the second half of the eighteenth century,[76] and it was in the period from 1750 to 1850 that lime was in its hey-day. The difficulty was to get the finished product to the places where it was most needed. The presence of lime and anthracite coal close together made it easy to burn the lime with culm at the limestone quarries. Arthur Young noted in 1776 that it was then carried away from the Narberth neighbourhood in panniers on the backs of horses, for twenty-five miles, into the hill districts.[77] Sometimes either the lime, or the culm, or both, were brought in coasting vessels to convenient places along the coast. Young speaks of sixteen to eighteen kilns in St. Clears, the culm having been brought by water,[78] for St. Clears was a little port in his day. Almost every little haven where a small ship could safely enter still has its ruined limekiln.[79] In the Rebecca period there were at least twelve limekilns along the seaboard of Cardiganshire from Newquay to Llanddewi Aber-arth, a distance of only eight miles, and they were in constant operation during the summer months.[80] But it remained difficult to transport the lime inland, and turnpike roads were therefore built from the hills to the limekilns. That is one reason why so many of the turnpike roads in West Wales ran in a southerly or south-westerly direction. When the lime-burning season began, in May or June, farmers with their carts would assemble at the nearest toll-gate at midnight, hoping to make their journey to the kilns, at Lawrenny or Ludchurch or Llandybie, and return before the next midnight, in order to avoid a double toll. Long strings of carts traversed the roads every night throughout the season, cutting in and out upon the parish roads to avoid the turnpike tolls.[82] These carts ruined the roads, especially in wet summers, but the farmers complained bitterly at having to pay tolls. For on a cart load of lime, which cost 2*s.* 6*d.* or 3*s.* at the kiln, tolls of 5*s.* or 6*s.* might have to be paid within a distance of eight miles.[83] The first Rebecca Riot broke out on 13 May 1839, just as the lime-burning season was beginning, with the destruction of a gate at Efail-wen which had been erected to catch lime-carters who were evading the tolls.[84]

For the payment of his rent, however, the Welsh farmer depended not upon his crops but upon his stock. At an earlier day his mainstay had been his cattle, of the black Pembrokeshire breed. These were small and hardy, able to survive in the upland regions, and also able to travel well on their long journeys to Kent and Essex.[85] For they were in great demand by the drovers, whose brutal and evil-smelling occupation[86] has been much romanticised by recent writers. Welsh butter was salted, and exported in casks to Bristol,[87] or taken in their carts by higglers and butter-dealers all the way from Pembrokeshire, over the Black Mountain, to Merthyr Tydfil.[88] In the eighteenth century, sheep came to predominate over cattle as the main stock of the Welsh farmer. These also were small, and very wild, and their wool was exceedingly coarse.[89] From October to April they were brought down to lower levels for pasturing. This seasonal

movement may be the vestige of the transhumance of semi-
nomadic, pastoral days, when the family with all its stock of
cattle and sheep moved from its winter *hendre* to its summer
hafod in the hills.[90] If so, the ties between the upland settle-
ments and the lowland farms had long been broken, even
before the enclosures of the eighteenth century. At least, the
present writer has been able to find no evidence of transhumance in South Wales in this period.

The establishment of separate upland farms was part of
a continuous upward trend of habitation which, in the course
of centuries, slowly brought the waste under cultivation.
For the enclosure movement in Wales in the eighteenth and
nineteenth centuries was but an acceleration of a process
that had been continuing for a long time, and it was almost
exclusively concerned with the waste. There were no
cultivated 'open fields' to be enclosed in West Wales at this
period, if there ever had been any. A great deal of inter-
mixture of tenements there certainly was. This was particularly marked where lands had remained for centuries in the
possession of the church, as, for example, in the neighbourhood of St. David's,[91] for such property would not often
change hands and thereby provide an opportunity for the
consolidation of holdings. Besides, Walter Davies noted the
extreme reluctance of the Welsh to sell or exchange 'a square
yard of their great-grandsire's land'.[92] But this inter-mixture
almost certainly arose out of the subdivision of property
through gavelkind, and not out of any system of co-aration.
Arthur Young noted that the country through which he
passed in 1776 was all enclosed, 'without such a thing as
a common field'.[93]

On the other hand it is difficult now to realise how much
of Wales was marginal land in the eighteenth century.
There were great tracts of moorland which settlers were
bringing under cultivation by a process singularly like the
colonisation of the frontier in new countries. As we shall see,
the growth of population was forcing crofters ever further

up the hillsides. During the long war from 1793 to 1815, the fall in imports made it imperative to produce more food or starve, while, at the same time, the rise in prices due to the war and to a succession of bad harvests made it economically profitable to cultivate these areas. The encroachment upon the waste therefore became accelerated, and this was particularly true on the lands of the Crown. In Pembrokeshire, the Crown had few manorial rights (although this did not prevent a scion of the house of Orielton from drawing a salary of £142 10s. as Crown steward),[94] but in Carmarthenshire they were extensive, and in Cardiganshire Crown lands constituted about two-thirds of the shire.[95] They were administered with 'the grossest incompetence and neglect'.[96] In some manors the rent rolls had been lost for many years, and the quit rents were collected 'by hearsay';[97] in others they had fallen into oblivion. Anyone who liked could encroach on Crown land,[98] and the greatest culprit of all was Thomas Johnes of Hafod. Although, as Crown steward, it was his duty to prevent encroachment, he, himself, appropriated nearly seven thousand acres of waste immediately adjoining his estate. He died in debt to the extent of about £50,000, and the estate passed to others. When the Crown officials did begin enquiring into the rights of the Crown, the landowners became alarmed, but, in 1843, the duke of Newcastle, who then owned Hafod, settled for these lands by the payment of the small sum of £800, although, even so, under protest.[99]

It must be stressed that it was only the freeholders who had any right to the waste, and that this was usually restricted to the pasturing of as many beasts as their holdings could support in winter. In other words, the right of common was not a personal privilege, but was attached to land, and was roughly proportionate to the amount of land held. But the number of occupiers had become so large that it was impossible to determine their rights, and a great many had ceased to exercise them.[100] The decay of the manorial courts had adversely affected the commons even in the sixteenth century.[101] For unscrupulous persons took advantage of the absence of any control to turn so many beasts on to the waste that it became over-stocked and of little value.[102] Others attempted to gain their erds by bribing the members of the court leet.[103] It was a frequent practice to take a farm adjoining the waste for the sole purpose of bringing cattle from a distance and turning them on to the common.[104] Generally the farmers used the grassy banks near their tenements, but the boundaries between these were naturally vague, and there was endless strife between farmers on this account. Night after night they would be up driving each other's flocks away from fertile or sheltered spots.[105] Frequently these men had no legal right whatsoever to the common. Before an enclosure act of 1828, the hillside around Rhayader (later the scene of some of the most violent acts of the Rebecca rioters) was monopolised by two men who had no legal right to it at all.[106] As we have seen, the smaller proprietors were no match for the larger ones, who employed shepherds on account of their prowess as bullies. These were the men who 'coursed' the sheep of their rivals with dogs, drove them into torrents, kicked them till their ribs were broken, or scattered them irrecoverably over the moorland.[107] Occasionally these 'shepherds' were brought before the magistrates,[108] but the fear of revenge, the constant undertone of life in rural Wales at this period, was usually strong enough to prevent this from happening.

In course of time numerous small homesteads were established by encroachment upon the wastes both of the Crown and of other manors. When the Crown officials eventually paid attention to this, they allowed occupation for sixty years to establish ownership, but they brought a great number of suits against other encroachers. In 1820 they sued certain of the inhabitants of Fishguard, among them Richard Fenton the historian, for encroachment, but abandoned the case when the Crown sold the manor of Fishguard in 1823 to a private owner. This person then proceeded to build three cottages upon what he considered to be his property, but in August of the following year several hundreds of the inhabitants assembled to 'defend their rights', and tore down the cottages, the historian's widow removing the first stone.[109] In a great many instances, especially in Cardiganshire and Carmarthenshire, the Crown sold parcels of land to encroachers. Sometimes these encroachments amounted to no more than an acre (or even less), but others were substantial.[110] Difficulty arose most frequently when, as at Fishguard, the Crown sold the manor itself, for the new owner immediately found himself at variance with the encroachers. This almost assumed the proportions of a widespread riot in south Radnorshire (again in the hinterland of Rhayader) when James Watt, the son of a famous father of the same name, bought three or four Crown manors in 1826 and brought several suits against occupiers. There is no doubt that real hardship was involved, for it led a high sheriff of Radnorshire to write to the prime minister (Lord Melbourne): 'If the assumed rights of the lords of the manor be allowed, it is impossible to describe the extent of misery which must inevitably follow to the families of that numerous class of men who for many years have been in quiet and peaceful possession of the little sheltered houses they have by their own labour secured from the waste lands'.[111] The discontent in Radnorshire was still smouldering in the period of the Rebecca Riots. Other lords of manors, of considerably longer standing, met with similar difficulties. For example, there were controversies throughout the first half of the nineteenth century between the inhabitants of Newport (Pembrokeshire) and the Lloyds of Bronwydd over encroachments, and this, in 1833, developed into a concerted attempt to refuse payment of quit rents, abetted, strange to say, by the neighbouring landowner, George Bowen of Llwyn-gwair.[112]

Objection to squatters came also (and, indeed, primarily) from freeholders and tenants. As we have already seen, these squatters were frequently undesirable persons, notorious pilferers and sheep stealers. The practice of putting up a miserable shack in one night (*tŷ unnos*), in the belief that freehold was thereby acquired, was widespread in Wales, especially in upland areas such as Radnorshire.[113] It was probably a late development,[114] but, like many other things, was widely held to be sanctioned by the laws of Hywel Dda.[115] When the road from Llandovery to Lampeter was built over Pencarreg mountain, it became lined with these hovels.[116] It was natural that the squatter should build his hut where there was a bit of good land. But in so doing he deprived his neighbours of the use of this land, and their attitude towards him from the start was one of animosity. This, in turn, made him an outcast, an Ishmael in society, living on the verge of destitution, and predisposed him towards criminal acts. Periodically the commoners would go in a body and destroy these shacks.[117] One squatter in Radnorshire brought an action against his neighbours for doing so, but lost his case.[118] In 1843 a squatter built a shack on the fertile common adjoining the town of Cardigan, but the freeholders immediately pulled it down.[119] Another, whose shack on Llangyfelach common was destroyed by his neighbours, turned informer against them and involved them in one of the most spectacular incidents during the Rebecca Riots.[120] On 28 September 1843, inhabitants of Llandybie actually disguised themselves as Rebeccaites before entering a house built on the common and occupied by an old woman. They made her kiss a gun and swear she did not know any of them before they ordered her out of the house and destroyed it.[121] In other instances, as for example at Begelly, due process of law was observed and the encroachers brought before the assizes.[122]

In addition to encroachment, the commons could be enclosed by two methods, namely by common consent or by act of parliament. Walter Davies asserts that in the decade between 1750 and 1760 'whole parishes (in Pembrokeshire) were enclosed by common consent'.[123] This is scarcely credible, for unanimity would be very difficult to obtain. Enclosure by act of parliament was surprisingly late in coming to West Wales. Before the outbreak of the war with France there had been only two acts, both relating to Pembrokeshire. The first of these had enclosed an extensive tract of Narberth Mountain (1786), which, within a very few years, was under cultivation;[124] the other enclosed a part of the marsh at Castlemartin (1788). It was nearly twenty years (1807) before another act was passed relating to West Wales, and then all the legislation which enclosed the open moorlands of this area before the Rebecca period was concentrated within one decade. Three of these acts dealt with large areas in Cardiganshire. Pembrokeshire was little affected, apart from the Carmarthenshire border, but there were some dozen acts relating to the latter.[125] Soon after the war was over the movement to obtain enclosure acts ceased altogether, and the only two remaining acts in our period were concerned with commons in the immediate neighbourhood of towns. The first of these, the Kidwelly Act of 1830, enclosed two thousand acres of land. It proved to be a very disorderly transaction, for the commissioner appointed to administer the act became bankrupt, although he continued to advertise sales of common land. The borough had thereupon to appoint another commissioner, and for a time there were two rival commissioners, both of them selling pieces of the common.[126] The other act (Portfield Enclosure Act, 1837) enclosed six hundred acres of good land at Haverfordwest, which was soon laid out in roads and fields, and sold to private owners.[127] Nevertheless there still remained, in 1843, a total of over sixty-five thousand acres of waste in the three shires (over half of this being in Carmarthenshire), and much of it was capable of being cultivated.[128]

The main reason why there was so little enclosure by act of parliament was the expense which this involved. Even when a bill was not opposed, the fees in both houses of parliament were enormous. The surveyors appointed to administer the acts (prominent among whom was Charles Hassall) found them a profitable line of business, and often took years to complete their work. Apart from the lords of the manor and the tithe owners, they were the ones who profited most. 'If the whole common were sold', said a Welsh occupier in 1844, 'it would not pay the expense of the act of parliament and the expense of the surveyor, and we should lose it all.'[129] As early as 1814 the burgesses of Cardigan wished to enclose their two hundred acres of common, but they had refrained from doing so on this account,[130] and they did not obtain their act until 1854. The Rhayader act of 1828, referred to above, although unopposed, cost £337 in parliamentary fees and £662 in surveyor's and other expenses.[131] The act to enclose the neighbouring waste at St. Harmons and Llan-hir, the scene of James Watt's difficulties, which did meet with opposition, cost £1,728 to pass through parliament (1840), and £6,400 to administer (£3,000 being spent, it is true, on making roads, which was frequently a primary concern in obtaining an enclosure act).[132] A particularly scandalous instance was the enclosure (1808, 1815) of the Great Forest of Brecknock, the eastern barrier to our area. Of the forty thousand acres concerned, thirteen thousand were allocated to the Crown and only seventeen thousand went to the commoners. For the total cost of the act, and of the proceedings under them, amounted to £16,000, and seven thousand five hundred acres of the best land had to be sold to meet these expenses. Owing to the cost of setting up fences, the commoners decided not to divide up their portion, but the parcels of land which had been sold now hindered them in gaining access to it. As a final indignity, a grantee of the Crown claimed manorial rights over what was left to the commoners. The position, therefore, amounted to this, that, before the acts, the commoners had forty thousand acres on which to graze their cattle; after enclosure, they had only seventeen thousand acres and no additional benefits whatsoever.[133]

We have seen that enclosure by squatters was resisted with violence; it is strange how little violence resulted from enclosure by act of parliament. This may have been due partly to the fewness of such acts, and partly to the difficulty in resisting constituted authority, but one is forced to the conclusion that there was, in fact, little opposition.[134] An act of 1815, which enclosed the mountain behind Maenclochog, in Pembrokeshire, led to a riot in May 1820, when fences were razed, and a house built on the enclosed land was set on fire.[135] The rioting on Mynydd Bach in Cardiganshire (resulting from an act of the same date) was more serious. Some eight hundred and fifty acres of enclosed land were bought by one Augustus Brackenbury, but a house which he built upon it was burnt to the ground in July 1820. 'The little Englishman', as he was called (*y Sais bach*), persisted in building another house, which he sought to fortify with a moat and in other ways, but in May 1826 this again was destroyed. He returned yet a third time, and was allowed to build his third house undisturbed, but he thought well to leave the inhospitable neighbourhood within two years.[136] The riot at Maenclochog and the 'war of the little Englishman' (*Rhyfel y Sais bach*) are the only incidents of this kind in West Wales.

Yet the enclosure movement was part of the general background of the Rebecca Riots. How far, then, did it produce a definite degradation in the condition of the rural population? The opinion of Arthur Young, who was, nevertheless, one of the chief exponents of enclosure, that 'by nineteen enclosures out of twenty the poor are injured, in some cases grossly injured'[137] is well known. The poor, it is true, had no legal right to the common unless they held freehold land; a moral right they may, nevertheless, have had. This is illustrated by a lengthy letter written ostensibly by an old man of eighty-four in anticipation of the visit of the commissioners enquiring into the causes of the Rebecca Riots.[138] He had enclosed an acre of common and built his house on it. He had spent every spare hour in cultivating it, and had been awarded first prize by a horticultural society for his garden. Yet when the enclosure act was passed (the Kidwelly act of 1830), he had been in occupation for eight weeks short of the twenty years which would have given him possession, and his house and garden had been sold over his head. He felt that the enquiries of the commissioners would not extend to men of his class, and so had written his letter. The commissioners were not unaware of such problems, for the chairman, Thomas Frankland Lewis, only a few months later gave the remarkable evidence to the commission of inquiry into enclosures which has been used in this chapter. He may not have had sympathy with squatters, and it might be argued that this is why the report of the Rebecca commissioners does not mention enclosures at all. But the enquiry was far-reaching, and extended to all classes, and the evidence is printed verbatim. Yet throughout this large volume there are only two references to enclosures, and these are to the desirability but expense of enclosure acts.[139] Even more remarkable is the fact that the evils of enclosures did not figure in any one of the many petitions and lists of grievances drawn up by the rioters themselves. As a cause of the Rebecca Riots, the problem of enclosures may be disregarded.

The economic life of the countryside was diversified by rural crafts, which provided alternative employment although still associated with agriculture. The census returns, as might be expected, show a wide distribution of blacksmiths, masons, carpenters, coopers and millers; but, in addition, there were surprisingly high numbers of boot-makers and tailors, which prove that the rural areas were independent of the great manufactories even in such essential commodities as clothing and footwear.[140] Of the rural industries, the most important was the making of various kinds of light woollen cloth, notably flannel. Spinning was done in the farm-houses, and most agricultural societies offered premiums for the best yarn. Many farmers had their looms, also, and their labourers would be engaged in weaving during inclement weather and in the winter months. But most of the weaving was done by independent weavers in their own cottages. These men either wove wool brought to them by customers, or bought their raw material and sold the product on market days.[141] In 1831 there were two hundred and forty male weavers in Cardiganshire, one hundred and thirty in Pembrokeshire and two hundred and sixty in Carmarthenshire, but they were widely scattered, the largest return being that of seventeen weavers in the neighbourhood of St. David's. It is probable that there were, in addition, as many female weavers. Even so the numbers were small, yet they were important in the social economy of a thinly populated rural area.[142] It was for carding and spinning that the first tiny woollen factories of the countryside were established, and not for weaving, but the weavers, although independent workers, were of the same social status as farm labourers and other wage earners. Their numbers had dropped in 1841 to seventy-three in Pembrokeshire, but remained stable elsewhere. The introduction of improved machinery in the large woollen mills of Yorkshire had almost eliminated them in some areas even before the coming of the railway brought an influx of manufactured goods.[143] Other rural occupations ancillary to agriculture were tanning and the stripping from trees (generally by women) of the bark which was used in preparing hides at the tanneries.

In the small country towns there were a few diminutive industries. Hats were made at Narberth, and the census of 1821 accounted for an increase in the town's population by the flourishing state of the hat trade.[144] Carmarthen, also, had a hat-making industry. The reason for the prevalence of this trade in West Wales was, apparently, the good felting qualities of the wool produced there.[145] But, by 1847, a change in taste had brought ruin to the hat-makers both of Narberth and of Carmarthen.[146] Boots were made at Narberth, Haverfordwest and Lampeter, but this industry,

also, was in decay.[147] A last attempt by the cordwainers'
guild of Haverfordwest to exercise their rights in 1831 had
failed. The wardens of the guild distrained upon the goods
of a shoemaker of Prendergast because he practised his
trade without being a member. He brought an action for
trespass against them at the Pembrokeshire assizes and won
his case, for the judge ruled that the bye-laws of the guild
were bad in law because they were in restraint of trade.[148]
Towards the end of the eighteenth century a Manchester
manufacturer named Scowcroft had established a cotton
factory at Haverfordwest, hoping to take advantage of the
town's abundant labour, its damp climate and its favourable
position for the export trade. When Malkin visited Haverfordwest in 1807 it was the largest factory in Pembrokeshire,
employing some one hundred and fifty men, but before the
end of the war the founder had been forced to close it down,
and it was not reopened after the return of peace.[149]

The country towns, however, were social and commercial
rather than industrial centres, and, in this respect, Carmarthen had so far outstripped the others that it had become the
metropolis of the area. It was centrally situated, and had
been the old administrative capital of the principality of
West Wales. It was thus the focus of its social life, and the
neighbouring gentry had their town houses there. Several
of these still remain, their elegant proportions disfigured by
shop fronts or by neglect. That so many of them are Georgian
in character is because Carmarthen underwent its most
rapid expansion (79.4 per cent) in the first three decades of
the nineteenth century, reaching a population of ten
thousand in 1831[150] (as against six thousand for Cardiff and
seven thousand for Newport). Ships of a hundred tons
berthed at its quay, and carried on an extensive coasting
trade with Bristol and other ports. The Irish mail connected
the town with London, to begin with via Swansea and
Bristol but afterwards by road to Gloucester and thence by
train. Moreover, two waggons set out from London every
Saturday, from the George, Snow Hill, and the King's

Head in the Old Change, arriving at Carmarthen on the
following Tuesday week, and starting the return journey on
the next day. The regular journeys of local carters linked
Carmarthen with most places in West Wales, and made it
the chief marketing centre.[151] But Carmarthen had already
reached the peak of its expansion. The rapid increase in its
population in the first three decades was followed by
stagnation between 1831 and 1861 (an increase of only
0.4 per cent), and this remained true throughout the
century.[152] Haverfordwest, also, had minor metropolitan
status.[153] It had its town houses, its market and its shipping
trade,[154] while its position as a county borough, with its own
parliamentary representation, gave it a unique distinction.
Other small seaports, such as Kidwelly, Laugharne, and
St. Clears, decayed when the sea receded or the river
became silted up.

Industries unconnected with agriculture flourished here
and there, such as fishing at various places along the coast,
notably in and around Milford Haven. The dockyard had
been removed in 1814 from Milford to Paterchurch which
became Pembroke Dock,[155] but ships continued to be built
there, as well as at the most unlikely places, such as
Lawrenny, Saundersfoot, and St. Clears.[156] Lead mining in
Cardiganshire experienced a return of prosperity from about
1836 onwards. In the year 1841, a single firm in this area
paid no less than £40,000 in wages.[157] This prosperity not
only provided employment to the people of the locality but
enabled the farmers to sell their produce. Almost certainly
it accounts for the fact that the Rebecca Riots did not
spread as far north as the Aberystwyth district. Small
metallurgical industries, such as iron works at Whitland
and Carmarthen,[158] and tin-plate manufacture in the Teify
valley,[159] relics of the pre-industrial age, were now dis-
appearing with the development of the coalfield. The
building of a railway at Saundersfoot in 1829 inaugurated
a brief period of prosperity for the Pembrokeshire coalfield,
but the undertakings there remained diminutive in size.

The Gwendraeth valley of Carmarthenshire, the scene of some of Rebecca's most violent exploits, was being developed now that its anthracite coal, hitherto used almost exclusively for lime-burning, could be used for smelting iron as well, although even here the industrial concerns, though numerous, were still very small. Further east, at Llanelly, the building of a dock in 1836 and the opening of a railway into its hinterland in 1841 heralded the growth of its heavy industries. Llanelly, and the Loughor valley beyond, mark the eastern limit of our area. Their development, also, marks the change-over to industrialism which radically altered the old way of life, of the decay of which the Rebecca Riots were an outcome.

Chapter IV

SOCIAL CONDITIONS

THE most outstanding social phenomenon in the first half of the nineteenth century in West Wales was the remarkable growth of the population. Admittedly, this was not peculiar to West Wales. The population of England and Wales as a whole doubled itself in the same period.[1] This increase, however, is related to the growth of great industries, to the influx of masses of people into the towns, and to the extension of medical knowledge and better sanitary conditions within those towns; and the increase in the first half of the century was still further accelerated in the second. What makes the position in West Wales so remarkable is, in the first place, that it was inhabited almost entirely by a rural population, and, in the second place, that the number of people engaged in agriculture within this area fell considerably in the second half of the century. It is impossible to distinguish strictly between rural and urban populations, but this presents no great difficulty, for the towns were small and were closely integrated into the life of the countryside. Moreover, although the western end of the South Wales coalfield was now being developed, industrialisation, as we have seen, had not progressed very far. The railway, for example, did not reach Swansea until 1850. Besides, the industrial workers, the lead miners of Cardiganshire, the coal miners of Pembrokeshire, and even the iron and copper workers of Carmarthenshire, were still not entirely divorced from the soil. A great proportion of them tilled their own bits of land. The problem, therefore, lies in the rapid but temporary increase of a population chiefly dependent upon agriculture, and in the far-reaching social repercussions of this occurrence.

Statistical accuracy is out of the question, particularly for the period before the first census was taken in 1801.

Nevertheless, a reasonable estimate can be made on the basis of information derived from parish registers.[2] If it can be assumed (and this is by no means certain) that the proportion of baptisms to the total population was the same in 1750 as in 1801, then the population of the three shires had increased by 20 per cent in this half-century. The first three censuses, again, are not quite reliable, but are sufficiently so to provide a basis for an estimate. A comparison of the figures of the first census with those of 1851 shows that the population had increased by 65 per cent. Finally, if the estimated population of 1750 is compared with the enumerated population of 1851 it will be seen that the increase in population amounted to 98.5 per cent. In other words, the population of the three shires had doubled itself in the course of a century.[3]

It must be emphasised that this was due to natural increase; it was in no way due to immigration into the area. There was, it is true, a slight influx of Irish workers who had crossed from southern Ireland by the shortest sea route, and their numbers increased during the Irish famines of 1817–8 and 1822, and especially after that of 1846, which occurred, however, when the Rebecca Riots were over. But the Irish were generally on their way to the industrial areas, or returning home in a state of destitution during industrial depressions, and their numbers were so small that they are negligible. Nor does migration into the growing industries of West Wales account for the increase, for, in this period, this was still 'short-distance migration', within the three shires themselves. In fact, immigration was more than offset by emigration. No figures for emigration are available, except, strangely enough, those for the five months from 1 January to 7 June 1841, which are included in the census report of that year.[4] The total shown for Cardiganshire in these months is considerably higher than for any other shire in Wales. Emigration was, indeed, widespread in the area of south Cardiganshire, north Pembrokeshire, and north-west Carmarthenshire, where the Rebecca Riots had begun some eighteen months previously, and were soon to break out again. Some parishes record a surprisingly large number of emigrants in this brief period of five months (fifty-three from Llannarth in Cardiganshire, twenty-five from Llanfihangel-ar-arth in north Carmarthenshire, and thirty from Meline in north Pembrokeshire), and there is no reason to believe that the period was exceptional. In the following census returns of 1851 numerous parishes, for the first time, record the migration of labourers to the mines of Glamorgan or the ironworks of Merthyr Tydfil; that is to say, they note the beginning of 'long-distance' migration to places entirely outside their area, and, once again, it is the three shires which show the greatest loss of any part of Wales.[5] In view of the continued net increase in the population of these shires, despite loss through migration and emigration, it is clear that its natural increase was greater even than the census figures show. If a dozen Carmarthenshire parishes can be taken as typical of the purely rural area within West Wales, then the population reached its highest peak in 1831, and afterwards diminished steadily throughout the century.[6]

The phenomenal rise in the population of industrial England is generally attributed to a fall in the death-rate due to increased medical knowledge and better sanitary conditions. But social conditions in West Wales were widely different, and bore a far greater resemblance to those prevailing in Ireland.[7] That there was any improvement in sanitation is difficult to believe, in view of the living conditions which will be described later. Nor had the nascent temperance movement yet had time to have much effect. The census return of 1821 for the parish of Llangeler in Carmarthenshire does attribute the increase in population to the absence of 'malignant fevers', which formerly had been 'common and destructive', and especially to 'the almost total extirpation of the small-pox', and the return for the parish of Llanwinio in the same neighbourhood speaks of the absence of 'any severe fever or other illness' in the

previous decade. How far this was due to better medical
attention is difficult to say. The return for Kidwelly states
that vaccination had become more general. The country-
folk had, in fact, always had their own crude methods of
inoculation. A Haverfordwest physician noted, as early as
1722, that they rubbed pustular matter taken from persons
suffering from smallpox on to the arms of others, after
pricking them with pins. 'I cannot hear of one instance of
their having smallpox a second time', he adds.[8] But the
practice cannot have been widespread, and, in the early
nineteenth century, when provision was made for free
vaccination, it was few who took advantage of it for their
children, and that through sheer improvidence.[9] Nor was
there adequate medical attention. Most medical men
acquired their knowledge through apprenticeship,[10] and it
cannot have been extensive. There were, in 1851, forty-four
doctors in Cardiganshire, forty-five in Carmarthenshire,
and fifty in Pembrokeshire.[11] There were also a few medical
dispensaries, 'to afford gratuitous advice and medicines to
the poor'.[12] But these, like the practitioners, were located in
the towns. In remote villages, and particularly in upland
farms and cottages, the sick had to rely on such help as they
could get from the more knowledgeable people of the
locality. Nor could their neighbours, who were in the same
state of destitution as themselves, afford the time to give
them much assistance, and the amount of suffering and
misery endured must have been very great.[13] It is difficult
to believe that, through increased medical attention, there
was any appreciable fall in the death-rate, though it may
be that more women lived through their child-bearing
years.

If there was no fall in the death-rate, the increase in
population must have been due to a higher birth-rate. The
tendency of country-dwellers to raise large families is well
known. A number of children may well be an asset to a small
farmer, if he is dependent upon their labour for the cultivation of his land. They may also afford him some protection

against sickness, and insurance against old age. Without a most intensive study of parish registers, it would be difficult to prove statistically that families were larger at this time than they had hitherto been, but other evidence seems to point in that direction. The number of children born out of wedlock was undoubtedly large, as we shall see, and this fact was not unrelated to the remarkable excess of females over males in the population of the three shires.[14] But this does not appreciably affect the problem, which is primarily one of early marriages. The census return of 1821 for one Cardiganshire parish (Llanfihangel Ystrad) does, in fact, attribute the increase in population to 'too frequen⁺ early marriages', and adds the illuminating comment that this 'took place in order to enable the parties to have a better claim to parochial relief'. It is a commonplace that early marriage takes place when the maximum income is reached soon in life. Those who have a prospect of improving their lot usually postpone matrimony. Of such a prospect there was little or none in this period in rural Wales. Thrift was out of the question; living conditions were so wretched that they could not well become worse; there was no hope that they would improve in the future. Men married early with the expectation that the parish would assist them with their large families. Once married, there was little, if any, restriction on reproduction, so that early marriage, by extending the child-bearing period, inevitably led to a growth in population.[15]

Early marriage was facilitated by a social custom known as bidding (*neithior*) which was almost universal in West Wales but seems to have been little known, except by hear-say, outside this area.[16] Before a wedding, a printed announcement would be sent around soliciting gifts, and informing those who had received such gifts in the past from the parents or relatives of the bride or bridegroom that they could now be repaid. The bidding was usually accompanied by a bid-ale (*cwrw bach*), for a quantity of beer would be brewed (without a licence) and sold for considerably more than its market price in order to raise money. Such occasions generally ended in dissipation, as might be expected. The practice, however, was deplored for other reasons than that, and specifically because it led to early and improvident marriages. A young pair would be induced by the prospect of obtaining a little money in this way to get married and furnish a cottage, and possibly take a small farm. But the gifts were in the nature of a loan, and, moreover, were totally inadequate. As a result the newly married couple would start with insufficient capital. They would struggle on wretchedly for a few years, in ever-increasing poverty as their family grew, and frequently ended by having their possessions distrained upon for rent, and losing their farm.

Yet another contributory cause of the growing population was the adoption of the potato as a universal article of diet. As we have seen, its introduction into Wales was late. The comparative prosperity of the first half of the eighteenth century made its progress slow. It was the distress of the war years which led to its general use, so that by 1814 it had become a cheap substitute for bread for most of the nation,[18] and in the next thirty years its progress was remarkable. Potatoes could be grown on land which had hitherto been of little use, while a quarter of the acreage required to maintain a family on wheat would maintain it on potatoes. Besides, contrary to general belief, they provided an adequately sustaining diet, at any rate in conjunction with milk or butter-milk. This reliance on one cheap article of diet was primarily a consequence, or symptom, rather than a cause of the prevailing distress, but, in its turn, it contributed substantially to this distress. For it enabled country people to raise large families more cheaply than had been possible in the past, and this produced still greater poverty. 'Poverty, potatoes, larger families, more potatoes, and greater poverty',[19] represented the interaction of cause and effect in Wales as in Ireland.

It was the pressure of an increased population which led to settlement higher up the hillsides, and this also, in turn, enabled the population still further to expand. In the census returns of 1821, the parishes of Llanegwad and Llanarthney in Carmarthenshire; in those of 1831, the parish of Llanfyrnach, across the border in Pembrokeshire; and the parishes of Llansanffraid and Llan-non in Cardiganshire in 1841, all attribute their increased population to the enclosure and cultivation of the waste, and, in all these cases, this followed an act of parliament. It may be true that enclosure acts relating to the open fields of lowland England sometimes led to depopulation; those which enclosed the upland wastes of Wales never did so. On the contrary they made possible an increase in the population. Besides, the expenditure involved in erecting cottages or farm buildings high up on the hillside was small, except in labour, which would be supplied by the family. Hence the number of upland cottages built in these years. The ordnance survey of 1822 shows an upward limit of cultivation on the Presely hills in Pembrokeshire which had already fallen by the time of the tithe maps of 1846. Fields marked in 1822 are shown as waste on later maps.[20] By the time of the Land Commission of 1893, an unbelievable number of small holdings in upland Carmarthenshire had disappeared, and even more cottages had fallen into ruin.[21] Their remains may still be seen scattered over the hillsides, bearing witness to a pitiful and futile attempt to wrest a livelihood from an inexorable environment.

This rapid increase in population had overtaxed the economy of the countryside. The agricultural practices of West Wales, backward though they were, had been adequate as long as the population was small, and as long as people had been satisfied with a low standard of living. Now there was imminent danger of catastrophe if any untoward circumstances arose. For a considerable proportion of the inhabitants existed on the verge of destitution, in a plight which bred sickness both of body and of mind. The outbreak of rioting was due, to a great degree, to these intolerable conditions of life, to extreme discomfort, and to the recklessness born of despair.

Descriptions of the social life of West Wales in this period are numerous and detailed. The attraction of Wales to tourists during the romantic era is well known, and it produced a considerable body of published literature. This is supplemented by a wealth of unpublished material of the same nature, as well as of private letters from visitors. The attention of government investigators was eventually drawn to the prevailing distress, and there are a number of official publications which provide valuable information. The riots themselves led to an exhaustive enquiry, as well as to a remarkable series of articles in the *Times*. Above all, a commission to enquire into the state of education in Wales (which was a by-product of the Rebecca Riots) produced three enormous folio volumes of reports and evidence in 1847. These 'Blue Books' are sufficiently notorious to anyone who is at all acquainted with the history of Wales in the nineteenth century. Nothing, indeed, can justify the employment of three young barristers, who knew little of education, or of Wales, and who were anglican in religion, to investigate a people which was now predominantly nonconformist. They produced a terrible indictment of the Welsh nation on grounds of morality, attributing the state of affairs which prevailed to the growth of Nonconformity. In consequence of the passions which were aroused, any use of these reports has become suspect, and evidence drawn from them is immediately questioned on account of its origin. Yet the amount of factual information given in them on social phenomena is enormous, and this is generally reliable. Even in matters of opinion it is necessary to distinguish between the investigators. The report which covers Carmarthenshire and Pembrokeshire was the work of R. R. W. Lingen (the future Lord Lingen, a friend of the Celtophil, Matthew Arnold), and, critical though it is, this is unexceptionable in tone. It is the report of J. C. Symons (including Cardigan-shire), which caused most offence, because of its con-temptuous attitude and its reliance on the evidence of anglican controversialists who were imbued with bitter sectarian prejudice. But the descriptions given of social conditions even by Symons are detailed and specific, and, moreover, they are corroborated by other writers who had no preconceived notions, whose work, in many instances, was not meant for publication. Besides, much of the obloquy attached to the reports arose from the fact that the three investigators were Englishmen. The curious will note that many of their strictures are repeated, sometimes in stronger terms, in the official reports of (Sir) Daniel Lleufer Thomas later in the century. But no exception was taken to his criticisms, for he devoted his long life to unremitting effort on behalf of every movement to ameliorate conditions in Wales.

The most obvious feature of rural life described by tourists was housing. It must be admitted that their descrip-tions vary. An unpublished tour in 1826 comments on the general cleanliness of neat cottages near Carmarthen whose slate roofs, even, were white-washed.[22] Another writer was enraptured by the same characteristic. These cottages, she said, were covered with roses and buried in apple trees. Their white-washed roofs made the villages appear, in the distance, like drifts of snow on the hillsides, and their cleanli-ness would do honour to a Dutch housewife.[23] But such descriptions are exceptional, and, in any case, few farm-houses or cottages in West Wales had slate roofs which could be white-washed; they were nearly all thatched. The typical cottage, so frequently described, had mud walls about 5 feet high, covered by a low thatched roof out of which there barely emerged a wattle and daub chimney, which was kept together by hay-rope bandages and was usually far from upright.[24] Such buildings inevitably became rat-infested.[25] The windows generally had no glass, and the floors had no paving.[26] Inside there was but one room, but this was usually partitioned into two by a box-bed or a chest of drawers.[27]

Conditions of life in these dwellings were unbearably distressing. When Arthur Young landed in Pembrokeshire from Ireland in 1776, he found 'the cottages many of them not a whit better than Irish cabins';[28] Sir Thomas Cullum, in 1811, thought the houses of Pembrokeshire and Carmarthenshire (in contrast with those of North Wales) 'the worst mansions of human beings on this side of the Tweed'.[29] A very sympathetic observer has described what he considered to be 'a superior cottage for a Welsh peasant', three miles from Aberystwyth, in which he took refuge from a heavy shower in 1819. The husband was at work in the fields, and the wife was scraping a few potatoes for his supper and that of her six children, who looked half-starved. There was but one chair in the house, and the only bed for the whole family was some straw laid on a few boards and covered with a blanket, on which lay a girl of five suffering from fever.[30] Evidence was given to the Rebecca commissioners of a family which had brought up fourteen children although they had but two beds in the house. 'Some of the children', said the witness, 'never slept in a bed for twelve years.'[31] Cleanliness was difficult in these circumstances. Soap was very little used by the farmers.[32] The usual fuel was turf, for it could be obtained free (although much labour was needed in cutting it),[33] and its acrid smoke pervaded everywhere. Even within the memory of persons now living there were no sanitary arrangements within or without the farm-houses of mid-Cardiganshire.[34] The place usually used for this purpose was the gable-end of the house,[35] and at the other end there was generally a pig-sty.[36] The villages were no better. The poor of Llansawel were said to use the churchyard as a privy. Nor can this be dismissed as the prejudiced remark of an English observer. The parish vestries themselves, as at Llangynllo, directed their overseers 'to cause the heaps of filth to be removed as far as possible'.[38] Pigs and poultry were allowed inside the houses,[39] and wrought havoc with their earthen floors. Twenty years after the Rebecca Riots, a sympathetic observer could speak of the existence in Cardiganshire 'of perhaps a greater number of cottages unfit for the habitation of human beings than is to be found within an equal area in any part of Great Britain'.[40]

Travellers remarked, also, on the insanitary condition of the country towns. Malkin, who was not slow to commend when given an opportunity, was particularly critical of this. He found the streets of Llandovery 'filthy and disgusting',[41] and he singles out Fishguard especially for censure. 'It is the only town I ever met with', he says, 'from which dunghills —I do not mean mere heaps of dirt, but literal and bona fide dunghills—are not excluded.'[42] The streets of Carmarthen were paved, and lighted with gas, and there was an adequate water supply,[43] but this was exceptional. Even in Aberystwyth, a seaside resort, water was brought in casks on horse-drawn sledges, and sold in the streets.[44] The new corporations, under the Municipal Corporations Act, were concerned with the primitive sanitation of their towns, with the lack of privies and with pigsties in the streets.[45] The description of Tregaron by the education commissioner of 1847 is graphic enough to be credible: 'I saw a huge sow go up to a door (the lower half of which was shut), and put her forepaws on the top of it and begin shaking it: a woman with a child in her arms rushed across the road from the other side of the way and immediately opened the door, and the animal walked into the house grunting as if offended at the delay, the woman following and closing the door behind her'.[46] Disagreeable though this picture may be, it is mild compared with the indictment of the town of Kidwelly, and of his fellow townsmen, by the Chartist leader and defender of the Rebecca rioters, Hugh Williams.[47]

The lack of comfort in their homes was increased by the fact that Welsh women shared in all farm work, and had little time to attend to their houses. They could be seen in the fields, driving the oxen at the plough and leading the horses in harrowing, planting and digging potatoes, or cleaning out the stalls in the farm-yard and loading the dung carts. They started milking at five o'clock in the morning and did not cease their duties until nightfall.[48] Some observers, indeed, contrasted the industry of Welsh women with the idleness of the men.[49] Early in the century the women were generally without shoes and stockings, but by the forties this was seldom seen.[50]

If one can believe George Owen, the people of south Pembrokeshire in his day lived well. 'At certain seasons and labours', he said, 'they will have five meals a day, and if you bestow the sixth on them they will accept it very kindly, and if they be but a little intreated they will bestow labour on the seventh meal.'[51] Allowance must be made for that entertaining writer's sense of humour, but Arthur Young, two centuries later, seemed to detect a superior diet in south Pembrokeshire,[52] and the *Times* observer in 1843 asserted explicitly that 'the people of Little England beyond Wales lived well and comfortably', in contrast with their neighbours 'the pure Welsh, who live as miserably as the poor Irish'.[53] The diet of the Welsh peasant was so poor as to be scarcely credible, but its very insufficiency drew the attention of writers to it. He ate coarse barley bread, which looked more like lead than food for human beings, but was possibly an improvement on the rye bread of the previous century.[54] For breakfast he had a preparation of oatmeal and water; for dinner, potatoes and buttermilk with barley bread, and some cheese in summer; for supper, again potatoes and buttermilk.[55] Butter he seldom tasted, for it was sold to pay the rent, and so were his eggs. Every farmer kept a pig, but this also was usually sold. 'I never knew them to consume it', says Edward Crompton Lloyd Hall, adding, 'I believe the cottagers of this country never taste meat unless it is at harvest time'.[56] There was little difference between the diet of the small farmers and of their labourers, and all writers comment on the absence of meat. And it was regarded as a joke in Cardiganshire to say that if there was

8

any sort of pudding they would begin the meal with it to make sure of it, for someone had been known to die before reaching that course. But this low diet had a serious effect on the countryman's health and energy. When ill, he took a long time to recover,[57] and a sympathetic observer thought the general strength of a Welsh labourer so much inferior to that of English labourers, on account of insufficient diet, that a Lincolnshire workman at half-a-crown a day was cheaper to employ than most Welsh labourers at a shilling a day.[58]

One inevitable consequence of the malaise engendered by these conditions was the prevalence of insobriety. Certainly there was adequate provision for the sale of drink. Incredible though it may seem, there were in 1822 no less than eighty-two public houses within the town of Carmarthen.[59] There were six on the road between Llandeilo and Llangadog and fourteen in the village of Llangadog itself, while, still higher up the valley, there were forty-seven in Llandovery.[60] There is no reason to believe that the Towy valley was exceptional, and the concern caused by this was now leading to the growth of a temperance movement.[61] Yet there was a notable absence of the more serious crimes. As J. C. Symons is the chief traducer of the Welsh people on grounds of morality, let him be witness to this. Serious crimes, he says, were five times as numerous in Herefordshire as in Cardiganshire.[62] Nor did all the poor try to find solace in drink. The sole woman witness before the Rebecca commission gave poignant evidence of hardship. She had nursed sixteen children and struggled to pay the rent and the tithe. Her family could not go to church or to chapel for want of decent clothing; yet her husband, she stated, had not spent sixpence on beer in twenty years.[63]

The rapid rise in population inevitably had a serious effect on the demand for farms, and thereby on the livelihood of the whole rural community. For the number of farms was reasonably stable, and, far from meeting the increased demand by a sub-division of holdings, the tendency was towards their consolidation into larger units. All writers seem to be agreed that farms were too small. The numerous sales advertised in the weekly newspapers in the second quarter of the nineteenth century show a remarkable variety in size, and do not bear out this opinion, but it is difficult to know how much of the larger farms was waste land, and impressions derived from sale notices are unreliable. A trustworthy witness in 1847 stated that of the eighty-six farms in the parish of Llandingat (which includes the town of Llandovery) twenty were under thirty acres, fifteen were between thirty and fifty acres, twenty-seven between fifty and a hundred acres, thirteen between a hundred and a hundred and fifty acres, and only eleven were larger than this.[64] Accurate statistics become available only in 1882, but these show that no less than two-thirds of the farms in the three shires of West Wales were under fifty acres in size at that date.[65] It is probable that the proportion was still higher in the forties.

The smaller farms barely provided a livelihood. It was estimated that a farm carrying a rent of £60 would produce, on an average, about £180 a year in 1843. But, in addition to the rent, there would be an outlay on tithes of £9, on church and road rates of 10s., on poor rates of £1 10s., on lime and coal of £7 10s., on two labourers (at 7s. a week) of £36 8s., in addition to interest on capital of about £10, and an allowance of £5 for wear and tear, that is, a total outlay of £129 18s., leaving only £50 2s., or less than £1 a week, for the support of the farmer and his family.[66] Inevitably the smaller farmer would become distressed; he would then apply to a bank for a loan, on which he might have to pay 10 or 15 per cent interest, and he would soon become destitute. It was generally agreed that he was worse off than an independent labourer who earned ten shillings a week.[67]

The merging of small farms into larger holdings was profitable to the landowners, for it saved them from the perpetual

expense of restoring so many small homesteads, and allowed
for improvements in agriculture. But it was a serious matter
for the country people, since there was little alternative
occupation in the countryside, and fewer farms meant less
opportunity of earning a livelihood. From the beginning of
the century there was an outcry against this.[68] 'Woe', they
cried with Isaiah, 'unto them that join house to house, that
lay field to field',[69] and their anger was turned more against
those of their neighbours who profited by the practice than
against the landowners. When the government requested
all incumbents to make a return of the acreage of crops in
their parishes in 1801, many drew attention to the evil
consequence of the practice, and a study of all the returns
for Wales will show that it was far more prevalent in the
three shires than elsewhere.[70] Several incumbents noted that
the 'byhold' was generally used for grazing and not for
tillage, and thus required less labour, thereby increasing the
prevailing distress. The depression in the countryside in
the 1840's was partly attributed to the consolidation of
farms,[71] and, as we have seen, it was the occasion for the
use of the *ceffyl pren*.[72] Threatening letters were sent to
culprits by Rebecca and her daughters, and, in some
instances, their ricks were set on fire.[73] In more than one
meeting to air their grievances, the supporters of Rebecca
protested against the engrossing of farms.[74]

Competition for farms had the inevitable consequence of
keeping rents high. Primarily, these high rents were due to
the inflation of the Napoleonic War period, and how great
the increase was on that account can be vividly illustrated
by the position on Lord Lisburne's Crosswood estate, since
there happen to be extant three complete rentals, farm by
farm, for these years. In 1801, the total rent on this estate
amounted to £3,397 9s. 8d.; by 1807 this had risen to
£6,134 8s. 6d.; in 1814 it was £11,286 13s.[75] In other
words, a farmer who paid £100 in rent in the first year of the
century was paying £332 at the end of the war. The landowners had in fact over-reached themselves, as this instance

shows, for tenants were giving up their farms because they were unable to pay their rents. The earl of Lisburne of the day was an imbecile, and the consent of the Lunacy Commissioners had to be obtained for the lowering of rents on his property. His guardians found themselves obliged to seek this consent, to prevent the departure of more tenants, and, in submitting their case, they produced the three rentals to which reference has been made. They proposed a reduction to a total of £9,044 8s., and an order to this effect was made by the lord chancellor. Other landowners, while not reducing their rents, made substantial rebates on rent days, and both the weekly newspapers and the vernacular press record frequent instances of such generosity in the years succeeding Waterloo.[76] But such rebates were very serious matters for landowners whose estates were encumbered by mortgages, possibly up to half their value, and by legacies and annuities and marriage portions, and many were unable to relieve their tenants even if they desired to do so.[77] And, in fact, rents continued to rise. The total rental of the three shires rose by over 35 per cent in the period of depression between Waterloo and the outbreak of the Rebecca Riots.[78] It is significant of the excessive rents then paid that they showed an actual decrease in the following decade in both Carmarthenshire and Pembrokeshire, while in Cardiganshire, also, they remained almost stable.[79]

The *Times* reporter seized upon high rents as one of the chief causes of distress. They were 'screwed up', he said, 'till they can be got no higher'. In particular he condemned the system by which farms were let by tender. A farmer would call upon an agent and make an offer; he would be told to call back, and, in the meantime, others would be interviewed. The farm would then be let to the highest bidder.[80] As soon as a farm became vacant, a dozen or more would bid for it.[81] It was the reckless bidding that kept rents high, and also poisoned the life of the countryside. The Welsh peasant was attached to his land, and was

prepared to pay a ridiculous rent rather than give up the
farm held by his forefathers, but (as in the case of the
Bronwydd lease mentioned in the last chapter) he would
have to hasten to his landowner on the day of his father's
funeral, for others might already have been there before
him.[82] For the decay in rural industries, in conjunction with
the growth of population, made it impossible for farmers to
find other means of livelihood, unless they left the district.
It was too great a temptation for an impecunious squire, at
his wits' ends to find money to meet his commitments, not
to accept the highest bid for a farm, but his tenant might
find himself in a position in which neither honesty, sobriety
nor privation would save him from pauperism.

The farmers were well aware of this evil, but their attempts
to remedy it were fitful and ineffective. The subject was
discussed at every mass meeting held by the Rebeccaites
in the summer and autumn of 1843. In the meantime an
anonymous writer in the *Welshman* (who called himself
'Lex', and may well have been Lloyd Hall) had outlined an
elaborate plan for parochial unions of farmers, which might
be affiliated into district unions, a plan which seemed to
foreshadow an incipient agrarian movement. He called upon
the farmers to form 'a fraternity of true socialists, brothers
in all but blood', and reminded them that 'the multitude is
physically the most powerful in the state'. He suggested
numerous co-operative schemes, but in particular he
advocated that the unions should determine the fair rent of
every farm, and bring pressure, by boycott and other means,
on any landlord who let a farm at more than a fair rent,
and on any tenant who occupied it.[83] In midsummer,
a magistrate reported to the Home Office that Rebecca's
emissaries were, in fact, going around Carmarthenshire
assessing the value of farms, and threatening with incendiarism any farmer who paid more than they considered to be
just.[84] There is no evidence of this, but later in the year
farmers in the parish of Pen-boyr received a threatening
letter from Rebecca, enjoining them to approach their

landlords in a body to obtain a reassessment of their farms. If they did not do so, added Rebecca, 'as the Lord God knoweth, you shall see more fire than you have ever seen in your lives. It is probable I may visit some of you in Penboyr ere long'.[85]

One very remarkable consequence of the increase in population in West Wales was the excessive number of farm labourers. In a considerable percentage of farms the tenant was assisted by his grown-up sons, and, in view of the smallness of most holdings, this amount of labour might have been thought sufficient. But the census of 1851 distinguishes between three categories, namely farmers, their sons and other close male relatives, and male agricultural labourers, and shows that, in West Wales, the last category was larger than the other two put together. In fact, if the last two categories are merged, the total is more than double that of farmers. In other words, although the great majority of holdings did not exceed fifty acres, every farmer, on an average, had rather more than two men to help him.[86] The reason for this is obvious. As the number of farms remained reasonably stable, and there was little alternative occupation in the countryside, the sons of farmers, as well as those farmers who had failed, must, of necessity, become farm labourers unless they left the district. The excess of farm labourers was, in fact, so great that migration proved to be the safety valve which alone saved Wales from a labourers' revolt similar to the one which had occurred in south-east England in the early thirties. For while the agricultural population of Wales declined steadily with each succeeding census after 1851, the decline in the number of farm labourers was still more rapid, and it is significant that this decline was greatest in the two decades after 1851, in a period of relative agricultural prosperity. This decline was due to the migration of farm workers to the great industries, attracted by higher money wages, better conditions of living and better prospects of advancement.

An excess in numbers meant low wages, and this was true both of farm-servants who were boarded and lodged on the farms, and of labourers, generally married men, who lived in cottages. It is, however, difficult to express these wages in terms of money, for in so many instances they were supplemented by other allowances. There had been cases in the previous century where no money was paid at all, as in respect of a boy hired for a whole year, in 1708, by a yeoman in the parish of St. Dogmaels 'for a pair of close and a lam', in addition, presumably, to his food.[87] Frequently a woman servant would be given a pound of wool, or flannel for a shift, and a man the ground to set a bushel of potatoes, or possibly two loads of potato manure, in addition to wages.[88] There does seem to have been a marked rise in the wages of those servants who 'lived in' in the second decade of the war against France, but there was a fall, again, at the end of the war, and there was little improvement afterwards until the middle of the century.[89] Allowing for a great diversity of circumstances, it may be said that, at the time of the Rebecca Riots, the principal servant would earn between £6 and £7 a year, the next servant about £4, and a boy between £2 and £3. The first maid would get, perhaps, £3, the next about £2 10s., and a young girl about £1.[90] Various account books give poignant details of the pence and shillings doled out to them by their employers in the course of the year to meet shoemakers' and tailors' bills, or a shilling or two to go to a fair, or even, indeed, 'to buy books 2s', for the ploughman, and smaller sums for boots and clogs, or a few pence for collection in Sunday School, or a shilling 'for a hat at Carmarthen' for the maid. At the end of the year there might be only ninepence left 'to go home'.[91]

Labourers, both men and women, were engaged at hiring fairs, of which there were many in the late autumn.[92] These events were much looked forward to, both because they were pleasure fairs as well and introduced some colour into the monotony of life, and because they gave an opportunity for a fleeting hope of better conditions in the ensuing

year. On such occasions the narrow streets of the country
town would be crammed with cattle, with booths and with
shows, and on wet days (they were so often wet) the inns
would be filled with noisy, drunken crowds. The hiring was
done in the open streets, where the older men and women,
the servant girls and the lads, would all stand in a row, in
the rain and the cold, jostled and crushed and subjected to
coarse jokes, while the humiliating process of haggling went
on.[93] The agreement was a verbal one, but a shilling would
be paid as an 'earnest' of the contract, and would be returned
if the servant decided to change his mind.[94] One late Pembrokeshire fair was called the 'runaway fair', because it
gave an opportunity to those who had left their places
after a few days to engage themselves with other
employers.[95]

There was no great social gulf between the farmer and his
labourers as there was, for example, in south-east England,
where a rising standard of living made most farmers
reluctant to have their labourers at the same table. In Wales
they shared the same inadequate diet, and worked the same
interminable hours, from sunrise to sunset, often rising at
4.30 in the morning.[96] But the living accommodation of
labourers was even worse than that of their employers.
The women servants generally slept in the farm-house, but
the men and the lads slept in the outbuildings, in dark,
badly-ventilated lofts over stables or cowsheds, or even in
carthouses. Their bedding consisted only of clothes spread
on straw. Many a boy started his life of unremitting toil
sleeping at nights on straw spread over the bottom of
a cart.[97]

Those labourers who lived in cottages were also hired by
the year, though they were generally paid fortnightly.[98]
In the late eighteenth century, a Cardiganshire labourer
who provided his own food earned only about sixpence
a day; where his employer supplied him with food, his
wages might be as low as twopence or threepence a day.
These had risen slightly in the early days of the war to

tenpence in summer and eightpence in winter (without food) in the lowlands of Pembrokeshire and Carmarthenshire, and about twopence less in the upland regions and in Cardiganshire.[99] By the end of the war the usual wage was about a shilling a day,[100] which Sir Thomas Cullum thought 'astonishingly low',[101] though wages remained still less in the hill districts. For the time of the Rebecca Riots we have accurate figures, since Lingen, the education commissioner, noted in great detail the wages paid in every parish in his area.[102] His figures show that wages had risen, on an average, by little more than twopence a day over a period of thirty years.

Lloyd Hall wondered how labourers were able to live at all on these wages, and could only suggest that it was by depending to a great extent on potatoes.[103] It is instructive to compare the weekly budget (in September 1841) of a coal miner living at Llangennech who earned 14s. a week and had a family of a wife, two girls and two boys, one of whom earned 4s., with that of a farm labourer living nearby at Llan-non who earned 10s. a week and had a wife and one child. Their rents were much the same (1s. 2d. and 1s. 4d. a week). Both grew their own potatoes, and both reared a pig, though the miner, who killed the pig in November, depended upon the sale of a part of it to help with the rent and to buy clothes for his family, and was therefore forced to spend 10d. a week on bacon. Both bought a considerable quantity of barley flour (20 lbs. and 18 lbs. at 1½d. a lb.), and the miner also bought 20 lbs. of wheaten flour to the labourer's 6 lbs. The miner's family consumed 7½ lbs. of cheese (which he and his son probably took with them underground) and the labourer 3 lb. The miner bought 1½ lbs. of butter and the labourer ½ lb. Naturally the miner used more soap (1½ lb. to ½ lb.). Both had a little tea (1½ oz. and 1 oz.) and tobacco (2 oz. and 1 oz.). The miner spent 1s. 6d. a week on candles, but this was a luxury which did not figure in the labourer's budget at all. By the end of the week the wages of both were spent to the last penny.[104]

The lack of adjustment between a growing population and a backward economy was brought to a head by the period of depression at the end of the Napoleonic war. The causes of this depression are familiar enough.[105] The change-over from war to peace was catastrophic. There was a sudden cessation of employment directly dependent upon the war, and unemployment in the industrial areas on account of this had the immediate consequence of restricting the market for agricultural products. Britain's continental customers were themselves impoverished because of the devastation of war, and trade was difficult because of high tariffs both in this and in other countries. The enormous national debt and public expenditure kept the cost of living high. All these factors were common to the country as a whole, but their effects varied from time to time and from place to place. In fact, the chancellor of the Exchequer could speak, in 1823, of a 'flood of prosperity'. In West Wales the depression was more unrelieved. Even the return to relative prosperity in other parts of the country was felt, in this area, mostly through its unfortunate consequences, for the boom of 1823 led to reckless speculation, and to the excessive issue of notes by country banks which caused a banking crisis affecting the whole population.

Another factor, which might be considered an external one in the sense that it did not arise from social conditions, was the inclemency of the weather. A wet and unproductive harvest is often the *deus ex machina* of the economic historian, an act of God which does not itself require explanation but which explains many things. But the weather, also, can vary from place to place, and the harvest may be bad in one part of the country and good in another. Nor was this a new phenomenon; Welsh ballad singers had often signalised both drought and excessive rain.[106] Yet the immediate post-war years, which are well-documented in this respect, seem to have experienced uncommonly bad weather,[107] and this was especially true of 1816. It was 'extremely cold and wet throughout; one of the worst harvests ever known',[108] and it came to be called 'the year without a summer' because its temperature was the lowest on record.[109] In consequence, the following year was one of extreme shortage, and there were meetings of landowners to see what could be done to relieve the prevailing distress.[110] The months of July and August of 1817 were 'very cold and wet', though the weather improved in September.[111] The summer of 1818 was 'intensely hot and dry',[112] but, possibly on that account, there was thunder in September, with tremendous gales and heavy rain which unroofed houses, destroyed farms and converted the flats in the Towy valley into a sheet of water.[113] After that, the weather improved somewhat.

A farmer's prosperity must depend mainly on the market prices of his products, and since West Wales was an area of pastoral farming it was the price of dairy produce which mattered most, and not that of corn.[114] Before the outbreak of war, beef, mutton and pork sold at about 3*d.* a pound; butter at 6*d.*; cheese at 2½*d.* or 3*d.*; while eggs were three a penny, and a couple of fat chickens could be obtained for a shilling. Prices remained much the same in the early days of the war, but then rose a little, falling again in 1802, possibly on account of the Peace of Amiens. After that there was a considerable rise, beef selling at 6*d.* or 7*d.* a pound and butter at 11*d.* to 1*s.* 6*d.* Farmers were therefore tempted to hold back their produce,[115] and the coming of peace took them unawares; even today there is a faint memory in West Wales of how they were caught by the fall in the price of butter. By 1816 wheat was said to have fallen in South Wales to one-third of the former price, barley and oats to a quarter, cattle to one-third and sheep to a half.[116] Farmers were compelled to sell off their cattle to pay their rents, so that they became understocked and had smaller returns. In some instances they had to give up their farms. There were in this year about sixty farms in Cardiganshire unoccupied (ranging from fifty to two hundred and fifty acres), among them twelve of the largest farms in the Lampeter district.[117] Butter was sold in 1817 'at whatever price they could get'.[118]

Wheat fetched a lower price in Pembrokeshire in 1820 than in any other county, probably because supply greatly exceeded demand in this remote area.[119] Thereafter prices became steadier, but they remained at a low level for a quarter of a century, while rents, as we have seen, rose by as much as 35 per cent.

Depression had a disastrous effect on the country banks, and this, in turn, had important consequences.[120] These banks had come into existence in the first decade of the war with France, after the Bank of England had, in 1797, suspended cash payments. They issued a considerable quantity of notes, which provided most of the currency circulating in the countryside. When the slump came, many stopped payment, while others were afraid to issue notes through fear of a run on the bank.[121] What was worse, several became bankrupt or dissolved partnership, among them being the Aberystwyth and Tregaron Bank (*Banc y Ddafad Ddu*),[122] *Banc y Llong* of Aberystwyth,[123] and the Union Bank of Haverfordwest.[124] Some were able to reconstitute themselves, but all were caught up in the blizzard which overtook them in 1825–6,[125] wiping out every single bank in Pembrokeshire.[126] The most notable of the failures was the Haverfordwest bank of Nathaniel Phillips, the son of a Jewish pedlar of Frankfort who, with his brother, had settled in Haverfordwest and become a Christian, and who was the progenitor of several distinguished Calvinistic Methodists. Fifty years later the failure of 'Natty Phillips's bank' was still only 'too well remembered' in Haverfordwest.[127] Even the important Carmarthen bank of Waters, Jones and Company found it wise to have public meetings held to express confidence in its solvency,[128] and, although it weathered the storm on that occasion, when there was a return of panic in 1832 it, also, succumbed[129]. It was then said to have issued notes to the extent of about £100,000 upon unmarketable securities, and to have lent money contrary to every principle of common sense and common safety.[130]

The consequences of these banking crises were momentous. They wiped out innumerable small savings, and may have had a decisive effect on the disappearance of the class of yeomen farmers. They nearly ruined the small savings banks which were striving to improve conditions of life in the countryside.[131] Even the smaller turnpike trusts were seriously affected by the loss of their deposits.[132] But more important was the scarcity of currency which was generated by these failures. The industrialist, Lewis Weston Dillwyn, wrote that the withdrawal of £240,000 'abruptly locked up from our circulating medium . . . threatens the whole country with ruin'.[133] Employers in Swansea were unable to get money to pay their workmen, while deflation had its usual effect in restricting trade, and this indirectly affected the countryside adversely. Farmers were paralysed by their inability to find ready money. This was at the root of much of their objection to the new poor law, for they had often hitherto relieved the poor by gifts of provisions and clothing. The poor law commissioner reported that the guardians of Cardigan Union were seriously discussing the propriety of even paying the poor rate in kind. This was certainly why they objected to the compulsory commutation of the tithes in a period of scarce currency. It also had a bad effect on rural industries, which, as we have seen, had done much to diversify the life of the countryside, and had provided alternative employment in periods of depression. For, at a time, for example, when the flannel trade was being seriously affected by competition from Yorkshire, the small rural firms were hampered, if not ruined, by the restriction of their credit through the failures of the banks.[135]

It was the persistence of almost unrelieved depression which accounted for the increase in emigration from West Wales as the century progressed, a movement of which some figures have already been given in this chapter. Parish vestries, indeed, found in emigration a partial solution to their difficulties, and sometimes contributed very substantial sums, even as much as £30, to aid a pauper and his family to emigrate to America.[136] Far more numerous were the emigrants, 'small farmers and the better order of peasantry'[137] as well as labourers, who left without assistance. Notices of shipping companies began to appear regularly in the weekly press. The usual practice was for small ships to pick up passengers in the ports along the coast, at Carmarthen, Fishguard, Cardigan, Newquay, and Aberaeron, and even in tiny harbours such as Llan-non near Aberystwyth,[138] where it is surprising that a ship could enter, and take them to Liverpool, whence a passage to New York could be obtained in the steerage for £4.[139] Soon, ships took passengers direct from Cardigan and Carmarthen to Quebec or New York.[140] Frequently emigrants left in groups together; for example, about eighty left in one group from the neighbourhood of Clydau in the summer of 1840.[141] There were poignant scenes at the quay-side as the emigrants took leave of their relatives, whom they could scarcely hope ever to see again, and listened, possibly for the last time, to a sermon preached in their mother tongue.

Conditions improved a little in the mid-thirties, but they deteriorated seriously towards the end of the decade. Primarily, the cause, again, was a series of bad harvests. Those of 1837 and 1838 were poor in the country as a whole, and led to a drain of gold to pay for foreign corn.[142] In West Wales the following three seasons were appallingly bad, so much so that they form the dominant recurring theme in the evidence given before the Rebecca commission.[143] Nine out of every ten farmers even in Pembrokeshire were forced to buy corn for their own use.[144] The harvest of 1842, on the other hand, proved remarkably abundant; it was the best in Pembrokeshire and Carmarthenshire for seventeen years.[145] Ironically enough, this did not benefit the farmers, for it coincided with a severe industrial depression, especially in the iron trade, which was caused, apparently, by overspeculation, by the competition of foreign manufacturers and by foreign tariffs, and by a banking crisis in the United States.[146] This depression had already begun in the late autumn of 1841,[147] and it became progressively more severe. Soon the furnaces of Glamorgan and Monmouthshire were being blown out, miners were being discharged and industrial workers generally were returning to their homes in rural Wales.[148] The climax was reached in South Wales with the failure in June 1843 of the Ebbw Vale ironworks, which employed some 3,000 men.[149] The connection of this depression with the disturbances in West Wales was not lost on the authorities.[150] For the fall in the demand for provisions which it immediately engendered brought prices down. Wheat, which averaged 63s. a quarter in January 1842, fell to 58s. 4d. in March, and to 47s. in the following January.[151] Barley dropped from 6s. a bushel to 3s. 6d.[152] Butter was sold in Narberth market at 6½d. a pound, half its normal price,[153] and even when taken in casks all the way to Swansea fetched only 8d. a pound.[154] Farmers from Newcastle Emlyn who carried their butter every fortnight to Merthyr Tydfil found that they could scarcely sell it.[155] The fairs were slack, for there was no demand for the horses and cattle of West Wales,[156] and their prices fell by a half,[157] so that there immediately arose a clamour against the importation of foreign cattle.[158] The depression in West Wales was almost unprecedented.

So great was the poverty and suffering which ensued that it engendered spiritual malaise and recklessness.[159] The isolated assault on two gates on the border between Carmarthenshire and Pembrokeshire in the summer of 1839, symptomatic though it was of a general restlessness in the countryside, had not been followed by further acts of violence. It was in the winter of 1842 that the Rebecca Riots really broke out, and their cause was poverty. It was distress and semi-starvation which led the country people to march under the banners of Rebecca. 'The people', read a letter which was secretly left in the office of the *Welshman*, and was signed only by Rebecca, though it is difficult not to see in it the hand of Hugh Williams, 'the masses to a man throughout the three counties of Carmarthen, Cardigan, and Pembroke

are with me. Oh yes, they are all my children. When I meet
the lime-men on the road covered with sweat and dust,
I know they are Rebeccaites. When I see the coalmen
coming to town cloathed in rags, hard worked and hard fed,
I know they are mine, these are Rebecca's children. When
I see the farmers' wives carrying loaded baskets to market,
bending under the weight, I know well that these are my
daughters. If I turn into a farmer's house and see them
eating barley bread and drinking whey, surely, say I, these
are members of my family, these are the oppressrd sons and
daughters of Rebecca.'[160]

Chapter V

THE GROWTH OF OPINION

SOCIAL distress, however aggravated, will not of itself produce organised discontent. It may, and often does, lead to rioting, when privation causes hysteria, and people become desperate through despair of obtaining any alleviation of their suffering, if not even deranged in mind through semi-starvation. This, according to the *Times* correspondent, was the explanation of the Rebecca Riots. 'I am convinced', he wrote, 'there is nothing like political disaffection, opposition to the Government, or any Chartist crotchets instigating the present disturbances. Distress—growing distress—and want, only, are at the bottom of all. I do not think anything beyond the hope of shaking off an intolerable load—burdens too great for them to bear—influences them. I have never, whilst here, heard anything whatever approaching to political disaffection.'[1] The situation, however, was not as simple as that. Economic depression always throws specific grievances into high relief, and these grievances become formulated by the more politically-minded members of a community. Although it will be seen that there was no organised conspiracy in West Wales, no clear leadership, above all no one man who personified Rebecca, it is nevertheless necessary to examine the climate of opinion, the welter of confused beliefs and emotions, in which the movement grew.

The analysis of the social structure given in an earlier chapter has shown that society in West Wales comprised, broadly speaking, only two classes, the gentry and the peasantry. It is also true that the Rebecca Riots were almost entirely an affair of the small farmers. Therefore it is the standard of education of this class which is of importance in this connection. This standard should not be difficult to determine, for the rioting itself led to the notorious education commission which produced, in 1847, three enormous volumes examining in exhaustive detail the schools in every parish in Wales. But the whole question has been bedevilled by the controversy caused by the appearance of these volumes. Exaggerated statements were made by both sides. The cumulative impression of the appearance in print of thousands of ignorant answers, extracted from bewildered children by the commissioners and their assistants, is one of appalling illiteracy. On the other hand a tutor at a nonconformist academy could write in a memorandum to the commissioners: 'I have several times (within the last twenty years) met men working upon the roads in Cardiganshire who could repeat passages from Horace or Homer'.[2] If the reverend gentleman is to be believed, one must reflect sadly on the deterioration which has taken place within one hundred years, for, today, not one in ten of the professors of the university college located within the same shire possesses a knowledge of the classics comparable to that of those remarkable roadmen.[3]

Now that the dust of the controversy has begun to settle a clearer picture emerges, and few would deny that the provision for education was woefully inadequate. A century or more earlier Pembrokeshire had compared favourably with any shire in Britain in the number of its charity schools because of the support given to that movement by the philanthropist, the 'good' Sir John Philipps of Picton Castle, but these had nearly all disappeared. The circulating schools which had followed them lapsed because of law suits, but were revived in 1809 as 'Madam Bevan's Charity'. In 1833 there were twenty-nine such schools in South Wales, periodically circulating from one parish to another, and the model school, at which teachers were trained, was at Newport in Pembrokeshire.[4] The British Schools and the National Schools had made little headway in Wales, and it was not until 1843, the year of the Rebecca Riots, that the British and Foreign School Society appointed an organiser

in the principality. The statistics of the education commissioners reveal, on the other hand, an incredible number of
'private adventure' schools, the great majority of which,
however, had little merit. It is not necessary to give here any
details of the squalid rooms in which these were held, of their
almost total lack of ventilation and sanitation. Nor need one
dilate upon the inadequate attainments of the teachers,
who had been engaged in every conceivable occupation
before undertaking what was 'one of the least esteemed and
worst remunerated' of employments.[5] Many continued to
combine teaching with other jobs, and it is of interest to this
study to note that one man, at least, was both a schoolmaster
and a turnpike gate-keeper.[6] Yet, despite the number of
these schools, there were fifteen parishes in Carmarthenshire, twenty in Cardiganshire, and fifty-six in Pembrokeshire, with no day-school of any kind,[7] and it is particularly
noticeable also that a great many of the schools which were
listed in the reports had been founded only in the early
forties. For, once more, one of the reasons for the inadequacy
of the schools was the rapid increase in the population, and
the Rebecca Riots occurred at a time when the old provision
for education had broken down, but before the efforts which
were being made to improve conditions had taken effect.

The educational standards of the small farmers were
summed up by a highly intelligent and, it would appear,
unprejudiced magistrate, John Johnes of Dolau Cothi, who
wrote *An Address to the Inhabitants of Conwil-Gaio* during the
rioting, and kept his own district free from disturbance.
'The majority of the small farmers', he wrote to the education commissioners, 'can read and write very imperfectly;
the writing seldom extends beyond signing the name . . .
Farmers of this class are almost on a level with labourers . . .;
they possess no surplus sufficient to give their families
superior education. Their children are generally sent to
a day-school, if there is one within a moderate distance, but
not during the whole year; they get, however, more
schooling than those of labourers.'[8]

For the children of the growing middle class of professional men and tradesmen there were several grammar schools,[9] notably at Carmarthen and Haverfordwest, together with a surprising number of boarding establishments, both for boys and young ladies. Many of these were kept by clergymen in order to supplement their stipends, though some were more ambitious undertakings. Their advertisements in the local newspapers, twice a year, give a quaint insight into by-gone refinement and pretentiousness.

The establishment of local newspapers had, itself, a marked effect on the growth of public opinion. The first English newspaper to be published in South Wales was the Swansea *Cambrian* which appeared in 1804. It was independent, if not Liberal, in its politics. In opposition to it, the *Carmarthen Journal* was founded in 1810. This, also, was independent to begin with, but it soon became the avowed Tory newspaper of West Wales. The growth of a reading public and the excitement over the Reform Bill led to the appearance of yet a third paper, the *Welshman* of Carmarthen, early in 1832, which was liberal, indeed radical, in its standpoint. The price of these weeklies was high (it remained $4\frac{1}{2}d.$ a copy even after the reduction of the newspaper tax in 1836), and this restricted their circulation. Yet, if the number of government stamps issued to each paper can be taken as a reliable guide, their readers were remarkably numerous. The *Cambrian*, which served a wider area, purchased some eight thousand stamps a month, and the *Journal* and the *Welshman* each about half this number, though their clientele was confined to the three shires.[10] This would give a larger number of subscribers than might have been expected, and readers were probably still more numerous.

The publisher (and part proprietor) of the *Welshman*, John Lewis Brigstocke, was a member of an important Carmarthen family, but the main editorial work was done by John Palmer, who combined this with his other duties as mathematics tutor at the Presbyterian College and minister to a Unitarian congregation in the town.[11] The controversial methods of both men were lively, especially in their attacks on the *Journal*, and they were soon involved in a series of prosecutions for libel which brought Brigstocke a prison sentence and several substantial fines.[12] Palmer left the town, and in time Brigstocke became bankrupt, so that the paper changed hands. It continued to be most outspoken, especially in matters relating to the state church and to the Crown. Its radical standpoint influenced its attitude towards the Rebecca Riots, concerning which it is a primary source of information.

But the predominant factor in the growth of opinion in these years was a remarkable increase in Nonconformity. There has been a tendency to ante-date this development, and to believe that the majority of Welsh people had become nonconformist immediately after the religious revival of the eighteenth century. This is far from being true. Such figures as are available are fragmentary and difficult to interpret, but it can at least be said with certainty that Nonconformity accounted for a very small minority in the first decade of the nineteenth century. The Methodists became a separate denomination only in 1811. Thereafter there came a period of intense activity, which coincided with the growth in population and with the industrialisation of the South Wales coalfield. One aspect of this activity was the work of the Sunday Schools. On the evidence of the education commissioners there were, in 1847, four times as many children in dissenting Sunday Schools in Pembrokeshire as in those of the Church of England, six times as many in the schools of Cardiganshire and eight times as many in those of Carmarthenshire.[13] Lingen, the commissioner in Pembrokeshire and Carmarthenshire, was quite evidently impressed by these efforts (inadequate though they were) on the part of the people to educate themselves without aid from anyone.[14] Others were not so favourably disposed towards the schools, and one egregious writer warned the

Home Office that they should be carefully watched as they were used for subversive purposes.[15] How successful the efforts of the Nonconformists were can be appreciated with reasonable accuracy, for an official religious census was taken in 1851. This shows, among other things, the number of attendants at public worship on Sunday, 30 March 1851, and, although it was the subject of some controversy during the bitter struggle for disestablishment later in the century, the result in Wales was so startling that even a wide margin of error would not affect the argument. For an analysis of the figures for the three shires of West Wales shows that, of the worshippers on that day, only 21 per cent attended the services of the Church of England whereas 79 per cent attended those of the Protestant dissenting denominations.[16] In half a century West Wales had become predominantly nonconformist.

The fundamental reason for this change (apart from the exertions of the nonconformist leaders) was the dissolution of society, the unloosening of old ties, which is the theme of this book. The Church of England, so perfectly planned for one set of circumstances, was extremely slow in adapting itself to new conditions. It made inadequate provision for the growth in population. If, for example, by some happy miracle, every man, woman and child in the town of Carmarthen felt moved on Easter Sunday in 1841 to attend divine service as by law established they would have found accommodation for less than one in four.[17] The failure of the Church in this respect was even more marked in the new conurbations of the coalfield, where the uprooting was greatest because of a change from village to urban life and from a rural to an industrial economy. In the absence of an adequate parochial organisation in these new areas, workers attached themselves to small religious societies. These gave them the comfort of associating with their fellows, and, as well, by a democratic atmosphere, developed in them courage and self-respect, for here, if nowhere else, they felt that they still counted. But Nonconformity was to prove the main, if not the sole, emotional link between rural and industrial Wales, and this democratic ethos, generated in the industrial areas, overflowed into the countryside where, also, the Church had shown itself too closely associated with the landowning gentry and indifferent to the social condition of the poor. Thereby the class struggle was intensified, for a religious difference between the gentry and their tenants was now added to the already existing differences in social standing and in language. Moreover, within the dissenting congregations, there was a great measure of equality which helped to integrate the peasant class, for servants could take an equal share in the affairs of their meeting-house if they were suitably gifted. (It should be noted, however, that the nonconformist leaders who voiced the grievances of tenant farmers in the second half of the century were singularly silent on those of farm labourers.) The older Nonconformity of the eighteenth century had been radical through tradition, through a rationalistic attitude and a minority mentality. The democracy of rural Wales in the nineteenth century, on the other hand, was primarily social rather than political in origin. So it was that the peasantry, usually a conservative force, had in Wales become radical. Moreover, in becoming the religious persuasion of the majority within society, Welsh Nonconformity, while it lost something of the intellectual basis of eighteenth-century Dissent, acquired strong self-confidence and an impatience with disabilities. It is important to bear in mind that this ferment of opinion was taking place when the Rebecca rioting occurred.

Welsh Nonconformity became articulate in a number of monthly magazines which, in turn, greatly influenced opinion and, also, reflected the varying attitudes of the different denominations. An attempt in 1814 to start a weekly newspaper in the Welsh language, *Seren Gomer*, proved unsuccessful, but after some vicissitudes it reappeared as a monthly from 1820 onwards. It was published in Swansea and priced sixpence. Its editor, Joseph Harris, who

wrote under the pen-name of 'Gomer', was a Baptist
minister and a native of Pembrokeshire. He was a moderate
reformer, but did much to break down the apathy of the
Welsh peasantry in political matters. The vanguard of
radicalism was taken by the Independents, who acquired
their own monthly in West Wales in 1831, *Yr Efangylydd*,
published in Llandovery and edited by David Owen
('Brutus'). He had begun life as a Baptist minister, but
unbearable poverty and an erratic temperament led him into
actions which brought expulsion from his denomination.
A misfit in Welsh society, his great ability as a writer was to
make him the foremost satirist that Wales has produced.[18]
Under his editorship, *Yr Efangylydd* advocated the reform of
parliament (while warning its readers against expecting too
much from this)[19] and even the ballot.[20] But it soon became
apparent that the editor was not in sympathy with his
subscribers. *Yr Efangylydd* therefore ceased publication in
1835, and the Independents of West Wales issued a new
monthly, *Y Diwygiwr*, published in Llanelly. Its editor,
David Rees, was a native of Tre-lech, a stronghold of
Nonconformity which was soon to become one of the centres
of the Rebecca movement in Carmarthenshire. In 1829 he
had taken as his first pastorate an Independent church in
Llanelly, and there he was to remain for forty years,
exercising an authoritative influence on the public life of
the growing industrial town. For the motto of his magazine
he took O'Connell's slogan, 'Agitate!', and he lived up to it,
while strongly deploring violence. On the other hand, when
Yr Efangylydd ceased in 1835, Brutus took over a new
Llandovery publication, *Yr Haul*. This was moderate at
first, but within a year it became a champion of the established church. In it, at last, Brutus shed all his inhibitions
and found his métier. He lashed his former associates with
a savagery which the anglican clergy may have welcomed
but would have scrupled to employ themselves. He accused
the Nonconformists of wishing to overthrow the throne,
destroy the Church and appropriate private property. The

polemics of Brutus and of David Rees assumed the proportions of a gladiatorial contest, which drew all the more attention because of the clash of personalities involved. It served to educate West Wales in politics. Throughout these debates the Independents were the most radical of the nonconformist denominations. The Baptists occupied an intermediary position, while the Methodists, both Wesleyan and Calvinistic, who, if taken together, were more numerous than any other denomination in West Wales in 1851, remained conservative. Their insistence upon the salvation of individual souls and upon the salutary discipline of adversity rendered them indifferent to social reform.[21]

The Nonconformists were still subject to certain positive and practical disabilities even after the repeal of the Test and Corporation Acts in 1828, notably with regard to baptism and the registration of births, to the solemnisation of marriages and to burial in the parish graveyards. These matters related to the most poignant occasions in life, and ranged the Nonconformists emotionally on the side of the reformers. They received considerable attention in the dissenting periodicals. Much was expected of the Reform Act of 1832, and the disillusion that followed was, therefore, all the greater on that account, so that Nonconformists showed much apathy in registering themselves as voters under the new franchise.[22] The Dissenters' Marriage Act of 1836, which allowed them to solemnise marriages in their own chapels, and the Civil Registration Act of the following year, brought some relief. Yet Nonconformists could still be compelled to act as churchwardens, either in person or by deputy (an obligation which they were to exploit to the utmost for their own purposes), and they still had to contribute to church rates to defray parochial expenses and maintain the fabric of the church. They therefore resorted to the practice of flooding the parish vestry meetings in order to outvote the Anglicans, and thereby they succeeded in 'postponing' the declaration of a rate for years on end.

Thus the parish system, like so many other aspects of public life, had broken down.

This development was not peculiar to West Wales,[23] but West Wales provided one of its most startling episodes. The vicar of Llanelly, who also held the livings of Llan-non and Llanddarog, the Reverend Ebenezer Morris, was a very striking figure.[24] He was a man of great physical strength, and was, quite literally, a fighting parson, for in 1832 he assaulted William Chambers, senior, and was fined £20 and bound over for two years to keep the peace.[25] He stood no nonsense from Nonconformists. When the Llanelly vestry elected one of David Rees's congregation, John James, as churchwarden in 1838, the vicar had him prosecuted in the ecclesiastical court for neglecting his duties and refusing to provide the wine necessary to administer the sacrament, and when he persisted in his obstinacy and refused to pay the costs of the action, he was imprisoned.[26] Worse was to follow in Llan-non. There a Unitarian, David Jones, a weaver by trade, was elected churchwarden in 1837. It was stated that this was done against his will,[27] but that may be doubted. The vicar's warden was Rees Goring Thomas, the local landowner and patron of the living and an extensive tithe impropriator, but he was an absentee. So, with David Jones as chairman, the vestry 'postponed' consideration of a rate. The vicar thereupon called on Jones to provide the elements and, on his refusal on a plea of poverty, had him prosecuted in the ecclesiastical court. The costs of this action amounted to the outrageous sum of £80, which Jones was unable to pay, with the result that he was imprisoned for debt.[28] The matter was brought to the notice of parliament, where it was discussed at great length,[29] but there the vicar found an able advocate in his friend, John Jones of Ystrad.[30] Public subscriptions were invited to secure David Jones's release,[31] and in June 1839, Lord Denman, on circuit at Carmarthen, liberated him because of a technical error in the warrant for his arrest.[32] He had been in gaol for nearly seven months.

The indefatigable vicar thereupon had the error rectified and a new warrant issued, but Jones, in great agitation at the prospect of another term in prison, hurriedly left home, and died in a house in Gorseinon where he had sought shelter on his way. This brought feelings on both sides to a high pitch. All the local periodicals, Welsh and English, were full of this episode. The *Welshman* found itself once again in court for libel, but got away with an apology.[33] A subscription was started to relieve the widow and children of the dead man.[34] But the vicar stood his ground. He published a letter in the *Carmarthen Journal* informing the new churchwardens in 1840 that if they had any opposition from 'the friends of Infidelity and Popery falsely calling themselves Protestant dissenters' they need only apply to him.[35] Yet he, also, had overtaxed his resources, and the weary details of his petition of bankruptcy were soon appearing in the local press.[36]

Meanwhile the question of church rates continued to agitate the countryside. The violent expressions of the *Welshman* on the one side were equalled by those of the *Journal* on the other; envy, hatred, malice and all uncharitableness were freely attributed to their opponents by both periodicals. Vestry meetings sometimes became disorderly scuffles.[37] In Cilgerran, in the heart of the *ceffyl pren* and Rebecca area, the rate was 'postponed' year after year, and the parish meetings there were a powerful agency in developing public opinion.[38] Some incumbents, as at Narberth, relied on voluntary subscriptions;[39] elsewhere the goods of objectors were distrained upon.[40] One instance was brought forcibly to the attention of the Rebecca commissioners. The church rate in 1835 in the parish of Minwear was no less than five shillings in the pound, and one farmer found himself called upon to pay £64 8s. 6d. He delayed doing so, and died two years later. No steps were taken to recover the money till 1841, when his executor was summoned before the ecclesiastical court at Carmarthen and ordered to pay. He, however, appealed to the Court of Arches and obtained a verdict in his favour, but this had involved him in an expense of £30.[41] Bills were brought into parliament for the abolition of church rates, but with no success. Sir James Graham felt that if such a bill became law 'not five years would elapse before the bishops would be expelled from their places in the House of Lords, and five years more would not elapse before episcopacy would be wholly abolished in England'.[42] These forebodings did not, however, prove to be justified when church rates were at last abolished in 1868.

The problem of tithes was closely associated with that of church rates, but was of even greater importance, for in it economic depression combined with religious dissent to aggravate a dissatisfaction which had long existed. Hitherto, friction had been caused mainly by disputes about methods of payment, and by the extortionate practices of individual tithe-owners. Now the objection had become more fundamental. Tithe was a charge which increased with any improvement in farming, and the better farmers objected to it because it was heavier on arable land, so that they were loath to cultivate in parishes where the tithe arrangements were unsatisfactory to them.[43] It was still more obnoxious to the poorer farmers. In law it was the landowner who paid the tithe, but this was a fiction; the burden fell upon the tenant farmer, and in the years after Waterloo this burden seemed too heavy to bear. When there was added to this the disinclination of the growing nonconformist majority in a parish to support a Church frequented by only a handful of parishioners, the payment of tithes became a subject of discussion in every parish in the countryside.

In West Wales the position was still more anomalous, for there, to a greater extent than anywhere else in southern Britain, tithes, and the advowsons which generally went with them, had passed into the hands of laymen.[44] They were advertised for sale in the local press like any other commodity. The advowson of Maenclochog, for example, was declared to be 'a novel and safe investment', so that 'gentle-men desirous of making a certain provision in the church for a son would find this an opportunity seldom to be met with'.[45] Generally the added attraction was specified that 'the present incumbent is far advanced in years', so that the purchaser would not have long to wait.[46] It was otherwise when a life-lease was offered for sub-letting. The living of Lledrod was in the gift of the holder of the tithes, and these, it was stressed, were leased 'on the life of a healthy lady of fifty-nine'.[47] Nor was it only the advowson which could be bought. When John Jones of Ystrad died in 1842 there was offered for sale, in addition to the tithes of St. Peter's, Carmarthen, the proprietorship of the north chancel, entitling the purchaser to the pew rents and 'an exclusive right to the burial fees within the said chancel'.[48] The sale of such spiritualities in the nineteenth century was a gross impropriety.

Whatever may have been the origin of the alienation of the tithes, and this differed from place to place, it served to impoverish the parish clergy and to drain away the wealth of the countryside into the pockets of absentee owners. It was usually the great or rectorial tithes, of corn and hay, which were alienated; the little, or vicarial tithes, of calves, lambs, eggs and so on, remained more often to the incum-bent. But the latter were relatively insignificant. For example, John Jones's share of the tithe of St. Peter's was £971 12s. 6d.; the vicar received only £7.[49] In the nearby parish of Llan-gyndeyrn the impropriator, Rees Goring Thomas, drew an annual revenue from tithes of £1,000; the vicar £13 3s. 4d.[50] The tithes of fifteen parishes around Aberystwyth had passed into the possession of a Devonshire family, the Chichesters, whose income from this source in the mid-nineteenth century amounted to £6,000 a year, while the incumbents received less than a third of that sum between them.[51] Devout churchmen, at this time, were building new churches in the wide and sparsely populated area of these fifteen parishes in order to counteract the spread of Dissent, but it was stated that the tithe impropriators had contributed nothing.[52] The behaviour, also, of the tithe-owners and their agents was often harsh and vexatious. Their 'arrogance and rapacity' said a Pembrokeshire landowner, were a greater grievance even than the turnpike trusts.[53] Some tried to revive tithes which had fallen into abeyance, among them, again, Rees Goring Thomas. In the parish of Llanelly he sought to recover the tithe on potatoes, on wood cut under twenty years' growth, on mills and gardens, on milk and other items,[54] and became involved in much litigation. Moreover his agent, who 'added insult to unnecessary severity', according to William Chambers, junior,[55] refused to allow even the most deserving persons extra time to pay.[56] This harshness was soon to procure for him the personal attentions of Rebecca.

The collection of tithes had given rise to endless, and often amusing, disputes. The rector of Mathry brought an action in 1757 against a farmer who refused to allow the rector's cart to cross his fields to fetch the tithes unless the oxen were muzzled to stop them from nibbling his grass.[57] The tithe of milk was particularly troublesome, as the vicar of Llanstadwell found in 1818 when a farmer claimed that his cows grazed partly in the parish and partly in another.[58] Sometimes the tithes were taken in kind, sometimes in money. As long as they were paid in kind, there was a possibility of bargaining with the tithe-owner, and there was a tendency to revert to this when the harvest was bad. In those circumstances the country people exercised the most amazing ingenuity in evading the tithes. The vicar of Llangrannog in 1836 took his parishioners at their word and collected the tithe in kind. He claimed that he had made a profit thereby, but his parishioners would not believe it. 'We have heard that story many times', they said.[59] In several parishes there were moduses, ancient commutations of certain tithes, and these were highly intricate in nature. They had become advantageous to the farmers through the fall in the value of money. But in times of depression, as a south Pembrokeshire farmer said in 1818, 'money was harder to come by than tithe'.[60] The Board of Agriculture's report of 1794 for Pembrokeshire claimed that all classes, tithe-owners, clergy, landowners and farmers, were already in favour of the commutation of all tithes.[61] Action was, indeed, taken in some parishes to have this done by act of parliament. In Llanelly, Rees Goring Thomas secured an act in 1831 which commuted the tithes at £2,100 a year, but this led to endless argument, for the farmers claimed that they had been grossly misled when they agreed to this sum.[62] The whole system of tithes had become so complicated that the reformed parliament decided to reduce the chaos to some order by the Tithe Commutation Act of 1836.

This act provided the machinery for the substitution of an annual tithe rent charge, based on the average prices of wheat, barley and oats for the previous seven years, in place of collection in kind. What it is important to realise, for the purpose of this study, is that this took years to operate, and that during the actual rioting tithe meetings under the act were being held in a large number of the parishes of West Wales. The assumption was made that tithe, in the words of the home secretary, was a 'tax on property',[63] that it was the landlord who paid in so far as he received a lower rent because of tithe. Commutation was therefore a bargain between the landowner and the tithe-owner. But it was a matter of common knowledge that, at least in Wales, tithe was paid by the occupier and not by the owner.[64] No doubt it was on this account that landowners showed such indifference towards the problem, as several witnesses were to complain to the Rebecca commission.[65] Frequently they had not troubled to attend meetings at all. In other instances the greatest landowner in a parish was himself the tithe impropriator,[66] and he could therefore, under the terms of the act, arrange matters to suit his own convenience. For the first meeting was one between those persons who owned collectively not less than two-thirds of the total land in a parish and those who together had not less than a two-thirds interest in its tithes. At this meeting maps and receipts were produced, and the total amount of tithe was ascertained. Almost invariably, however, it was found necessary to appoint a surveyor and to have a tithe map drawn. Like the contemporary enclosure acts, tithe commutation proved a lucrative business for land surveyors, many of whom were appointed for personal reasons and were grossly incompetent.[67] When the total sum was determined it had to be apportioned among individual occupiers, and the map and draft apportionment were deposited at a convenient place in the parish. It was only then that a meeting was called at which an assistant tithe commissioner would hear any objections. Such meetings were inclined to be stormy, for there was much discontent not only with the total amount of the tithe but also with the apportionment between individual occupiers. If the landowners and tithe-owners failed to agree, the Tithe Commission could announce a compulsory award. As the years went by, and the problem of tithes still remained unsettled in many parishes, the proportion of these compulsory awards increased considerably.[68]

It is evident that commutation proved a great mystery to the farmers. Even the *Times* correspondent fell into the error of thinking that farmers were injured because prices in West Wales were lower than those for the country as a whole, on which the averages were based.[69] These averages, in fact, merely determined the annual fluctuation in the tithes, and not the initial sum. What was important was that the price of corn was depressed in 1843, so that the average for seven years was higher than the current price. This would right itself in time, but that, as the *Times* representative argued in the correspondence into which his fallacy had drawn him, was small consolation to a farmer unable to pay in that year.[70] It was a grave misfortune that the act should have coincided with a period of depression, especially since the distress of the country banks had led to a scarcity of currency, so that payment in money had become increasingly difficult.

10

Moreover, the act allowed the commissioners to increase the tithes by as much as 20 per cent where it was found that the sum did not fairly represent what ought to be taken. This was frequently done in Wales, for the tithe commissioners reported that the tithes were 'very peculiarly low'.[71] The *Times* correspondent argued, on the other hand, that they were low only because the cost of collection from inaccessible upland farms made them by no means worth their nominal value. He characterised the increase as 'legalised robbery'.[72] On the calculation of the Rebecca commissioners, the tithes of South Wales were increased by 7 per cent through commutation,[73] and their figures show that the percentage for West Wales was considerably higher. In no instance does a landowner seem to have reduced his rents on account of this increase, thereby disproving Sir James Graham's contention that tithe was a tax on property.

The position in two parishes may be briefly outlined. The tithes of Penbryn (a parish bordering the sea, a few miles north of Cardigan), belonged one-third to the vicar and two-thirds to an impropriator. The commutation was carried out in a most slovenly manner. There was much disagreement as to what really happened, but at least it seems clear that the surveyor estimated the acreage to be 10,000 whereas it amounted to 8,827 acres. The average of the tithes for the years from 1829 to 1835 was £525, but they were commuted at £700; why, it is not clear. The apportionment took some three years to complete, and was eventually announced in the summer of 1842. Immediately there was trouble. The parishioners were Dissenters almost without exception. One of them was either unable or unwilling to pay, and an order was made to distrain upon his goods. There was very little to distrain upon, but, with incredible ineptitude, the family Bible of this Dissenter was sold to pay the vicar's tithes. This made the name of Penbryn celebrated 'all the way from Holyhead to Newport'. On 16 June 1843 Rebecca wrote to the vicar her best-known letter, addressed from Penyrherber in the neighbourhood of

Newcastle Emlyn. She gave him a few days to return the farmer's Bible, and also all tithes paid in excess of the previous year's amount. If he did not do so, she promised him a visit when she would mutilate him in body and burn all his possessions. This reduced him to such terror that a detachment of marines had to be sent to guard his house.[74]

The parish of Aber-nant lies some six miles to the north-west of Carmarthen. There the commutation was agreed to voluntarily, the lay impropriator accepting £270 a year and the vicar £25. The latter was an old man of eighty-four, and was well-to-do and possibly disinclined to bother. But the assistant tithe commissioner ruled that this did not represent the true value of the vicarial tithes, and that even if the vicar was prepared to accept the sum, it would be unjust to his successors. He fixed these tithes at £102, including a tithe on potatoes, which he admitted had never been paid before. Representations were made to him that he had not taken into account a modus on milk and some other articles of produce, and so he reduced the tithes to £67 10s. Local farmers, among them Captain Lewis Evans of Pantycendy (of whom more later) still protested, and two meetings were held at Carmarthen in December 1843 to hear appeals, but the assistant tithe commissioner held his ground, even though the incumbent was still prepared to accept a much smaller amount.[75] It was from this area that the march on Carmarthen had taken place six months previously.

Thus the problem of tithes contributed to the turmoil in these months. Meetings to memorialise the clergy and tithe impropriators, and also to petition the queen, were held even in the hundred of Castlemartin in south Pembrokeshire which remained undisturbed by Rebecca.[76] They were much more numerous in the disturbed area,[77] and the subject was discussed at length at every one of the massed meetings which came to replace Rebecca's nocturnal outrages. One witness before the Rebecca commission attributed the peaceful condition of north Cardiganshire 'to the fact that the tithe commutation is not yet apportioned'.[78] He 'dreaded to see the day' when this was done, and well he might, for the tithes of Lledrod, to take one instance from the neighbourhood, were being raised from £110 to £206.[79]

The Tithe Commutation Act was one of the attempts of the reformed parliament to set the country's house in order; the Poor Law Amendment Act of 1834 was another. Religious and sociological considerations were inseparably entangled in both acts, but the consequences of the latter were far more serious, for pauperism was itself gravely aggravated by the intense economic depression of the time, and, moreover, parliament approached this problem with a doctrinaire rigidity which has seldom been equalled. The sudden and complete break with the past, which was the result of this attitude, precipitated a crisis. Yet it took a considerable time to put the new act into operation, so that the bitter opposition which it engendered served to increase discontent in the years which witnessed the Rebecca Riots.

The evils of the old poor law are sufficiently notorious, and need not be discussed here in any detail.[80] Once again an antiquated system had not been adapted to meet rapidly changing circumstances and had broken down. Individual parishes had been able to look after their own poor as long as these were few in number and were confined to the sick and the aged. But the growth in population, and especially in the number of able-bodied men unable to find employment, gave rise to a problem which was entirely beyond the competence of parish overseers, for they were appointed for one year only and were both unpaid and unwilling to do their work. It was the impossibility of providing adequate employment which had given rise to the allowance system, which had, in turn, depressed wages and demoralised the poor. The poor rate had increased from about £2 million for the whole country in 1785 to over £10 million in 1817, and from £13,000 in the three shires of West Wales to over £57,000;[81] in the depression of the following years its rate of increase seemed catastrophic. Faced with this situation, parish officers applied the law with increasing harshness in a vain attempt to keep down their own rates. Persons likely to require assistance were removed to their original parishes without mercy, while the laws relating to the apprenticeship of poor children and to bastardy were brutally enforced. The central authorities also panicked, and decided to take drastic action.

The Poor Law Amendment Act was the outcome of the reforming passion of Edwin Chadwick. He regarded pauperism as a problem in administration only, and not in social responsibility. The allowance system, which he rightly considered to be the basis of evil in rural areas, must be wiped out regardless of the cost in human suffering. He succeeded in convincing the authorities that this would not merely reduce expenditure but would be in the interests of the labouring poor themselves. Reform was to be accomplished by uniting parishes into larger and more efficient unions, by substituting for the overseers new and elective bodies called the Guardians of the Poor, by building workhouses and refusing outdoor relief, by making conditions in the workhouses worse than those of the lowest-paid labourers outside, and, finally, by establishing strict control through a body of commissioners sitting in London. Chadwick's quarrels with the commissioners do not concern us, but it is important to notice that their chairman was Thomas Frankland Lewis, a member of an old Welsh family, the Lewises of Harpton in Radnorshire. He had served as member of parliament for various constituencies from 1812 onwards, and had held minor offices in Tory administrations. His interest in the poor law dated from 1817, when he drafted the report of the select committee of that year which first brought the abuses of the old system to the attention of the public.[82] It was on this account that his political opponents selected him as chairman of the Poor Law Commissioners in 1834. His difficulties with Chadwick, whose uncompromising rigidity he sought to modify, have led to much abuse from Chadwick's apologists.[83] Yet he was an enlightened landowner and agriculturalist,[84] and an able administrator. He resigned his post in December 1838, and was succeeded by his brilliant son, George Cornewall Lewis. Thus he was free to accept the onerous and unpaid post of chairman of the commission of inquiry which followed the Rebecca Riots, a duty which he discharged with uncommon efficiency and success. It should be noticed, also, that the chief clerk of the Poor Law Commission in these years was Hugh Owen, whose 'Letter to the Welsh People' in the year of the Rebecca Riots was to prove of momentous importance in the history of education in Wales.[85]

The act passed through parliament by the surprising majority of 319 to 20.[86] There was therefore no division on party lines. Yet opposition soon came from a variety of sources. The reform was a heavy blow to the country gentry; possibly a heavier blow than the Reform Act of 1832. As magistrates they had supervised the work of the overseers and exercised much authority in the distribution of relief in their localities. Now they found themselves, as De Tocqueville remarked, 'either excluded from influence in the management of their own parishes, or forced to accept a seat on the Board of Guardians and to debate and vote among shopkeepers and farmers'.[87] They detested the centralisation which was Chadwick's panacea. Their ideas found expression in the furious onslaughts of the *Times*, whose proprietor, John Walter II, devoted his time in parliament primarily to a criticism of the poor law. This is what accounts for the attitude which the *Times* was to take towards the Rebecca Riots, for it evidently regarded them as an extension of anti-poor-law agitation. The act also hurt religious susceptibilities. Charity, however inadequately dispensed, was a religious duty; its regimentation was repugnant to many people, and above all to those who resisted interference by the state even in education, as did the Welsh Nonconformists.

The act tended to regard poverty, if not even old age, as a crime; it envisaged the breaking up of families; its attitude towards unmarried mothers was brutal. Opposition became articulate, therefore, on humanitarian grounds, and this long before the first workhouse was built, or even the first union formed. The actual working of the new system produced a reaction which was widely different.

The first union in West Wales, that of Carmarthen, came into existence in July 1836, and was succeeded in the following months by Llanelly, Llandeilo, Llandovery, Narberth, Pembroke, Haverfordwest, Aberystwyth, Aberaeron, Cardigan, Lampeter, Tregaron and Newcastle Emlyn, the last-named being formed in May 1837, so that by this time all parishes had been allocated.[88] Guardians were then elected, their numbers being roughly in proportion to the ratable value of each parish. They had to be in occupation of property of £25 annual rental,[89] but in practice it was found difficult to get persons to serve because of the obloquy which this involved.[90] In general, therefore, it was the poorest farmers who were elected, so that the majority of them could not read, and some were surreptitiously paid for their service.[91] It is significant that many of them in West Wales were of the same class as the paupers whom they relieved.[92] Frequently they were elected under a pledge to refuse to build a workhouse, and some Welsh Boards of Guardians had to be coerced before they would comply.[93] Even before the workhouse at Narberth had been completed, an attempt was made, on 16 January 1839, to burn it down. This was five months before the Rebecca Riots began with an outbreak in the same neighbourhood. Substantial rewards were offered for information, together with a free pardon, to any accomplice who would give evidence, but with no success.[94] In 1841 workhouses had still not been built in Aberystwyth, Tregaron or Lampeter;[95] even two years later that of Lampeter remained unerected.[96]

During this transitional period the old system, and the old abuses, continued. In the winter of 1835, fifty able-bodied

men and their families were being relieved in the
parish of Conwil alone. Five men from the parish of
St. Ishmael, although they were in full-time employment in
Merthyr Tydfil, received an allowance, for otherwise they
would return home and be entirely dependent on the parish.
Several of the paupers of Abergwili were likewise non-
resident. The able-bodied poor of Llanstephan were set to
work upon the roads, but they did not earn their pay. The
vestry of the same parish had, in that year, paid £90 in rent
for its paupers. The practice of 'bidding' and the consequent
early marriages had their usual effect. 'Young people rush
headlong into matrimony', said a report from Llanpumsaint, 'all look to the parish and they are upon it as soon
as they have a child.' Yet the parishes of the Carmarthen
union supported four hundred bastard children in that
year.[97] Nevertheless, a highly confidential memorandum on
the state of public opinion, submitted by Thomas Frankland
Lewis to the Home Office in December 1838, shows that the
changes then being introduced were less unpopular than had
been anticipated. It is significant that all three assistant
commissioners reporting from Wales stated that the aged and
infirm thought themselves more liberally dealt with than
under the old law, and considered that there was a decided
improvement in the medical attention they received.
Opposition to the changes came from 'the upper class',
jealous of its loss of influence, from parish officers who had
been displaced and small dealers who had lost their custom,
from the able-bodied who were now deprived of their
allowances and from those who had received rent for
cottages let to paupers, but, above all, from the ratepayers.[98] In other words, the grounds of opposition were not
so much humanitarian as pecuniary.

The work of implementing the changes fell to assistant
commissioners. Their territories varied in the early days, but,
in time, the whole of Wales, apart from Monmouthshire,
became the province of William Day.[99] He was a Sussex
farmer and a justice of the peace, and was thirty-six years

of age when the Poor Law Amendment Act was passed. He had already, in the previous year, published a pamphlet on the subject of the poor law,[100] and it was on this account that he was invited to become an assistant commissioner. His reports show that he was a man of outstanding ability and ceaseless energy, but, if that were possible, he was even more rigid in the handling of men than Edwin Chadwick. Not that Chadwick allowed much latitude to his assistants; his instructions to them were enormously detailed,[101] and few can have dared to infringe them.

Day was constantly in attendance at meetings of guardians up and down the country, attending to the innumerable details of the change-over to the new system, such as the appointment of relieving officers and medical officers, the building of workhouses and the engagement of their staffs, and the obtaining, by contract, of a remarkable range of commodities from bread to elm coffins. He went in danger of personal injury, and on one occasion in 1837 a troop of cavalry had to be called out to escort him when he was driven from Llanfair Caereinion, in Montgomeryshire, by the violence of the mob.[102] He met with stubborn resistance from Boards of Guardians. The expenditure on the poor had diminished in the years immediately after the passing of the act of 1834, but by 1838 it had once more begun to increase in Pembrokeshire, and by the following year in Carmarthenshire and Cardiganshire.[103] This was primarily due to the return of economic depression, but the guardians attributed it to the payment of the salaries of poor law officials, notably those of the relieving officers and the medical officers.[104] Relieving officers were, in fact, better off than the smaller farmers,[105] and Day had to intervene on several occasions to veto a reduction in their salaries.[106] The collection of the rate, on the other hand, still had to be done gratuitously by the parish. But the farmers resisted paying, often pleading intimidation, and the unions were soon heavily in debt. On the other hand the guardians could not issue distress warrants, for the defaulters were so numerous and the countryside so disturbed.[107] With no money to pay, the relieving officers could not relieve the poor. Parishes with few paupers of their own objected to paying into the general funds of the union, for they felt that they were contributing to the support of the poor of the larger towns. They wished to return to the system by which they could relieve their own poor, preferably in kind.[108] Immediately the first workhouse was built at Carmarthen, instructions were issued to the guardians of that union to discontinue forthwith outdoor relief to any able-bodied persons whatsoever, except widows with dependent children.[109] But the guardians, by a large majority, passed a resolution, proposed by Captain Evans of Pantycendy and seconded by Hugh Williams, that outdoor relief should be continued.[110] Even Day felt that the transition was too abrupt and must cause dislocation and disturbance.[111] Frequently the meetings of the guardians ended in confusion, and, at one of them, Captain Evans and another guardian came to blows, the gallant captain, in good schoolboy fashion, offering to fight his opponent with one arm, and both men had to be bound over to keep the peace.[112]

The disputes, as in this instance, were usually between those who wished to grant relief more generously and those who did not. For the guardians were also ratepayers, and were often themselves in arrears with their payments. Many became parsimonious on this account, and soon *Y Diwygiwr* was blaming the people themselves for electing unsympathetic guardians.[113] The suffering which this involved can be illustrated by the case of William Thomas, an invalid living with his two boys at Ffynnonfadog, between Meidrim and Aber-nant. His cottage was dilapidated, the front part having fallen in. The occupants had no bed-clothes at all. A daughter who was in work tried to look after them. Thomas received a total of three shillings a week relief in respect of himself and his two boys. This sum was always mortgaged in advance to the local shopkeeper, and the three generally spent one day a week with no food at all.

He had frequently asked for more relief, and the relieving officer had recommended it, but at the instance of a guardian of the parish of Meidrim this was refused, on the grounds that the elder of the two boys should be in service, and that three shillings a week was the wage received by farm labourers in the district in addition to their food. When he died on 19 November 1843 there was no money, food or fuel in the house. The coroner's jury returned a verdict of death through starvation.[114]

In Wales, as in the north of England,[115] one of the chief grounds of complaint against the new poor law was the change in the regulation relating to the support of illegitimate children. This subject, above all others, has been bedevilled by the bitter controversy which followed the education reports of 1847, and it is worthy of note, in passing, that it was the unspeakable Brutus, ex-Baptist, ex-Independent, now staunch Anglican, who maintained to the commissioners that incontinence was due to the excitation of the religious revivals of the Dissenters, and that their week-night prayer meetings provided the occasions for it.[116] It is undeniable that illegitimacy had increased in Wales, as in England,[117] but, fortunately, accurate figures are available for many registration districts in 1842, the year which saw the renewal of the Rebecca Riots, and these show that South Wales compares very favourably indeed with, say, Cumberland or Shropshire.[118] Under the old law, if a mother on oath charged anyone with paternity, a magistrate could commit him until he gave security either to maintain the child or to appear at quarter sessions to dispute the fact. But Chadwick's report of 1834 declared that 'a bastard will be what Providence appears to have ordained that it should be, a burden on its mother, and where she cannot maintain it on her parents'.[119] The task of proving paternity was therefore placed entirely upon the mother, and became so difficult that the father often escaped scot-free. Since unmarried mothers could not receive outdoor relief they were forced into the workhouse. It is clear that Chadwick and his associates had in mind such cases as that of Squire Bramble in Smollett's *Humphrey Clinker*, who had nine bastards sworn to him by women whom, he said, he had never seen. The commissioners may, also, have been misled by thinking of conditions in towns, but there was little or no prostitution in rural Wales; the women there were usually deceived by a promise of marriage. The new regulation produced a storm of protest. Religious bodies held that it led to an enormous increase in illegitimacy, to the desertion of infants by their mothers and to infanticide.[120] This theme runs throughout the evidence taken before the Rebecca commissioners, [121] but when challenged to produce instances of infanticide the witnesses were unable to do so. Yet the home secretary, possibly because of the rioting in South Wales, thought good to introduce a bill in 1844 relieving the poor law of any connection at all with bastardy.[122] It should be borne in mind, moreover, that the Poor Law Amendment Act in no way affected the law relating to settlement. Under the old poor law the removal of unmarried expectant mothers had formed the most obnoxious part of the duties of the parish overseers; these still provided a large proportion of removal cases until the law was changed in 1876. In the meantime, as we shall see, Rebecca had her own way of dealing with the problem.

Finally, among the complaints against the poor law were conditions in the workhouses.[123] The 'workhouse test' was brutal, especially for people who had seen better days, and some endured incredible privation rather than enter the workhouse.[124] Yet, as Day pointed out, it was humane compared with the old practice of farming out the poor in an annual auction to those who would take them for the least money.[125] Much was made of the separation of man and wife, though witnesses before the Rebecca commission could produce few instances of this having been done.[126] The diet in Carmarthen workhouse was described in detail by the *Times* reporter. It comprised, almost exclusively, black barley bread, potatoes and soup, with $1\frac{1}{2}$ oz. of cheese on

Mondays and Thursdays and $3\frac{1}{2}$ oz. of cooked meat on Sundays and Wednesdays. On Fridays the inmates had a 'fish dinner', that is to say one salt herring each ('and very large ones they are too', said the matron). The reporter had the clever idea of comparing this diet, item by item, with that in the county gaol in the same town, and was able to show that the latter was superior in all respects.[127] Yet Rees Goring Thomas claimed that the guardians were reluctant to send persons into the workhouse because they lived better there than the farmers did out of it,[128] and the *Times* reporter, himself, writing from Ireland later on, recalled that in Narberth workhouse the farmers of south Pembrokeshire, used to good living, felt half-starved, but those of the uplands did not do so badly.[129] The guardians of Newcastle Emlyn refused to authorise soap for the workhouse, for they used very little of it themselves.[130] In Brecon the old men and women had been given a little tea, but the guardians ordered this to be discontinued.[131] The irascible William Day complained of the lack of cleanliness in the workhouses. 'Their beds were dungheaps', he stated, 'and everything else in keeping.' Nor was this a solitary instance; 'from the Kington Union to Cardigan and Haverfordwest, they were all alike.' He had come across the practice of covering a filthy bed with a clean sheet in anticipation of his visit, but he had soon put a stop to that, and had summarily sacked the masters of both Haverfordwest and Pembroke workhouses.[132] Yet the schools in the workhouses were better than those attended by the children of the poorer farmers,[133] and the medical services were better than anything they had been used to.[134] It is difficult to reach a final conclusion, but George Rice Trevor's report that all the adult paupers refused to leave Carmarthen workhouse when it was ransacked on 19 June 1843 seems at least credible.[135]

Few, if any, of the witnesses before the Rebecca Commission wished to return to the old system, yet the subject was discussed at all Rebecca's massed meetings, and numerous memorials were sent to the Home Office and to the queen requesting that the law be changed.[136] Chadwick had warned the Poor Law Commissioners against allowing the idea to get abroad that the Rebecca Riots were a reaction against the poor law,[137] but the commissioners themselves evidently shared this idea. They made a scapegoat of William Day. Immediately after the attack on the Carmarthen workhouse he had submitted a memorandum on the state of South Wales which is incomparably the best analysis of the situation.[138] In August he met with an accident while staying at Lord Cawdor's mansion at Golden Grove and was incapacitated for five weeks. Soon after he had recovered, the commission of enquiry into the Rebecca Riots was appointed with his old chief, Thomas Frankland Lewis, as chairman. Evidently complaints were made to the commissioners of Day's tactlessness, of his creating difficulties instead of solving them, and, although Lewis was taken by surprise by subsequent developments, these complaints were passed on to his son, George Cornewall Lewis, by William Cripps, another member of the Rebecca Commission. Cornewall Lewis thereupon dismissed Day in December 1843. The affair could not have been worse handled. It was represented to Day that action had been taken because his injury had incapacitated him, whereas he had now fully recovered; that it was because the number of assistant commissioners was to be reduced, whereas he was replaced. Sir James Graham made matters worse by declaring in the house of commons that Day's administration of the law had been among the prominent causes of the disturbance, whereas the Poor Law Commissioners had never asserted this. So, when the Andover scandal broke and a select committee was appointed to enquire into it, they investigated the case of William Day, and came to the conclusion that the Poor Law Commissioners had 'altogether failed to justify their removal of Mr. Day from his office'. Day thereby became a man with a grievance (a minor copy of Edwin Chadwick) and poured letters on the home secretary and the duke of

Wellington. There is no doubt that he had been unjustly treated; had the commissioners dismissed him because of his prolixity and his bad handwriting the historian might more easily have forgiven them.[139]

There is much truth in the statement of the *Cambrian* newspaper that 'Chartism was but a development of the Poor Law agitation'.[140] Certainly the Chartist movement, although it found expression in a demand for political changes, the 'six points' of the People's Charter, was primarily directed to the removal of social distress. It is highly significant that, in so far as Wales is concerned, Chartism was not the outcome of industrial conditions but first appeared as an aspect of agrarian discontent in West Wales. The first branch of the Working Men's Association in Wales was formed not in the coalfield but in Carmarthen. There is thus an inherent connection between the Chartist and Rebecca movements, and this connection is personified in Hugh Williams, who has already flitted across these pages and must now be properly introduced.

Hugh Williams was born near Machynlleth in 1796, his father being a timber merchant who later became interested in slate quarrying and lead mining. He was therefore of middle class origin, and his sister was to become (in May 1840) the wife of Richard Cobden. He qualified as a solicitor and settled in Carmarthen. There he married a woman, twenty-five years his senior, who was possessed of considerable property in the village of St. Clears, some nine miles away.[141] He lived, however, at Kidwelly and not at St. Clears (a fact which it is important to bear in mind in assessing his responsibility, for the Rebecca Riots, when they re-started in the winter of 1842, did so in St. Clears). There is no doubt that he had married because of his wife's property, but she cheated him by living till she was ninety.[142] He was maritally unfaithful to her,[143] and his reputation generally was somewhat unsavoury. Cobden's daughters were accustomed to refer to him as 'our bad uncle'.[144] How

he became an extreme radical in politics is uncertain.
A younger brother was a London solicitor, practising in
Gray's Inn Road, and Hugh Williams was frequently in
London on business. Possibly it was in this way that he
became acquainted with the London radicals. Certainly he
was a close friend of Henry Hetherington, the hero of the
struggle for a free press, and it was Hetherington who, in
1840, printed Williams's *National Songs and Poetical Pieces*,
an anthology of patriotic verse, some of it by Williams
himself, which he facetiously dedicated 'to the Queen and
her Countrywomen'. The literary merit of his poems is small,
but Sir James Graham thought them worth bringing to the
attention of the prime minister as they were 'very mis-
chievous and exciting'.[145] In 1841, Williams was able to
render Hetherington substantial assistance during his
celebrated trial for blasphemy.[146]

   The London Working Men's Association, the parent body
of Chartism, was founded in June 1836, with William Lovett
as its secretary and Hetherington as its treasurer, and
a branch was soon formed at Carmarthen. Hugh Williams,
who was clearly the moving spirit, became its secretary.[147]
He was elected an honorary member of the London body in
January 1838, and was present at Palace Yard, Westminster,
on 17 September 1838, when it was decided to hold
a convention of the working classes and present a petition
to parliament. He assured the meeting that the radicals of
South Wales 'were prepared to assert their rights at any
time and in any manner they might be called upon by the
London committee'.[148] Naturally he was chosen as member
of the convention for Carmarthen. This took place at
a monster meeting on 9 January, attended it is said by
four thousand people and held by torchlight around Picton's
monument. The town council had refused the use of the
Guild Hall, so that the Chartists had to meet out-of-doors on
this winter's night.[149] Their milling around with torches and
lanterns in the badly lighted streets must have caused much
apprehension to the townspeople. Williams was elected also

for Merthyr and for Swansea, but was not able to take his seat at the convention until 10 May, when he was introduced by Lovett.[150] In the meantime he had sent an emissary, William Jenkins, around the villages of Carmarthenshire and Pembrokeshire and into the Teify valley. At Narberth Jenkins deplored the attempt to burn the workhouse which had taken place there some weeks previously. The magistrates tried to hinder him from holding meetings, and it is difficult to know what success he had, but he must have contributed to the turmoil of opinion in this area, which saw the first outbreak of the Rebecca Riots three months later.[151] At almost exactly the same time as this incident at Efail-wen a Chartist riot broke out in Llanidloes, soon after Hetherington's visit to the flannel towns of mid-Wales. Hugh Williams hurried down from London and gave his services gratuitously in preparing the defence of the Chartist prisoners at the Welshpool assizes.[152] He celebrated the riot in a poem, 'The Horn of Liberty', which was found on the person of William Jones, one of the three leaders of the Chartist march on Newport in the following November.[153] That march proved a fiasco, and marked the eclipse of Chartism in South Wales. Hugh Williams's activities as a guardian of the poor, and his attempt to frustrate the application of the Poor Law Amendment Act, have already been noticed. Despite all his notoriety he was elected a member of the Carmarthen town council in 1841, and was prominent in promoting schemes for the development of the town's economic advantages.[154]

Welsh Nonconformity had welcomed the Chartist movement. *Y Diwygiwr* claimed that the Charter was consistent with Christianity, although it urged on the workers the desirability of co-operation with the middle class.[155] The need for the ballot had, in fact, become more urgent, since the enfranchisement of tenant farmers by the Act of 1832 had greatly increased the possibility of intimidation for political reasons.[156] *Y Diwygiwr*, however, was doubtful about the expediency of universal suffrage; certainly it was opposed to violence, although its motto, 'Agitate', laid it

11

open to a charge of fomenting disturbance. Published in Llanelly, *Y Diwygiwr* was a link between the industrial and rural sections of West Wales, so that the rapid spread of Chartism in the coalfield must have reacted on the countryside. Besides, the renewal of the Rebecca rioting in the winter of 1842 and throughout 1843 coincided both with the revival of Chartism and with industrial depression, with the prolonged strike of the Swansea copper workers and especially the failure of the Ebbw Vale works. Colonel Love, the officer commanding troops in West Wales, reported in July 1843: 'Great numbers of discharged workmen from Merthyr and Dowlais have come into this county and are active in persuading the people to mischief'.[157] Even Liberals, such as Captain Evans of Pantycendy, attributed the disturbances to 'revolutionary demagogues that traverse the country instilling their poisons into the minds of the thoughtless and unwary of our countrymen', and spoke of their being 'harboured' in two houses in Carmarthen.[158] Yet Lloyd Hall was able to convince Symons, the education commissioner, that the Welsh countrymen would have nothing to do with Chartist emissaries because they were English; 'dim Sassenach' was the surly reply to all their overtures.[159] And Harriet Martineau thought that 'from the time that Chartist emissaries directed Rebecca's movements nothing went well with her'.[160]

The Chartist leaders themselves were inclined to adopt a disparaging attitude towards country-people. The Gloucestershire villages, said Henry Vincent, were 'steeped in ignorance, beer and superstition'.[161] Bronterre O'Brien's *Poor Man's Guardian*, published though it was by Hugh Williams's friend, Hetherington, was evidently mystified by what was taking place in Wales. It rightly pointed out that the Rebecca Riots were a revolt of the farmers and not of the workers, for artisans and farm labourers paid no turnpike tolls. It advised the labourers to let the farmers fight their own battles. Clearly it was misled by thinking in terms of the large farms of England, and assuming that there was an equal antipathy between the small farmers of Wales and their servants.[162] Local industrial workers, also, were not slow to point out that the farmers had never joined them in fighting for their rights.[163]

It is therefore of the utmost significance to realise that the approach between the two movements was made by the Rebeccaites to the Chartists, and not the other way about. When the Chartist movement was revived in 1843, a secret lodge was formed at Merthyr, meeting at the Three Horse Shoes tavern. It was highly subversive in character, for its members made weekly contributions towards the purchase of firearms and drew lots to determine who should buy a gun when sufficient money had been collected. Yet from the start there was a spy in the inner councils of this arms club. He reported on 2 July that a letter had been received from the Rebeccaites asking the Chartists to join them, and that two of their number had reached Merthyr the previous night.[164] This information was immediately conveyed to Colonel Love and to George Rice Trevor.[165] The disturbances were discussed at subsequent meetings of the lodge, and on 6 August another letter was read from a Carmarthenshire blacksmith requesting them to send down two or three lecturers 'who would be conveyed into the middle of the Rebeccaites to lecture where there would be no danger'.[166] It was reported on 20 August that Feargus O'Connor and W. P. Roberts (the celebrated 'Miners' Attorney General') intended visiting Tenby 'for the purpose of agitating the neighbourhood', although they thought it would be 'of no use to go up amongst the Welsh in the upper part of the country'.[167] The Home Office asked Colonel Love to trace, if possible, the connection between the Merthyr Chartists and the Rebecca leaders,[168] and at the same time instructed the Post Office to open the letters of Rees Davies, Pontygelly, Llandeilo, and John Thomas, Pontystorehouse, Merthyr, who were evidently suspected of being the go-betweens.[169] In the meantime the Merthyr Chartists were keenly interested in events in Carmarthenshire,[170] and even

contemplated imitating them by destroying their own
Pandy and Cefn gates, but abandoned the idea when they
found that their plan had leaked out.[171] Two Chartists were
reported to have left Merthyr in October, one a native of
the town of Carmarthen and the other of Llanarthney.[172]
When the Pontarddulais rioters were tried at Cardiff in that
month, several of the jurymen were from Merthyr. Their
names were read out at a secret meeting of the lodge, and
serious threats were made against them.[173] Some Chartists
made contact with Hugh Williams, who was defending the
prisoners, and the lodge sent him a letter of 'instructions'.
His reply, which was copied and forwarded to Colonel Love,
was highly seditious. The jury, he said, was packed.
'I need not mention who the rogues were who found them
guilty', he added. 'No doubt the liberty-loving men of
Merthyr know them very well, and I do hope they will do
their best for them.'[174] Two jurymen did receive threatening
letters,[175] and other letters were left about the levels at
Cyfarthfa works threatening to 'scotch' anyone who traded
with them,[176] but no reprisals appear to have been taken.
By this time the rioting itself had died down.

The anti-Corn Law movement was regarded by the
radicals as 'a red herring trailed across the path of
democracy', and it was essentially a middle-class movement.
On this account it found more favour in the nonconformist
press than did Chartism.[177] Yet it, also, made its contribution to the turmoil of ideas in the Rebecca period. The
Anti-Corn Law League became active in Wales only in
1840, when a young organiser, Walter Griffith, was
appointed. His activities were mostly confined to North
Wales, but in the winter of 1840 he held two meetings in
Carmarthen, although he was refused the use of the Guild
Hall.[178] It was nearly two years before he again appeared
in Carmarthen, where he was once more refused the Hall, as
well as at Haverfordwest.[179] He lectured in other West
Wales centres, among them Narberth and Pembroke

Dock.[180] At the same time a second organiser, John Jenkins, was appointed by the League, more particularly for South Wales. He held a meeting at Carmarthen a month before the attack on the workhouse.[181]. Both *Seren Gomer* and *Y Diwygiwr* had in the meantime been urging their readers to sign petitions for repeal.[182] Hugh Williams was also 'active in the service of the League'.[183] His relations with his brother-in-law are rather obscure; probably Cobden did not wish to be compromised by him. It is difficult to think of Cobden as a conspirator, but the Home Office issued instructions that his letters should be opened,[184] and Colonel Love was told that the 'Repeal Emissaries' in his area 'must be carefully watched'.[185] Repeal was advocated in several of Rebecca's mass meetings. The significance of the anti-Corn Law movement in Wales lay, however, not in its subversive possibilities but in its wider implications, for it did much to wean the peasantry away from their semi-feudal loyalty to the older families by proving that the interests of landowners and of their Welsh tenants conflicted even in agricultural matters.

The Rebecca Riots placed Welsh Nonconformity in a quandary. The early stages of the rioting did not attract much attention from the denominations; its renewal, and especially its gathering momentum in the early months of 1843, coincided with yet another emotional outburst, this time against Sir James Graham's education bill, which would have placed the education of children employed in mines and factories under the control of the established church. Protest meetings were held, for example, at Haverfordwest, and petitions forwarded to members of parliament, no less than thirty-four of them from the Aberystwyth district alone.[186] For a time this topic entirely displaced anti-Corn Law agitation in the denominational press. While this excitement was going on, the religious leaders had to make up their minds about the disturbances nearer home. They did not find it easy. Two new periodicals, destined to be among the most important in Wales, were started in 1843, *Yr Amserau* edited by William Rees (Gwilym Hiraethog) and *Y Cronicl* edited by Samuel Roberts of Llanbryn-mair. Both men were Independent ministers, but both were North Walians and had little understanding of the situation in West Wales and less sympathy with the rioters. They expressed strong and disdainful disapproval.[187] Another North Walian, a newly ordained minister, John Thomas, who later became one of the leaders of political Nonconformity, had the courage to address his flock at Bwlchnewydd in Carmarthenshire on Sunday night, 18 June 1843, on Jeremiah xxix, 7: 'Seek ye the peace of the city'; early the following morning, nevertheless, the congregation assembled for the march on Carmarthen.[188] On Tuesday, 26 September 1843, a meeting at Pen-y-groes in north Pembrokeshire was called to solicit the guidance of the Almighty in the agitated and alarming state of Wales.[189] There was present a native of the locality, Caleb Morris, the minister of Fetter Lane, London. He was a genius in the exposition of religious truth, and the inspirer of Browning and Mark Rutherford, the latter of whom came to regard him as the greatest orator he had heard, Gladstone not excluded. Morris did not justify Rebecca's outrages, but he showed an insight into the meaning of the movement as an awakening of the Welsh peasantry, and as an assertion of its rights which heralded the dawn of a new era.[190] Meanwhile, yet another London-Welsh minister of the same denomination, Henry Richard, a native of Tregaron, had used his influence with the London Peace Society to have ten thousand handbills distributed in Wales urging the Rebeccaites to renounce violence.[191]

David Rees, especially, found himself in difficulties. His incitement to agitation had produced a Frankenstein. However much he might call on the rioters to cast off 'carnal weapons', he had laid himself open to the charge of fomenting sedition. This charge *Yr Haul* brought relentlessly against him, claiming moreover that the prayer meetings of the Nonconformists were a cloak for their subversive purposes.[192] The *Times*, as if to make up for its unexpected attitude towards the rioting, vehemently attacked the Nonconformists in general and David Rees in particular. It accused ministers of preaching on the text: 'And they blessed Rebekah and said unto her . . . let thy seed possess the gates of those which hate them' (Genesis xxiv, 60), and quoted David Rees's article 'The Great Tyranny' as an encouragement to the rioters. Even William Chambers, junior, though a Churchman and one who had suffered at the hands of Rebecca, was moved to write to the *Times* in Rees's defence.[193] Meanwhile *Blackwood's Magazine* characterised him as 'an illiterate fanatic . . . a little pope within his little circle of the great unwashed', who would benefit greatly from a sojourn in Newgate or Cold Bath Fields, while to another writer his periodical was 'vile trash, published by a preacher at Llanelly, a sort of little bishop in his dirty diocese of colliers and copper men'.[194] Moderate clergymen such as Tegid, a poet and scholar, made fervent appeals to their parishioners to avoid violence.[195] Thomas Carlyle was at this time staying with the bishop of the diocese, the redoubtable Connop Thirlwall, at his palace of Abergwili, near Carmarthen. 'The sight of gates and houses lately demolished by Rebecca', says the bishop, 'did not appear to distress him in the least.' But the bishop himself, although he appreciated that the rioting was due to poverty, to bad harvests, rain and floods, and was prepared to admit that grievances existed, had no sympathy with the hooliganism of the peasantry.[196]

The extremes within Nonconformity, both in politics and in theology, were represented by the Calvinistic Methodists and the Unitarians. The former, at their association meeting at Newport in Pembrokeshire on 3 October 1843, formally condemned 'the lawless and anarchical spirit' of Rebecca, and published in the press a notice urging their societies to expel not only those who participated in the outrages but even those who merely concurred in or sought to justify such acts.[197] Across the border in Cardiganshire there exists the only large rural community of Unitarians in Britain. They have always been in the vanguard of liberalism, and at Rebecca's mass meetings at Pen Das Eithin and Llannarth it was a Unitarian minister, Thomas Emlyn Thomas of Cribyn, who formulated her programme and drew up her petitions to the queen.[198] According to the *Morning Herald*, 'Hugh Williams the Chartist, Walter Anthony the Socialist, and Thomas Emlyn Thomas the Unitarian Minister' were 'the chief disturbers of the principality'.[199]

Finally, among the factors contributing to the growth of opinion was the remarkable number of friendly societies established in these years in West Wales. Their primary purpose was to provide burial, accident and sickness bene-fits. There had been several in the previous century,[200] but most of these were local and many became insolvent through inadequate funds. The eighteen-thirties saw an astonishing outcrop of lodges, particularly of branches of English orders. Of these the most notable were the Oddfellows. In 1836 an entirely Welsh order, the True Ivorites, was established in Wrexham, and in 1838 its headquarters were moved to Carmarthen.[201] There were also the Rechabites, established to promote temperance, and, for persons of a slightly higher class in society (if not of higher intelligence) there was a marked revival of Freemasonry.[202] Every market town in West Wales had two or three lodges, and these catered not only for men but also for women; there were, for example, Oddsisters (the Rose of Cambria Lodge) at Carmarthen.[203] It is particularly important to realise that even small villages had their lodges; the movement had penetrated into the remotest recesses of the countryside. There were three lodges in the village of Llandybie.[204] In the two years, 1838 and 1839, no less than seventy-six lodges of Ivorites were opened in the Carmarthen district.[205] Week by week the local papers gave particulars of their activities, their processions with banners and medals and sashes, and their celebrations.

The lodges had their ritual, their secret signs and their passwords. These, according to the Ivorites, were to prevent them from being imposed upon by strangers. But the Home Office feared that they might be used for subversive purposes,[206] and the Calvinistic Methodists distrusted them so much that, in 1840, they forbade any of their members to join the Oddfellows.[207] Yet the orders were eminently respectable. The purpose of the Ivorites, for example, was 'to encourage the Welsh language, to preserve its members as far as possible from want, and to unite every Welshman as one man to support each other'.[208] They promoted literacy, for they insisted that their members should write their names,[209] and although their secrecy may have accustomed their members to clandestine association, they also developed in them habits of self-respect and self-reliance. Their attitude towards Rebecca differed little from that of the nonconformist bodies. The Oddfellows at Llanelly, on 19 September 1843, deplored the destruction of property and pledged themselves to discourage nightly meetings.[210] Their brethren at Carmarthen went further, and at a special meeting on 27 September forbade any member to take part in them.[211] More remarkable still, the Ivorites of Talog, where the march on Carmarthen of 19 June originated, six months after that event passed a series of resolutions which provided for the expulsion of any of their members known to have participated in illegal meetings.[212] The respectable elements in the community were fairly solidly ranged against Rebecca.

Chapter VI

THE ROADS OF WEST WALES

THE Rebecca Riots were the growing pains of a new society, an example of the disturbances which so often accompany any change in the social structure. They were accentuated by the isolation of the area in which they occurred. The promontory of West Wales was distant from all great centres of population, and its inaccessibility was increased by its indifferent roads. Its economic development was thereby retarded; moreover, a solution for its social problems had to be sought within its own borders because of its isolation. In time, the railway lessened the pressure caused by a growing population in a backward area by facilitating migration to the industries of Glamorgan and Monmouthshire, and it is arguable that if the railway had reached West Wales a decade earlier the riots would not have taken place. That they took the form, primarily, of an attack on the turnpike toll-gates was almost accidental; the gates were tangible objects which people could destroy. It is scarcely credible that they hoped thereby to relieve their economic condition, except perhaps temporarily. Their relief was emotional, and the spread of the rioting was a symptom of mass hysteria.

The history of road legislation is as tortuous as a Pembrokeshire lane, but, fortunately, a bird's eye view of its intricacies is all that is necessary for the purposes of this study.[1] As long as traffic was small, and goods and persons were carried by packhorse or by horse litter, there was little need to repair the roads. By common law, liability for their upkeep lay with the holders of land within each manor, although from the earliest times tolls were raised, especially at bridges, on the principle that those who used them should pay for doing so.[2] But the sixteenth century saw both the decay of the manorial courts and an increase in traffic. An act of 1555, in the reign of Philip and Mary, therefore transferred responsibility for the roads to the parish, which was then replacing the manor as an administrative unit. Every parishioner who held land within a parish was called upon to provide a cart with horses or oxen, together with two able men, for four days in the year to work on the roads, and every other householder or cottager had to devote the same time to this work or supply a deputy. Shortly afterwards the period was extended from four days to six. Thereby the system of compulsory labour on the roads, the *corvée*, was introduced. It lasted for three centuries, all but twenty years, for it was abolished only by the General Highways Act of 1835, passed four years before the first outbreak of the Rebecca Riots. Supervision of this labour was entrusted to two surveyors appointed annually by the parishioners. These men were not paid for their work, and their period of office was too short to enable them to acquire any skill. Needless to say, they exercised very little authority over their neighbours. At the end of the seventeenth century their appointment was transferred to the magistrates sitting in special highway sessions, though still from a list supplied by the parishioners. At the same time the parishes were allowed to levy a highway rate to meet the cost of repairs. Yet the following decades showed very little improvement. The six days were regarded as holidays; *diwrnod i'r brenin* (a day for the king) is still synonymous with a holiday in West Wales. Magistrates frequently had occasion to call upon both surveyors and parishioners to mend their ways. Parishes were indicted at quarter sessions, but they could be fined only if it could be proved that the road had previously been in a better state, and, even so, the fine was usually delayed for three months to enable repairs to be carried out.[3]

This system of compulsory labour proved adequate in parishes where most of the traffic was local, for the wear and tear of their roads was small, and the parishioners would be prepared to repair them when it was to their advantage to do so. In the promontory of West Wales this was the case; there was little through traffic. It is true that Pembrokeshire provided access to southern Ireland by the shortest sea passage, and more than one English king made the journey by way of Milford Haven. But the growing importance of Dublin gave precedence to the direct route between the two capitals through North Wales, so that West Wales remained in its isolation.

In course of time, however, two routes into our area had become well-defined. The road from London to Gloucester continued to Brecon and proceeded up the Usk valley to Trecastle. The traveller then could either cross the moorland barrier between Brecknockshire and Carmarthenshire and descend into the Towy valley at Llandovery, continuing down that river to Llandeilo, or he could take a mountain road from Trecastle to Llandeilo over multitudinous hills. From Llandeilo the road descended the valley to Carmarthen and continued its way through St. Clears to the borders of Pembrokeshire at Tavernspite. Here there was a parting of the ways, for one road turned southwards to Tenby and Pembroke and another continued to Haverfordwest, subdividing there again, with one branch going to St. David's and the other to the northern shore of Milford Haven. The second main road descended the Severn from Gloucester through the Forest of Dean to Chepstow, following the coast through Newport and Cardiff, and on across the Vale of Glamorgan to Neath. Beyond Swansea, a traveller on horseback could, at low water, cross into Carmarthenshire at Loughor. Otherwise he ascended the river of that name to Pontarddulais and descended it again towards Llanelly. Beyond Kidwelly he crossed by ferry to Llanstephan, thereby avoiding the town of Carmarthen, but a few miles further on there was yet another ferry to Laugharne. Thence the road proceeded to join the upper road at Tavernspite.[4] This lower route was beset with many perils when Gerald of Wales traversed it in the twelfth century. Six hundred years later marshlands and estuaries still presented difficulties, but the industrial development of the coalfield and the growth of towns along the coast gave it an increasing importance.

Expanding traffic on the great roads of England made them a burden to the rural parishes through which they passed. It was therefore natural that the parishioners should wish to transfer the cost of repairs on to the users of the roads, and the mid-seventeenth century saw a revival of tolls and the passing of acts of parliament to authorise the setting up of gates, or turnpikes, across certain roads.[5] But it was not until fifty years later, in the first decade of the eighteenth century, that the first road trusts were established.[6] These were composed of local gentlemen who obtained private acts to enable them to borrow money on the security of turnpike tolls and use it to improve the roads. Once established, the system of turnpike trusts spread quickly over the country. But it was soon seen that the tolls were not the blessing which the country-people had anticipated. For objections to the tolls came mostly from them and not from through travellers. Periodically some gate or other would be pulled down. In October 1735 the gate at Ledbury was destroyed, although it was guarded by armed men who killed two of the rioters. The late summer of 1749 saw widespread riots in Somersetshire and Gloucestershire, and on the night of 3 August nearly all the gates in the neighbourhood of Bristol were demolished. Four years later there were disturbances in Yorkshire.[7] As moonlighting takes much the same form in all places, it is of interest to note that some of these rioters were disguised in women's clothes, as were the Rebeccaites almost a century later. So frequent did such activities become that the destruction of toll-houses was made a felony, punishable by death.

All turnpike acts conformed to a type, although they varied greatly in detail.[8] They named the trustees, who were, presumably, those who were prepared to advance money in the first instance. There was usually a large number of them, but great difficulty was later encountered

in getting a sufficient attendance at trust meetings to form
a quorum. The roads which they took over were indicated
in great detail, and the maximum tolls which they could
levy. The duration of a trust was limited to a number of
years, usually twenty-one, for it was anticipated that the
road could be improved and the loan repaid in this period,
so that the trust could be disbanded. But this was never the
case, and the acts were invariably renewed. It was never
intended that the trusts should relieve the parishes from
their duty of maintaining the roads. Their purpose was to
improve the roads, and the money they borrowed was for
this initial outlay. The *corvée* continued as before, except
that, in some instances, trusts accepted from the parishes
an annual sum in lieu of statute labour. As responsibility
for the state of the roads still rested with the parishes, it
followed logically that no trust could be indicted for bad
roads; the only legal remedy still was to indict the parishes
through which such roads passed.

One of the reasons for the ultimate failure of the turnpike
system was the haphazard way in which it grew. Yet it
began, in West Wales, as could have been expected, with
the improvement of the upper route. The Carmarthenshire
gentry, indeed, took action four years before their Brecknockshire neighbours who usually forestalled them in any
new ideas. Early in 1763 they submitted a petition to
parliament, in the stereotyped form of such documents,
stating that the road from the Brecknockshire border through
Llandovery, Llandeilo, Carmarthen and St. Clears to
Tavernspite was in a ruinous condition and could not be
repaired by the methods provided by law. They asked leave
therefore for their representatives to bring in a bill for the
purpose of repairing and widening this road. Their petition
was submitted to a committee of the house of commons
comprising all the Welsh members and those for the border
shires, and as there was no opposition a bill was introduced
which, in due course, became law.[9]

This act, which established what was to be known as the
Main Trust, indicated in precise detail the roads which
were affected. It listed the numerous trustees, all of whom
must own land worth £50 a year or be heirs to persons with
twice that estate, or have personal estate to the value of
£1,000. Five of their number could form a quorum. The
tolls were fixed at 3*d.* for each horse drawing a carriage or
cart, 9*d.* for a carriage and pair, a penny for a horse not so
employed, 10*d.* per score of cattle and 5*d.* per score of sheep
passing through a gate. No person should pay toll at more
than three gates of the trust in the period from midnight to
midnight, or pay on return through the same gates in this
period, and there was to be no toll on coal or lime, on
manure, or on hay, corn or straw which was not for sale.
Neither should a farmer pay for proceeding not more than
three hundred yards along a turnpike road for the purposes
of husbandry, and any carriages going to or coming from
church or a funeral were exempt. The first charge on the
tolls and on the money borrowed on their security was to
meet the expense of securing the act; the second to erect
gates and toll-houses, and the third to repair, widen and
amend the road. The act removed any doubt there might
be by expressly stating that the inhabitants of the various
parishes were still responsible for the repair of their roads,
and that lists should be supplied by them differentiating
between those who had to supply a team of horses and those
who were liable to statute labour only. The act even provided
for the levying of fines upon those who refused to comply
or did their work imperfectly.[10]

Two years later, the gentry who were interested in the
lower route presented their petition. They detailed the road
from Pontarddulais through Llanelly to Kidwelly, and
then on by way of the two ferries to Tavernspite. But this
latter part they were never to take up, for they also specified
a road from Kidwelly to Carmarthen which was to displace
it, as well as a direct road from Llanelly to Carmarthen
through Pontyates, and another from Pontarddulais to

Carmarthen through Llan-non. These were to form the roads of the Kidwelly Trust. Presumably for no other reason than to avoid the expense of obtaining a separate act of parliament, the petition (and the act which followed it) included an entirely different set of roads, based on Llandeilo, which linked up with the former only at Pontarddulais. This section of roads became in time the concern of the Llandeilo and Llandybie Trust; separate lists of trustees were, in fact, included in the act. It differed in details from the previous one (the property qualification was lower, for example, and coal was not exempt although it still paid only half toll). It would, however, be more than tedious to particularise.[11]

The Cardiganshire gentry were the next to move. They obtained a comprehensive act in 1770, which covered the whole shire, although from the start it was divided into a section based on Cardigan and another on Aberystwyth.[12] But of more significance was the petition of the Pembrokeshire gentry in the following year relating to what they called the 'London Road' in its Pembrokeshire sections. They outlined the road from Tavernspite through Narberth to Haverfordwest and then on to Hubberston Hakin on the north side of Milford Haven, together with another road branching from it beyond Tavernspite to Pembroke and the south shore of the Haven. Thereby the Tavernspite Trust came into existence.[13]

The 'great road to London', to quote the petition of 1771, was thus accounted for throughout its whole length in West Wales. But improvements were soon found to be necessary. The ancient bridge over the Towy at Llandovery, a vital point in the route, was swept away in a violent flood, and a new bridge had to be erected in 1772 at a cost of £4,000. But this, in turn, lasted less than a year, and so the gentry obtained parliamentary sanction to build another, this time at the expense of the county.[14] As the old site had proved so unsatisfactory, the new bridge was erected a mile or so above the town. It was a handsome stone structure of one arch,

83 feet in the span, and was typical of the work of its builder, Thomas Edwards, son of the self-taught architect, William Edwards of Pontypridd.[15] At the other end of the route, a growing appreciation of the importance of Milford Haven led to a duplication of roads, for Lord Milford and other gentlemen sponsored the establishment, in 1788, of the Pembroke Ferry Trust, to improve the road from Haverfordwest southwards along the estuary of the Cleddau to the ferry across the Haven.[16] And only three years later, Charles Francis Greville, who had just secured a private act of parliament to build the new town of Milford, also obtained an act to establish the Milford Trust to build a road linking the town to Haverfordwest, and he advanced nearly the whole of the money necessary to do so.[17] Thus Haverfordwest was joined to the Haven by three different turnpike roads.

The second motive for establishing turnpike trusts in West Wales was already apparent in the formation of the Llandeilo and Llandybie Trust. For the purpose of its roads over the hills southward from the Towy valley was to reach the lime kilns at Llandybie and the coal of the Amman valley beyond. It is the lime traffic which accounts for the fact that so many of the turnpike roads in our area run directly from north to south, for lime, as we have seen, was to be found only along the rim of the coalfield. As the purpose of the roads was to facilitate the transport of lime, it was unreasonable that lime should be free of toll. Besides, a stream of lime carts in a rainy spring or early summer churned the country roads into mud and did more damage than any other form of traffic. Yet when the act of 1765 came up for renewal in 1786, the omission of the clause exempting lime brought a protest from parishes north of the Towy, as far afield as Llanybyther in the Teify valley.[18] Lime and coal were also the *raison d'être* of the Llandovery and Llangadog Trust, which was formed in 1779 to link the uplands beyond Llandovery with Llangadog and the Amman valley by way of the Black Mountain.[19]

12

The farmers of mid-Carmarthenshire, north of the Towy, were hindered in their journeys to get lime by the absence of any bridge across the river between Llandeilo and Carmarthen. An act was therefore obtained, in 1784, for building a bridge at Llandeilo Rwnws, below the junction of the Cothi and the Towy, specifically to obtain access to the lime kilns in the parish of Llanddarog.[20] Unlike the road trusts, this bridge trust was a permanent one, and the tallies issued (for £1,600) all became, in time, the property of John Jones of Ystrad. He rented the bridge for various periods to the Three Commotts Trust, but he did not derive much financial benefit from his investment, for at the time of his death the arrears of interest amounted to £2,350.[21]

This bridge became the hub of two other trusts, of which the Three Commotts Trust was one.[22] This was established in 1792,[23] its sponsor being Sir William Paxton.[24] Its main line of road ran from Llandeilo to Carmarthen, south of the Towy, passing Lord Cawdor's seat of Golden Grove and Paxton's own mansion at Middleton Hall. It thus competed with the Main Trust for this part of the route. But its purpose was to provide access to the lime kilns and coal pits, and to facilitate this the act envisaged two further bridges, at Dryslwyn and at Golden Grove. From these three bridges the roads of the trust ran southwards, interlacing with those of the Kidwelly Trust, to Pontarddulais, to Llanelly, and even to Kidwelly itself. Northwards from the Llandeilo Rwnws bridge to Brechfa ran the road of the Brechfa Trust, subdividing there, with one branch ascending the River Cothi towards Llansawel and the other climbing into the hills of north Carmarthenshire. It was founded in 1809,[25] and enabled the farmers of the hill districts to descend to the Towy on their way to the lime kilns. But its history was unfortunate from the start, for the trustees either lost or mislaid their copy of the act itself, and, in 1830, were not aware that it had expired.[26]

Last of the lime trusts, and possibly the most celebrated of them, was the Whitland Trust, founded in 1791.[27] Its main road ran westwards from St. Clears through Whitland to join that of the Tavernspite Trust at Robeston Wathan. This provided a more direct route to Haverfordwest than the road through Tavernspite, and it forms the main highway into Pembrokeshire at the present day. But from this axis no less than six roads penetrated northwards into the hills of west Carmarthenshire and into the Presely range. It was on two of these roads that the first outbreaks of the Rebecca Riots occurred as the lime carting season was beginning in 1839.

In addition to improving the main roads going westwards, and the lime roads running from north to south, the turnpike trusts had a third purpose in linking the market towns. An act of 1788 joined Carmarthen with Lampeter, and, also, Lampeter with Llandovery, thereby linking the Towy valley with that of the Teify.[28] When this act came to be renewed in 1809, the two sections became distinct, forming the Llandovery and Lampeter Trust,[29] and the Carmarthen and Lampeter Trust.[30] Lampeter thus became an important road centre, for it was also the meeting place of the roads of the Cardigan and Aberystwyth districts. The Carmarthen and Newcastle Trust, formed in 1803,[31] similarly joined Carmarthen to Llandysul and Newcastle Emlyn in the lower Teify valley.

Two trusts, at the extreme ends of our area, remain to be noticed. The old coach road from Cheltenham to Aberystwyth ran through Rhayader, and then on through a mountainous district for thirty miles via Devil's Bridge. This was virtually impracticable as the mail coach line. The Aberystwyth Trust effected a great improvement in 1812[32] by constructing an upper road through Ponterwyd to the base of Plynlymon, where it joined an old parish road from Devil's Bridge to Llangurig and Llanidloes. The existing road from Rhayader to Llanidloes (although belonging to the Radnorshire Trust) was merely a narrow lane. So, in 1829, a Llangurig Trust was formed to build an entirely new road up the valley of the Wye from Rhayader to Llangurig.[33] Thereby the route from the Midlands across the Plynlymon range to Cardigan Bay was immensely improved, but thereby, also, Rhayader became an important road junction and the scene of some of the most violent of Rebecca's exploits.

There remained the roads of north Pembrokeshire. These were bedevilled by false starts and unfulfilled intentions. A petition of 1790 envisaged a trust to take over the road from Haverfordwest to St. David's, as well as a few miles along two other roads out of Haverfordwest, one towards Fishguard and the other towards Cardigan.[34] But this brought an immediate protest from no less than twenty-four parishes, some of them surprisingly far afield, whose own chief road branched from the road to Cardigan a mile out of Haverfordwest.[35] They claimed that it would be a great hardship to have to pay sixpence in tolls on carts traversing only a mile of road. They asked that they should be exempt from this toll, or that the trust should take over their own road from Haverfordwest to Maenclochog at the foot of the Presely hills. A new bill was therefore introduced which included this road, as well as the whole length of the road to Fishguard and the coast roads from Fishguard to St. David's, and from Fishguard to Newport and beyond in the direction of Cardigan.[36] When the act came up for renewal in 1812, there were further protests against the Haverfordwest to St. David's road.[37] In fact, the trust became responsible for only one road, that from Haverfordwest to Fishguard, the road in which the trustees themselves were personally interested. North Pembrokeshire, therefore, remained singularly free from turnpike trusts.

The importance of bridges in an area where the roads were constantly intersected by rivers and streams need not be emphasised, and notice has already been taken of some bridges in a previous paragraph. Administratively their position was anomalous. Remarkably few bridges had been built since the later middle ages, for packhorses and riders

on horseback could ford most streams. There were many
country parishes with no bridges at all.[38] It was the growth
of wheeled traffic in the second half of the eighteenth
century which drew attention to their inadequacy. With
increasing frequency, bridges came to be 'presented' at
quarter sessions as being out of repair. But, while a parish
could be indicted for bad highways, it was often difficult
to state what authority was responsible for the repair of
bridges, for the common law of England took no cognisance
of them.[39] Therefore, unless it could be proved that a parish
or a hundred had repaired a bridge in times past, responsibility came to be placed on the county. Soon the erection
and maintenance of bridges became the main item discussed
by magistrates at quarter sessions, and accounted for the
greatest expenditure out of county stock.[40]

No subject gave rise to more acrimony. A bridge obviously
enhanced the value of a landowner's property, and William
Chambers, junior, roundly accused the magistrates of
building bridges out of county stock for their own convenience. He instanced the suspension bridge at Llandovery,
completed in 1832, to which the county had contributed.
This was not on the main road, and it had, he said, no
purpose other than the convenience of magistrates living in
the neighbourhood.[41] He accused Lord Cawdor of having
a new bridge built at Golden Grove at public expense.[42]
There was much rivalry between the southern, industrial
part of Carmarthenshire and the rural areas. When John
Johnes of Dolau Cothi sought, in 1842, to get a bridge built
out of public funds across the Cothi, he was strongly opposed
by R. J. Nevill of Llanelly, and Lord Cawdor gave it as his
opinion, in this instance, that the voting of money in respect
of bridges not previously on the county was illegal.[43] It was
otherwise with the bridge in Llandeilo, which was presented
in the same year as being a danger to the public. A new
bridge to replace it was built for £6,000, despite the
opposition of R. J. Nevill and Rees Goring Thomas. Lord
Cawdor, whose interests were closely involved, argued, with

some asperity, that as the county had pleaded guilty to the indictment it must assume responsibility.[44] Circumstances evidently altered cases.

Frequently the county made payments to individual trusts for keeping bridges in repair. In other instances, trusts made substantial contributions towards the building of new bridges.[45] The suspension bridge at Llandovery, to which William Chambers, junior, objected, was built by a small trust, the Towy Bridge Trust, which was a subsidiary of the Llandovery and Lampeter Trust. For this purpose a government loan of £1,500 was obtained, while £1,600 was taken in bonds by the local gentry. The county's only contribution was to take out a bond for £1,000, although the wooden footbridge, which was now replaced, had been its responsibility.[46] Its affairs were administered by the parent trust. As we have seen, an entirely independent trust erected a bridge at Llandeilo Rwnws. But more remarkable was the enterprise shown by trusts in building bridges along their routes. The Tavernspite Trust sponsored a new bridge at Haverfordwest.[47] Above all, the Kidwelly Trust undertook, in 1831, to build a bridge across the Loughor at an expense of some £10,000, £4,000 of which it borrowed from the government. The county contributed nothing. The bridge never paid its way, and the tolls were high (ninepence for each horse drawing a carriage both on the outward and on the return journey) but it reduced the distance from Llanelly to Swansea by four miles, making it unnecessary to ascend the river to Pontarddulais. At the same time, the Kidwelly Trust contributed £1,000 to the building of an embankment and a road over the Gwendraeth Fawr at Kidwelly.[48] The trusts have been greatly maligned and the tolls which they levied have been condemned as iniquitous, but at least it can be said that they provided the countryside with the bridges which it sorely lacked.

The initiative in establishing a trust naturally came from the landowners, for turnpike roads enhanced the value of their property. Lord Cawdor, for example, whose estates bestrode all three shires, subscribed to no less than twelve trusts in West Wales.[49] It is unlikely that either he or any of the other landowners expected ever to see their money again.[50] Yet their position was a difficult one. Although their contributions were admittedly due only in part to their concern for the common good, and although, also, they frequently made grants of land for the making of roads, yet any action taken by a trust which might be thought to be more in the interest of a landowner than of the community was likely to be narrowly watched. Besides, the rivalries of landowners were held to be responsible for the interlacing of turnpike roads and the consequent multiplication of gates. A prominent witness before the Rebecca commission accounted in this way for the rivalry between the 'Red' (Tory) Kidwelly Trust and the 'Blue' (Whig) Three Commotts Trust. 'They even got the tickets printed their colours', he said.[51] Yet an examination of the financial accounts of the trusts does not seem to bear this out, for Sir William Paxton, the sponsor of the Three Commotts Trust, contributed to both, and so did his powerful opponent, Lord Dynevor.[52]

Several trusts had difficulty in getting their sponsors to redeem their promises, and some had to threaten them with legal proceedings.[53] The bonds, or 'tallies' as they were called, could be sold like ordinary stock, and were occasionally advertised in the press.[54] Nominally they bore interest at the rate of 5 per cent, but the practice grew up in most trusts of paying interest only when it was asked for.[55] Some trusts were twenty years behind with their interest,[56] and, in some instances, unpaid interest was converted into capital by allocating additional bonds to persons to whom interest was due.[57] Yet road bonds seem to have been regarded as a profitable investment even by charitable institutions. Albany Chapel, Haverfordwest, for instance, held considerable sums in two trusts, as did the vicar and churchwardens of Llandeilo. Madam Bevan's charity schools, also, had money invested in a turnpike trust.[58] But the most notable fact which emerges from an examination of lists of bond-holders is the number of small investors among them. This is particularly true of the notorious Whitland Trust, whose oppressive actions are held to have started the rioting. At the time of the Rebecca Riots no less than fifty-one out of its ninety-three bondholders held sums of £10 and under, some holding very small sums indeed. Among them were several labourers, so that, if it be true that the riots were due to the oppression of the trusts, in this case it was the poor who oppressed the poor.[59] Whenever any exceptional expenditure was called for, the trusts had to rely on treasury loans through the Public Works Loan Commissioners. On these loans, interest at the rate of 4 per cent had to be paid in addition to regular payments in redemption of the loans.[60]

The success of a trust depended upon the public spirit and ability of the trustees, which varied enormously. They were not paid for their services, and their task was often arduous and thankless. Hence arose the difficulty in getting a sufficient number to attend trust meetings, except when appointments were to be made, or, possibly, when tolls were to be let. Of the one hundred and twenty meetings of the Brechfa Trust, called during its inauspicious career from 1809 to 1843, no less than fifty-eight had to be adjourned because of insufficient attendance. Often not a single trustee appeared, even at the annual meeting for letting the tolls.[61] Needless to say, the trust was in financial difficulties from the start, and these became desperate when the trust's bankers became bankrupt in the crisis of 1832, and the trust's clerk went to gaol in 1836.[62] Adjournments were frequent, also, in the history of the Fishguard Trust (in one year there were no less than seven consecutive adjournments) and, in time, its members came to meet only once a year.[63] It was soon in financial chaos. By 1814, its accumulated interest almost equalled the original debt.[64] This interest was then converted into tallies, but this procedure was of doubtful legality, and counsel's opinion had to be obtained on it.[65] The final blow came with the failure of Nathaniel Phillips's bank at Haverfordwest in 1825. The Rebecca commissioners found it utterly impossible to unravel the affairs of this trust.[66] Not all trusts were in as bad a state as those of Bréchfa and Fishguard, but at the time of the rioting no less than thirteen of the twenty-nine trusts in the whole of South Wales were bankrupt, and in some instances their bankruptcy was 'irretrievable'.[67]

Road administration was evidently beyond the competence of the local worthies who had made themselves responsible for it. Their officers, also, were local men who were given their little posts for personal reasons. The clerk to the Carmarthen and Lampeter Trust was illiterate.[68] Even worse, the clerk to the important Main Trust absconded to America in 1823 with £650 of the trust funds.[69] The surveyors were equally intractable. The Fishguard Trust had much difficulty with Charles Hassall in its early days.[70] The surveyor of the Llandeilo and Llandybie Trust was generally drunk and had to be dismissed.[71] The surveyor of the Kidwelly Trust was a tenant of one of the leading trustees. His work was so bad that he was indicted for neglect by a local magistrate under the Highways Act of 1835, but he was defended by the trustees at the expense of the trust.[72] In the Llangurig Trust, the surveyor was allowed to contract for work which would be surveyed by himself, and, even so, had to be removed for disobeying orders.[73] Many surveyors were unable to state precisely what roads belonged to their particular trusts.[74] Frequently local politics entered into the decisions of the trusts, and their meetings were held in an atmosphere of bickering and recrimination. This was particularly true of the Kidwelly Trust,[75] possibly because one of its leading trustees was William Chambers, junior. In all these matters, the trusts were probably no worse than local authorities generally, but, like them, they had become out of date.

The tolls, as we have seen, were specified in each turnpike act, and could not be raised, although in some trusts they could be lowered.[76] It was anticipated that they would produce sufficient revenue to liquidate the loans and expenditures incurred, so that the trusts could be disbanded. In no case did this happen. The expense of obtaining a turnpike act was outrageously heavy, and the payment of interest together with administrative costs absorbed most of the revenue of the trusts after the initial improvement of the roads had been made. Turnpike acts, therefore, invariably had to be renewed. When this occurred in the inflationary war period, advantage was generally taken to increase the tolls. Various expedients were adopted, such as a higher toll in winter or a double toll on Sundays. Several trusts varied the toll according to the breadth of the wheels, or 'fellies', in an attempt to regulate the traffic to suit the roads, instead of making the roads suit the traffic, for narrow wheels were more injurious to the roads. In all trusts one payment at a toll-gate covered twenty-four hours, however frequently the traveller passed through it, but the Cardiganshire act of 1833 introduced a novel device by which payment was made 'every third time', that is on every outward journey.[77] This caused intense dissatisfaction. There were slight variations in all trusts, but the tolls of the Main Trust can be taken as typical in 1839, namely 6d. per horse drawing a carriage, 4d. per horse drawing a cart with broad wheels, but 6d. for narrow wheels (and nearly all Welsh carts had narrow wheels), 1s. 6d. per score of cattle passing through a gate and 1s. per score of sheep. Despite this increase in the tolls, it is important to appreciate that they were, still, lower than in other parts of the country. The tolls in Brecknockshire, for example, were considerably higher,[78] and yet Brecknockshire remained almost free from rioting.

The toll on lime has become inseparably associated with the Rebecca Riots in the traditions of the countryside. On the trunk roads served by the Main and Kidwelly Trusts, lime was, at first, entirely exempt from toll, and this was also true of the two Cardiganshire districts. But with the greatly increased use of lime towards the end of the eighteenth century, together with the inflationary rise in prices, and especially because of the damage done to the roads by the lime carts, this exemption was discontinued.[79] Even so, lime paid only a half-toll, at least in the summer months (in a vain attempt to distinguish between lime used for agricultural purposes and for building). The change did not go without protest.[80] Moreover, many of the trusts were established primarily to facilitate access to the limekilns. To have exempted lime altogether on these trusts would have ruined them.[81] On the other hand, to have abolished the trusts would have crippled the parishes near the limekilns by forcing them to repair the damage done by lime carts coming from distant places.[82] All the acts varied in details, but the majority charged only a half-toll for lime. Those of the Three Commotts Trust granted no exemption on lime, but the trustees, in response to public clamour, let their gates on the understanding that lime should pay half-toll.[83] They undoubtedly acted illegally in doing so, and rendered themselves open to prosecution by any disgruntled tally-holder whose interest was in arrears.

Most trusts adopted the practice of letting their gates annually, and advertisements of meetings at which they were to be let appeared in the weekly newspapers. Generally the gates were put up in lots, the advertisements almost invariably indicating the sums paid by the lessees of the previous year. These sums show a small but steady rise, although there was much haggling at these meetings and much collusion between prospective lessees to keep down the price.[84] Sometimes the poorer trusts entirely failed to let their gates and had themselves to arrange for the collection of tolls. The lessees usually were local men, but the situation was radically changed by the appearance of a class of professional toll-farmers. Of these the best known is Thomas Bullin,[85] who is sometimes made the scapegoat for the Rebecca Riots.

Bullin first made his appearance in South Wales about 1830. He came of a family of toll-farmers, for he and his uncle leased gates in various parts of the country. They held the gates on the Hackney and Portsmouth roads in London, as well as others in the home counties, in addition to many gates in and around Bristol. Thomas Bullin is usually described as of Swansea or Neath. His letters are a trifle illiterate, but his credit was always good.[86] His brother and his son also figure in the business, either as lessees or collectors. At one time or another, the Bullin family held gates in all parts of South Wales.

Their appearance must have been a god-send to the harassed trusts, for they usually took over all the gates of a trust *en bloc*, and at a remarkable increase in rent.[87] When the Rebecca Riots broke out in 1839, Bullin held all the gates of the Main, Kidwelly, Tavernspite, Cardigan, Milford, Carmarthen and Newcastle, and Whitland Trusts. For those of the Whitland Trust (on which the rioting began) he paid £300 more than the previous letting.[88] He was able to pay such high rents by attending closely to his business and refusing credit, by changing his collectors at frequent intervals and by rigidly applying the respective turnpike acts.[89] Bullin admitted that where there was doubt he collected toll until the magistrates gave a decision against him.[90] Otherwise there is no evidence that he ever acted illegally. This was not true of his chief competitor in West Wales, a lesser but not unimportant toll-farmer bearing the authentically Welsh name of William Lewis, who took all the Kidwelly gates in 1841 and 1842. He was convicted of setting up an unauthorised chain at Porth-y-rhyd on the roads of that Trust. Fortunately for him, six of the nine magistrates who tried him were also trustees, and he got away with a fine of £50 which he promptly produced and paid into court.[91] Many a man had been transported for less.

The work of collecting was done by humble men earning a weekly wage. A toll-farmer, John Evans by name, employed some twenty-five at a time, paying them eight shillings a week in summer and two shillings more in winter, with perhaps an extra shilling a week if they were honest, 'to keep them honest',[92] for it was very difficult to check their accounts. According to Mr. Weller, senior, they were misanthropic by nature, 'men as has met some disappointment in life, consequence of vich they retires from the world and shuts themselves up in pikes, partly with a view to being solitary and partly to revenge themselves on mankind by takin tolls'. At least, they were unpopular. Some earned as little as two shillings a week, and eked out a livelihood as shoemakers or tailors or schoolmasters.[93] Even so the income at some gates was insufficient to pay the collectors.[94] Possibly tolls would be taken at such gates only on days when there was a fair or a market or a wedding. At some places where a toll could be levied there was neither gate nor chain, and country life would be enlivened from time to time by a race between a farmer, urging on his horses, and a collector, with his toll-board and his chain under his arm, panting as he struggled to get first to the proper spot.[95] The toll-houses, so many of which were easily destroyed later on, were flimsy structures, some of them on wheels,[96] except here and there, as at Abergwili, where it was thought good to have 'something ornamental' because of the bishop's palace nearby.[97] The delightful toll-houses which still adorn the countryside are mostly of a later date.

The country people, for their part, showed much ingenuity in evading tolls. They would unhitch an extra horse some distance away and lead it through a gate, for a horse not drawing paid less. They would hide a load of bricks by covering it with manure which went free, or a load of corn with straw. There were frequent prosecutions, some of which are recorded in the weekly newspapers,[98] but details are lacking for there seem to be very few petty sessions records for West Wales.

Tolls in West Wales were low, but gates were frequent. It must be borne in mind, however, that each gate of a trust 'cleared' several others; payment was not made at all of them. But the gates of one trust did not 'clear' those of another, and there were frequent 'plague spots' where the roads of different trusts interlaced. The parish of Llanarthney had three gates and eleven bars belonging either to the Kidwelly or the Three Commotts Trust.[99] Some towns were surrounded by toll-gates like besieged cities, such as Llanelly with a gate on every one of its five roads,[100] or Rhayader with a gate on all of its six entrances.[101] In Thomas Bullin's wide experience, Carmarthen was unique in having the roads of five trusts radiating from it.[102] In this way it was possible for a traveller to have to pay twice or even three times in as many miles.

Road administration had reached a state of confusion by the early nineteenth century. An attempt was made to bring some order out of the chaos of turnpike law by a general act of 1822, which was piloted through parliament by Thomas Frankland Lewis.[103] It repealed all existing laws, and, amongst other provisions, authorised the inclusion of all magistrates on the board of every turnpike trust within a shire, and provided for the depositing of their financial statements annually with the clerk of the peace. But it was soon confused by a multitude of amendments. Select committees of the house of commons repeatedly advocated that trusts be consolidated.[104] There were undoubtedly too many of them. Cardiganshire, as we have seen, had only one trust, although it was divided into two districts. Pembrokeshire had four trusts, while Carmarthenshire had no less than eleven.[105] Obviously the trusts were too small to be profitable. Yet, here again, the situation in West Wales was in no way exceptional. The average length of road operated by a trust throughout the whole country in 1839 was only twenty miles.[106] Flintshire, which was considerably smaller than Carmarthenshire, had its thirteen trusts; Gloucestershire had fifty. But nothing came of the proposals to consolidate, for the solvent trusts naturally objected to bearing the burdens of the insolvent.

Great confusion was caused in the minds of the Rebecca rioters by the existence, side by side, of turnpike roads and parish highways, and subsequent writers (particularly in Welsh) have written as if all roads were subject to toll.[107] Reasonable statistical accuracy is possible in determining the relative proportions of turnpike roads and other highways capable of being used by wheeled carriages, because of frequent government enquiries, and it can be stated with certainty that at no time did the trusts control more than one-fifth of the roads of West Wales,[108] a proportion which corresponds to that for the country as a whole.[109]

Equally confusing was the extent of parish responsibility for the upkeep of the turnpike roads. No act abolished statute labour; the parishes, as we have seen, were still responsible for repairs. But the acts differed in detail as to the use of the revenue from tolls. In the Cardiganshire act, repair was a prior charge on the tolls; in most other acts it came after the discharge of the interest on the tallies.[110] Nevertheless several trusts, Whitland among them,[111] had used their revenues to keep their roads in repair, even though they were in arrears with their interest payments, and busybodies like Edward Crompton Lloyd Hall were not slow to point out to them that they had acted illegally in doing so.[112]

The extent to which the trusts did call upon the parishes for statute labour in 1834, or for payment in lieu of it, can be gathered from an enquiry conducted in respect of that year.[113] The Main Trust had received no help from the parishes, in money, materials or labour, for twenty-five years. Nor was the maligned Whitland Trust receiving any help, except the carriage of some materials by the parishes. Nor did eight of the smaller trusts in West Wales. Of the remaining seven, the only trust receiving substantial help was the Kidwelly Trust, which had statute duty to the value of £230 performed in 1834, in addition to a £50 composition from certain parishes. The Tavernspite Trust had statute duty to the value of £180 performed, and the

Three Commotts Trust to the value of £157. The other returns are trifling.

It is strange that the over-rated Reform Parliament, which applied its doctrinaire rigidity to human beings in the Poor Law Amendment Act, did not overhaul the road system, where it could have found scope for its tidiness of mind without causing human suffering. The Highways Act of 1835 missed a great opportunity of establishing a national, or at least a regional, system of roads. Instead, it still retained the parish as the road authority. It did, however, abolish both statute labour and all payments in lieu of it. Therefore the oft-repeated grievance that the parishioners had to pay tolls on turnpike roads and, also, had to repair them, had ceased entirely four years before the first incident at Efail-wen, even in respect of those trusts where it had previously prevailed. Yet so great a loss was this to the trusts of the country as a whole (it is estimated at £200,000)[114] that a new act had to be passed in 1841 by which the magistrates could order the surveyors of a parish to pay to a trust a proportion of the highway rates. Recourse was had to this procedure by some trusts,[115] and it has been suggested, though with no great plausibility, that this had something to do with the renewal of rioting in the winter of 1842.[116]

The establishment of a turnpike trust did not necessarily mean an immediate improvement in the roads. Those of Cornwall were said to be in the eighteenth century what Providence had left them after the Flood; those of West Wales were not much better, and the early trusts did little more than the parish surveyors had done. A traveller in Pembrokeshire described the 'uniform manner of making or mending' roads there in 1814 as 'overturning upon them cartloads of stones as big as one's head, which, in a track where wheels seldom roll, are never forced down into the earth, but form, as the old woman at the toll-gate observed, a fine hard road.' 'Nothing but love of glory', he added, should induce anyone to travel along them.[117]

Developments in communication and transport had made this state of affairs no longer tolerable. In 1784 the first mail coaches in the country were introduced; in 1785 a packet service was started between Milford (Hubberston Hakin) and Ireland;[118] in 1787 the Irish mail was carried along the South Wales route for the first time.[119] And so, in 1789, a 'South Wales Association for the Improvement of Roads' was established to promote the improvement of roads all the way from the New Passage (across the Severn) to Milford Haven, and to prosecute all parishes along this route where the road was out of repair.[120] It was, however, primarily a Glamorgan association, interested in the lower road in opposition to the one through Brecon, although its chief surveyor was Charles Hassall of Narberth. This rivalry was soon superseded by a more formidable one. In 1810 a parliamentary committee was appointed to enquire into the route from London to Holyhead, and Thomas Telford was commissioned to survey it. Government grants, to the extent of some three-quarters of a million pounds in all, were then made to improve this road, including the building of bridges over the Conway River and the Menai Straits.[121] Thereby the South Wales route to Ireland was entirely outclassed, and it became increasingly the practice for travellers, even for Cork and Waterford, to go through Dublin.

So bad were the South Wales roads that the postmaster-general threatened to withdraw the Irish mail altogether from this route, or, alternatively, to indict the parishes, but as the mail coaches paid no tolls, although they cut up the roads badly, he wisely decided to do neither.[122] A select committee of the house of commons then enquired into communication via Milford Haven, and, once more, it was Telford who was commissioned, in 1827, to survey the route. He recommended the consolidation of all trusts both from Gloucester to Milford and from Cardiff to Milford. But, to

13

the great chagrin of Haverfordwest,[123] and of the new town of Milford, Telford decided upon Hobbs' Point (Pembroke Dock), on the south side of the Haven, as the place of departure for Ireland, and recommended the construction of a new road leading to it.[124]

Both the Main Trust and the Tavernspite Trust acted on Telford's recommendation. The former built an entirely new road, branching off from its original road a little beyond St. Clears, proceeding through the delightfully named village of Red Roses into Pembrokeshire, and joining the Tavernspite Trust's road on Kingsmoor. Thence a new Tavernspite road proceeded through Redberth, past Carew, to Hobbs' Point. Thereby a virtually straight road was provided all the way from Carmarthen to the Haven, and the mail travelled over it for the first time on 6 April 1839. 'Pontifex Maximus Telford' designed this road; 'Macadam the Magician' was called in to make it.[125] Between them they ruined the two trusts. John Loudon Macadam had already entered into a seven years' contract as surveyor to the Tavernspite Trust a year before he died in 1836, and his work was carried on by his son, John Loudon Macadam, junior. But the son never came near south Pembrokeshire, and his deputy scarcely ever looked at the road.[126] The son's estimate of the expenditure necessary on the Main Trust was £3,197.[127] He was wildly wrong. The cost to the trust proved to be £22,600.[128] Besides, Macadam's deputy on the Kingsmoor road admitted fabricating the accounts to deceive the trustees and had to be removed.[129] The Main Trust spent yet another £11,700 on other plans put forward by Telford.[130] Meanwhile the Kidwelly Trust had spent £10,000 on Loughor Bridge, again one of Telford's recommendations. All this expenditure was of great benefit to the nation as a whole, but the increase in tolls which it produced for the trusts was very small. Ironically, as we have seen, the mail coaches themselves were exempt from tolls, thereby decreasing the revenues of the trusts of the three shires by about £2,000 a year.[131]

This great outlay on both roads and bridges had to be met by government loans at 4 per cent interest. Small wonder that the trusts of West Wales looked with envy on the government subsidies for the Holyhead road, and on the grant of a quarter of a million pounds in these years to improve the roads of Scotland.

The general attitude of the country people towards the turnpike trusts was one of suspicion and of irritation. They were suspicious of jobbery. Roads were kept in a good state of repair, they felt, if they were near the houses of the gentry. A gate on a Three Commotts Trust road was believed to be placed so that Lord Cawdor could go from Golden Grove to Llandeilo without payment.[132] The Tavernspite Trust was thought to have made a length of road to a magistrate's house at its own expense, and so also were the Kidwelly and the Llangadog Trusts.[133] Such matters had a prominent place in the discussions of the countryside and in the reports of the *Times* correspondent.[134] Certainly, when the Carmarthen and Newcastle Trust raised its tolls by one-half in February 1837, as it was legally entitled to do by its particular act, it omitted to do so in respect of gentlemen's carriages. This appeared to a government investigator to be 'a fraud upon parliament, and glaringly partial and unjust'.[135] The location of a gate just within a town, as at Prendergast in Haverfordwest or Water Street in Carmarthen, was a source of great irritation, although the usual cause was that the town had grown beyond the gate, and its boundaries had been extended by the recent Municipal Corporations Act. When a gate at Cardigan was moved for this reason it was placed so as to catch the farmers coming into town from Verwick who would travel along a turnpike road for only four hundred yards.[136] The numerous side bars were set up to catch the lime carts which dodged in and out of the turnpike roads, and the irritation was none the less because the bars were justified. In places, at Adpar, for example, travellers paid for only crossing a turnpike road.[137] Many of the actions of the trusts seemed arbitrary, and their accounts, even when published, were incomprehensible. More fundamental was the loss of confidence in the administration of the law itself, whether it related to turnpikes or to other matters. As magistrates, turnpike trustees were often judges in their own cases. One and the same person was agent to the Nanteos estate, clerk to the petty sessions and surveyor for the Aberystwyth Trust; his brother was clerk to the trust, and both were important tally-holders.[138] Yet when the country people were asked by the Rebecca commission, as they frequently were, what they would substitute for the tolls, they invariably became embarrassed and sought to discuss their grievances in general, and, when pressed for an answer, they invariably preferred the tolls.[139] But the turnpike system, introduced on the equitable principle of making those who used the roads pay for them, had, like so many other aspects of administration in the early nineteenth century, ceased adequately to serve the needs of an expanding and rapidly changing community.

Chapter VII

THE OUTBREAK OF RIOTING

THE winter of 1838–9 was one of fitful disturbance and uneasiness in the countryside. Successive bad harvests had produced a state of semi-starvation and of spiritual malaise. The *ceffyl pren* stalked the Pembrokeshire hills. Dissatisfaction with the commutation of the tithes and with the new poor law found expression in endless discussions in the winter evenings, and, in mid-January, in the attempt to burn the new workhouse at Narberth. After the mass demonstration by torch-light at Carmarthen on 9 January, Chartist emissaries went around the country, adding to the welter of confused opinions. In April, the magistrates of Newcastle Emlyn were forced to swear in special constables in order to preserve the peace,[1] and before the end of the month the serious Chartist riots at Llanidloes had occurred. It would have been strange if the toll-gates had escaped unscathed. The incidents in which two gates were involved would, however, have had no particular significance had it not been for the renewal of rioting three and a half years later.

The Whitland Trust, as we have seen, sponsored several roads which existed primarily for the carting of lime. One of these, running from Efail-wen in the parish of Llandisilio southwards past Narberth to the Ludchurch limekilns, had been included in the original act of 1791. Another, from the mansion of Maes-gwyn in the parish of Llanboidy to St. Clears, was added when the act was renewed for a second time in 1832. On neither of these did the trust take any steps to repair the road, nor did it set up a toll-gate. But the renewal of the act had proved expensive. Moreover Thomas Bullin, the toll contractor, offered in 1838 to take all the roads of the trust for three years at a very substantially increased rent provided the number of gates was increased.

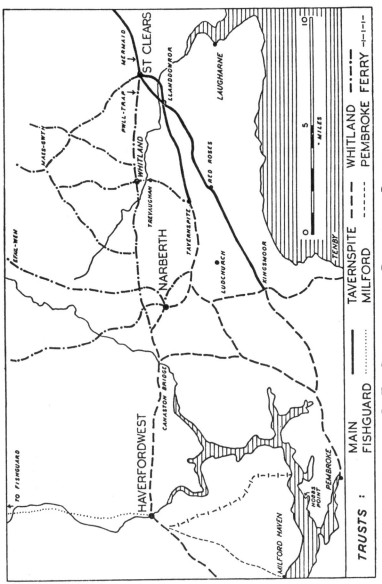

TRUSTS : MAIN ———— TAVERNSPITE –––– WHITLAND ————
FISHGUARD ············· MILFORD ------ PEMBROKE FERRY –·–·–

I. The Carmarthenshire—Pembrokeshire Border

So, at their meeting on 24 January 1839, the trustees decided upon four new gates, one being at Efail-wen and another at Maes-gwyn.[2] These took some time to erect, and they were ready just as the lime-carting season was about to begin. On the night of 13 May, scarcely a week after it had been erected, the gate at Efail-wen was destroyed and the toll-house set on fire. The trust re-erected the gate, whereupon notices were posted on public doors facetiously summoning a meeting on 6 June 'for the purpose of considering the necessity of a toll gate at Efail-wen'. The magistrates hastily swore in seven special constables and sent them to protect the gate. The mob, three to four hundred strong, arrived at 10.30 p.m. on the appointed night. They made much noise, clamouring that they would have 'free laws'. They were all disguised, some having their faces blackened and some being dressed in women's clothes. They drove away the special constables and chased them into the neighbouring fields. Then they set to work, smashing the gate with large sledge hammers and dismantling the house to within a yard of the ground. On the Saturday night of the following week some two hundred disguised rioters appeared at the Maes-gwyn gate, and, with much firing of guns, destroyed it also.[3]

The magistrates were seized with panic. Their immediate response was to ask the Home Office for troops, but they were strangely uncertain of their powers. They begged to be told, for example, whether they could order the troops to fire without reading the Riot Act, for, they said, if they waited to do so the mischief would be done. The Home Office complied with their request, and ordered a detachment of twenty-five foot soldiers to proceed from their barracks at Brecon to Narberth. These reached the little town on Sunday morning, 7 July, just when the inhabitants were going to their places of worship, and they marched through the streets with fixed bayonets, a piece of imbecility which scandalised the neighbourhood and brought a resounding protest from one of the leading Dissenters.[4] But the magistrates had already held their petty sessions at Tavern-spite, nearby, on the previous Friday. They had feared a riot, and as the infantry could not arrive in time they had called out the Castlemartin Yeomanry Cavalry, the heroes of the 1797 affair at Fishguard, 'the last invasion of Britain'.[5] Whether or not it was because of the presence of the soldiers in their resplendent uniforms, there was no disturbance at Tavernspite. Persons suspected of having been concerned in the rioting were acquitted because, when the day arrived, the witnesses against them could not be found. But several who had resisted paying tolls at the chains which had replaced the destroyed gates were fined.[6] Even so, the authorities fared badly. Benjamin Bullin (the toll keeper at Efail-wen and brother of the contractor) had ordered two constables to arrest two farmers for non-payment, and these had been handcuffed and kept in custody overnight. The farmers were fined the large sum of £5 each for the offence, but they rightly brought an action against the constables for trespass, and were each awarded £6 damages at the subsequent Pembrokeshire Spring Assizes. The constables then found themselves imprisoned for debt as they were unable to pay the costs of the action, but the Whitland Trust came to their assistance, thereby depleting its strained resources by a further £175.[7] When the magistrates met again on 18 July they did commit one Morris David, an aged black-smith, for trial at the Carmarthen Assizes for his part in the riot, but the grand jury threw out the bill.[8]

In the meantime yet a third riot had taken place at Efail-wen. On Wednesday afternoon, 17 July, a large crowd assembled, again with blackened faces and in women's clothes, but this time in broad daylight. The constables who were guarding the chain took to their heels, except a lame man who failed to get away and was severely manhandled.[9] On this occasion the leader was addressed as Becca,[10] and the name 'the Rebecca Riots' thereby came into use. Local tradition has always identified him with Thomas Rees, a pugilist who farmed the little homestead of Carnabwth nearby, in the parish of Mynachlog-ddu. It is said that there had been difficulty in finding women's clothes large enough to fit him until he succeeded in borrowing those of Big Rebecca, who lived in the neighbouring parish of Llan-golman. From that day to this the name of Twm Carnabwth has been inseparably associated with the Rebecca Riots in popular tradition, but the truth is that he played no further part whatsoever in them, nor did any subsequent riot take place within eight miles of Efail-wen.

The outcome of these incidents proved to be a surprising anticlimax. An emergency meeting of the Whitland trustees was called at the Blue Boar Inn, in St. Clears, in the following week (23 July), and a large number of magistrates who had never hitherto taken an interest in turnpike roads exercised their right to attend. There were some forty people in all, and the meeting was held in public.[11] Among those present was John Jones of Ystrad, the member of parliament for Carmarthenshire, and there is a strong suspicion that what happened was due to his wish to gain popularity for electioneering purposes.[12] There may have been some slight doubt whether adequate notice had been given of an intention to erect the gates, but there could be little question otherwise of their legality.[13] Yet, on a motion by John Jones, the magistrates overruled the trustees and resolved that the order establishing the four gates should be revoked.[14] Rebecca had won a remarkable victory, and had implanted in the minds of the country people a conviction that obnoxious gates could, with impunity, be removed by violence.

There was no further attack on toll-gates until the winter of 1842. Throughout the summer of that year there had been constant unrest in the industrial areas of the Midlands and the North.[15] A cursory glance at the Home Office papers shows how frequently the military were called upon, and how great was the demand for the services of the metro-politan police. Even in far-away West Wales, the *Welshman* carried second editions with 'Latest News from the Disturbed Districts' which lost nothing in the telling.[16] The words of Jeremiah that 'they that perish by the sword are better than they that perish by hunger' took on a very real meaning for many people. In August there were strikes at Cyfarthfa in a futile attempt to resist lower wages, and both infantry and cavalry were brought into the coalfield.[17] In the countryside the summer was a glorious one, and the harvest much improved, but, ironically, the lowering of demand from the industrial areas still further depressed the prices of agricultural products.[18] There was a revival of Chartism, and in October the Anti-Corn Law League appointed a lecturer to devote his attention solely to South Wales. There were even, as we have seen, adumbrations of an agrarian law with its sinister reminders of the French Revolution. The countryman's secret weapon on a summer's night is fire, and in October the corn stacks of some of the squires of south Cardiganshire were burnt.[19] Despite the offer of an award of £100 by the home secretary, and another of the same amount by the magistrates, the incendiaries were not found. There can be little doubt that they were tenant farmers, and when rioting began again in November at St. Clears it was definitely the work of farmers and not of farm labourers.[20]

As in 1839, it was a new gate which started the trouble. St. Clears was the junction of the Main and the Whitland Trusts. The former, it will be recalled, had completed its new road from St. Clears to Kingsmoor in 1839 at great expense. But it found that farmers and cattle drovers coming on to its road at St. Clears from the Whitland road on their way towards Carmarthen were able to evade payment for a considerable distance. Therefore, on 20 October 1842, it ordered the erection of a gate at the Mermaid, a few hundred yards east of the village.[21] As soon as it was erected it was destroyed (18 November), together with a bar on the bridge across the River Taf at St. Clears belonging to the same trust. The Whitland Trust had its gate at Pwll-trap, to the west of the village, and travellers coming from Haverfordwest and Narberth would have had to pay twice, at Pwll-trap and the Mermaid, in less than a mile, if the new gate had been left standing. So, on the same night, the rioters destroyed Pwll-trap as well.[22] It is clear that they had the Efail-wen 'precedent' in mind, for the name Rebecca was immediately brought into use.[23] The magistrates hastily met, and offered a reward of £30 for information in addition to another £20 offered by the Main Trust, but, as if to show their contempt, on the very night of the quarter sessions (24 November) the rioters destroyed a gate some six miles away at Trevaughan, Whitland, on a side road of the Whitland Trust.[24] The gates were re-erected, but within less than three weeks, on 12 December, a crowd of seventy to a hundred men, armed with scythes and guns and in women's clothes, entered the village of St. Clears at midnight and destroyed all its gates.[25] The magistrates swore in special constables, but they were useless, if not, indeed, in league with the rioters. A frantic request for troops and for metropolitan policemen was then sent to the Home Office, and Police Inspector George Martin, who had already had experience of riots in Yorkshire, and who, remarkably enough, knew Welsh,[26] was sent down with two men. They reached St. Clears on 20 December, but, before they had arrived, the Mermaid gate had been destroyed for the third time.[27]

At Pwll-trap, Rebecca had acted a pantomime after the fashion of the *ceffyl pren*. As she approached the gate she said in Welsh: 'My children, this gate has no business to be here, has it?'; to this the crowd replied that it had not. Then she asked what was to be done with it, and was told that it must be levelled to the ground.[28] This was reminiscent of the meeting to 'consider the necessity of the tollgate at Efailwen', and it illustrates the frolic side of the rioting, at least in its early stages, but the pantomime can hardly have been usual later on, when secrecy and haste were essential, and the rioting itself had become more sinister.

Rebecca threatened those who were sworn in as special constables by putting letters under their doors at night. Two of the original letters survive, and, as threatening letters were to become frequent in the following months, they are worth examining.[29] They are in English, in different hands, but are identical except for numerous spelling errors, and they look as if they had been taken down from dictation by uneducated men. Rebecca warned the special constables not to interfere. She referred bitterly to 'Bowlin' (the contractor), and stated that he would not succeed in continuing the new gates. Gates on the queen's road, she said, would be allowed to stand, but not those on the small roads. She evidently objected to Bullin because he was English. Was it not a shameful thing, she asked, for the sons of Hengist to have dominion over Welshmen? Did the Welsh not remember the long knives with which Hengist had killed their forefathers?[30] She cared no more for Martin and his two policemen than for the grasshoppers in summer. There were several marked men whom she could name, and if they did not obey the notice she would call on them. She signed herself 'Becca & children'.

Christmas passed without further disturbance. Martin continued to make enquiries, but found it quite impossible to obtain information. He thought that he and his men should be armed with cutlasses.[31] Fifty-four special constables had been sworn in at St. Clears, and half of them were on duty every night. Martin divided them into three reliefs of nine men, who took their turn on guard for two hours at a time.[32] Their reflections as they walked the roads of St. Clears on these wet December nights, in complete darkness, hardly bear imagining. The magistrates knew that they could not be relied upon; besides they had already cost the shire £114 by the end of the first week in January, in addition to £5 19s. 6d. a day for the three policemen.[33] The magistrates begged the Home Office to send troops, but this the government was reluctant to do because of its dislike for using the regular army in civil disturbances.[34] Nevertheless, in mid-January, because of rumours of another attack, the magistrates, on their own responsibility, summoned thirty marines from Pembroke Dock. They arrived at St. Clears on 15 January.[35] The following night, Rebecca, with impudent bravado, sent them a message that she proposed to visit Trevaughan once again. The marines hurried there as fast as they could, only to find the gate completely demolished.[36]

The exasperation of the magistrates was increased when the government withdrew the marines.[37] They were replaced by Major Bowling and his gallant men of the Castlemartin Yeomanry Cavalry, a company of three officers and twenty-five men in all.[38] But these, also, found their duties singularly harassing, for some were kept under arms continuously for two successive nights.[39] Besides, they were expensive to maintain. So, when the magistrates realised that the Trevaughan gate was actually on the Pembrokeshire side of the River Taf, they dismissed the yeomanry, and did so late one afternoon, forcing them to do the long march home of twenty-four miles at night in the depth of winter merely to save a day's pay, a bit of scurviness which the Pembroke-shire men rightly resented and which led to some acrimonious correspondence.[40]

Rebecca had, in fact, transferred her attentions to Pembrokeshire. There were rumours of a threat to Narberth workhouse unless the paupers were given better food.[41] Then, with dramatic suddenness, the gate at Prendergast, on the Fishguard road, was removed on the night of 1 February, and when the keeper awoke on the following morning he saw only the stumps of the posts level with the ground.[42] This startling incident drew much attention. The gate was within the town of Haverfordwest, and there was some doubt of its legality on that account.[43] When the chaotic affairs of the Fishguard Trust were discussed later on, one of its bitterest critics was William Edwardes of Sealyham, a local landowner and close relative of Lord Kensington.[44] Is it possible that his son, Owen Tucker Edwardes, took part in the work of destruction at Prendergast? For, only a week later, the *Illustrated London News*, which had already shown much interest in the rioting, declared that Rebecca was 'said to be a county magistrate',[45] and the tradition has persisted until the present day that one of the Edwardes brothers, an officer in the militia, was able on occasion to negotiate a few days' truce with Rebecca so that he could do some hunting. In October, William Edwardes found it necessary to offer a reward of £50 for information 'to discover the person who had circulated the malicious report' that his son, Owen, had assisted the rioters.[46] Certainly no one man directed Rebecca's activities, for three nights later she destroyed the Garreg gate on the Three Commotts road outside Kidwelly, forty miles away.[47]

At midnight on 13 February, the night when the disgruntled yeomanry were riding their horses homewards through the muddy Pembrokeshire lanes, Rebecca struck again at Trevaughan a few hours after they had passed the gate, but this time two of her children were identified. It was the night of Whitland fair, and a pig dealer from Haverfordwest was sleeping off the effects of the evening on the floor of the Golden Lion in Whitland when he was awakened by having beer thrown over his face, and was told: 'Becca is come'. He went with others to the gate. It was a clear, moonlit night. There were only some fifteen or twenty rioters on this occasion, and it may well be that the numbers said to have been present at other incidents were exaggerated because of the darkness and the rain. The pig dealer informed on two of his companions, one of them a very respectable farmer living nearby. The informer was loudly hissed when these were examined by the magistrates, and it was suggested that his motive was to get the reward offered. But the two men were refused bail and placed in Haverfordwest gaol to await trial at the assizes. There, however, the jury discredited the evidence of the pig dealer, as he was both drunk and an accomplice, while other witnesses had absconded, and the men were acquitted.[48]

Three weeks later (6 March) Rebecca was at Narberth and at Robeston Wathan a mile or so away, and four nights afterwards she returned and destroyed the remaining two gates at Narberth. Here the roads of the Whitland and Tavernspite Trusts met; hence the multiplication of gates, which interfered seriously with the lime traffic. Every single gate of the Whitland Trust had now been pulled down. The old woman gatekeeper at Robeston Wathan told the magistrates that the leader of the rioters was 'a person of most gentlemanly address and voice', and that another rioter, mounted on a 'splendid horse', had made it leap right over the gate.[49] Had she, perhaps, heard rumours of the Edwardes brothers? Certainly it was not only the farmers who refused to pay toll at the destroyed gates. The wife of Colonel Colby, an officer in the Engineers (and later a major-general) whose family ranked with the more important gentry in the upper part of Pembrokeshire, refused to pay at the north (Plaindealings) gate at Narberth. Worse still, a few days later the colonel's servant hitched his horse to the chain there and dragged it away. The exasperated colonel took forcible possession of the warrant issued for his servant's arrest for 'this trifling offence'; furthermore he interrupted the magistrates at Tenby, resisted being ejected from the courtroom, and insulted a magistrate in the street. Meanwhile the colonel's lady had a miscarriage, brought on by the chagrin which the incident had caused her. Yet when the servant appeared before the Pembrokeshire Quarter Sessions in October the grand jury threw out the bill, to the surprise of the court who feared it would create an impression that the poor were punished for what the rich could do with impunity.[50]

The rioting, so far, was restricted mainly to the roads between St. Clears and Narberth, and, in view of its later development, it is remarkable how slow it was in gathering momentum. Even in mid-spring it was the re-erected gates which suffered most: Pwll-trap for the fourth time (7 April),

Prendergast (12 April), Trevaughan (22 April), and the Mermaid again (28 April). Isolated incidents occurred elsewhere, at Garreg, as we have seen (4 February and again on 13 March) and at Llanddarog beyond Carmarthen (16 February). Here the toll-keeper had refused to accept five shillings to compound for the passing of a wedding party through his gate, and the two culprits were easily identified. They were fined £10 and £5 respectively, together with costs, in the hope that these severe penalties would prevent the rioting from spreading into that neighbourhood.[51] The gates at the Fishguard end of the road from Haverfordwest were also destroyed, and, once again, doubt was cast on their legality for it was argued that the turnpike act had long expired.[52]

Yet, as spring wore on, the incidence of rioting moved distinctly into the hilly country to the north of the town of Carmarthen and down into the Teify valley. First came the Nant-y-clawdd gate in the parish of Conwil Elfed on the road of the Carmarthen and Newcastle Emlyn Trust to Llandysul (15 March); then Bwlch-y-domen on the branch of the same road to Newcastle Emlyn (13 April), and, a few days later, Bwlch-y-clawdd on the northern side of the hills from Nant-y-clawdd (19 April). On this occasion the rioters assembled at 11 o'clock at night, marched through the village of Conwil Elfed led by a man with a drawn sword, coolly ordered the toll-collector and his wife to leave the toll-house or be shot, holding the muzzle of a gun to his breast while they did so, and proceeded to demolish the house from the roof downwards. Their work done, they returned for some miles along the turnpike road and knocked up an innkeeper to get ale.[53] Early in May Rebecca made her first appearance in the Teify valley, on the Carmarthenshire side of the river at Llandysul, and destroyed the two gates of Pont-tyweli and Troedrhiwgribyn, where the roads of the Newcastle and Lampeter Trusts met.[54]

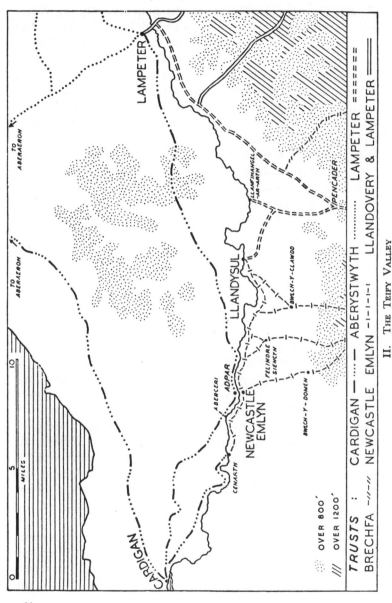

II. The Teify Valley

TRUSTS :   CARDIGAN ———— ABERYSTWTH ⋯⋯⋯⋯ LAMPETER ======
BRECHFA ~~//~~ NEWCASTLE EMLYN –ı–ı–ı LLANDOVERY & LAMPETER ————

14

But far more significant was the destruction of the Water Street gate in Carmarthen on the night of 26 May. The Carmarthen and Newcastle Trust had recently completed an admirable new road from Carmarthen past Abergwili to Conwil Elfed. Its old road to Conwil, which started at Water Street, therefore ceased to be much used by persons going any distance. But the trust had to keep its toll-gate there, otherwise travellers would avoid using the new road. This gate was particularly obnoxious to the farmers to the north-west of Carmarthen, whose parish roads joined the old turnpike road just outside the town, and they objected strongly when the toll was increased in 1837. According to the local historian, Alcwyn Evans, who knew him, it was one of their number, Michael Bowen, a young farmer of Tre-lech, who acted the part of Rebecca on the night of 26 May.[55] With his second-in-command, Charlotte, he and some three hundred followers arrived at the gate shortly after midnight. They posted sentinels to keep away the townspeople, and kept firing down Water Street. They treated the gate-keeper with civility, and were anxious not to alarm his family, but they unroofed his house and destroyed the gate. The town constables, meanwhile, kept safely out of the range of their fire.[56]

Early in June the rioters destroyed the gate at the Llandeilo Rwnws Bridge over the Towy, and the Penllwyni gate near by on the road into the hills towards Brechfa, both of them obnoxious to the lime carters from south Cardiganshire.[57] The ensuing week was one of intense activity, all concentrated in the lower Teify valley. Here, at Newcastle Emlyn, dwelt Edward Crompton Lloyd Hall, and on 15 June he wrote the first of his remarkable series of letters to the Home Office, but the government so little appreciated his information and advice that it repaid him only by getting secret reports on his own activities. The previous night (Wednesday) the rioters had destroyed a gate at Newcastle Emlyn itself on the road towards Carmarthen, and another, four miles away, at Felindre Siencyn.[58] On Thursday night they were back, destroying a gate of doubtful legality within Newcastle Emlyn on the road to Cardigan.[59] On Friday night Bwlch-y-clawdd was down again. According to a local magistrate, J. Lloyd Davies of Alltyrodyn (later a member of parliament), there were between two and three thousand rioters on this occasion, a figure which must reflect his panic more than it does the actual number present. Some five to seven hundred of them then marched the four miles from Bwlch-y-clawdd to Llandysul, seized the four special constables who had been placed there to guard the re-erected Pont-tyweli gate and compelled them to join in the work of destruction, meanwhile firing in all directions.[60] They even announced that their next visit would be to Llanfihangel-ar-arth, further up the river. Rebecca was a strict Sabbatarian; she broke the Sabbath neither in its early hours nor on Sunday nights. But on Monday night she kept her word. About one hundred and fifty men appeared at the gate, all in female clothes, some masked and others with their faces painted. They formed a circle around the special constables, who had been hurriedly brought there, and ordered them to destroy the gate, for this was evidently Rebecca's humour in these parts. As the constables had only their staffs, they were ordered symbolically to strike the gate with them. The leader laid his hand on the face of one of the constables, who reported that 'the hand was as soft as a female's and evidently that of one unused to work'. However this may have been, the solitary rioter indicted for this incident was the tenant of a small farm of sixty acres. His trial was delayed until the Carmarthen Assizes twelve months later, when, although two eminent barristers appeared for the prosecution, he was very ably defended by Lloyd Hall and was acquitted.[61] By that Monday night, 19 June, there was scarcely a gate standing on the roads of either the Newcastle or the Lampeter Trusts, but, that afternoon, a far more startling occurrence had taken place elsewhere.

During these months public opinion was solidifying for and against Rebecca. Both the Whitland and the Tavern-spite Trusts issued addresses and made public their balance sheets in the hope of making their position clear. They were at pains to explain the uses to which money derived from tolls must be put by law, as well as their rights under the act of 1841, which entitled them to a portion of the highway rate.[62] The destruction of the gates was disastrous to their finances. They could, of course, sue the hundreds for compensation, and this they did in some instances; for example, the hundred of Elfed was sued in respect of the gate at Bwlch-y-clawdd, and an order was made against it for the amount of the damage done.[63] But the position of the trustees was an unhappy one. Men who knew the law better than they did, such as Hugh Williams and Lloyd Hall, were quick to take advantage of their errors. Hugh Williams disconcerted the Newcastle Trust by proving, in an action against the toll-keeper at the Water Street gate—which he, himself, had probably instigated—that the decision to raise the tolls in 1837 had been taken when there were only four trustees present, whereas the act required a clear majority of five.[64] Moreover, when seven lime carters were prosecuted for passing over the Llandeilo Rwnws Bridge without payment, Hugh Williams undertook their defence and proved that the lessee demanded $4\frac{1}{2}d.$ for a two-horse cart laden with lime, whereas the act only allowed a charge of $3d$. In this case the magistrates urged the lessee to reach a compromise, for he had rendered himself liable to a fine of £5 for every time he had levied the toll, and the lessee could only plead that 'there must be another act'.[65]

The magistrates, for their part, also issued addresses to the public. They stressed that rioting was contrary to religious principles, and impressed upon the rioters the serious penalties to which they were liable, including trans-portation, with all the misery that this would mean to their families. They pointed out that the damage would have to be paid for, and that the cost of the special constables and metropolitan police would fall on the rates.[66] All the while they were strongly resisting the establishment of a rural police on the grounds of expense. They were exasperated at their inability to gain information, and realised that only very large rewards would overcome the fear of retaliation. The government did offer such rewards, three of £50 each in respect of most incidents, with free pardons to accomplices who turned informants,[67] but they had singularly little effect. Threats were made to the lives of magistrates who were active against Rebecca, and their property was set on fire.[68] In the end, the government acceded to their request for troops. The War Office, on Friday, 16 June, gave instructions that a troop of the Fourth Light Dragoons should proceed from Cardiff to Carmarthen. They were due to arrive there on the following Monday morning.[69] They were a few hours late; when they did arrive, it was at a very critical moment.

The movement itself was becoming sinister. The indiscriminate use of firearms was potentially evil, and if there was no loss of life this was due more to good fortune than to discretion. Threatening letters were becoming more outrageous, and were no longer restricted to turnpike matters. This was the time when the vicar of Penbryn was ordered to return the Bible impounded in lieu of tithes or be mutilated.[70] A few days later the master of Newcastle Emlyn workhouse received a notice in Welsh, written in red ink and headed 'the Vengeance of Blood', warning him to vacate the workhouse immediately or he 'would be taken care of'. This was no longer a joking matter the notice added, though it was signed 'Rebecca (L.S.), Miss Brown (L.S.)'.[71] On the same day Rebecca wrote a letter, ostensibly from Mynachlog-ddu (thereby recalling Twm Carnabwth), to William Peel of Taliaris, high sheriff of Carmarthenshire. She accused him and other landowners of oppressing their tenantry. She warned him to lower his rents by next rent day or she would visit Taliaris, in which case he had better prepare a secure place for his soul, for she would see to his body and give his flesh to the Glansevin hounds.[72] Nor did Rebecca reserve her threats for her enemies; there is ample evidence of intimidation. From the early days she had levied contributions towards her expenses, whatever they may have been, even making clandestine door to door collections.[73] The farmers, impoverished though they were, feared to refuse. Still less did they dare to stay away from the nocturnal meetings.[74] They were summoned by word of mouth or by letter. A boy then in service in the parish of Cilrhedyn vividly recalled later in life the terror of his master when he had received such a summons. The farmer trembled like a leaf, said the boy; he took to his bed on the pretence of being ill and immediately sent the boy to fetch a doctor in order to provide an excuse for not obeying.[75] Even Lloyd Hall received a notice in Welsh, summoning him to attend a meeting. He was told to bring his servants armed with guns, swords, pickaxes or mattocks, and the notice ended with the sinister words *'onid e'* (otherwise).[76] An ever-present fear of revenge haunted the lives of countrymen in their lonely farms and made them risk the dangers of imprisonment and transportation.

The attack on the Water Street gate started an important train of consequences. Notices in scriptural Welsh were immediately posted (on the door of Bwlchnewydd chapel, for example, and on a stable in Blaen-y-coed village) warning those who paid toll henceforth at this gate that they would have their possessions burnt and their lives taken from them 'at an hour when they thought not'.[77] In the next few days three men were brought before the Carmarthen petty sessions for refusing to pay. All were from this neighbourhood, one being John Harries of Talog Mill, some seven or eight miles distant from Carmarthen in the parish of Aber-nant, where the tithe dispute was then at its height. The three men were fined 40s. and 8s. 6d. costs, although all three pleaded intimidation, saying that they preferred to be punished by the magistrates than endanger their lives and their homes. They did not pay the fines into court, and with unusual speed the magistrates sent four special constables on Friday, 9 June, to collect the money or distrain on their goods. But when the constables reached Blaen-y-coed village they heard a horn sounded, and found their way blocked by forty or fifty men with blackened faces, armed with scythes and other implements. Wisely the constables returned to Carmarthen, watched by sullen groups of men standing here and there along the road.[78]

The magistrates responded to this reversal with a pseudo-military expedition, which they entrusted to the borough road surveyor. He assembled a force of four special constables and some thirty or more aged pensioners, together with Inspector Martin and his two metropolitan policemen. They left Carmarthen at the incredible hour of 2.30 on the Monday morning, hoping, no doubt, to accomplish their task before daybreak and thus forestall any interference. They were mistaken. A mile from Talog they were spotted by a man standing on a bank. He ran to give warning; a horn was sounded and a gun fired, and thirty to forty persons immediately appeared, some of them armed with guns. Nevertheless the police seized four boxes belonging to the miller and started for Carmarthen. They had gone about three hundred yards when they found their retreat cut off by a large crowd. A local shopkeeper offered to go surety for the fine, and Harries's goods were surrendered. But the mob then proceeded to divest the militant road surveyor of his two pistols, and roughly handled the special constables. These were jostled along the road, and when they reached the property of a magistrate who had signed the warrant against Harries, they were compelled to dismantle the wall around his plantation. The pistols were then returned, and the party allowed to go, but after they had proceeded a few hundred yards the crowd fired at them and spattered them with gunshot. The pensioners, all the while, had taken no active part and rendered no assistance. The expedition returned to Carmarthen at eight o'clock, in time for breakfast.[79] Eventually, though not until the Carmarthen Spring Assizes, five men were prosecuted for this riot. They were defended by Hugh Williams but received sentences of eight months' imprisonment.[80]

It was the disturbance at Talog which finally decided the government to send troops into the area. Rebecca, for her part, also took an equally important step. On the night immediately after the riot a meeting was held in the parish of Conwil Elfed, though where exactly is not known. According to the jittery magistrate (and future member of parliament), J. Lloyd Davies, there were about a thousand present, 'an unprecedented number' in the three shires, but it is clear that he had no head for figures. He said that the ostensible purpose of the meeting was to discuss grievances, but he feared that its real purpose was different.[81] Among the papers of William Chambers, junior, there exists an undated draft of resolutions which undoubtedly are those of this meeting at Conwil. They show that the chief concern of those present was with the toll at the Water Street gate. The abuses of the Newcastle Trust and the increase in its tolls, stated the resolutions, were the sole cause of the disturbances which had taken place. If the trust produced a satisfactory account of its expenditure, and if the tolls were reduced, every farmer in the parishes of Conwil, Aber-nant, Newchurch, Tre-lech and Cilrhedyn would join in putting down the disturbances. This agrees with the assertion in Alcwyn Evans's account that the Conwil meeting resolved to demand a financial statement for the last eighteen years from the Newcastle Trust. But the farmers went on to complain also of the overbearing attitude of the magistrates; 'we are treated like dogs', they said, a reference, no doubt, to the resentment felt at the Water Street prosecutions.[82]

A knowledge of what transpired at this meeting would go far to explain the events of the following Monday, when the Carmarthen workhouse was ransacked. It is noticeable that neither the draft nor Alcwyn Evans's account makes any reference to the workhouse. Threats to workhouses in general were certainly being made,[83] and the leader at the Water Street riot, on 26 May, according to the depositions of the gatekeeper, had said that Carmarthen workhouse would be down in two months 'because they starved the people there'.[84] At Talog, also, some of the mob had stated that they would 'take the workhouse down'.[85] J. Lloyd Davies understood that eight to ten thousand people were to assemble to pass resolutions against the poor law, and pull down the workhouse.[86] Yet the mayor of Carmarthen, in a well-informed letter, told the Home Office that the plan for the following Monday was to stage a great demonstration. The crowd was to enter Carmarthen at noon 'to the number of many thousands . . . for the purpose of intimidating the magistrates by a display of physical strength and inducing them to return the fines paid by two parties for refusing payment of the toll at the Water Street gate'.[87] Alcwyn Evans adds that the procession was to be formed at eleven o'clock at the Plough and Harrow Inn, in the parish of New-church. Rich and poor were to be compelled to attend, or, in case of illness, to provide a substitute, and all owners of horses were to be mounted. No one, he says, was on any account to be disguised either in person or in dress.[88]

The following days were marked by great activity. The willing and the unwilling alike were summoned by word of mouth and by letter. Among the most active in doing so was John Harries of Talog Mill. On the Saturday he was in Carmarthen telling the farmers that they would stay home at their peril.[89] Other emissaries rode far afield on horseback, bearing the same threat of a visitation and of fire.[90] Letters were sent even to Newcastle Emlyn and the Teify valley. Lloyd Hall was consulted by a score of farmers who had received them, and who appeared terrified.[91] Among the recipients of threatening letters was an Englishman living in the parish of Meidrim. He had apparently shown him-self unsympathetic to Rebecca; yet he was charged to attend personally on horseback and bring with him every man in his employment. 'Non-compliance will bring vengeance on your head,' read the notice, in unusually literate English, 'and most likely you will be landed into eternity without the least warning.' 'If you exert yourself in the people's cause,' it concluded, 'all well and good, if not, Monday will decide your fate.'[92]

Other notices were posted on church and chapel doors. On Sunday morning, the clerk of Aber-nant parish church read such a notice out, threat and all, among the announcements after the morning service. He had been induced to do so, he said, by John Harries of Talog.[93] This also happened in Bwlchnewydd chapel,[94] where the young minister, John Thomas, had the courage to preach that evening against Rebecca, though his admonitions were to have no more effect than those of the magistrates.

Monday proved to be a glorious June day. In the early hours small groups were to be seen coming from the hill farms and the villages and merging on Newchurch, at a spot where the roads from Tre-lech, Talog, Blaen-y-coed and Conwil joined. Soon the narrow lanes were thick with people. The magistrates were now aware of what was going on, and J. Lloyd Davies, to give him his due, had the courage to ride out to Newchurch accompanied by Captain Evans of Pantycendy, the blustering opponent of the tithe and the poor law, but they failed to dissuade the crowd from proceeding. They had to listen to a list of grievances regarding the tolls, the tithe, the poor law and church rates, which the Rebeccaites were determined to lay before the magistrates. The two men did succeed in persuading them to leave their firearms behind, and these were stacked up in a house in Newchurch. Then, having formed up in some sort of order, the vast concourse moved on, and entered Carmarthen appropriately by the Water Street gate. First came the band; then the men on foot, one of them bearing a placard with the words: 'Cyfiawnder a charwyr cyfiawnder ydym ni oll' (Justice, and lovers of justice are we all); then the horsemen. As is usually the case, it is difficult to determine the numbers present, but a conservative estimate would place them at three hundred on horseback and two thousand on foot.[95] Among the former, John Harries was conspicuous. Contrary to popular tradition,[96] only one rider was disguised;[97] possibly he symbolised Rebecca. He wore a woman's clothes and had long ringlets of horsehair. The future historian, Alcwyn Evans, was present, as a boy of fifteen, watching the procession. As the fantastic horseman passed he winked at the boy, who recognised him as Mike Bowen of Tre-lech.

The behaviour of the crowd was quite orderly, and the route taken entirely discounts the theory that an attack on the workhouse was intended. For the procession turned westwards towards Picton's Monument, where it was joined by a contingent from St. Clears, then went down to the Quay, came back up Castle Hill, went along Spilman Street and around St. Peter's Church, on to the Cross (Nott's Square), and into the Guildhall Square. It had thus perambulated the whole town before reaching the Guildhall, where the resolutions were to be presented to the magistrates.

But here things got out of hand. The procession had been joined by unruly elements from the town who poured out of the congested back alleys and the slum houses along the quay. Many of them were fishermen who, on occasion, had had a taste of workhouse fare. These linked arms at the head of the procession and led it on to the workhouse. There they called on the frightened master to surrender his keys in order to let all the paupers out, and he complied. The mob then rushed into the courtyard and broke into the house. Frances Evans, a farm servant from the parish of Newchurch, who had recently given birth to her illegitimate child in the workhouse, led them in. She did a wild dance on a table in the hall as she urged the men upstairs.[98] The noise was deafening as they shouted and smashed the furniture and threw the bedding out of the windows, while the children screamed in terror in the schoolroom. Suddenly there came a cry: 'the soldiers are here'.

For the dragoons were on their way to Carmarthen under
the command of Major Parlby. They had been misdirected
at Pontarddulais (possibly intentionally) and this had
caused them some delay. But a despatch from William
Chambers, senior, informed them of what was taking place,[99]
and they rode on furiously through the broiling sunshine.
They galloped over the bridge and up into the town,
scattering the amazed bystanders. A local magistrate had
joined them.[100] It was long remembered against him that
he had shouted to the dragoons to 'slash away' and that
Major Parlby had told them to take their orders only from
him. Their arrival at the workhouse led to a scene of
indescribable confusion. The mounted rioters stampeded
wildly up Pen-lan Hill behind the workhouse. Others,
including John Harries, were trapped in the courtyard.
Some scrambled over the walls, abandoning their horses,
which they were afterwards afraid to claim, and among
these was Mike Bowen, with his curls in his pocket. The
board, with its noble device 'Cyfiawnder', lay symbolically
trodden underfoot by the dragoons. Hundreds of demonstrators scattered in all directions, over hedges and ditches,
through fields and woods. Fifty years later, the widow of
Michael Bowen had not forgotten her husband's ashen
face when he returned home.

In the workhouse yard the horse of one of the dragoons
fell dead from exhaustion, and another died the following
day, for they had covered the last fourteen miles in an hour
and ten minutes. While the soldiers rested, the magistrates
immediately began the examination of some sixty prisoners
taken in the workhouse. They committed a number to gaol
while others were bound over to appear if required. At the
Summer Assizes a true bill was found against twelve men,
but their trial was deferred and they were remanded on
bail. Among them was John Harries, and it is noticeable
that his bail (£200 with two sureties of £100) was twice
that of the others.[101] It was not until the following Spring
Assizes that they were brought up for trial with the other

Talog rioters, when Lloyd Hall and Hugh Williams appeared for their defence. Harries was then sentenced to a year's hard labour, and five other men to eight months' hard labour, but the remainder were discharged.[102] For by that time the authorities were taking a very lenient view of the disturbances.

Chapter VIII

MIDSUMMER MADNESS

THE affray at Carmarthen attracted wide attention and caused much speculation. The national dailies had already given brief news items of the rioting, generally borrowing them from the local press. Thereafter they carried full reports and editorial comment, and the London *Times* became, itself, a factor in the situation which developed. It is well to remember that the *Times* was not yet the champion of respectability and spokesman for the stately homes of England which it afterwards became. It had been most outspoken in its comments on the riots of 1830 in the south-eastern counties, and had used surprisingly violent language on that occasion. In that area the peasantry, whom the government suppressed with hangings and transportation, had been driven into revolt by famine, said the *Times*, 'maddened by insufficient food and clothing, and by the utter want of necessaries for themselves and their unfortunate families', and it characterised as 'a foul iniquity' the self-indulgence of the gentry in the face of this suffering.[1] Besides, the new poor law of 1834 became the chief object of attack by its proprietor, John Walter II. The ransacking of Carmarthen workhouse was, therefore, of unusual interest to the *Times*, and its issue of 22 June included a report of the incident running to two and a half columns. Even before its appearance, the editor had sent a special representative to South Wales.

Thomas Campbell Foster, to whom this assignment was entrusted, was a young man of thirty.[2] The voluminous dispatches which he wrote during his six months' stay, and which appeared almost daily, provide a remarkable picture of the social scene in Wales.[3] By profession he was a legal journalist. Later he was called to the bar, and became a distinguished barrister and queen's counsel. When he unsuccessfully stood for parliament in later years, he did so as a 'liberal conservative'. His politics in 1843 were those of his newspaper, but he managed to combine an understanding of the grievances of the Welsh peasantry with a detestation of Nonconformity. His aspersions on the county magistrates roused the indignation of the gentry. They challenged the accuracy of his facts and deplored his ideas.[4] They went so far as to insult him 'in an unwarrantable and outrageous manner' when he had the temerity to present himself at their ball at Aberystwyth.[5] Men as diverse as George Rice Trevor and Thomas Bullin considered that his articles had helped to foment discord in Wales,[6] and the prime minister even said that the *Times* seemed to be 'usurping the functions of government'.[7] But the farmers welcomed his unexpected support, and his well-wishers presented him with 'a silver goblet and waiter' on his departure.[8] Besides, his employers were well satisfied with his services. When an outbreak of incendiarism took place in Norfolk and Suffolk after the rioting in Wales had died down, Foster was immediately sent to investigate.[9] More important still, the *Times* sent him for five months to Ireland in 1845, and his bitter attacks on Irish landlords in general, and Daniel O'Connell in particular, caused enormous stir. His dispatches were reprinted in a volume entitled *Letters on the Condition of the People of Ireland*, and they provide a valuable comparison with the state of Wales.[10]

Public opinion could not believe that the rioting was not organised by someone, and there was much speculation as to who Rebecca was. The wording of the threatening letters, in particular the use of legal phrases, seemed to point to an educated man, however much this might be disguised. The authorities made searching enquiries into the conduct of Lloyd Hall.[11] They must have been puzzled by his action in sending them almost daily reports, and especially by his offer to stop the nocturnal meetings if he were given the use of a dozen soldiers.[12] Much as they disliked his extreme views, they found nothing subversive in them. They thought that 'he was by no means as dangerous a man as Hugh Williams',[13] and popular tradition, also, has always attributed the role of leader to Williams. It is worth noting that his personal friend, W. J. Linton, who visited him during the rioting, thought that Hugh Williams was the organiser of what he called 'the one successful uprising in England since the Great Rebellion'. Linton was the lithographer of the *Illustrated London News* (and possibly the best lithographer of his day), and was a member of the group of London radicals with whom Hugh Williams was associated. But the information which he gives about Williams's activities, though valuable, is very meagre.[14] Over half a century later, a native of Hugh Williams's home town, and a business associate of his during the period of the rioting, engaged in a controversy on 'the real Rebecca', and sought to identify her with Hugh Williams. The writer, however, had become senile, and could not substantiate his assertions.[15] As the rioting began in the neighbourhood of St. Clears, where Hugh Williams's wife had her property and where he subsequently made his home, it is well to remember that he did not live there at this time. Certainly the multitude of Home Office papers on the rioting offer not a single suggestion that Hugh Williams participated in it. For it was not until October 1843 that an order was given to open all letters addressed to him, either at Carmarthen or at Hatton Garden, and even this brought no result.[16] Moreover, the popular belief that he was struck off the rolls for his part in the rioting[17] has no foundation whatsoever.[18] It is true that he defended the rioters in the courts; it may be that he gave them clandestine advice as well. On the whole it is best to conclude that the rioting had no master-mind directing it, that it spread like a contagion as the success of the rioters in one area led others to imitate them elsewhere.

The task of capturing the elusive Rebecca was entrusted to a very able soldier, Colonel James Frederick Love, a man fifty-four years of age. He had had a very distinguished career. He had fought in Spain under both Sir John Moore

Take Notice

I wish to give you notice espesial to those which has
sworn to be counstable in order to grab of Becca and her
children but I can sure you that it will be to hard
matter for Bowlin and comp~ to finish the job that they
began, and that is to keep up the Gate at Stanengel
and wire sach gat—
Now take this few lines as information for you to mind
yourselves, you that had any corection with Bowlin
Mr Mc Lies, Wm thom as Blue Boar, all thire property
in one night shale be in conflagration if they will not
obey to this notice. and that to send them vagabonds away
wich you are favourable to, I alway like to be plain in
ale my engagement—is it a reasonable thing that they in—
pose so must, on the county only picking poor labours and
farmers pockets, and you depend that all the Gates that are
on these smale roads shale be destroyed. I am willing for
the gates on the Queen Road to stand it is shameful thing
for us welchmen to have the sons of Hengust have a domirion
over us, do you not remember the long knives which Hengust
hath invented to kile our fore fathers and you may depend that
you shall recieve the same, if you will not give up, when I shall
give you a visit and that shale be in a short time, and now
I would give an order to leave the please before I will come;
for, I do determin that I will have my way ale through;
As for the counstable and the polies men; Becca her children heed
no more of them than the Grass-hopers which fly in the summor
there are others which as masked with Becca, but they shale
not be named now but in case they will not obey to this notice
she shall cale about them in a short time.

Town Mansionith
Dec, 16 1842

Faithfule to Death
with the county
Becca & children

V. THE FIRST REBECCA LETTER

and the duke of Wellington. Then he had been sent to fight the Americans, and had two horses killed under him in the attack on New Orleans, but returned and fought again at Waterloo where he was severely wounded. He was as experienced in civil disturbances as he was in war. It was he who had charge of the troops during the rioting in Merthyr Tydfil in 1831 and in Monmouthshire in the subsequent years. He commanded a troop of horse in Canada in the insurrection of 1838, and was back in South Wales in time for the Chartist march on Newport in November 1839. He was sent to Bradford to cope with the disturbances of 1842. On the day of the Carmarthen riot he was instructed to take command of the troops in Carmarthenshire, Cardiganshire and Pembrokeshire.[19] Love was to find his duties most exasperating, but he brought to them admirable qualities of mind. His lengthy reports throw much light on the circumstances which prevailed. His preconceptions were those of his class, but he was by no means unsympathetic towards the peasantry nor blind to the faults of landowners and industrialists. It was his duty to restore order. In his subsequent career he became major-general, lieutenant-general, and general, before he died in 1866 at the age of seventy-seven.[20]

The hilly, wooded country of West Wales, with its deep-sunk roads and thick hedges, was difficult for cavalry to negotiate, so the dragoons were reinforced by a detachment of infantry from Love's own regiment, the 73rd. Foot, which reached Carmarthen on 23 June.[21] In addition, the marines at Pembroke Dock were strengthened and placed at Love's disposal.[22] The Castlemartin Yeomanry Cavalry were again called out and stationed at Narberth.[23] Meanwhile, the lords-lieutenant were urged to stay in their shires,[24] and, under pressure of circumstances, the Carmarthenshire magistrates agreed to establish a rural police.[25] To assist them, two plain-clothes policemen who knew Welsh were sent down from London.[26] Such aged pensioners as there were in West Wales were placed under the command of the military in order, significantly enough, 'to prevent the possibility of their joining the disturbers of the public peace'.[27] Strangest of all, the War Office sent two field pieces to Carmarthen at Colonel Love's request.[28]

Rebecca, therefore, had a formidable force arrayed against her, and the movement of these troops kept the countryside in a state of great excitement. The dragoons, for example, were rushed to Newcastle Emlyn because of a threat to the workhouse there,[29] and were then relieved by the yeomanry when the expected attack did not take place.[30] The marines were taken by steamer from Pembroke Dock to Cardigan for the same reason.[31] Even so, the force was not thought adequate. Cavalry from Clifton and Taunton was drafted into South Wales early in July,[32] and a staff officer, Major Scott, was sent to assist Colonel Love.[33] It would appear that Love sought to throw a cordon around the area, in order to prevent union with any rising which might take place in Glamorgan and Monmouthshire, while concentrating his main forces on Carmarthen, Narberth, Cardigan and Newcastle Emlyn.[34]

Love's difficulties were increased because the rioting now became more sporadic. The night after the Carmarthen riot, Rebecca was again at St. Clears.[35] But the ubiquitous lady on the same night also destroyed the bars at the Llandeilo Rwnws and Dryslwyn bridges across the Towy and began operations to the south of that river as well, at Llanddarog and Castell Rhingyll.[36] The following night she was at Newcastle Emlyn. This time she made a clean sweep of the three gates of the Cardigan Trust on the north side of the Teify.[37] She had sent a notice summoning Lloyd Hall himself, 'for I was gave to understand that you are on my side,' and also warned him to 'look out for some unpleasantness' if he disobeyed.[38] He disregarded the warning, and, instead, hid himself among the trees to watch operations, afterwards sending a detailed report, in eight quarto pages, to the Home Office. Rebecca's forces, he said, were arranged in military fashion. There was an advance guard of about twenty men, armed with guns. Then came the main body of about two hundred men, most of them carrying axes and other implements, though some had firearms. Lastly there was a rear guard, also armed. Lloyd Hall realised that it was the main body which made all the noise and did the firing. From the sound he knew that their guns were loaded only with powder, but since the advance and rear guards did not fire a single shot he assumed that theirs were loaded with ball. The words of command, 'given in a fine, manly voice', were all in English.[39]

Two nights later (23 June), Rebecca moved down the river and destroyed two gates of the same trust at Cardigan. First the rioters demolished the gate on the outskirts of the town on the road to Aberaeron, and then marched through the streets to another gate where a road branched off to Llangoedmor. Significantly, the gate on the main road to Newcastle Emlyn at the same spot was left untouched, for Rebecca was still destroying only those gates which she considered unjust.[40] As usual, the week-end was quiet, but in the early hours of Tuesday she destroyed the Pen-y-garn gate on the Main Trust road between Carmarthen and Llandeilo. A local farmer—a very substantial freeholder and poor law guardian—was foolish enough to boast that he was Rebecca on this occasion. He was promptly arrested, and for a time was refused bail for very considerable amounts. The authorities evidently thought that they had made an important catch, but the jury at the Carmarthen Winter Assizes charitably came to the conclusion that he had been too drunk to know what he was saying.[41] On the following night (Wednesday) Rebecca was at Llangadog.[42] Thus her activities were evidently extending up the Towy valley into parts which had hitherto been untouched. But the unpredictable lady had the previous night destroyed the gate at Scleddy near Fishguard, on the road to Haverfordwest, at the other end of her territory.[43]

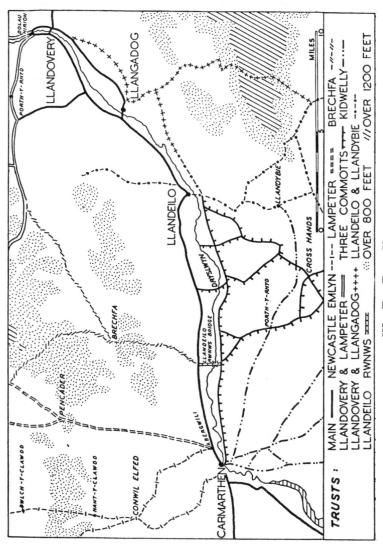

III. The Towy Valley

TRUSTS: MAIN ▬▬▬ NEWCASTLE EMLYN ─··─ LAMPETER ─·─ BRECHFA ─//─
LLANDOVERY & LAMPETER ▬▬▬ THREE COMMOTTS ┯┯┯ KIDWELLY ─···─
LLANDOVERY & LLANGADOG +++ LLANDEILO & LLANDYBIE ─···─
LLANDEILO RWNWS ═══ :::: OVER 800 FEET ///OVER 1200 FEET

In the meantime the magistrates were fumbling for some way to check Rebecca. Exaggerated reports added to their difficulties by further unsettling the countryside. The hurried departure of the dragoons for Newcastle Emlyn, for example, produced a vivid description in the London *Standard* of a battle there on Monday, 26 June, when fifteen to twenty thousand rioters met the dragoons at Newcastle Emlyn bridge, unhorsed them and threw them into the river, where some swam for their lives and others were dashed against the rocks.[44] Actually no incident took place there at all, but such rumours added impetus to the rioting and spread it into other areas.

There had, indeed, been an important but less spectacular development at Newcastle Emlyn on the previous Friday. The enigmatic Lloyd Hall had been asked by the farmers of the hundred of Elfed to place their grievances before the Newcastle Trust, which had called a meeting for that day.[45] He had also replied to Rebecca's threatening letter by issuing a handbill, 'To Rebecca and her Daughters', in Welsh and English.[46] In this he condemned her violence and non-sensical extravagance but invited each parish to select two delegates to meet him. There was thus both a meeting of the trust and a public gathering on the same afternoon. George Rice Trevor was present at the former, when a committee was set up to investigate the finances of the trust. Lloyd Hall was so well satisfied by this that he issued a second handbill, 'Welshmen, here is a glorious beginning', urging them to remain peaceful until the committee had seen what it could do.[47] But he had taken the opportunity of addressing the public gathering on the ballot and related topics, which, as Trevor complained, 'were not well calculated to lessen excitement'.[48] The trust met again with commendable speed a week later. Lloyd Hall had made a searching enquiry into their finances and found no misuse, except, indeed, that the trust had spent £2,000 on the repair of the roads which they should have used to pay interest, an action for which the farmers were not likely to blame them. But the trust resolved to reduce the toll to what it had been before 1837, except on the new road.[49] Three of the gates which Rebecca had destroyed were not to be re-erected, and others were to be moved to less objectionable sites. The tally-holders were asked to accept a reduction in interest from 5 to 3½ per cent. These resolutions were published as a handbill, and Lloyd Hall thought them such a victory that Rebecca would disappear from the area of the trust. Colonel Love, on the other hand, regretted that Rebecca had won through violence concessions which should have been granted in justice before the rioting had begun.[50]

There were other handbills. A local clergyman, the Reverend Augustus Brigstocke, issued one in Welsh, in which, with much scriptural allusion, he urged his readers to submit to those in authority, and even suffer oppression, rather than use illegal means. For had not the Hebrews done so? He thought that 'bad men', strangers to the neighbourhood, were at the bottom of it all, and there is no doubt that he had the Chartists in mind.[51] A neighbouring landowner, Lloyd Williams of Gwernant, was by no means so gentle. He had been threatened with incendiarism if he did not reduce his rents, and in a handbill addressed 'To the person calling himself Rebecca', he promised an equally 'warm' reception to her if she came. He would also see that the cost of any damage would fall on the hundred, and would himself leave the neighbourhood, thereby ceasing to give employment to thirty or forty persons.[52]

But the magistrates were taking no chances. The quarter sessions of all three shires met towards the end of June, and all three bodies issued proclamations warning the people of the heavy punishment for nocturnal outrages. The magistrates decided to hold meetings in different villages to explain the position and hear grievances. But they also asked the Home Office to tighten up the law, for although the destruction of a toll-house was a felony, that of a toll-gate was only a misdemeanour and was not punishable by transportation. The government refused to alter the law. But they did agree to the offer of further rewards, and authorised the magistrates of the individual shires to pay sums up to a total of £500 for information.[53] Within a fortnight Colonel Trevor had been authorised to spend a further £300 in Carmarthenshire alone.[54] Funds were thus available which must have seemed like untold wealth to any farmer or farm labourer who was willing to betray his fellows and risk the wrath of Rebecca, as some were prepared to do.

While summer wore on, the rioting entered upon a new phase. It still continued to be scattered, and even spread further afield, but its main incidence now fell in the hilly country which lies south of the stretch of the Towy between Llandeilo and Carmarthen towards the coast. This was the area where the roads of the Kidwelly and Three Commotts Trusts interlaced, with the consequent multiplication of gates. Here, also, were the lime quarries, especially at Llandybie. But of greater importance were the adjoining coal measures and their growing industrialisation. This had not proceeded so far as to obliterate the rural character of the area, and the farmers who lived here objected to toll-gates for the usual reasons. But the industrial workers had few interests in common with them. They were themselves depressed through falling wages and unemployment. This depression was even more acute in the Glamorgan coalmines and ironworks. Unemployed workers from Merthyr were drifting back to their homes in West Wales throughout the summer.[55] Others sought employment in this part of Carmarthenshire, and some of them were very strange men indeed, as we shall see. They were quite prepared to earn a few shillings for a night's work smashing gates or setting ricks on fire. In the early autumn came the strike of the Swansea copper men.[56] Rioting therefore spread into this area through sheer increased momentum, and because of industrial depression; in its later stages it had little to do with the grievances of tenant farmers.

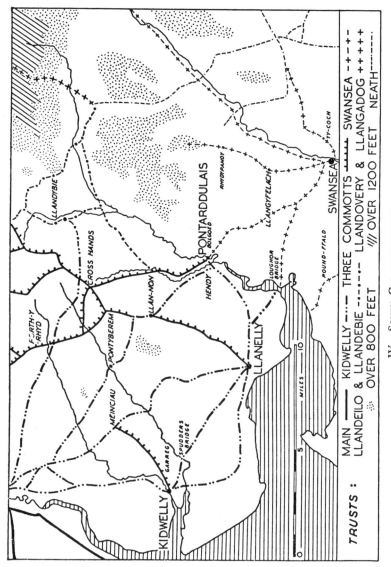

IV. SOUTH CARMARTHENSHIRE

Four gates in this district—at Kidwelly and Garreg (the latter for the third time), at Meinciau where the roads of the two trusts crossed each other, and at Pontyates—were destroyed on Tuesday night, 4 July.[57]

On Thursday night Rebecca was at Bolgoed, at the other end of the area. The River Loughor here forms the boundary with Glamorgan, and the gate was situated in that shire, a mile or so from Pontarddulais on the road to Swansea.[58] Its destruction, together with that of the gate at Rhydypandy (five miles away, beyond Llangyfelach on a lesser road from Swansea) exactly two weeks later (20 July), proved to be of unusual importance, for an informer claimed to have been present on both occasions. He bore the name of John Jones, and his case is interesting, for he was one of those dwellers on the fringes of the uplands whose hands were always against their neighbours.[59] He had sought to build a *tŷ unnos* on the slopes of Darren Fawr, but the local farmers objected to this invasion of their sheepwalks and pulled down the hovel. Among these farmers was Morgan Morgan of Cwm Cile Fach.[60] There is no doubt, therefore, that the informer was actuated by a desire for revenge as well as by the hope of financial reward.

At the first of the two gates, according to the informer, there were present about two hundred and fifty men, of whom about a hundred had guns. All were disguised but only one was mounted, namely a local weaver, Daniel Lewis, who rode a white horse and was addressed as 'mother'. In the crowd was Griffith Vaughan, the landlord of the Red Lion in Pontarddulais and postmaster of that town.[61] After he had been arrested, a consignment of firearms arrived for Griffith Vaughan. This took some explaining, but he stoutly denied that they were intended for the rioters. There were only forty men on the second occasion, one of them again riding a white horse. The informer identified two of these rioters as Mathew and Henry, the sons of Morgan Morgan of Cwm Cile.

Both gates were in Glamorgan which already had a police force, so the informer went to an inspector of police in Swansea on the Saturday (22 July). He discussed with him the prospect of a reward and his own immunity for his share in the incidents. The chief constable, Captain Napier, immediately procured warrants, and in the early hours of Sunday morning went with the inspector and two policemen to Llangyfelach. They seized Mathew Morgan a few hundred yards away from the homestead of Cwm Cile, and left him in the custody of the two policemen. Then they went to the house. The family objected vigorously to being disturbed on the Sabbath (was not Rebecca herself a Sabbatarian?). Henry, who asserted that he was ill, managed to escape upstairs.[62] Napier tried to seize him, whereupon the whole family set about the two police officers. The father belaboured them with his stick and the mother with a bar of iron which she snatched from the fire, while the sister threw a saucepan of boiling water at them. Out of doors they got Napier on the ground, and in the struggle the sister cut his head open with a reaping hook. They tried to seize his pistol, but he succeeded in freeing his arm and shot a younger brother, John, in the stomach. This increased their fury. Yet another brother, Rees, attacked with a hammer, and Henry, who had come downstairs, with a hatchet. Napier, who was now on his feet, floored the former with his fist and then fired his pistol again, so that Henry ran away. The shots brought one of the other policemen on the scene. With his help the two officers secured the wounded boy, and took him and his elder brother, Mathew, to Swansea. In the afternoon a company of the 73rd. Foot reached Cwm Cile and arrested both mother and daughter and the brother, Rees. The father was recognised in Swansea on the following day, enquiring about his wounded son, and he, also, was arrested.

Napier was subjected to much ridicule in the London papers for what the *Atlas* called his fight with 'the old woman with a frying pan'. But the authorities took the matter seriously. They sent Maule, the Treasury solicitor, to Swansea to conduct the prosecutions;[63] they resisted bail (although this was granted later), and ordered Colonel Love to move a force into the town to prevent a demonstration.[64] Yet when the trial came on before a special commission in Cardiff, on 28 October, the father and mother, on account of their advanced age, were discharged on their own recognisances to keep the peace, but the sister, Margaret, was sentenced to six months', and the two brothers, Rees and John, to twelve months' detention in the House of Correction in Swansea. Meanwhile, both the informer's wife and his brother had sworn on oath that he could not possibly have been present either at Bolgoed or Rhydypandy, and there is little doubt that they thereby committed perjury to ward off the wrath of their neighbours. Therefore, when the cases of the rioters involved in those two incidents came up for trial at the Glamorgan Spring Assizes, in March 1844, the government withdrew the charges, and both Mathew and Henry Morgan thus escaped scot free, as, also, did Griffith Vaughan, the innkeeper, and Daniel Lewis, the weaver, of Pontarddulais.

Throughout July there were riots in other places which do not fall into any sort of pattern. When Rebecca was at Bolgoed she was also at Pumsaint on the road from Llandovery to Lampeter, and, two nights later, at Bronfelen, beyond Llandovery on the way to Builth. The Cardigan gates and the one at Pont-tyweli were down again,[66] and so, also, was the bar at the Llandeilo Rwnws Bridge for the second time (7 July). Here Rebecca was particularly violent, for she horsewhipped the lessee of the gate as well as two other men who were probably acting as special constables.[67] The next night, Saturday, Rebecca destroyed the gate on a new road of the Tavernspite Trust at Canaston Bridge near Narberth. Early in the following week she was at Gwarallt, in the parish of Llanllwni, on a road of the Lampeter Trust (10 July). A local farmer had been active

in intimidating his neighbours on this occasion, and he was
arrested on their evidence. His trial, however, did not
come on until the Carmarthenshire Summer Assizes,
twelve months later, and Lloyd Hall, who defended him,
made great play of this delay and of the inconsistencies of
the witnesses. The jury, who retired to consider their verdict
at eleven o'clock in the morning, did not reach an agreement
until fifteen hours later, at two o'clock on the following
morning. Even so, when the judge was roused from his
slumbers and brought to the courtroom, it was to find that
the jury had disagreed again. After another seven hours
they were still not agreed, so the judge dismissed them and
discharged the prisoner.[68] It is not unlikely that Rebecca
had friends among the jurymen.

Newcastle Emlyn,[69] Llanddarog and Meinciau were all
revisited in the same week; and so also were Porth-y-rhyd,
a very important junction of the Kidwelly and Three
Commotts Trusts roads, and Poundffald, the only gate to
be destroyed in Gower[70] (14 July). The gate at Cenarth
Bridge across the Teify was destroyed on 21 July,[71] and
a gate at Narberth on the following night,[72] but the
main activity seemed once more to be in the Towy valley,
near Llangadog,[73] at Pen-y-garn, and near the town of
Carmarthen.[74]

Rebecca was also varying her activities as well as extending them. There were repeated threats to workhouses at
Newcastle Emlyn,[75] at Llanelly,[76] at Haverfordwest,[77] and
at Narberth.[78] Colonel Love reported that about five
hundred men had assembled to attack the Narberth workhouse, and claimed they had dispersed only because they
were forestalled by the arrival of a troop of cavalry which he
had sent there,[79] but William Day, the poor law commissioner, strongly denied that any such gathering had taken
place,[80] a good illustration of the contradictory rumours
which were circulating. Many guardians of the poor would
probably have welcomed the destruction of the workhouses,
which, moreover, were becoming more obnoxious as they

were invariably chosen to house the troops sent into the
various districts.

Rebecca was just as much concerned to remove obstructions on the rivers as to destroy gates on the turnpike roads.
Among these obstructions were the weirs. There had been
salmon weirs at various places on the Teify from time
immemorial,[81] and they had always been an annoyance to
those living higher up the river. Threats were made to the
weir at Llechryd in June,[82] and on the night of 18 July
a crowd assembled to destroy it but found that the soldiers
had arrived before them. This weir was held under a lease
of three lives by one of the local gentry, Abel Lewes Gower,
a director of the Bank of England.[83] He immediately issued
a handbill with the usual threat to dismiss his workmen if
his property were damaged, and brought his own police
from London to protect it.[84] A week later the weir on the
River Nevern at Felingigfran was destroyed (26 July).
Lloyd Hall had heard of a threat to do so, and issued yet
another address 'To Rebecca and her Daughters', but failed
to dissuade them. Some one hundred and fifty men met on
Eglwyswrw common on this occasion and marched to the
weir.[85] Later in the autumn (12 September) there was
another threat to the mill at Felingigfran, but it was not
carried out.[86] On the next night, however, a mob completely
destroyed Llechryd weir, within forty-eight hours of Gower's
departure for London. A reward of £100 was offered for
information, but with no success. The local gentry realised
that the weir was a public grievance, and they started a fund
to buy the leasehold but they received very little support.[87]
A month later (14 October) yet another weir, at Blackpool
below Canaston Bridge, the property of the Baron de
Rutzen, was destroyed.[88]

Love kept patrolling the countryside night after night, but
Rebecca had the initiative and he could not know where
she would strike. His difficulty is well illustrated by the
threat of another attack on Porth-y-rhyd on the night of
21 July. Love was forewarned, and set out in the evening

with a patrol from Carmarthen, accompanied by George Rice Trevor. He also sent word to Llandeilo, and directed another patrol to move southwards. The parties met and wove their way through the roads and lanes. Nothing happened at Porth-y-rhyd, but every movement of the troops was watched, and as soon as they had gone through a village or hamlet they heard shots fired, evidently to let people know they were out. Within an hour after the troops had passed the spot, the colliers of Tumble destroyed a gate near that village. Love had to report that he could do little except protect towns and workhouses and guard such gates as were within a reasonable distance of the places occupied by the troops.[89]

Love's failure was thrown into high relief by the startling success of the *Times* representative. For, on the night of 20 July, Foster succeeded in attending a meeting of Rebecca-ites at Cwm Ifor, a little hamlet some three miles from Llandeilo, and about half a mile off the main road to Llangadog. The meeting began about 9.30 in the burial ground of a Baptist chapel, and was continued until midnight by candlelight in the schoolroom over the chapel stable, a little room, twenty-one feet by ten, which was filled to suffocation. Foster had great difficulty in gaining admission, but, by a show of hands, was allowed to stay when he assured those present that his sole purpose was to obtain a knowledge of their grievances. All the discussion was in Welsh, but Foster secured the assistance of an interpreter, who also translated the resolutions agreed upon. These were dated 'the first year of Rebecca's exploits, A.D. 1843', and the preamble quoted, in anticipation of John Stuart Mill, the aphorism that the price of liberty was eternal vigilance. An army of principles, said Rebecca, will penetrate where an army of soldiers cannot. The grievances included the toll-gates, the tithe, church rates, and high rents. But Rebecca also resolved that no Englishman should be employed as a steward in Wales (for the landlords had made a practice of importing English and Scottish stewards who would be out of sympathy with their tenants). Farmers were urged not to get into debt, but, if any man endeavoured treacherously to obtain his neighbour's farm, or took a farm which had been given up because the rent was too high, 'the Lady' must be acquainted and encouraged in her exertions. No youth under eighteen was to be admitted into Rebecca's secret counsels, and no female 'except Rebecca and Miss Cromwell'. Little did Rebecca think that, early next morning, Foster would supply an account of the proceedings to George Rice Trevor, without naming anyone, it is true, and that Trevor would send it immediately to the Home Office.[90] There was a note of asperity in Sir James Graham's comment that if the account were genuine, and a reporter could attend such a meeting, it should not be difficult for the magistrates to obtain the information they wanted.[91]

The magistrates were doing their best. They invariably placed chains where gates had been destroyed, and heavily fined those who refused to pay at them.[92] They swore in special constables,[93] but found the greatest difficulty in getting anyone to serve. No less than a hundred and ninety men were summoned to a petty sessions at Carmarthen on 2 August, but only six came, and four of these refused to take the oath. The four men were fined £5 each, but George Rice Trevor thought it unwise to enforce the penalty, for this could only be done with the aid of the military and it would further unsettle the countryside.[94] The magistrates tried reasoning with the people by calling together meetings of villagers, as at Pen-boyr.[95] They thought that the judge's charge to the grand jury at the Cardiganshire Summer Assizes would have such a salutary effect that they asked the local clergyman and poet, Tegid, to translate it into Welsh, and distributed a thousand copies.[96] The judge (the future lord chancellor, R. M. Rolfe) had warned the rioters of the serious punishments to which they rendered themselves liable, and had urged the magistrates to enquire into grievances. The magistrates did, in fact, examine the affairs of the trusts,[97] and the Cardigan trustees followed the example of the Newcastle Trust in lowering their tolls. They also abandoned the unusual practice of levying a toll 'every third time', and that exasperating person, Lloyd Hall, was not slow to point out that they thereby infringed their own act of parliament.[98] The Main Trust invited the public to bring forward its complaints.[99] It became clear that a searching enquiry was desirable. Colonel Love reported that such an enquiry would help to allay discontent,[100] and the Carmarthenshire magistrates petitioned the government to appoint commissioners for that purpose.[101] The home secretary therefore gave his consent.

Sir James Graham's choice fell on T. J. Hall, the stipendiary magistrate at the Bow Street police station. His appointment clearly indicates that the Home Office still suspected the rioters of subversive intentions, and it came in for much criticism from the *Times*. But with him was associated G. H. Ellis, a member of a London firm of solicitors which had experience in turnpike trust affairs. The two men left London on 26 July, and their mission took them eighteen days. Their enquiry was a confidential one, but knowledge of it soon leaked out, and they received deputations which laid grievances before them. Both men travelled together, although it was agreed that Ellis should report on the trusts and that Hall should deal with other matters. Ellis did, in fact, produce a valuable report of forty-nine pages which has been extensively used in this book. Hall's recommendations, as we shall see, had important consequences.[102]

August opened with a dramatic occurrence in Lampeter. The little bridge town on the Teify was an important focus for the lime traffic southwards to the kilns, and, also, for the farmers who took their produce to market all the way to the industrial towns. But it was the junction of the roads of no less than four trusts, and it was hemmed in by five gates.

Rebecca destroyed them all in one night (1 August), marching unhindered through the streets from one gate to another with music and much firing of guns.[103] The next night the two gates at Aberaeron fell,[104] and the following night the gate at New Inn on the road from Aberaeron to Cardigan. At this place the toll-keeper's wife indiscreetly opened a window to look out, and a rioter promptly put the muzzle of his gun to her face and fired. The gun was loaded only with powder, but the woman was rendered totally blind.[105] There were rumours of an attack on Aberaeron workhouse, and the magistrates hastily summoned the dragoons.[106]

In the meantime Rebecca had appeared in the Llanelly district, which had hitherto been quiet. On the night of 2 August, rioters destroyed the Sandy gate on the road out of the town to Pembrey. They fired into the toll-house, and it was with difficulty that the toll-keeper's wife got her children out through a back window. The keeper managed to rescue his clock, on which he set much store, before the house was pulled down and his furniture smashed. The rioters then proceeded to the Furnace gate on the road towards Pontyates and Carmarthen; they destroyed the gate but spared the house because the keeper's children were inside and were terrified. In the morning the keeper at Sandy made a statement to the magistrates incriminating a local innkeeper (who was also a coach proprietor) and two other men. The three were arrested, but the keeper, who was at all times given to drink, returned next day and begged the magistrates to disregard his evidence as he was drunk when he had given it; otherwise, he said, he would surely be murdered. The magistrates found themselves in a quandary. They indicted the gatekeeper for perjury when he swore that his first depositions were false; in the end, they decided to abandon the prosecution both against him and against the rioters.[107]

At the same time, rioting had spread over the border into industrial west Glamorgan. A gate at Aberafon was destroyed on 1 August, when the toll-keeper and his wife were ill-treated,[108] and on the following night, a few hours after the strike of the copper men had begun, rioters appeared in the outskirts of Swansea itself, at the Ty-coch (Red Lion) gate on the road to Neath. The old woman who kept this gate was brutally injured. She identified her assailant as a local collier, and he was indicted at the Glamorgan Assizes.[109] The Chartist leader, Feargus O'Connor, was in Swansea at this time, but his opinion of Rebecca does not seem to be recorded.

Rioting continued throughout August, although it now became more intermittent. At Pontarllechau, on the road from Llangadog to the Black Mountain, special constables were compelled to destroy the gate and toll-house. Three of the rioters were identified and received sentences of a year's imprisonment (1 August).[110] The Burton gate at the Ferry across Milford Haven was down on 3 August.[111] The following night Porth-y-rhyd was again attacked by a noisy crowd of some three hundred men, led by a man on horse-back. The parish constable here had made himself very unpopular. He was known as 'Llew Porthyrhyd' (the Porth-y-rhyd Lion) on account of his boastfulness, but when Rebecca appeared he took to his heels and found refuge in a cow shed. A local poet thereupon celebrated his discomfiture in verse.[112] Five youths, the eldest being only twenty-one years of age, were indicted for this riot; at the Carmarthen Winter Assizes, however, they were all discharged on their own recognisances to keep the peace.[113] The Three Commotts Trust immediately began to rebuild, but precisely two weeks later Rebecca returned. This time she caught the Lion in bed and made him get up and assist in the work of demolition.[114] Within nine days (27 August) Rebecca had returned to Porth-y-rhyd yet again.[115]

Rebecca was certainly not lacking in boldness. Although the dragoons were stationed in Llandeilo she appeared there on Monday night, 7 August, and destroyed the Walk gate on the outskirts of the town. The next night she appeared once more at Pen-y-garn, half-way between Llandeilo and Carmarthen, and not only destroyed the gate but set the toll-house on fire, as well as the belongings of the gate-keeper which he had hastily removed outside before going into hiding.[117] Foelycastell, on the road of the Kidwelly Trust beyond Porth-y-rhyd, fell the same night.[118] The Whitland Trust had now been undisturbed for some months, although it had continued to levy tolls at the destroyed gates. On Saturday night (12 August), some twenty-five horsemen, all clad in white, suddenly appeared at Trevaughan. They demanded from the toll-keeper the account books in which he kept the names of those who had refused to pay, and, before going away, made him swear that he would not collect any more tolls.[119] Bwlch-y-clawdd was destroyed for the third time on Wednesday night (16 August),[120] and on the Saturday night Rebecca made one of her very rare appearances in Brecknockshire, when she destroyed the gate at Tair Derwen, two miles from Brecon on the road to Builth.[121]

The Croeslwyd gate near Carmarthen town on a road of the Kidwelly Trust, which had been destroyed on 25 July, was down again on 23 August, the guards, as usual, having fled at the approach of Rebecca.[122] The next night, Thursday, 24 August, came an attack on the Glangwili gate, also on the outskirts of Carmarthen, where the road of the Lampeter Trust branched off from the new road to Conwil. The gate-keeper here, a bookbinder named David Joshua, was strongly disliked, for before taking up his unsocial occupation he had been a radical orator. At the great torch-light demonstration at Picton's Monument on 9 January 1839 he had been one of the principal speakers, discoursing on the people's grievances. He was strongly suspected also of being an informer.[123] When he heard that the rioters were coming, he hid himself in a field, and he claimed that he had recognised four men who were immediately arrested and bound over to appear at the assizes. On the following morning the future historian,

Alcwyn Evans, walked out to Glangwili and found the gate down, the house demolished, and Joshua's stock-in-trade of books and his furniture strewn over the fields. Joshua collected what he could of his belongings and persuaded a local farmer to take them on the Saturday afternoon to a yard in town. But the Carmarthen townsfolk were so bitterly hostile to Joshua that they again scattered his goods in fragments about the streets, and it was only the intervention of Nott, the innkeeper of the Ivy Bush and father of the general, which saved the farmer himself from lynching. A temporary shed was erected at Glangwili, but the next day, although it was Sunday, it was set on fire about three o'clock in the afternoon, possibly the only occasion on which Rebecca broke the Sabbath. Joshua was so exasperated that he attacked and injured a person who refused to pay at his gate, and was himself indicted for wounding and maiming. The four rioters were brought before the December Assizes, but the prosecution there was conducted by the brilliant and humane lawyer, Sir Frederick Pollock, and they were discharged without a trial.[124]

While the Glangwili riot was on, another was taking place at Haverfordwest where there had been no disturbance since 12 April. Doubt had been cast on the legality of the Prendergast gate, since it was within the town, and Ellis, the turnpike expert who had accompanied T. J. Hall, had advised its removal a few hundred yards away. This had now been done, but the local farmers were no better pleased. The magistrates got information on Thursday, 24 August, that it was intended to destroy the new gate that night. They hastily sent to Narberth for the yeomanry and to Pembroke Dock for the marines, but neither detachment arrived in time. The meeting place of the rioters was to be at the Three Corner Piece Inn, some four miles out of Haverfordwest, where a road branched off towards Little Newcastle (the village where Bartholomew Roberts, the greatest pirate of all time, was born). A Haverfordwest constable was bold enough to make his way out to the meeting place, and saw the groups assemble from different directions, some twenty to thirty of the men being on horseback. They called for beer at the inn and drank a quarter of a caskful. According to the innkeeper and her daughter, the leader spoke 'excellent English like a gentleman' (it was suspiciously near to Sealyham); at least, the beer was paid for. The crowd moved on in silence towards Haverfordwest, but broke into a blacksmith's shop on the way and took his sledge-hammer. At the gate the magistrates and constables had hidden themselves. They leapt out to seize the leader and managed to secure his gun which went off in the struggle and killed one of the horses. There was general panic in which the horsemen got away, but the constables, after a hard fight, secured two men, both of them farm servants. Threats of violence were made to the magistrates in the next few days unless the prisoners were released. Nothing came of them, but some ten days later the Haroldston gate outside the town on the Pembroke Ferry road, and the Scleddy gate on the way to Fishguard, were destroyed. The two rioters did not come up for trial until the Pembrokeshire Spring Assizes. Unless she was well acquainted with the niceties of the legal profession, Rebecca must have been astounded when she found that the brief for their prosecution had been accepted, in the normal way of business, by Lloyd Hall. His success in obtaining for the two men a year's imprisonment for unlawful assembly must also have raised in her mind some doubt as to the sincerity of his protestations.[125]

The month of August ended, as it had begun, with an attack on one of the re-erected Lampeter gates.[126] But the fever was now showing some signs of abating; its nature also began to change both for the better and for the worse.

Chapter IX

SMOULDERING EMBERS

THE success of Rebecca's bands in eluding capture over a period of months, and the refusal of special constables to act against them, clearly indicated a general breakdown in society. But the inevitable consequences of this defiance of the rule of law was that the forces which engendered it were perverted to other purposes, for, in a social upheaval, the scum may rise to the surface as readily as the cream. The more law-abiding members of the community were kept in constant fear of a summons to attend at the destruction of a gate, and of the lurid threat of retaliation which accompanied it. Moreover, the sending of threatening letters itself became contagious, and the summer produced an astonishing crop of them which frequently had no connection with toll-gates. Some were sent on to the Home Office and are preserved among its papers; others appear in indictments at the assizes, and a few have survived in the countryside. They are clearly all of a pattern; for example, several advise their recipients to prepare a place for their souls as Rebecca would see to their bodies. Their quaint expressions and extravagant terms have, with time, made them amusing to read, but those who received them had good reason not to be amused by them.

Clergymen of the established church, or 'ministers of the national whore', as Rebecca chose to call them, were obvious targets. The vicar of Penbryn's ill-advised seizure of a Dissenter's Bible in distraint for his tithes, and his terror at the receipt of Rebecca's letter, have already been noticed.[1] His neighbour at Llangrannog was also singled out. He was doubly unpopular, both on account of his tithes and because he had collected money from Dissenters towards the erection of a schoolroom and had then used the building as a place of worship. He received two letters enjoining him to return the money, as well as all additional tithes paid under the new assessment, or be visited by Rebecca.[2]

Still more frequent were the letters to landowners and their agents. A Teifyside landowner was accused of having defrauded a tenant in respect of certain improvements and was ordered to repay the money or be visited.[3] The squire of Cwmgwili was warned to accept a reasonable rent for a particular farm, and a notice was posted locally threatening vengeance on anyone who offered a higher rent.[4] An Aberaeron man, evidently an agent, 'a gape-mouthed Devil . . . ripe to go to Tartarus', was warned, in a particularly violent letter, against the sin of coveting his neighbour's house.[5] The farmers of Pen-boyr, as we have seen, were instructed to demand a revaluation of their farms or Rebecca's vengeance would fall on them.[6] One property owner was accused of taking food out of the mouths of timber-cutters and their children by sharp practices, and was ordered to make restitution.[7] Another had distrained upon his tenants' cattle for rent.[8] The Irish owners of a Whitland estate were invited to return to Ireland and take their agent and gamekeepers with them.[9] A farmer of the same neighbourhood was warned against holding three farms, and told to surrender two of them.[10] Solicitors and auctioneers, also, were among the recipients. A Newcastle Emlyn solicitor who had had a widow imprisoned for debt was threatened,[11] and a Carmarthen solicitor was told to prepare a place for his soul if he did not do justice to a countryman.[12] Advice in the same form of words was given to a Llandovery auctioneer who was accused of lending money to farmers at the extortionate interest of 30 per cent.[13] He received two letters and brought actions against two men, one of whom was defended by Lloyd Hall and was acquitted, while the other, who had actually handed in the letter at a neighbouring post office, was sentenced to nine months' imprisonment.[14]

Other letters were of a miscellaneous nature. A poor woman at Cenarth, who could neither read nor write, had a letter sent to a neighbour in Rebecca's name, but she was

easily identified and received a sentence of four months'
imprisonment with hard labour for her temerity.[15] In
another instance, Rebecca took it on herself to be a censor
of morals in warning two women at Llangeler not to have
undesirable company in their house,[16] while the mother of
an illegitimate child induced a Narberth schoolmaster to
write, in the name of Rebecca, to a local farmer warning
him to pay towards the maintenance of the child, an action
which brought the mother six months' hard labour and the
unfortunate schoolmaster four months' imprisonment.[17]
Naturally, in the towns, the letters voiced the grievances of
the industrial workers. For example, Rebecca condemned
the system of 'long pay', by which the 'worker slaves' were
paid monthly,[18] and a Swansea Rebecca reminded those
workers 'tied down to slavery and doomed to bondage by
the insolence of the brutal English' that 'man is born free
and is endowed by his Creator with the inalienable right of
life, liberty, and the pursuit of happiness'. She urged them to
act without any fear of the soldiers, who would discard their
red coats and join them when they overthrew 'the privileged
class'.[19]

Nor did Rebecca content herself with sending anonymous
letters; she frequently carried out her threats. Her vengeance
fell particularly on those who opposed her, notably on the
magistrates. One of these, a doctor living near Newcastle
Emlyn, a strong Tory and an opponent of the Dissenters,
had been outspoken in his condemnation of the rioting.
He was staying, early in August, with his family at a farm
which he owned on the coast at Aber-porth. On the night
of 4 August, a number of men stealthily surrounded the
house and, without warning, fired slugs in through the
windows, and then took deliberate aim at the doctor when
he appeared at one of them. After that they gave a shout
and departed. The doctor issued a handbill offering a reward
of £100 for information, and the government took so serious
a view of the incident that it also offered another £100.[20]
Later in the month, wheat stacks were set on fire at Dynevor

Castle, no doubt because of the activity of George Rice Trevor. Both the government and Lord Dynevor offered rewards of £200. An informer eventually came forward in this case and implicated a local farmer. The magistrates at Llandeilo deliberated for several hours on the evidence brought before them but decided not to proceed with an indictment, and the informer was severely manhandled afterwards.[21] On the night of 12 September, Edward Adams of Middleton Hall (where his family had succeeded Sir William Paxton) returned from quarter sessions to find his ricks on fire, and the plantation around the mansion alive with armed men.[22] The haggard of yet another magistrate, Captain Davies of Dôl-haidd, near Newcastle Emlyn, was set on fire on 21 September. He had been a guardian of the poor, and had even supported a petition against the new poor law, but he had apparently expressed himself too freely against Rebecca. The rewards of £50 offered by him and by the government brought no information.[23] Lesser men who dared to oppose Rebecca also incurred her vengeance; this, for example, was the reason why the haggard of a farmer in the parish of Conwil was fired in July.[24] Even worse, the vicar of Llangrannog's curate was waylaid and beaten, until several of his ribs were broken, because he had given evidence before the magistrates.[25]

Naturally, the services of Rebecca were called for in the ordinary disputes of the countryside. A farmer in the parish of Llandysul who had taken a farm against the wishes of his neighbours was beaten by a number of disguised men in August,[26] and in September a homestead in the hamlet of Gwynfe (Llangadog) was fired on this account.[27] Two farmers, one in Llanegwad and another living near Haverfordwest, were visited on the same night (25 August) and warned to dispose of the corn which they were hoarding in expectation of a rise in price.[28] The holding of more than one farm was anathema to the land-hungry tenant-farmers. On 21 October Rebecca set fire to the outhouses of a farm near Carmarthen for this reason.[29] The following night she demolished an unoccupied farmstead in the parish of Llanfihangel-ar-arth because its owner was accused of encouraging farmers to bid against one another for farms.[30]

Sheriff's officers (or bum-bailiffs, as they were popularly called) went in peril of their lives throughout the summer, and especially after Michaelmas had brought its usual number of rent-defaulters. The parish pound at Newcastle Emlyn, where stray cattle and distrained goods were detained until they were redeemed, was destroyed in July.[31] On the night of 26 August, the pound of the manor of Slebech, near Haverfordwest, was the scene of a considerable riot. The Baron de Rutzen had seized no less than eighteen cattle, three mares and six colts belonging to one of his tenants for non-payment of rent. He must have anticipated trouble, for he sent two gamekeepers and three other men to help the pound-keeper in keeping watch over them. About midnight, a large crowd arrived at the pound from the direction of Canaston Bridge, and, after a scuffle, released the animals. A local shoemaker was tried at the Winter Assizes for his part in the incident, but was ably defended by Lloyd Hall and was given the benefit of the doubt through the proverbial mercifulness of a Pembrokeshire jury.[32] At Llanarthney (29 August), Llanegwad (30 August) and Kidwelly (10 September), Rebecca drove bailiffs away from farms, and, in the last instance, spirited away the distrained goods.[33] The bailiff acting for the undersheriff of Carmarthen (a Llandeilo attorney, James Thomas, known locally by the delightful nickname of Jemmy Genteel), who had distrained upon the goods of a Llanfynydd farmer, was himself bound hand and foot and placed in Brechfa pound (22 September), and was released in the morning only on payment of the customary fourpence for redeemed strays. Ever afterwards, it is said, he was a strong opponent of cruelty to dumb animals.[34] Two bailiffs who took possession of a farmer's goods in the parish of Llangunnor were thrashed by a crowd of twenty-five to thirty men, who made them swear on the Bible never to distrain again (8 October).

The farmer and his son were tried for this assault at the assizes. They were defended by Lloyd Hall, but the farmer, though an old man, was sentenced to twelve months' imprisonment, and the son to twelve months' hard labour.[35] Three hundred disguised men drove out the bailiffs in occupation of a farm in the parish of Llanfyrnach on the night of 10 October,[36] and on the following night a bailiff in a farm at Llandyfaelog was found by Rebecca and her daughters hidden under a bed, but was allowed to go unharmed.[37]

Tithe disputes produced one startling incident. Rees Goring Thomas, the squire of Llan-non, was, as we have seen, an extensive tithe impropriator. His agent, John Edwards, 'added insult to unnecessary severity' in the collection of tithes, according to a letter which William Chambers, junior, wrote to his employer. Edwards lived at Gelliwernen, a mile or so from Llan-non in the direction of Llanelly. At midnight on 22 August, a crowd of several hundred assembled in the village of Llan-non and proceeded with much noise towards Gelliwernen, being joined on the way by groups from other directions. When they reached the house they fired in through the windows. The agent was ill in bed, but his wife and daughter had the courage to speak to the crowd, which eventually left after having smashed the greenhouses and uprooted the trees in the orchard. Some of the rioters had, meanwhile, gone to the gamekeeper's cottage nearby, but he had taken himself into the woods, leaving his wife and children behind. Both Goring Thomas and the government offered sums of £250 for information, and a handbill was issued drawing attention to this enormous reward of £500, with the usual pardon to any accomplice who would turn informer. It met with no response.[38]

It is significant that no riot took place on account of any enclosure of common land by act of parliament. On the other hand, the common at Llandybie was the scene of three incidents arising from encroachments. A tenant of

Lord Cawdor's had enclosed some acres a dozen years previously, but on the night of 29 July Rebecca and her daughters destroyed the fences. When these were re-erected they were again destroyed on the night of 23 August.[39] Even more significant was the incident on the night of 28 September. An old woman had had a cottage built for her on part of the common. She was herself not very respectable for she had been in gaol for theft, and she was typical of the dwellers on the fringes of the common land. A number of disguised men entered the house on that night. They made her kiss a gun and swear she did not recognise any of them, then ordered her out of the house and pulled it down. Four men were indicted for this riot, and their trial at the Winter Assizes was prolonged. They all pleaded alibis, one producing a witness who swore that he had been with her 'courting her all night as is the custom of the country'. In the face of such evidence no jury could convict.[40]

From the redress of public grievances it was a short step to the remedy of private wrongs. This could be amusing; it could also be sinister. One such incident arose out of a wedding. Two maiden ladies of fortune but of uncertain age lived at Glanmedenny, Newcastle Emlyn. One day in summer they fell in with a wedding party, and a farm lad, in the exuberance of the moment, kissed one of the old maids for a bet. He was fined £1 for this assault, a sum which may have represented his money wages for two months. On the night of 4 September a riotous crowd surrounded Glanmedenny and demanded that the lady should reimburse the boy or they would burn the place down. She wrote next day to the Home Office, and both she and the government offered rewards of £50. No further incident took place, but having tasted of the joys of writing letters of complaint to a government department the lady continued to do so, and within some weeks she had raised to £500 the reward for information relating to 'this murderous attack'. Six months later she was still writing.[41] A second instance concerned a dispute over a will. A number of men, armed with guns and reaping hooks, entered the home of an old man in Llanfihangel-ar-arth at dead of night on 12 August, and compelled him by threats to sign a promissory note in favour of a claimant under the will. Eight men were indicted for this riot and were found guilty at the Carmarthen Spring Assizes. In stern contrast to the leniency with which most of the gate breakers were treated, the instigator was sentenced to twenty years' transportation and the other seven to ten years' transportation. There were heart-rending scenes as their relatives thronged the dock after the sentence was passed and when a large crowd gathered to witness their removal on their way to the hulks.[42]

One other aspect of Rebecca's activities, that of guardian of public morals, must be noticed. As we have seen, the punishment of marital infidelity was peculiarly the function of the *ceffyl pren*. Rebecca took over this work. At dead of night she brought illegitimate children to their supposed fathers and enjoined them to look after them, sometimes, it would appear, to the amusement of their legitimate spouses. She sponsored cases where magistrates had refused affiliation orders. She threatened young men with punishment unless they married the girls they had betrayed. A dozen instances during the summer can be authenticated, and there were, no doubt, more, but it would serve no purpose to give details. Rebecca also visited a shopkeeper and a shoemaker in Newcastle Emlyn and warned them to give up beating their wives.[43] Strangest of all, she forcibly reconciled the vicar of Bangor Teify and his lady. They had been separated for several years, but one night, early in October, Rebecca called for the vicar's wife at the house where she was staying in a neighbouring parish, took the astonished woman to her husband and told them to cherish one another henceforth on pain of her severe displeasure.[44] This aspect of Rebecca's work has loomed large in popular tradition, so much so that a writer of reminiscences forty years later gives it almost as much space as the destruction of the gates.[45]

The most noteworthy feature of the late summer, however, was the gradual replacement of nocturnal outrages by mass meetings to discuss grievances and to petition the government. Desultory discussions had, no doubt, taken place at all gatherings, and the demonstrators at Carmarthen had intended to submit a list of grievances to the magistrates. It is difficult to know whether the purpose of the meeting which Foster attended at Cwm Ifor was to arrange attacks on gates, and whether it was deflected to a statement of grievances by his presence. Nor can one say if Hugh Williams was there (for who, one wonders, knew the aphorism that 'eternal vigilance is the price of liberty' in Carmarthenshire in 1843?). W. J. Linton, who believed Williams to be the instigator of the riots, states that he had from the first meant the destruction of the toll-gates to be 'a preparation for further political action', and when Linton accompanied Williams to the greatest of all these meetings, on 25 August, he spoke of it simply as 'a gathering in favour of universal suffrage'. Linton adds that Williams then believed the 'Rebecca movement' to be at an end, because the presence of so large a body of police made secret action impossible.[46] Certainly Williams took a leading part in the mass meetings which were now to take place.

Besides, the magistrates themselves were holding meetings to reason with the farmers and villagers. Their arguments are expressed in a very moderate and well-written pamphlet, *An Address to the Inhabitants of Conwil Gaio*, issued on 14 August, in Welsh and in English, by an enlightened magistrate, John Johnes of Dolau Cothi. He warned his readers that heavy punishments might fall upon them in years to come, even though they escaped now, if anyone, through malice or hope of reward, laid information against them. He spoke of the pecuniary loss to themselves as rate-payers which the riots involved, and tried to explain the position of the turnpike trusts. He called upon religious leaders to help in restoring peace in the countryside.[47] Various clergymen and pastors, as we have seen, did urge

moderation. So also did the Quakers. Joseph Tregell
and some female co-religionists arrived in Carmarthen on
25 August for this purpose. Their views and demeanour must
have seemed as strange to Rebecca as hers did to them, and
it is difficult to estimate the extent, if any, of their influence,
or of the effect of the ten thousand pamphlets which the
London Peace Society distributed in South Wales.[48]

Whether the farmers were amenable to sweet reasonable-
ness or not, there were more pressing arguments for caution.
The presence of the police and the sentences passed on some
of their fellows sobered them. They hid themselves where
they could, if necessary lying flat between rows of plants in
a potato patch or buried in the hay in their haylofts, when
Rebecca's emissaries came for them, and they concocted
threatening letters addressed to themselves to prove intimidation should the police visit their farms.[49] Besides, the approach
of the hiring fairs, when farm servants might change their
situations, led to a fear that these would inform upon
them.[50] For farm servants and labourers were beginning to
hold their own meetings to discuss increased wages and
allowances.[51] So alive did some farmers become to this new
danger that they welcomed the presence of troops.[52] For
however much they approved of the breaking of toll-gates,
the firing of ricks by farm labourers was another matter.

Two meetings, which took place on the same day
(Thursday, 3 August) within a few miles of each other,
illustrate different aspects of this change. In the afternoon
of that day, magistrates and farmers met at the Hand and
Shears Inn in Llanfynydd. George Rice Trevor addressed
those who were assembled, and resolutions were passed
against specific grievances: the toll on lime on the Three
Commotts Trust roads, for example, the injustice of the
Walk Gate within the town of Llandeilo, and the cost of the
new rural police.[53] But late that evening there was a far
more significant gathering in the barn of an isolated farm-
house (Pen-lan) in the hills off the main road from Llandeilo

to Llangadog, not far from Cwm Ifor. Once again, Foster, the *Times* representative, had somehow heard of it. He made his way to the meeting place, accompanied by a guide who acted as his interpreter, and succeeded in persuading the farmers to allow him to stay. Their purpose was to form a Farmers' Union with a view to obtaining fair rents. Detailed rules for the union were adopted, and it was agreed that in future only members should attend its meetings. It was anticipated that the union would be linked with similar bodies elsewhere. The discussion ranged over a variety of topics and continued until eleven o'clock. Foster gives no indication that it was resolved to destroy the Walk Gate on the following Monday night; if he knew, he kept the information to himself. When the meeting was over, the farmers dispersed in all directions in complete silence. Foster made his way across the fields to an inn on the main road which was, all the while, being patrolled by the dragoons from Llandeilo.[54]

Foster also attended a meeting of magistrates and farmers in the following week (8 August) at Llan-non. T. J. Hall, the Bow Street stipendiary, was present and heard a statement of grievances in private. In the public meeting the farmers were quite prepared to accept a resolution condemning nocturnal outrages; they were more concerned to press for reductions in rent and in the tithes. The two Chambers (senior and junior), who were extensive land-owners in this area, agreed on the spot to reduce their rents by 15 per cent, but Rees Goring Thomas, the tithe impropriator, would only promise to consider a reduction when the tithes were next due.[55] Within two weeks there was another meeting in Llan-non (21 August). Although the curate of the parish took the chair, the discussion turned mainly on tithes. Dissatisfaction was expressed because Rees Goring Thomas had not yet agreed to a reduction, and this no doubt explains the attack on Gelliwernen on the following night, for it must already have been arranged.[56]

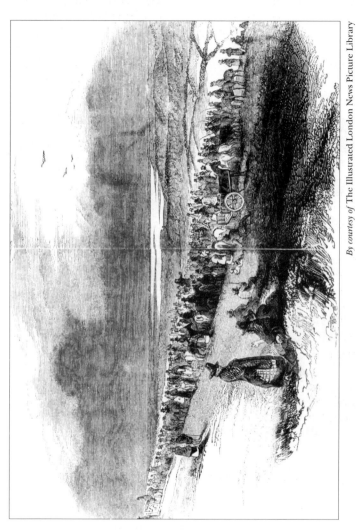

By courtesy of The Illustrated London News Picture Library

VI.   THE MEETING ON MYNYDD SYLEN

The lithographer, W. J. Linton, was present at the meeting

A LETTER.

"To the Public generally, and to our Neighbours in particular.

"WE, *John Hughes, David Jones,* and *John Hugh*, now lying in Cardiff gaol, convicted of the attack on Pontardulais turnpike gate, and the police stationed there to protect it—being now sentenced to transportation, beg, and earnestly call on others to take warning by our fate, and to stop in their mad course, before they fall into our condemnation.

"*We are guilty, and doomed to suffer*, while hundreds have escaped. Let them, and every one, take care not to be deluded again to attack public or private property, and resist the power of the law, for it will overtake them with vengeance, and bring them down to destruction.

"We are only in prison now, but in a week or two shall be banished as rogues—to be slaves to strangers, in a strange land. We must go, in the prime of life, from our dear homes, to live and labour with the worst of villains—looked upon as thieves.

"Friends—neighbours—all—but especially young men—keep from night meetings! Fear to do wrong, and dread the terrors of the judge.

"Think of what we *must*, and you *may suffer*, before you *dare* to do as we have done.

"If you will be peaceable, and live again like honest men, by the blessing of God, you may expect to prosper; and we, poor outcast wretches, may have to thank you for the mercy of the Crown—for on no other terms than your good conduct will any pity be shewn to us, or others, who may fall into our almost hopeless situation.

(*Signed*)

"JOHN HUGHES,
"DAVID JONES,
"The X mark of JOHN HUGH.

"Cardiff Gaol, Nov. 1st, 1843.

"Witness, JOHN B. WOODS, Governor."

VII. THE CONFESSION OF JOHN HUGHES, DAVID JONES AND JOHN HUGH

This handbill was issued in Welsh and in English

The farmers of Llanedy met on 15 August to complain of the tithes, the poor law, the Corn Laws and high rents.[57] The same day the magistrates got information of a secret meeting to be held in Llangyndeyrn. The dragoons were sent out and patrolled for three hours, but, although they passed within a field's distance from a copse where two hundred and fifty men were deliberating, they did not see them. These men, however, were colliers, and their interests were opposed to those of the farmers, for what they wanted was a reduction in the price of butter and other agricultural produce, and cheap beer.[58]

Whether Hugh Williams was deliberately bringing the Rebecca movement into line with Chartism or, more probably, only taking advantage of this new development, he now played an increasingly important part. He was invited to attend a meeting at the Bell Inn in Conwil on 16 August, where Foster, himself, took the chair. There, Williams outlined the history of Rebecca, attributing the Talog riot to the 'stupidity of a hot-headed road-surveyor' and the Carmarthen riot to the 'disorderly conduct of thoughtless persons in the town'. He expounded the usual grievances at length and strongly deprecated nocturnal outrages.[59] This was a small meeting of only a hundred persons, but preparations were already on foot for a monster demonstration to be held on Friday, 25 August, on Mynydd Sylen, the high open moorland between Llan-non and Pontyberem, only a mile or so from Gelliwernen where the riot had taken place on Tuesday night. It is estimated that there were no less than three thousand present on that August afternoon, among them being not only farmers but hundreds of colliers who had sacrificed a day's pay to attend. A carriage was drawn up to act as a platform, and William Chambers, junior, was induced to take the chair. Hugh Williams had been asked to prepare a petition to the queen for a redress of grievances. He expounded it at great length, and after some discussion it was adopted and was eventually submitted to Her Majesty through the good

17

offices of William Williams of Conwil, member of parliament for Coventry. The meeting then proceeded to formulate a series of resolutions, relating to the tolls and the expenditure of the county stock, commending several landowners for reducing their rents and condemning Rees Goring Thomas for his 'unfair and deceitful' behaviour with regard to the Llanelly tithes. Finally it 'pledged itself to discountenance all nightly meetings by every means in its power'. These resolutions were moved in Welsh with great eloquence by a local farmer (and local historian), Stephen Evans of Cilcarw. How seriously the pledge was to be taken can be judged by the fact that Stephen Evans, himself, is known to have acted as Rebecca on more than one occasion, and that conspicuous in the vast crowd by his vociferous approval of it was Shoni Sgubor Fawr.[60]

Lesser meetings were held at Newcastle Emlyn, where Rees Goring Thomas presided (he lived there and not at Llan-non) and the speakers were Foster and Lloyd Hall,[61] on the beach at Tre-saith, where a local magistrate, Edward Lloyd Williams of Gwernant, presided;[62] and at Llandyfaelog, where a most comprehensive list of grievances was produced, covering all matters in church and state from the duties of bishops down to income tax and dog licences, and ending with the opinion that 'soldiers are serviceable where they are wanted, but they are not wanted here'.[63]

It was possibly because the energies of the moderate leaders were being directed to protest meetings that the riots, while they became far less frequent, were now also much more violent. For this period witnessed the brief careers in the movement of the two stalwarts, Shoni Sgubor Fawr and Dai'r Cantwr. These two men, even more than Twm Carnabwth, have become associated with Rebecca in popular tradition. They have been greatly idealised, especially in the public lectures of pacifist nonconformist ministers, and they have been represented both as Robin

Hoods and as Tolpuddle Martyrs. The evidence does not bear out any such resemblance.

Shoni was the elder of the two men, and was thirty-two years of age in the summer of 1843.[64] His baptismal name was John Jones, and he was born in Merthyr, but he obtained his sobriquet from the farm, Sgubor-fawr, in the neighbouring parish of Penderyn, where he had probably been in service. Little is known of his early life, except that he joined the 98th. Foot, and that, while a soldier, he was useful to the authorities in obtaining information about the 'Scotch Cattle', the extremists among the industrial workers of Monmouthshire. This was advanced later on as an argument to gain some mitigation of his sentence, but it somewhat tarnishes his record as a labour hero.[65] He became a prize-fighter, and when the Taff Vale Railway was opened to Merthyr in 1840 the event was celebrated by a bare-fist encounter between Shoni and John Nash, the champion of Cyfarthfa.[66] Shoni was a tall man and wore a beard. He could read and could write a little, and by religious persuasion was a Baptist. In March 1843 he was brought before the Merthyr magistrates on a charge of being drunk and disorderly, but was discharged on promising 'to lead another life'.[67] Yet in the following May he was again brought before the magistrates at Swansea for the same offence and was once more reprimanded and discharged.[68] It is evident that the depression was driving him westwards in search of work, and this is what brought him to Pontyberem and into contact with Dai'r Cantwr. The authorities were inclined to believe that he had come to Carmarthenshire to take part in the riots, but his own statements make it certain that this was not so. What his occupation was is not clear. He worked for various employers, including the copper smelters, R. J. Nevill and Company, and probably took any labouring job he could get.

Dai was a finer type. He was two years younger than Shoni, but, like him, was a tall man, with brown hair and reddish whiskers.[69] His proper name was David Davies.

He was born in Llancarfan, in the Vale of Glamorgan, the son of a tenant-farmer. He had been a farm labourer and a quarryman as well as an industrial worker at Tredegar in Monmouthshire. When he moved to Pontyberem is not known, possibly not till the summer of 1843, but he is said to have been a 'contractor' there, that is, he acted as a middleman between pit-owners and a number of workmen. Certainly he had no fixed occupation during the brief period when he took part in the Rebecca Riots. In his time he had been a local preacher to the Wesleyans. He was a poet of some merit; he may, indeed, have been the person of his name who won the harp at the Abergavenny eisteddfod in 1838.[70] According to tradition he was also a ballad singer,[71] but this may only be an effort to explain his appellation 'y Cantwr' (the Singer); his own explanation of it was that he 'taught them to sing at church'. Both men were unmarried.

The first incident in which Shoni is known to have taken part is the attack on Porth-y-rhyd on 18 August, when the Lion was brought out of bed to assist in demolishing the toll-house.[72] As we have seen, he was present on Mynydd Sylen and loudly applauded Stephen Evans's motion condemning night meetings. (Yet after his arrest Shoni informed the authorities that Stephen Evans had himself attended on several occasions and had acted as Rebecca.[73]) That night there was much drinking in the neighbouring taverns. Shoni was soon drunk, and was seen wandering about Pontyberem carrying a gun, and dressed in what a witness called 'something like a petticoat which had been white'. He loudly proclaimed to everyone that he was Rebecca, and kept swearing that he would murder the man who had stolen his ramrod. Asked by someone why he had condemned night meetings if he was Rebecca, he promptly fired at him and chased him down the street into the New Inn. There he poked his gun in through a window, but, when a man named Walter Rees hastened to shut the door, he withdrew it and fired at him also, sending shots through his hat. Yet when he had quietened a little he was allowed into the inn where he found his ramrod. He drank a quart of beer, then left for another inn where he drank still more before going out into the night, firing his gun as he went along the village street.[74]

On the following Tuesday night, Shoni and some other men broke into a dwelling-house on the road between Cross Hands and Pontarddulais and robbed the occupants, taking away a gun among other things.[75] Exactly a week later (Tuesday, 5 September) he and Dai and a dozen other men were at Llanelly. The pilots of Llanelly had quarrelled with their harbour master, so they secured the services of Shoni and his associates in an attempt to intimidate him, on payment of half-a-crown to each man. The party arrived at the harbour master's house near the docks at 1.30 in the morning. Shoni alone was mounted, but all were disguised and several were armed. They roused the harbour master and threatened to kill him, until he swore that he would leave Llanelly within a week. Then they fired their guns in through the windows of his house and departed.[76]

Yet when one of the most important riots in the whole series (second only in importance to the attack on Carmarthen workhouse) took place on the following night at Pontarddulais, Shoni and Dai were not present.[77] The bridge across the River Loughor at this point was a meeting place of roads from Llanelly, and from Carmarthen and Llandeilo, on the route to Swansea. The magistrates[78] obtained reliable information in the afternoon of a proposed attack on the gates at Pontarddulais and at Hendy, about half-a-mile away where a road crosses the Gwili, a tributary of the Loughor. After nightfall William Chambers, junior, proceeded with a few infantrymen as far as the Hendy bridge where they hid themselves. Captain Napier, now recovered from his wound, took half a dozen policemen from Swansea to Pontarddulais, and with them went the two Penlle'r-gaer brothers, John Dillwyn Llewellyn and Lewis Llewellyn Dillwyn. They were followed by a body of

dragoons who, also, seem to have succeeded in reaching the
Pontarddulais gate unobserved. Shortly after midnight
Rebecca arrived, to the noise of bugles and the firing of
guns. There were about a hundred to a hundred and fifty
in the crowd, most of them on horseback and all disguised,
but only one, apparently, was clad in white (or, it may be
that his dress was whiter than that of the others). It was
a clear moonlit night, and the police and soldiers watched
for a minute or two in silence as the rioters destroyed the
gate. Then Napier called on them to stop and a general
mélée ensued. Who fired the first shot was to become the
subject of bitter controversy. The Rebeccaites had been
firing off their guns, though probably only those loaded with
powder. Napier claimed that he shot at the horses to prevent
their getting away. Three men rode towards him firing as
they came. There was a severe struggle before these were
brought down and seized. Four others were also captured
as the rioters dispersed. When he heard the fighting, William
Chambers, junior, brought his men from the Hendy bridge,
and the dragoons nearly fell on them thinking that they
were Rebeccaites.

The magistrates immediately began their examination of
the seven prisoners, and Hugh Williams was speedily sent
for to represent them. Their leader was found to be John
Hughes (Jac Tŷ-isha), a farmer's son, twenty-four years of
age, from the parish of Llan-non.[79] He was reasonably
well-educated, for he was able both to read and to write.
On his person was found a threatening letter which had
evidently not been sent, a sum of five shillings wrapped in
a paper which indicated that it was a contribution to
Rebecca, and various sums of money, possibly intended to
pay the rioters. He was wounded in the left arm. Much more
seriously wounded was John Hugh, a man who was a year
older than Hughes and was married. He could not sign
his name although he could read a little.[80] A third prisoner,
David Jones, was a lad of twenty. He could sign his name,
but could not otherwise write.[81] John Hughes was committed

for trial at the assizes for shooting at Captain Napier, and the other two for aiding and abetting him, and they were refused bail.[82] Two of the other prisoners, one of them a boy of fourteen, were charged with destroying the gate and were released on bail; the remaining two were discharged.

The capture, at last, of a genuine Rebecca leader caused great interest. Foster had hastened to Swansea, and he reported the exasperation of the people of the neighbourhood at the turn of events and the belief, well-founded or not, that it was the police who had started the firing. Interest became still more intense when it was realised that the government had appointed a special commission to try the prisoners and those of Llangyfelach, and had moved the trial to Cardiff because of local feeling. A Cardiff journalist even advertised beforehand that he would supply daily reports to subscribers. The trial took place seven weeks later (26 October). As members of the commission, the government had chosen an aged judge, Baron Gurney, who was in his seventy-fifth year, and a younger and more charitable colleague, Sir Cresswell Cresswell. The attorney-general, the great Sir Frederick Pollock, appeared in person for the prosecution, accompanied by the solicitor-general. But the defence also had retained a remarkable man, Matthew Davenport Hill, recorder of Birmingham, a law reformer and a radical who had himself purchased a gun in 1832 in case it might be needed against the duke of Wellington's troops.[83] With him were Lloyd Hall and two other barristers, all briefed by Hugh Williams. Even though the trial had been moved to Cardiff, several farmers called on the high sheriff of Glamorgan to beg that their names be removed from the jury list as they feared retaliation.[84] It became clear, also, that Pollock, by challenging several jurymen, sought to exclude all farmers from the jury, which was, in the end, composed of three gentlemen and nine tradesmen, drawn mainly from Cardiff and Merthyr Tydfil. Pollock conducted the case with great moderation, and when Hill had spoken at length, evidently arguing in mitigation of punishment, Pollock passed to him a note: 'You have just delivered one of the most appropriate, eloquent and feeling addresses I have ever heard. I dared not, could not add a word'.[85] The jury found John Hughes guilty but recommended him to mercy because of his unblemished character. Compassion, however, had no meaning for the aged judge, and he sentenced him to twenty years' transportation. On the advice of Hugh Williams, John Hugh and David Jones then pleaded guilty and were sentenced to seven years' transportation. Pollock announced that he did not propose to proceed against the two who were indicted only with breaking the Pontarddulais gate, and they were discharged. Furthermore, as if to forestall the judge, he indicated that he was prepared to accept the recognisances of Morgan Morgan of Cwm Cile and his wife to keep the peace, and reduced the charge against their daughter and two sons from felony to misdemeanour, thereby saving them from hard labour.

The contrast between the moderation of Pollock and the severity of the judge was widely remarked.[86] The *Times*, in particular, dealt scathingly with the judge's fatuous comment that all the farmers need do to obtain redress was to lay their grievances before the magistrates. Petitions for mercy were immediately set on foot, and the three prisoners in Cardiff gaol appealed to their friends, in a broadside issued in Welsh and in English, to keep the peace, for the good conduct of the Rebeccaites alone would bring a reduction of their sentence.[87] The prisoners were taken by packet to Bristol on 7 December on their way to Millbank. Sir John Guest crossed over on the same packet and spoke to Hughes. Guest was evidently impressed by his decency and his lively curiosity in his surroundings (he had never seen a packet steamer or indeed a train), and Lady Charlotte Guest (the romantic translator of the *Mabinogion*) shed a tear for this 'free child of the mountain, with all his faults and all his grievances and all his romance', now cooped up in a narrow cell.[88] One man alone had cause to rejoice for that night's work. The government, possibly to encourage others in the newly-founded rural police, lavished praise on Captain Napier, and the prime minister sanctioned as a reward to him the remarkable sum of £500.[89] Meritorious though his services may have been, they can hardly have been as great as that. Pollock tried also to get a knighthood for the elder of the Penlle'r-gaer brothers for the assistance he had given Napier, but the government demurred.[90]

The débâcle at Pontarddulais on the Wednesday night (6 September) did not restrain the hardier spirits among Rebecca's followers, for on the Saturday night some eight or ten of them returned to Hendy to set fire to the toll-house, a two-roomed thatched cottage. The gate-keeper was an old woman of seventy-five, Sarah Williams, who had been a toll-collector for years but had been at Hendy for less than a week. She ran to her neighbours to beg for help in putting out the fire, but they were afraid to go out of doors. Bewildered, she rushed back to her cottage to save a few of her belongings. Her neighbours heard four or five shots, then a scream, and the old woman crawled back to their doorstep and died. And so Rebecca had her first murder to her discredit. Yet the sympathy of the public (both then and, apparently, since) was not with the murdered woman but with her murderers; 'why had she run back, the dull old crittur?' was a typical comment. There was much specula-tion as to whether she had recognised one of the incendiaries who had killed her to avoid imprisonment or transportation, or whether she had been shot inadvertently, as Shoni Sgubor Fawr believed.[91] The coroner's jury added to the baseness of the whole incident by returning a verdict: 'that the deceased died from the effusion of blood into the chest, which occasioned suffocation, but from what cause is to this jury unknown', a verdict which was as evil in its anti-social implications as the murder itself, and which led the government to transfer the trial of John Hughes and his associates out of the locality. The magistrates, for their part, offered a reward of £500 for information.[92]

In the meantime Shoni and Dai and their associates were active in the country north-west of Llanelly which was their particular hunting ground. Two nights after they had visited the harbour master they destroyed the gate at Spudders Bridge across the Gwendraeth, between Trimsaran and Kidwelly.[93] They met at a farm named Topsail on Pembrey Mountain. The bailiffs had been in occupation there only a week previously, and the farmer, Thomas Phillips, was anxious to have his creditor's ricks on a neighbouring farm set on fire.[94] He repeatedly offered his servant boy 'a sovereign in his hand' if he would do it. The boy declined, but both he and his master went down to Spudders Bridge, calling on the way at midnight at a shop to buy powder and shot. When they had destroyed the gate they handed to the gatekeeper two threatening letters which were apparently written by Dai. One of these was intended for William Chambers, junior.[95]

This well-meaning young man was in a predicament. The authorities were dubious about his action in presiding over the meeting on Mynydd Sylen; on the other hand the wrath of Rebecca had fallen on him because of the general belief (unfounded though it was) that it was he who had shot John Hughes. He received a letter threatening to kill him unless the prisoners were released. His murder was frequently discussed at the Stag and Pheasant, at Pum Heol (Five Roads), where Shoni and his friends forgathered.[96] One of the company, David Thomas of Cilferi-uchaf, made an impassioned speech on the subject, lasting for ten minutes, and he and Thomas Phillips of Topsail offered £5 between them to anyone who would do the deed.[97] This discussion went on from day to day. Meanwhile two of Chambers's farms were set on fire on the Saturday night when Sarah Williams met her death at Hendy. Shoni had gone courting that evening but two men came and fetched him away. He proceeded with some eight others to Tyn-y-wern farm, turned the animals loose and set fire to the outbuildings.[98] Dai took another party to

Gelligylwnog and fired the ricks. As they were coming away one man said 'Here is a hare' and shot a horse. Another stuck his knife in it and all dipped their hands in the blood 'as a sacrifice', Dai saying that he had heard of a sacrament in many ways, but never before in the blood of a horse.[99] As it was now Sunday morning, Dai protested against any more shooting.[100]

Sunday or not, the friends were off in the evening again, although on different errands. Shoni and his mates went once more to Porth-y-rhyd in search of 'the Lion', who had evidently incurred the bitter hatred of his neighbours. His wife said that he was not at home this time again, but the rioters fired their powder-loaded guns into his house until it was full of smoke, and when she said that she recognised one of them, they fired shot into the room, some of which struck a child of ten months. A respectable farmer was indicted for his share in this riot along with Shoni, but at the Carmarthen Spring Assizes Lloyd Hall secured his acquittal because of a doubt in the identification.[101] Dai had gone a couple of miles in the opposite direction, across the Gwendraeth, to another of Chambers's farms called Maensant. The authorities had heard a rumour of this visit and sent the dragoons out on patrol, but when they arrived they found the farm half consumed.[102]

There is no doubt that the neighbourhood was terrorised during these weeks by this gang of miscreants. They represented the lunatic fringe of the Rebecca movement, for while they took 'Cyfiawnder' (justice or righteousness) for their password,[103] they were prepared to sell their services for half-a-crown[104] or five shillings a night,[105] each man supplying his own gun and ammunition. Years later Alcwyn Evans was told by the farmers of this district how Shoni and the others would walk into their farm-houses, demand food and lodgings for as long as they pleased, and even money, under the threat of informing on them or setting their ricks on fire.[106] Nor did they agree among themselves, Dai, apparently, being one of the moderates.

On Monday night, 18 September, while the gang were drinking at the Stag and Pheasant, Dai 'happened to go out to a young woman', and, when he returned, found that the others had decided to go to Tyn-y-wern again and burn the house with the occupants inside. Dai refused to go, so they quarrelled and parted,[107] but the others went and discharged their guns at the farmer.[108] Yet, although he again disapproved, Dai joined the others on Saturday night (23 September) in the last of their escapades. The manager of the Gwendraeth Ironworks at Pontyberem, a man named Slocombe, had incurred the enmity of his workmen for some reason, and the gang undertook to frighten him into leaving the country. They met at the Stag and Pheasant, and went in two parties by different routes to the manager's house. The manager's wife maintained that he was not at home, so they warned her that he should leave within a week or he would be 'a head shorter', Shoni adding that 'no Englishman should manage in Wales any more'. They then fired their guns into the house and departed.[109]

But a Trimsaran collier who was with them on this occasion decided over the week-end to turn informer. He went on Tuesday[110] to R. J. Nevill, who immediately issued warrants for the arrest of Shoni and Dai.[111] Thomas Phillips of Topsail had also been in the party and decided to come clean.[112] Some twenty policemen were sent to scour the hills and search the public houses. Careful watch was kept on the Stag and Pheasant, and news was brought to the police that Dai was there, but by the time they had arrived he had gone to the Plough and Harrow (another inn at Pum Heol), where he was arrested at midnight on Thursday night. Next morning Shoni was taken at Tumble. The two men were charged with the attack on the manager's house at Pontyberem and were lodged in Carmarthen gaol.[113]

There was consternation in the gang lest the prisoners should confess, and David Thomas, the impassioned orator of Cilferi-uchaf, kept repeating that he 'didn't know in the world what would come of it'.[114] Shoni wrote (or had written for him) a letter from Carmarthen gaol, asking for a little food to be brought him, in which he said: 'I have been offered £500 if I would split on any of my friends. I would rather have my head cut hof soner than I would say a word'.[115] He had, in fact, already split on them in great detail before he had reached Carmarthen gaol.[116] Months later another prisoner there was still busily eliciting information for the authorities from the Rebeccaites, in return for 'something for his trouble' when he was discharged.[117]

The trial of Shoni and Dai, together with that of thirty-nine other Rebeccaites who were being held for various offences, came on at the Carmarthen Winter Assizes immediately after Christmas (27 December). Throughout the week a strong force of the 76th. Foot were on guard in the town. Sir Frederick Pollock again appeared in person, and again challenged no less than thirty-two jurymen in order to eliminate any farmers, an action which remained on his conscience, for he thought it necessary to explain it in parliament.[118] There were numerous charges against Shoni, but he was tried only for shooting, on 25 August, in Pontyberem at Walter Rees, who had been induced to act as prosecutor and was given a gratuity of £20 for doing so.[119] Lloyd Hall valiantly tried to cast doubt on the evidence, and even quoted Shoni's vociferous condemnation of night rioting in his defence! But his task was hopeless and Shoni was found guilty. Dai was tried for destroying the gate at Spudders Bridge and was also found guilty. Pollock then withdrew the charge against another of the rioters at Spudders Bridge 'because he understood he had been compelled to join', thereby, had he but known it, securing the release of the man who had been the leader on that occasion and who had shot the sacramental horse at Gelligylwnog. The two prisoners received sentence together, Shoni to transportation for life and Dai for twenty years. They listened attentively to the judge's severe address to them, but both left the dock laughing.[120]

After the trial both men signed confessions and continued
to implicate their associates.[121] Dai also composed a threnody
on his fate while in Carmarthen gaol. He had become, he
said, a mirror in which the world might see its folly; the fame
which might have been his he had forfeited; no more would
he see Llancarfan and the haunts of his youth;[122] but an
unknown bard, remembering happier days, assured him
that while water ran in the rivers of Glamorgan his memory
would remain fragrant.[123] On 5 February 1844, Shoni and
Dai and a third convict were removed from Carmarthen on
their way to Millbank. They were chained together, and,
as the lot fell on Dai to be in the centre, he had a heavy
iron on both legs. Yet he seemed cheerful, while Shoni kept
sobbing bitterly.[124]

While attention was focused in these weeks primarily on
the Llanelly district, a few other riots were taking place in
widely separated places. The attack on the Prendergast gate
at Haverfordwest on 25 August had been followed by an
acrimonious public meeting at Wolf's Castle on Thursday,
7 September, presided over by William Edwardes of
Sealyham, when exception was taken to his criticism of the
trustees of the Fishguard Trust.[125] Yet on Friday night the
two gates at Fishguard, at the other end of the trust's road,
were destroyed. Furthermore, the rioters gave notice that
they intended to destroy the two toll-houses on the following
Monday night, and did so in the presence of a large crowd.
There was no resident magistrate in Fishguard, and, although
the disturbance continued for some hours, no attempt was
made to arrest its course. This brought scathing letters from
the Home Office to the lord-lieutenant. But in November an
accomplice, one Thomas Williams, turned informer, and
the magistrates were able belatedly to arrest thirty-three
persons. This number was too large for the local constables
to handle, so they had to be kept in the market house under
a triple guard of marines. Seven of the prisoners were
discharged and the others released on bail, but the informer

and his wife had to be conveyed to Haverfordwest gaol for safety. Yet when the men were tried at the Pembroke-shire Spring Assizes in March, no corroboration of the informer's evidence could be produced and they were discharged. The informer went in peril of his life, and the Home Office had to make him a gratuity of £20 to enable him to seek a livelihood elsewhere.[126]

Rioting also flared up suddenly in the upper reaches of the Towy. On Friday night (13 September) the three gates at Llangadog were down again.[127] On the following Wednesday night the men of Cil-y-cwm took down the gate at Porth-y-rhyd (five miles from Llandovery on the road to Lampeter)[128] and then proceeded towards Llandovery and destroyed the gate at Dolauhirion, although dragoons were stationed in the town a mile or so away. Exactly two weeks later they returned to demolish the toll-house. This was being carefully watched and the rioters were surprised before they had completed the job and scattered in all directions. Two farm labourers who were on the roof were unable to get away. Their trial strikingly illustrates the vagaries of Welsh juries in matters relating to Rebecca. At the Winter Assizes they pleaded not guilty either of destroying the gate or of the far more serious offence of demolishing the house. The jury declared that there was insufficient evidence with regard to the second charge (they did not explain what the men were doing on the roof) and the trial on the first charge was deferred to the following assizes. When the two men realised that Pollock was allowing those charged only with destroying gates to be released on their recognisances to keep the peace, they sought to change their plea to one of guilty, but the judge ruled that they were now too late. Despite this plea, the jury at the Spring Assizes insisted on finding them guilty only of being present when the gate was being demolished, and the judge directed that the men should be discharged.[129] On the night after Dolauhirion, Rebecca went still further afield and crossed the Brecknockshire border, destroying the gate at Cefn

Llanddewi, some eight miles from Llandovery on the road to Llangamarch. Her quarrel seems to have been a personal one with a new gate-keeper, but the Brecknockshire magistrates and the government offered rewards of £50 for information.[130] Next night, again, the gate on the Main Trust road at Pentre-bach, five miles from Llandovery on the road to Brecon, was destroyed, and one man who was involved in the incident was sentenced to six months' imprisonment.[131] Then the rioting died down just as suddenly as it had begun, and there were no further occurrences in the neighbourhood of Llandovery.

Equally unpredictable was Rebecca's appearance on the night of 15 September at Llan-non, Cardiganshire, the most northerly incident in the shire. Two months later a very respectable farmer's son, Isaac Evans of Gwern-llath, was arrested on the evidence of a boy from the Midlands who had been in service with Evans's father at the time. This caused great excitement in the neighbourhood, and, for his own sake as well as to avoid his being spirited away, the magistrates placed the witness in Cardigan gaol. But they did so against his will, and he refused to give evidence, so the case collapsed. The magistrates had acted illegally in placing the witness in gaol, and the Home Office wished to make him a gratuity of £3, but apparently he could not be traced.[132]

Towards the end of September, rioting spread beyond the geographical limits of the main affected area into the upper Wye valley around Rhayader. This outbreak was almost isolated from the rest of the Rebecca movement, but the neighbourhood provided in itself an epitome of all the Welsh grievances. Romantically situated among the hills at the junction of several valleys, Rhayader was a town of wretched mud hovels, invariably fronted with a pigsty or a dunghill or both. It was the only town in Radnorshire where Welsh was spoken, and it was the market centre for an extensive and wild countryside. The vicar of Nantmel drew an income of £600 from the tithes of his own and two

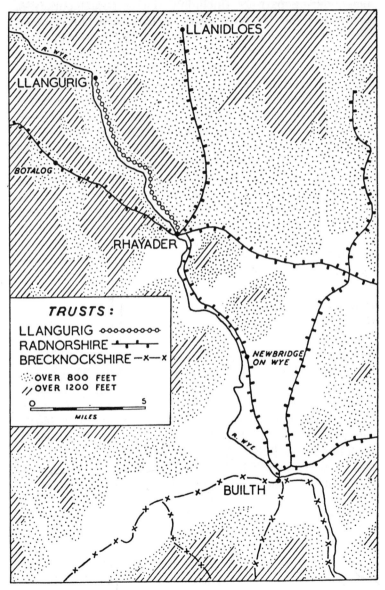

V. The Wye Valley

neighbouring parishes (including the perpetual curacy of
Rhayader) but for forty years he had been non-resident.
Nor had the adjoining parishes of St. Harmons and Llan-
wrthwl had a resident vicar or curate for forty years. Of the
poor rate of £800 in the parish of Nantmel in 1842, £200
had been spent on the relief of illegitimate children and their
mothers. There were six entrances to Rhayader; on them
there were six gates and a bar. The first outbreak occurred
on Monday night, 25 September, at the Llangurig end of
the new road from Rhayader which now formed part of
the route from Cheltenham to Aberystwyth.[133] On Thursday
night two gates, placed where a lane branched off from the
old Aberystwyth road beyond the bridge over the Wye at
Rhayader, were pulled down with all the pomp and
paraphernalia of Rebecca. Rewards of £50 were offered by
the county magistrates and by the government, but, as we
shall see, Rebecca was to return to the scene more than once
and with greater violence.[134]

When Rebecca made her last appearance in south
Carmarthenshire on the night of 30 September and removed
the Tir-fran gate in the outskirts of Llanelly (on the road to
Felin-foel), some forty farmers of the neighbourhood came
together the next morning, rescued the gate from a coalpit
where it had been thrown, and replaced it. They were,
according to Colonel Love, 'alarmed at the tone now
assumed by their labourers and servants' and wished to
'put a stop to the proceedings they had so injudiciously
commenced'.[135] Whether that was so or not, their action
certainly marked the turn of the tide. For as one farmer
said, Rebecca herself had become 'the greatest grievance in
the country' as she now 'burned the corn'.[136]

Despite this change of heart, the end of September saw
the beginning of a chain of events which illustrates the undertone of hatred and suspicion beneath the life of rural
Carmarthenshire in these years, and the opportunity which
Rebecca gave to private malignity and revenge. The village

of Brechfa lies surrounded by steep hills near the junction of two turbulent streams, the Marlais and the Cothi, a dozen miles north-east of Carmarthen. The farmer at Pantycerrig, a mile or so out of the village, was an old man, aged seventy-one, named Thomas Thomas. He was in difficulties with his neighbours. His cattle had strayed on to the land of Byrgwm, the next farm higher up the valley, and he had settled with his neighbour, David Evans, for ten shillings for the damage done. But his own sheep had been stolen, and a warrant had been issued for the arrest of Benjamin and Evan, the sons of Thomas Jones, blacksmith, of Clunllydan, a mile down the valley, both of whom had absconded.[137] Sometime after midnight, on Friday night, 29 September, a number of armed and disguised men appeared at Pantycerrig and demanded £5 for the damage done by Thomas's cattle. He protested that he had already settled for ten shillings, but was told that the matter was now 'in the hands of Rebecca' and had to promise to pay forty shillings within nine days. Even so the old man was forcibly dragged to Byrgwm and abused. He gave information to the magistrates against David Evans and his servant, James Evans, who, although only twenty-five, was five years older than his master and was the stronger character, and both were taken to Carmarthen gaol.[138] The following Friday Thomas went to Carmarthen to give evidence. The old man was afraid to go home at nights lest his neighbours should come for him, and on the Friday night, in his absence, a raging fire was started in the outhouses of Pantycerrig. It spread to the dwelling-house and consumed most of it, one of the servant girls being set on fire as the family tried to remove some of their belongings.[139]

The warrants against the sheep-stealers were still outstanding when, on Monday, 18 December, their father prevailed upon Thomas Thomas to come to Clunllydan to talk the matter over as he was too ill to leave the house himself. According to the father they parted in friendship in the late afternoon. But Thomas Thomas did not return home. He had to cross over the Marlais by a bridge which was merely the trunk of an ash tree and a handrail. When morning came, he was found in the brook beneath the bridge. Death was due to concussion and not to drowning, but whether this was caused by a blow on the head or by a fall against the rocks, the coroner's jury could not decide. The attorney-general, the vice-lieutenant and Colonel Love all agreed that the evidence was not sufficient to justify a charge of murder, but the tradition in the locality and in the dead man's family has always been that the old man was the victim of foul play.

James Evans and David Evans came up for trial at the Carmarthen Winter Assizes. They were defended by Lloyd Hall and another barrister, but so blatant was the perjury of their witnesses that their own counsel abandoned the case. Nevertheless, the jury recommended them to mercy because of their youth. The judge could detect no mercy in their treatment of the old man, and sentenced them to twelve months' imprisonment with hard labour. In December 1844, Benjamin Jones of Clunllydan was arrested. He was charged with robbery with violence in the desolate countryside near Trecastle, on the borders of Carmarthenshire and Brecknockshire. He was found guilty and was condemned to death, but this sentence was commuted to transportation for life. He was charged also with having set fire to Pantycerrig, but was acquitted 'in the teeth of very clear evidence'. He admitted that he had been guilty of sheep stealing, with which he was not charged; it was generally believed that he was guilty of the murder of Thomas Thomas. Justice had overtaken him, but the sordid events at Brechfa had provided the farmers of Carmarthenshire with a new object lesson of the evils which follow upon a breakdown in the rule of the law.

Chapter X

REBECCA TRIUMPHANS

In the first week of October, Queen Victoria sat in privy council at Windsor to consider the situation in Wales. Her Majesty was always disdainful where the principality was concerned, and although her opinion of Rebecca does not seem to be recorded it probably coincided with that of the gouty diarist, Charles Greville, who attended on crutches and felt that the government 'ought to have interfered with a strong hand long ago'.[1] For the moment the privy council contented itself with issuing a proclamation, in Welsh and English, calling upon the queen's officers to use their utmost endeavours to repress all breaches of the peace, and exhorting her liege subjects to render them prompt and effectual assistance. 'As a further inducement' the proclamation offered a reward of £500 to anyone who should arrest or give information leading to the arrest of the author of an incendiary fire or of an outrage involving loss of life, provided this resulted in a conviction, together with a free pardon to the informer if he had been an accomplice, and a reward of £50 in respect of lesser crimes, which presumably covered the destruction of toll-gates.[2]

There had been repeated rumours that the government intended to proclaim martial law.[3] This does not seem to have been contemplated at any time, but the home secretary's communications with the civil authorities, both lords-lieutenant and magistrates, showed an ever-increasing exasperation. These authorities kept clamouring for additional soldiers and metropolitan policemen, asking that the latter should be armed and that the law against nocturnal outrages be made more severe, while, at the same time, they stubbornly resisted the establishment of a rural police. Sir James Graham admonished them that 'new powers from parliament should only be applied for when the active

exercise of the powers of the law had been tried and failed'.[4]
The magistrates for their part resented this stricture on their
lack of activity; they were doing their best, they said, in
difficult circumstances.[5] Graham therefore called upon the
lords-lieutenant to supply lists of all magistrates in their
shires, and to nominate others if their number was
insufficient.[6] He also took the unusual step of sending
a Colonel Hankey to West Wales, with a recommendation
that he should be sworn in as a magistrate in the three shires,
so that he could relieve the older men in the onerous duty
of accompanying the troops on their nightly patrols.[7]
Graham refused to arm the metropolitan police,[8] but he still
further increased their number, until there were at least
a hundred and fifty in the three shires.[9] At the same time
he insisted that special constables should be enrolled. He had
agreed in July that it was unwise to levy the fines imposed
on those who refused to serve, in view of the disturbed state
of the country, but he held that the presence of so many
troops in West Wales now made it possible to enforce the
law.[10] In fact, insistence was no longer necessary because of
the changed attitude of the farmers. For example, some
three hundred were sworn in at Llanelly on 11 November.
These were drawn from the surrounding district, and it was
particularly noticeable that those from the parish of
Llan-non came forward voluntarily.[11] Their recent
experiences had no doubt chastened them.

The home secretary was also getting impatient with
Colonel Love. Graham wrote to the prime minister that
Love had one thousand eight hundred men under his
command, including a regiment of cavalry and a demi-
brigade of guns, 'enough to conquer the country, let alone
keep it in order'. 'If a crime is committed', said Graham,
'he instantly sends soldiers to the place the *following* day.'[12]
It is difficult to know what else Love could do, but Graham
decided to approach the duke of Wellington to have him
superseded 'without causing him needless offence or pain'.[13]
The duke's choice fell on the deputy adjutant-general,

Sir George Brown, and it is possibly the highest compliment paid to Rebecca that it was thought necessary to send a staff officer of his eminence to cope with her. Brown had been promoted major-general in 1841. Like Love he had fought at Corunna and in America, and had then spent a quarter of a century at the War Office where he had the reputation of a martinet, but he lived to see active service again in the Crimean War, and to be pilloried by a far more celebrated *Times* correspondent than Foster, namely William Howard Russell.[14] Brown arrived in Carmarthen on 6 October, and proceeded immediately on a tour of inspection. He did not, in fact, replace Love, and he stayed only for five weeks, but he used his time both to organise the military forces in West Wales and to bring pressure to bear on the magistrates of Cardiganshire and Pembrokeshire to induce them to establish a rural police.[15]

The plan which Brown elaborated in order to defeat Rebecca was to distribute his forces in small groups in a great number of places. In addition to his main forces, which were concentrated at Newport, Pontypool, Brecon, Merthyr, Cardiff and Swansea, and his artillery at Newport and Pembroke Dock, the Fourth Light Dragoons were distributed between Carmarthen (3 officers and 50 men), Llandeilo (3 +40), Newcastle Emlyn (3 +40), and Llandovery (3 +30) with smaller detachments at Llangadog and Llanarthney. The Royal Marines had been strengthened,[16] and the defence of Pembrokeshire was entrusted to them. They were placed at Pembroke (7 officers and 155 men), Haverfordwest (2 +50), Cardigan (2 +42), and Narberth (2 +40), with small units at Fishguard, Newport (Pembrokeshire), Eglwyswrw, Llandisilio, Llawhaden and Robeston Wathan. Most of the soldiers were infantry drawn from the 6th., 73rd. and 76th. Foot. There were large detachments at Carmarthen (6 officers and 120 men), Llanelly (2 +50), Aberaeron (3 +40), Newcastle Emlyn (2 +40), Rhayader (1 +40), Lampeter (2 +25), and Builth (1 +20), but smaller units were placed at an astonishing number of places, at

Pontarddulais, Cross Hands, Meinciau, Porth-y-rhyd, Llan-non and Pontyberem in south Carmarthenshire, at Conwil, Tre-lech, Brechfa, Pontargothi, Llansawel, St. Clears, Whitland and Llanboidy in north and west Carmarthenshire, and at Llandysul, Llanybyther, Tregaron, New Inn, Llwyndafydd, Llannarth and Llan-non in Cardiganshire.[17] In view of this large force, the Pembrokeshire Yeomanry, who had been under arms since the winter, were allowed to return to their homes for the harvest.[18]

So formidable an array of special constables, metropolitan policemen and soldiers would have made it difficult for Rebecca to continue her exploits. In fact the rioting was over. A great many rioters were by this time on bail awaiting trial, as we have seen earlier in discussing particular incidents, and, with the threat of imprisonment already hanging over them, they were not disposed to increase the gravity of their offences by further outrages. The farmers had changed their attitude, once their own property was threatened, and had come to favour mass meetings by day rather than clandestine gatherings at night. It is noteworthy that the remaining riots nearly all took place on the periphery of the area which had hitherto been affected. For nothing is more remarkable about the Rebecca Riots than their limitation to one geographical region. The same grievances existed beyond its boundaries; in fact, the tolls in Brecknockshire were higher than in West Wales.[19] An explanation for the absence of rioting in the neighbouring districts must therefore be sought in antidotes which were operative there. In Brecknockshire there was only one trust, so that there was no multiplication of gates because of the interlacing of roads. Besides, at the first indication of a spread of the disturbances into the shire, the Brecknock-shire trustees took down nine gates.[20] Colonel Love would have us believe that south Pembrokeshire was not involved because its inhabitants were not Welsh but were 'descended from the Flemings',[21] and this was also the explanation offered by a local magistrate for the peacefulness of Gower.[22] North Cardiganshire remained undisturbed because its lead mines were prosperous at this time, thereby providing employment and, as well, a market for agricultural produce.[23] The last fitful eruptions of disorder beyond the confines of West Wales only serve to emphasise the end of the main movement.

Two of these incidents occurred in Glamorgan. On 9 October the gate at Tonyrefail near Llantrisant, some fourteen miles from Cardiff, was destroyed, and, early in the following month, another at Croes-faen, a few miles away. They were isolated incidents, but, significantly, the gates were in the centre of the lime country on the rim of the coalfield.[24]

On 9 October, also, Rebecca destroyed the gate at Botalog, where the old road from Rhayader to Aberystwyth, via Devil's Bridge, goes for a mile or so through Montgomeryshire. At this most isolated spot, in a hollow among the hills, the solitary gate-keeper was an old woman. A rioter fired his powder-loaded gun in her face and injured both her eyes. She had recognised her assailants, but later denied all knowledge of them and 'acted like a raving maniac' through fear of reprisals. The authorities offered the usual reward of £50 for information.[25] Before the end of the month the gate at Newbridge-on-Wye, between Rhayader and Builth, was destroyed.[26] Early in the following week there was a renewal of serious rioting in Rhayader itself. Nothing had come of a meeting of the trustees after the previous riot in September, and there was bitter disappointment in the locality. The rioters entered the town on the night of 2 November in three contingents, each of about fifty men, marching in military formation. They met at the St. Harmons gate, demolished it, and then proceeded to the other gates. A metropolitan police sergeant who was at Rhayader assembled six special constables, but they could do nothing for they were unarmed and were kept at a distance by the rioters, whose front and rear guards had muskets loaded with ball and slugs. The other rioters, whose guns were loaded only with powder, kept firing them off continuously. In all, they destroyed four gates and a toll-house, but, even so, they discriminated, for they left standing two other gates which they did not consider obnoxious.[27] Around Christmas a gate at Glasbury, lower down the Wye, was destroyed, although, again, another at the same place was left standing. The authorities here, also, offered the usual reward of £50.[28] In the new year Rebecca destroyed the Llangurig gate for the second time. This gave rise to a pretty problem, for the gate belonged to the Radnorshire Trust but was within Montgomeryshire, and the Montgomeryshire magistrates sought to evade responsibility for its protection.[29] Another gate at Llanidloes, four miles away, was destroyed on 3 May.[30] Even as late as mid-September 1844, there were attacks on gates at Builth and Rhayader,[31] but with that the Rebecca movement flickered out in the Wye Valley also.

In the meantime a few isolated incidents were occurring elsewhere. A gate on a road from Llandovery towards the Black Mountain was destroyed on the night of 9 December for the third or fourth time, although a detachment of dragoons was stationed nearby at Llangadog.[32] A toll-house and bar midway between Lampeter and Carmarthen, in a thinly populated area where the road crosses the hills, were demolished on the night of 22 February 1844.[33] Evidently the heavy sentences passed at the Winter Assizes had not intimidated the hardier spirits among Rebecca's followers, for most remarkable of all was the destruction of a gate on the outskirts of Cardigan on the night of 26 March 1844, although there were forty marines in the town. The rioters were few in number, possibly under a dozen, but they were dressed as usual in women's clothes. They sawed the gateposts off a foot from the ground and carried the gate away.[34] Finally, in mid-summer, on 28 June 1844, for no very obvious reason, a gate at Steynton on the Milford Trust road was destroyed.[35]

Occasional meetings at night, to discuss tithes and rents and other matters, were reported to the authorities throughout the autumn and winter of 1843,[36] and numerous cases of refusal to pay tolls were tried at special sessions of magistrates and the culprits fined.[37] The hostility towards the magistrates had not abated. Shots were fired into the house of a magistrate living at St. Clears on 10 October,[38] and on 18 December a deliberate attempt was made on the life of a Pembrokeshire magistrate, the vicar of Robeston Wathan, who had been active in prosecuting Rebeccaites and who was the chairman of the local Board of Guardians. The outrage happened only a few hours after the judge had passed through the village on his way to hold the Pembrokeshire Winter Assizes at Haverfordwest. Several slugs were shot into the vicar's bedroom while he was undressing, and one of these pierced his arm. The authorities viewed the case so seriously that they offered a reward of £200 for information, and six months later enquiries were still being made.[39] The stacks of yet another magistrate, at Llan-non in Carmarthenshire, were fired on 26 December, and a reward of £100 was offered.[40] West Wales, therefore, was not yet pacified, but disturbances had become rare and soon were no more frequent than was normal in the countryside.

Undoubtedly, the main reason for the discontinuance of rioting was its replacement by a remarkable series of mass meetings. The great demonstration on Mynydd Sylen on 25 August had condemned night outrages, though, it must be admitted, with singularly little effect. Men as diverse as George Rice Trevor and Hugh Williams thought the new development should be encouraged,[41] and Williams may have welcomed the opportunity which it gave him to propagate his radical ideas. He was the principal speaker on 13 September at a meeting at Llyn Llech Owen on Mynydd Mawr. This romantic spot (the source of the Gwendraeth river) lies on high ground between the Towy and the

Loughor valleys and was equally accessible for farmers and for industrial workers. Despite the wet morning some six hundred men had assembled by mid-day, and this number increased to two or three thousand. William Chambers, junior, had again been asked to preside, but he indignantly refused to attend. Hugh Williams deplored the attacks which had been made on Chambers's farms, and exonerated him from any blame for wounding the Rebeccaites at Pont-arddulais a week previously. He submitted to the meeting a petition to the queen from six neighbouring parishes for the redress of the usual grievances, namely the tolls, the poor law, the tithes, the county stock, the inadequacy of the magistrates and high rents. Rents, claimed the petition, should be regulated by assessors on a sliding scale determined by the fluctuation of prices. The petition ended by stating that parliament was both disinclined and incompetent to meet the wishes of the community, a reflection, no doubt, of Hugh Williams's Chartism.[42]

A lesser meeting was held at Llanboidy on the same day,[43] and on 22 September, at Bryn Cwmllynfell on the southern slopes of the Black Mountain. Here, also, a petition was drawn up for submission to the queen. The chief speaker was John Jenkins, the anti-Corn Law organiser, and the Corn Laws naturally figured among the grievances discussed.[44] Hugh Williams addressed another meeting at Tre-lech on 25 September, when the tithe-impropriator, Rees Goring Thomas, presided. This was the area where the march on Carmarthen had originated. There were only some two hundred present, possibly on account of the harvest, but Hugh Williams discoursed at length on the usual topics. He again strongly deprecated recourse to violence, and even approved of the establishment of a rural police if this would put a stop to outrages. Despite the presence of the chairman, a petition to the queen which included the tithes among its list of grievances was adopted. Williams claimed that there was no hope of redress from a Tory government and the petition asked the queen to dissolve parliament.[45]

Two days later there was a great demonstration at Allt
Cunedda, near Kidwelly, when some two thousand
assembled despite the dismal day. This was Williams's home
town, and the mayor of the borough presided. The usual
petition was adopted, including a request for the dissolution
of parliament. There were other speakers in addition to
Williams, and some of the remarks made by them were
indistinguishable from those of the Chartist orators, for
example the attack on the expense of royalty.[46] The Allt
Cunedda petition was submitted six days later, on
3 October, to an even larger gathering of some three thousand
people, at Pencrwcybalog, near Newcastle Emlyn. As usual,
one of the local gentry had been asked to preside. He was
Lloyd Williams of Gwernant, who had issued an address
'To the person calling himself Rebecca' earlier in the year
and had threatened to meet violence with violence. He was
attacked by the *Carmarthen Journal* for consenting, and, even
so, the resolutions with regard to rents and fixity of tenure
in the petition were stricken out, no doubt at his insistence.[47]
On the same day, a lesser meeting of about five hundred
persons was held only a few miles away at Penrhiw-fawr in
the parish of Cilrhedyn, and here the chairman refused to
sign the petition.[48] There were similar meetings at Llanddowror (4 October),[49] at Llanfynydd (5 October),[50] and
at Llechryd (9 October), some seven miles down the Teify
from Newcastle Emlyn, where the salmon weir had been
destroyed a fortnight previously.[51]

Some twelve hundred farmers assembled at Cefn Coed
yr Arllwyd, on waste land near Llangadog, on 10 October,
and held a prolonged meeting despite torrential rain. The
petition was expounded in Welsh by a local farmer, and
a great many local grievances were aired. A Llandovery
solicitor who was present rebutted the charges against the
local gentry. He had, himself, arranged the commutation
of tithes for the surrounding parishes, and this he explained
in detail, evidently to a hostile audience. He read out the
queen's proclamation, but his listeners greeted with laughter

the idea that the rural police could catch Rebecca.[52] The proceedings at Mynydd Pysgodlyn in the following week were entirely in Welsh, when Stephen Evans, Cilcarw, erstwhile Rebecca, spoke powerfully against the poor law and the tithe act.[53] The farmers of north Carmarthenshire chose for their meeting-place the summit of Pen Das Eithin, the highest spot on Mynydd Pencarreg, three and a half miles south of Lampeter. Although it was difficult of access, and although rain fell intermittently in torrents, some three thousand assembled there on Monday, 30 October. Here it was Thomas Emlyn Thomas, the Unitarian minister of Cribyn, who prepared the petition and expounded it. It included a request for an extension of the franchise and for the ballot. A local farmer wished to substitute his own petition, in which he dealt with more specific grievances, such as exorbitant law charges, the employment of Englishmen as clerks to the magistrates and to boards of guardians, the severity of the game laws, the malt tax, excessive fees for marriage licences and the like. He failed to get the support of the audience, but on the following Thursday he was able to present his petition in person to the Rebecca commissioners. For, on the day of the Pen Das Eithin meeting, a Commission of Inquiry had opened its proceedings at Carmarthen.[54]

Throughout the autumn the trusts had been trying to set their affairs in order, stimulated to do so by the visit, early in August, of T. J. Hall, the Bow Street magistrate, and his companion, George H. Ellis, the expert on turnpike trust finance. The Main Trust invited the public to state its complaints, and received a number of petitions. It discontinued several gates and sought the consent of its creditors to a reduction from 5 to $3\frac{1}{2}$ per cent in the interest on their tallies.[55] The Kidwelly Trust removed no less than thirteen of its fifteen side bars. It arranged that payment at certain gates should 'clear' several others, and, to meet a loss in revenue, asked its creditors to accept a reduction in interest from 5 to 4 per cent.[56] Its rivals, the Three Commotts Trust, followed suit and removed ten gates and bars.[57] The Whitland Trust decided not to re-erect certain gates, and to seek a reduction in interest.[58] Similarly, the Cardigan and Aberystwyth Trusts removed certain gates and even reduced their tolls, though they were hardly empowered to do so by act of parliament.[59] Well might Foster, the *Times* correspondent, claim that had these concessions been granted only a few months previously there would have been no disturbances.[60]

Meanwhile the magistrates were anxiously awaiting the reports of T. J. Hall and G. H. Ellis. They had delayed taking action in order that they might do so in concert on the basis of Hall's recommendations.[61] Unless he produced a plan, said Trevor, his visit would have been useless.[62] Even the prime minister wrote to the home secretary expressing his doubts whether Hall's enquiry was an adequate fulfilment of a promise by the government to investigate 'the causes of insubordination in Wales'.[63] Graham replied on 4 September that the continued disturbances were a cause of great anxiety to him. He sent Peel a copy of Hall's report, and announced his intention of sending a letter to the three lords-lieutenant based upon it. But he, also, felt that Hall's enquiry should be regarded merely as a preliminary investigation, and that it was necessary to appoint a commission to report on the disturbances. He thought that Lord Cawdor was the obvious chairman for such a commission, but Cawdor was too deeply involved in the issues to be considered. Graham was therefore approaching Thomas Frankland Lewis.[64]

No doubt the content of Hall's report is incorporated in the letter which Graham sent to the lords-lieutenant on 15 September.[65] Graham stated that the complaints made by occupiers of land in West Wales against their landowners were well-founded in many instances, but this was difficult to remedy by legislation. The objection to the commutation of the tithes was due not so much to any defect in the law as to the fact that tithes had hitherto been much lower in Wales than in England, and that the burden in Wales fell entirely on the occupier and not on the landowner. The chief cause of complaint lay in the trusts. Side gates had been greatly multiplied, so that the cost of conveying lime had greatly increased. It was possible that the abuses of the trusts had been exaggerated, but it was necessary to examine their accounts and restore confidence through publicity. It was difficult to legislate without obtaining a detailed knowledge of the finances and management of all the trusts, and he was therefore advising the Crown to issue a commission for that purpose. He would seek to bring the perpetrators of outrages to justice, but he relied on the exertions of the magistrates and landowners in recovering the goodwill of the community and 'restoring peace by a kind consideration of the wants and feelings of those who were dependent upon them for protection and for the fair reward of honest industry'. This was a generous acknowledgment of the existence of grievances, and it set the tone for the enquiry which was to follow. It cannot have been pleasant reading for the gentry of West Wales. Trevor agreed that it would be well to make landowners responsible for the tithe rent charge. He was disposed to defend the record of the turnpike trusts, but he welcomed the appointment of a commission, and hoped it would pay special attention to the poor law which was the subject of much antipathy,[66] and which Graham (and probably Hall) had not mentioned.

There was a delay of another six weeks before Ellis submitted his report, but it proved to be a valuable document, and it has been repeatedly used in the preparation of this book. Ellis prefaced it with an examination of the causes of suspicion and irritation in respect of the trusts, and he acutely diagnosed their origin in a loss of confidence in the administration of the law. It was not so much that justice was refused to those who suffered at the hands of lessees and collectors of tolls, he said, as that the sufferers had made up their minds that it was useless to apply for redress. He

VIII. JOHN HUGHES IN TASMANIA

By courtesy of Mrs. Hughes, Tŷ-isha, Llan-non

By courtesy of Mr. Caleb Rees

IX. HUGH WILLIAMS

discussed in turn the affairs of every trust in the three shires. Before the report was submitted, the commission had already started its work, and a copy was sent confidentially to Frankland Lewis.[67]

The choice of Thomas Frankland Lewis as chairman of the commission proved to be an admirable one. He came of an old Welsh family and was familiar with the Welsh countryside. He had wide experience of public affairs, especially as chairman of the Poor Law Commission, a post which he had resigned in December 1838. The poor law was a vital element in the situation in West Wales, and few people knew more about it than he did, although the *Welshman* thought that his previous experience would prejudice his opinion.[68] He was given two colleagues. Robert Henry Clive was the second son of the earl of Powis and grandson of Lord Clive of India. He was a member of parliament for south Shropshire and was a keen agriculturist.[69] The third member was William Cripps, a barrister, thirty-eight years of age, and member of parliament for Cirencester.[70] Graham well knew that they had undertaken an arduous duty,[71] and they did so gratuitously apart from their expenses.[72] As their secretary, they were accompanied by George Kettilby Rickards, who was paid for his services.[73] He was a young man of thirty-one, destined to become celebrated for his writings on political economy and professor of that subject at Oxford. He became counsel to the Speaker of the house of commons, and was knighted in 1882. They were asked to inquire not only into the affairs of the turnpike trusts but into the circumstances which had led to 'acts of violence and outrage' in South Wales.[74] Unlike the far more celebrated Land Commission of fifty years later, they were empowered to examine witnesses on oath. Where necessary they employed interpreters.[75]

The commissioners reached Carmarthen on Tuesday, 24 October. They began to take evidence there on 30 October, and continued to do so for eleven days. They

19

then moved on for shorter stays at Haverfordwest, Narberth, Newcastle Emlyn, Cardigan and Aberystwyth. Then they crossed over the hills to Rhayader, descended along the border to Presteign and Brecon, recrossed the hills to Llandeilo, and proceeded via Llanelly, Swansea and Bridgend to Cardiff, completing their work with one day at Merthyr Tydfil on 13 December. In all, evidence was taken on thirty-five full days, and over ten thousand questions were asked. The commissioners took exactly seven weeks to complete their tour. Travelling as they did in winter, they had ample opportunity to appreciate the condition of the roads. All the way they were accompanied by Thomas Campbell Foster, the *Times* representative, conducting a running commentary and a commission of enquiry of his own.

Advertisements in the local newspapers invited the public to submit evidence[76] and handbills were circulated for the same purpose.[77] This gave a greater interest to the mass meetings which were still being held, for they now briefed delegates to meet the commissioners in addition to petitioning the queen. The farmers of Llandyfaelog who, early in September, had drawn up a list of grievances covering most things from the duties of bishops to dog licences, met on 31 October and prepared a remarkable statement for the commission. It was divided into three sections, namely 'causes', 'signs', and 'treatment', and was expressed in broken English with much legal jargon, ending by referring the commissioners for guidance to six passages of Scripture and Matthew Henry's commentary on them.[78] On 1 November there was a meeting at Llanddowror (presided over by Captain Lewis Evans of Pantycendy, the pugnacious opponent of the poor law) which prepared a statement and appointed representatives.[79] In anticipation of the arrival of the commissioners at Haverfordwest, the farmers of Wolf's Castle met on 7 November, and again a week later to receive a report from their delegates.[80] There were similar meetings at Narberth (8 November),[81] at Begelly (10 November),[82] and, next day, at Pembroke.[83] These last two meetings are significant because no outrage had taken place in their neighbourhoods, and the chief grievance discussed at both was the commutation of the tithes.

Meanwhile, the farmers of six north Pembrokeshire parishes had met at Eglwyswrw on 9 November to petition the queen. It was their chairman who had refused to sign the petition at Cilrhedyn a month previously, and, possibly on that account, theirs was restricted to the tithes, the poor law and exorbitant legal charges. They professed attachment to the person of the queen, deplored outrages, and pledged themselves to repress night meetings.[84] It was less than two months since they had destroyed the weirs at Felingigfran and Llechryd. Some three thousand persons, from ten parishes in mid-Cardiganshire, met at Llannarth on 20 November. Thomas Emlyn Thomas, the Unitarian minister, had prepared their petition, which included a request for the dissolution of parliament, an extension of the franchise and the ballot. Other speakers even advocated the separation of church and state, thereby introducing a new controversy.[85] Lesser gatherings, in anticipation of the visit of the commissioners, were held at Llanrhystyd,[86] Rhayader,[87] Llanelly,[88] and Llan-non.[89] But the meetings became less frequent as the weeks went by and the activities of the commission itself attracted less attention.

Foster criticised the commission because it took evidence mainly from the gentry and the magistrates.[90] This could scarcely be avoided, for it listened to anyone who chose to appear before it. The clerks of turnpike trusts were closely examined. But many witnesses were humble men. Some, like two farmers from the neighbourhood of Llanelly, were chosen by their vestry, 'because they have not the English language so well as we have';[91] others, at Carmarthen, Newcastle Emlyn and Cardigan, knew no English at all. Strange to say, Hugh Williams did not give evidence, but at least one witness is known to have put on Rebecca's white gown on occasion and acted as leader, namely Stephen Evans of Cilcarw.[92] Very wisely the commission decided to print its evidence verbatim. It constitutes a folio volume of over four hundred closely printed pages which are packed with information about the rural life of Wales.[93]

The commissioners took three months to sift the evidence and write their report. It appeared on 6 March 1844. It began with a general discussion of the dissatisfaction with the turnpike trusts and then proceeded to comment on the affairs of each trust, not only in the three shires but in Glamorgan, Brecknockshire and Radnorshire as well. Mismanagement and occasional abuse it recorded, but no deliberate attempt to defraud. After 'long and careful deliberation' it recommended that the trusts in each county should be consolidated, the marketable value of their tallies estimated and this sum tendered to their creditors, the money being advanced by the government on the basis of an annuity of fifty years. Road boards were then to take over the management of the turnpike roads in each shire. The commissioners reported an increase of 7 per cent in tithe over the whole of South Wales, and, believing as they did that tithe was a charge on land, they considered that some redress to their tenants should be granted by the landowners. The poor law they found to be reasonably well administered; its deficiencies arose out of the scarcity of ready money in the countryside and the unprecedented economic depression. Imperfections in the system of justice were admitted, notably an ignorance of Welsh on the part of the magistrates and their infrequent attendance at petty sessions, but the commissioners did not recommend the establishment of a stipendiary magistracy. The report was balanced and sympathetic, even paternal, in tone. It is strange to bear in mind that so different an attitude should have been adopted towards what was fundamentally the same problem, only three years later, by the notorious education commissioners in Wales.

The reception given to the report was lukewarm. The consolidation of the trusts was welcomed generally,[94] and much satisfaction was expressed that the Welsh grievances had, at last, been thoroughly aired and examined.[95] The *Times* naturally took credit to itself for the attention which it had given to them. It felt that Frankland Lewis could not do otherwise than place the poor law in a favourable light (although this section of the report was, in fact, written by Cripps)[96] but it attributed the intention of the home secretary to revise the bastardy regulations to 'the guns and cowhorns' of Carmarthenshire.[97] The rioting was now over, and interest in it had slackened, and the very moderation of the report made it uncontroversial, so that there was relatively little discussion.

Early in May the home secretary was asked if any legislative measures were to follow the report.[98] He was able to reply that a bill was already in an advanced stage of preparation. The government had acted with great promptitude, and 'An act to consolidate and amend the Laws relating to Turnpike Trusts in South Wales' received the royal assent on 9 August 1844. There had been a petition from Brecknockshire against inclusion in the act,[99] and some attempt was made in committee to exempt lime altogether from toll,[100] but the bill was accepted by both houses without any opposition. So much was this due to skilful direction by Lord Cawdor that it became known as Lord Cawdor's Act.[101]

The act was important but it was not revolutionary, for the turnpike system was still maintained. Graham argued that it would be unfair to throw the burden of the roads on the shires, that the principle whereby those who used the roads should pay for them was an equitable one and should be preserved.[102] The act therefore followed closely the recommendations of the commissioners. It consolidated all trusts within a shire, and provided for the appointment of a new commission, with three members, to determine the extent of their revenues and debts. Creditors were given twelve months from the date of the passing of the act to present their claims. A sum of £225,000 was set aside by the Public Works Loan Commissioners to meet their liabilities,[103] and this was to be repaid over a period of thirty years.[104] County roads boards, nominated by the magistrates in quarter sessions, were to take over the supervision of the roads, which were to be administered by lesser district roads boards.[105] Tolls were made uniform, namely 6*d*. for every horse drawing a carriage and 4*d*. for every horse drawing a cart, 1½*d*. for a horse not drawing, 10*d*. per score of cattle and 5*d*. per score of sheep. The coming of a new age was signalised by a toll of one shilling on any two-wheeled carriage drawn or impelled by steam and two shillings on any such carriage with more than two wheels. A toll once paid covered seven miles of road within a shire or two miles in an adjoining shire in a period from midnight to midnight. Revenue derived from tolls was to be applied in the first instance to the repayment of the debt and only then to the maintenance of the roads, for the parishes were still responsible for their upkeep.[106]

The government again asked Thomas Frankland Lewis to preside over the new commission,[107] and this he agreed to do without payment.[108] Cripps served with him; as a member of parliament he could not accept a salary. This time the third commissioner was their former secretary, George Kettilby Rickards, at a salary of £1,000 a year, and a Mr. Arthur Somerset replaced him as secretary, at a salary of £700.[109] For a second time they set out on a tour of South Wales, reaching Carmarthen on 1 October and visiting the headquarters of every trust to determine claims. Their work proved onerous, for there were so many tallies and for such small amounts. The claimants could, if necessary, appeal to arbitrators, and, finally, to an umpire, but this did not prove necessary in respect of any trust in West Wales.[110] Of the thirty-one trusts considered by the commissioners, fifteen were entirely solvent and their bond-holders were compensated at par, but in one case only 20 per cent of the nominal value of the tallies was awarded, and in another only 10 per cent. The total sum at which the debts of all the trusts were liquidated was £214,783 14s.[111] This was then allocated between the shires, to be repaid in thirty years by an annuity which combined both interest and a sinking-fund.

The first county roads board to be established was that of Brecknockshire. Like Radnorshire, this shire decided to have no district boards, whereas Cardiganshire and Pembrokeshire set up two each, and Carmarthenshire and Glamorgan three each. The boards then proceeded to determine which roads were to be continued as turnpike roads and where the gates were to be placed, to arrange for contracts for the supply of material, to engage surveyors and workmen and to let the tolls. The change-over took some time to accomplish, and there were innumerable problems to be solved, sometimes involving litigation.[112] In order to assist the local boards, Captain Harness of the Royal Engineers was appointed general superintendent for South Wales.[113] He was a highly efficient officer (he eventually became a general and colonel-commandant of the Royal Engineers)[114] and he soon put the affairs of the South Wales roads in order.[115] It was a remarkable consequence of the Rebecca Riots that, for the next thirty years, South Wales enjoyed a better general system of roads than any other part of the country.

The process of military disengagement, after the rioting was over, proved to be protracted and exasperating. On the one hand the government wished to withdraw the troops and the metropolitan police; on the other hand both Cardiganshire (until January 1844) and Pembrokeshire were resisting the establishment of a rural police. In December 1843 the inhabitants of Aberystwyth petitioned the Home Office to allow troops to remain in the town during the winter months for their protection,[116] at the very time when their own magistrates were maintaining that a rural police was unnecessary because the countryside was peaceful. Besides, at this time also, the Aberystwyth guardians were engaged in acrimonious correspondence with the military authorities over payment for the housing of these troops. The newly built workhouses had been used as barracks in some places, partly for convenience and partly because of the threats to destroy them. This had brought the military authorities up against the redoubtable Edwin Chadwick, who insisted that soldiers and paupers must be strictly segregated, and the former removed immediately the accommodation became necessary for its true purpose.[117] In most cases the workhouses were still empty. Both Colonel Love and George Rice Trevor thought that many guardians would have welcomed their destruction because of hostility to the new poor law.[118] They now attempted to pass on to the military authorities a part of their cost. All the Cardiganshire boards demanded payment for rent as well as compensation for wear and tear. Love thought the Aberystwyth charges 'so extraordinary' that he went there to investigate.[119] In their exasperation the government would willingly have left both guardians and magistrates to their own devices, but they had to see that law and order were preserved. They had to allow a reduced force of the metropolitan police to remain in Carmarthenshire until April and in Pembrokeshire until July.[120] It was not until October 1844 that Colonel Love was able to concentrate his forces in South Wales in their usual headquarters.[121]

Insurrection proved to have been an expensive interlude, and a considerable burden was placed on the rates of the three shires. Accommodation for the troops, whether in workhouses or in other buildings, had to be paid for by the civil authorities.[122] The Pembrokeshire Yeomanry cost between £60 and £80 a week, depending on how many men were kept under arms.[123] The swearing-in of every special constable cost the rates about ten shillings,[124] and all those employed in guarding gates had to be paid. Ultimately, the cost of re-erecting the destroyed toll-houses had to be borne by the public; the Carmarthenshire quarter sessions in January 1844 authorised a payment of over £500 in the previous three months for this item alone.[125] Above all, the assistance of the metropolitan police proved expensive. It has not been possible to ascertain the total cost, but for the period from 23 October 1843 to 31 March 1844, it was estimated that the metropolitan police would cost Carmarthenshire £2,324, Cardiganshire £968 and Pembrokeshire £1,014, a total of over £4,000. The Carmarthenshire magistrates made strong but ineffective representations that this expense should be borne by the Treasury.[126] The farmers of West Wales may well have wondered if they could not have attained their ends by less expensive means.

The only persons who made a profit out of Rebecca (apart from Captain Napier) were the informers. The home secretary did not favour the use of regular informers. This, he said, was both 'hazardous and inconvenient'. But he was aware that it was necessary in special cases and he authorised the sums expended by Colonel Love.[127] Love's payments were very small, a pound or two at a time, and similar amounts were paid by Captain Napier.[128] Rewards offered in respect of individual outrages and in virtue of the queen's proclamation were considerably larger. Their distribution was entrusted to the three lords-lieutenant in conjunction with the magistrates.[129] It proved a very difficult task. The queen's proclamation had extended the rewards to anyone who arrested or gave information leading to the arrest of a rioter, and so members of the metropolitan police might qualify. But it was necessary for the arrest to be followed by a conviction. This complicated matters in two ways. In some instances a rioter might be charged with several offences, but only tried for one of them, so that informers in respect of the other charges might be unlucky. In other instances the jury acquitted men who were clearly guilty. Both possibilities are illustrated in the case of Benjamin Jones of Brechfa. He confessed to sheep-stealing. There was a Home Office reward of £100 in respect of this crime, so that his captors might have claimed it. But he was not charged with sheep-stealing. On the other hand he was charged with arson in respect of the fire at Pantycerrig, and the chief witness against him, one of the servant girls, might have claimed a reward had not the jury acquitted him 'in the teeth of very clear evidence'. George Rice Trevor used his good offices both in respect of his captors and of the servant girl.[130] The informer at Fishguard was given a gratuity of £20 although his evidence did not lead to a conviction.[131] John Jones, who had informed on the Morgan brothers of Llangyfelach, was also given £20.[132] At the Carmarthen quarter sessions, on 5 March 1844, no less than £1,500 was distributed, of which £120 was paid to one informer, Richard Williams, though what his services were does not appear.[133]

Meanwhile, others were paying for the riots in a different way. Whether the prisoners in Millbank were able to forgather and discuss their exploits and their fate is not known, but John Hughes, John Hugh and David Jones were still there when Shoni Sgubor Fawr and Dai'r Cantwr arrived in February. Petitions were submitted to the queen asking for a reduction in John Hughes's sentence, including one from his mother and another signed by ten of the jurymen who had found him guilty. A public meeting at Llan-non also pleaded on his behalf, but all with no success.[134] Strange to say, Colonel Thomas Wood the member of parliament for Brecknockshire, submitted a testimonial in respect of Shoni, for he had been sworn in by the Brecknockshire magistrates as a special constable on the occasion of an election,[135] and the manager of a Monmouthshire ironworks also sought some mitigation of his sentence on account of Shoni's services, while a private in the 98th. Foot, in procuring private information for the authorities about the depredations of the Scotch Cattle and in protecting the writer's family.[136]

It was Shoni who was the first to be transported.[137] He was separated from the others. Possibly this was done because he had received a life sentence whereas they had terms of years, but the separation may have been deliberate as he was a far more violent character than they were. He embarked on the *Blundell* on 8 March 1844 and reached his destination on 6 July, after a seventeen weeks' journey around the Cape. To begin with he was placed on Norfolk Island, then a dependency of Van Diemen's Land and a 'model' station for the newly-established convict probation system. Three years later he was transferred to Van Diemen's Land, crossing the thousand miles of ocean in the ship *Pestongee Bomangee*. While on Norfolk Island he had already served sentences of two months' hard labour and ten days' solitary confinement for stealing potatoes and for fishing without permission. In Van Diemen's Land his life should have been easier for he was indentured to various employers, but their rapid succession (he served about twenty before his conditional pardon) and the frequency with which they 'returned him to service' show that they could do little with Shoni. He was imprisoned with hard labour for three months for refusing to work unless he got extra rations, given two days' solitary confinement for being absent without leave, two months' hard labour (with the tread-wheel) for disobeying orders, seven days' solitary confinement for being drunk and resisting a constable and one month's hard labour for not proceeding to Launceston as he had been directed to do. At last, on 19 September 1854, he was given his ticket of leave, but within a month it was revoked for he had committed an assault for which he was given eighteen months' hard labour. He seems to have been released before the end of this sentence, but, in December 1855, he was given a month's hard labour for drunkenness, and, in the following March, another three months for the same reason. He got his ticket of leave on 2 December 1856. Yet within two days he was reprimanded for misconduct, and this was repeated on two later occasions, and in March 1857 he was given a month's hard labour. He was conditionally pardoned on 20 April 1858, and with that his sad, if far from simple, annals terminate.

The other convicts embarked on the *London* four days after Shoni had left, and arrived in the antipodes also four days after he did. They were placed on probation on Maria Island (off the east coast of Van Diemen's Land), and there, only a week later, on 17 July 1844, David Jones died. He was just twenty-one years of age. Is it fanciful to imagine that he died of grief, twelve thousand miles from his native Carmarthenshire? John Hugh, who had been seriously wounded at Pontarddulais, fared better. He was soon given his probation pass (6 March 1846) and his ticket of leave (11 January 1848). In December 1850 he had served his seven years' sentence and was free. A solitary fine of five shillings for being drunk is the only penalty recorded against him. He was married and had a child in Carmarthenshire, but presumably his wife had died, for in August 1852 he applied for permission to marry Mary Maher, a convict transported on the *Duke of Cornwall*. With that he, also, passes from sight. John Hughes was admonished once or twice for misconduct during his probation, but he won the commendation of the authorities for capturing a fellow-convict who had absconded, and was given his pass on 18 July 1846. During his period of indenture he was given fourteen days' solitary confinement for feigning illness. He obtained his ticket of leave on 22 February 1853. Three years later this was revoked, but it was soon restored and, on 19 May 1857, he was given a conditional pardon, six and a half years before his sentence was completed. A letter which he wrote to his father on 18 April 1864 is still extant.[138] He was then a timber cutter and apparently hired men to work for him at times. He had forgotten most of his Welsh and wrote in English. Although he knew of some who had gone home and then returned to Tasmania because of the climate, he still hoped to be buried among his relations and friends. In October 1867 he was prosecuted in the Supreme Court of Tasmania for having stolen a bill of exchange valued £26 10s., but the jury exonerated him.[139] He married and settled down in Tasmania and never came home, but he corresponded with his relatives at Tŷ-isha until his death about 1900. Both his son and daughter were living and were in good circumstances in 1921.[140]

Finally, the Cantwr. He had a rougher passage. He emerged from probation within a year, but then ran into heavy weather. He was indentured to about a dozen masters and was fined for drunkenness several times and given twenty-one days' hard labour for this offence on one occasion. He served a period of three months' imprisonment with hard labour for gross insolence, and a similar sentence for using indecent language and assaulting a constable. It is clear that his weakness was drink. He obtained a ticket of leave in March 1852, but it was revoked, as also was the conditional pardon given him in October 1854. This was restored to him in August 1855, eight years before his sentence of twenty years had expired. In 1848 a man representing himself to be Dai'r Cantwr was soliciting alms in the Llanelly district.[141] But it was not Dai. Nor is it likely that the ballads attributed to him during his exile were his work.[142] In his freedom he tried to earn a living as a farm-overseer, a lime burner, a small road-contractor and a general labourer.[143] He was then known as Taff Davis. He died on 10 August 1874, in his sixty-first year. For several nights previously he had been sleeping in an outhouse of the hotel at Ross. He retired to sleep in an intoxicated state on the night of 10 August, and it is presumed that he set the grass on which he slept on fire by lighting his pipe, for he was found next morning suffocated and partly burnt. As he had foretold in his threnody he had never been able to return to his beloved Glamorgan: 'ddo'i byth yn ôl'.

Two months later died Hugh Williams, whom many believed to have been 'the real Rebecca'. The authorities had, if anything, become more suspicious of him after the rioting was over,[144] although there is no foundation for the statement which has frequently been made that he was struck off the roll of solicitors. In July 1844 Colonel Love instructed

Captain Scott, the chief constable of Carmarthenshire, that he should be 'closely watched', and when Williams visited Newcastle Emlyn in August, Love thought it might be well to go there himself. Williams was suspected of inciting both farmers and industrial workers. It was believed that he encouraged the attempt to inflict the punishment of the '*ceffyl pren*', at the time of the St. Clears fair in the autumn of 1844, on a person who had given information against the Rebeccaites, and the Home Office advised that he should be prosecuted if evidence could be obtained. He continued to live at Kidwelly, and early in 1847 he initiated a lengthy correspondence with the Home Office with a view to reforming that corrupt borough, despite the high praise he had bestowed on its corporation at the great meeting on Allt Cunedda.[145]

As we have seen, Williams was 'active in the service' of the Corn Law League,[146] of which his brother-in-law, Richard Cobden, was the moving spirit. Yet little is known of the relationship of the two men. When Cobden stayed for some weeks at his wife's home at Machynlleth in 1846, he complained that he was pestered by people from the locality who wanted him to get them jobs.[147] But when he invested a considerable proportion of his wealth in the Illinois Central Railroad,[148] Williams was associated with him. The affairs of the railway became embarrassed, and Cobden went out to investigate them in 1859. He was joined in New York by Hugh Williams.[149] At this time, Samuel Roberts, of Llanbryn-mair near Machynlleth, had established his ill-fated Welsh Settlement in Tennessee. Williams was in communication with Roberts, and Cobden offered him a square mile of land along the railway for a new settlement, but Roberts had to decline.[150]

Williams went to live on his wife's property, at Gardde, in St. Clears, some time before 1851. In that year he and his wife built a market hall in an attempt to develop the economic life of the village.[151] In the same year he was elected port-reeve of the borough, and became its recorder in 1853, an office which he retained till his death, despite frequent protests on account of his residence elsewhere.[152] His wife, it will be remembered, was twenty-five years his senior. She died on 5 August 1861 in her ninetieth year.[153] Hugh Williams lost no time. Two months after his wife's death, on 9 October 1861, at the Buckingham Baptist Chapel, Clifton, he married for the second time.[154] His new wife was thirty-nine years younger than he was.[155] They went to live at Ferryside, and started to produce a family as fast as might be.[156] In 1869 Hugh Williams put up for sale his property (as it now was) in St. Clears and its neighbourhood. It was a considerable estate, for, in addition to the house at Gardde and its seventy-five acres of land, there were no less than fifty-seven other lots.[157] He died on 19 October 1874, in his seventy-eighth year, at Cobden Villa, Ferryside, and lies buried in the parish churchyard of St. Ishmaels.

There is no doubt that Rebecca had won a substantial victory with the passing of Lord Cawdor's Act. No one appreciated this more fully than Thomas Frankland Lewis. When Nassau Senior stayed with him at Harpton in 1852, Frankland Lewis delivered, for the benefit of his guest, 'an eulogium on the Rebecca rioters'. He maintained that their cause was just, that the multiplication of gates had become an oppression. 'The people,' he said, 'saw that their only remedy was to take the law into their own hands. The Rebecca conspiracy was organised with much skill, and carried through with much fidelity. . . . It was never diverted from its original purpose, and the instant that purpose seemed likely to be attained, that is to say the instant that an enquiry into the Welsh turnpike system was instituted by the government, the association was dissolved and no one has ever proposed its revival.' 'The Rebecca Riots,' he concluded, 'are a very creditable portion of Welsh history.'[158] This was a striking tribute from a magistrate and a distinguished public servant.

Other legislation followed which alleviated the condition
of the peasant farmers of Wales, notably the general enclosure act of 1845, the repeal of the Corn Laws in 1846 and the
new poor law of 1847 which humanised the administration
of poor relief. With the fifties came the beginning of public
health legislation and a remarkable improvement in medical
facilities. These decades saw the return of agricultural
prosperity, when an increasing market for agricultural
products was found in the rapidly developing industrial
areas. Above all, the coming of the railway, which was to
ruin the turnpike trusts of England, provided a solution for
the problems of rural Wales by facilitating migration to the
great industries. The fundamental cause of the rioting had
been the rapid increase in population which had overtaxed
the economic resources of a backward area. It was poverty
which had driven the farmers to cultivate the barren
uplands. It was the pressure of population which had caused
the decay of the old social order and the breakdown of
obsolete systems of local government and administration.
But by the middle of the century the population of rural
Wales had reached its peak; afterwards, each succeeding
census showed a decline in the number of people engaged
in agriculture. Most notable of all was the decline in the
number of farm labourers, for they were attracted to the
towns by higher money wages and better conditions of life.
With the return of prosperity and the decline in rural
population the uplands were abandoned, and for some years
there was equilibrium in the countryside.

The mystique of Rebecca has itself changed with the
passing of the years. For a while there was some secretiveness,
through fear of exposure and an uneasy feeling of having
lived through a nightmare. The discomfort was soon
forgotten, and the tarnished heroes of the movement became
the subjects of countless stories as their escapades were retold
and magnified. Rebecca then came to symbolise the revolt
of an oppressed peasantry against human injustice, and the
struggle of men and women against inexorable poverty.

The farmers wresting a livelihood from a barren soil, and their womenfolk worn out by unceasing labour, accepted their lot in patience generally, but were at times driven to indignant protest. In those moments they all felt themselves to be the sons and daughters of Rebecca. And then they blessed Rebecca, whose seed had, at least for a time, possessed the gates of their oppressors.

BIBLIOGRAPHICAL NOTE

A BIBLIOGRAPHY of the Rebecca Riots is given in T. Gwyn Jones, 'Rebeccaism - Bibliography', *Carmarthen Antiquary*, I (1943–44), pp. 64–70. This is adequate except that it makes no reference to the wealth of material in the Public Record Office. This note is therefore limited to a review of the sources in general. It makes no attempt at a complete list of writings on the subject, the great majority of which are trivial, if not useless. The above number of the *Carmarthen Antiquary* is devoted entirely to the subject.

The only published account of the riots is Henry Tobit Evans, *Rebecca and her Daughters* (Cardiff, 1910). This appeared posthumously, edited by the author's daughter, Miss Gwladys Tobit Evans (Mrs. Huw J. Huws), who wrote an introduction, and to whom I am indebted for much kindness. The book presents the researcher with a strange bibliographical problem. It soon becomes clear that less than 10 per cent of it (possibly less than 5 per cent) is in the author's own words. It consists of extracts from newspapers (almost entirely from the *Welshman*), with some handbills and addresses inserted, all loosely strung together in chronological sequence but with no other order whatsoever. Had the extracts been printed as such, with references to their sources, the work might have been useful. Unfortunately, errors in transcription are innumerable.

Mr. Alcwyn Evans, the Carmarthen local historian, prepared several manuscript accounts of the riots. There are copies in the National Library of Wales (MS. 12368E), in the Carmarthen County Museum, and in the Tenby Museum. These accounts are in the form of chronological notes, and are, in fact, extracts from newspapers. In most cases they are taken from the *Welshman* and nearly all are identical with the accounts of the same incidents given by Tobit Evans, but without the errors in transcription. There are, also, some reminiscences of the writer's, who lived in Carmarthen at the time of the riots. The Tenby manuscript was prepared in 1893 for Miss Margaret James of Pantsaeson, Moylegrove, the author of a booklet, *The French Invasion of 1797* (published on the centenary of that event), who intended to write a book on the Rebecca Riots. For convenience, reference to Alcwyn Evans's transcripts has been made to the Tenby MS.

Miss Mabel Williams (Mrs. Bickerstaff) submitted a dissertation on the subject to the University of Wales in 1913 which she has kindly allowed me to consult.

Important original material in the Carmarthen County Museum, namely a series of forty-two letters from George Rice Trevor mostly to William Chambers, junior, has been printed in *Carmarthenshire Antiquarian Society Transactions*, XXIII (1932), pp. 60–77. (These are referred to as *Carm. Antiq. Soc. Trans.*, with number of letter.) In the National Library of Wales there is a series of eighty-three documents (MS. 14590E) which were in the possession of William Chambers, junior. These have been calendared in E. D. Jones, 'A File of Rebecca Papers', *Carmarthen Antiquary*, I (1943–4), pp. 21–63. (They are referred to as *Carmarthen Antiquary*, with number of document.) A series of twelve brief articles, the reminiscences of a participant in the riots, appeared in *Tarian y Gweithiwr*, 19 August to 4 November 1886. My attention was kindly drawn to them by Mr. Moelwyn Williams of the National Library of Wales.

The chief source of manuscript material for the rioting is in the Home Office papers in the Public Record Office. There is little Rebecca material in the H.O.40 series ('Disturbances') where one might expect to find it. This is because at some time it was transferred to the H.O.45 series ('Old Series'). The enormous bundles— 45/265, 45/453, 45/454 (three bundles), and 45/642—contain a wealth of material. Outgoing letters relating to the riots are in 41/17 and 41/18. My attention was kindly drawn to this material before the last war by Mr. W. Lloyd Davies of Bournemouth, who has since died. Mr. Davies began to prepare a schedule of it, now deposited in the Library of the University College of North Wales, Bangor, but it is far from being complete. An article by Mr. Davies, 'Notes on Hugh Williams and the Rebecca Riots', *Bulletin of the Board of Celtic Studies*, XI (1944), pp. 160–7, consists of a calendar of seventeen letters. There is considerable material in Assize Rolls 71/7, 71/8, and 72/1, with depositions of witnesses, in the Public Record Office. Prolonged and extensive search has been made in well over a hundred bundles in various series in the Public Record

Office, and reference to relevant material will be found in the footnotes.

Much manuscript material of a general nature is to be found in the Pembrokeshire Quarter Sessions Records (N.L.W.), and some in the Cardiganshire Quarter Sessions Records (N.L.W.), and in the Carmarthenshire Quarter Sessions Records (in Carmarthenshire County Hall). There are also Minute and Account Books of various trusts in Haverfordwest (communicated to me by Mr. G. A. Dickman, County Librarian), in the National Library of Wales, in the Carmarthen Museum, and in the Carmarthenshire County Hall (consulted through the courtesy of W. S. Thomas, Esq., the Clerk of the Peace; my attention was drawn to these by Mr. Jenkyn Beverley Smith). Detailed references will be found in the footnotes.

There is some valuable manuscript material in the Peel Papers in the British Museum.

Much use has been made of government publications, notably *Reports of the Commission for enquiring into the Administration of the Poor Laws*, 1834, and subsequent *Annual Reports*; *Report of the Commissioners of Inquiry for South Wales*, 1844; *Report of the Select Committee on Commons Inclosure*, 1844; *Reports of the Commissioners of Inquiry into the State of Education in Wales*, (three volumes), 1847; *Report of the Royal Commission on Land in Wales and Monmouthshire*, together with five volumes of *Evidence*, and a volume of *Appendices*, 1896. Numerous other parliamentary *Accounts and Papers* are referred to in the footnotes, as well as volumes of the *Journal of the House of Commons*, and Hansard, *Parliamentary Debates*.

Weekly newspapers presented a special problem. The essential newspapers are the *Welshman* and the *Carmarthen Journal*. There does not seem to be available a run of the *Welshman* for the years 1839 and 1840, nor of the *Carmarthen Journal* for the years 1841–4. In consequence, the *Carmarthen Journal* has been used for the two earlier years, and the *Welshman* for the following four years. Reference has also been made to the *Cambrian*, and to Welsh periodicals, notably *Seren Gomer*, *Yr Efangylydd*, *Y Diwygiwr*, and *Yr Haul*.

NOTES TO CHAPTER I

[1] *Royal Commission on Land in Wales and Monmouthshire, Report*, 1896, p. 390. The figures here given relate to a period later in the century, but they are roughly accurate for the earlier period.

[2] *Royal Commission on Land, Minutes of Evidence*, 1894, II, 551, 567; Charles Hassall, *General View of the Agriculture of the County of Pembroke*, 1794, p. 13.

[3] Henry Owen, *Old Pembroke Families*, 1902, p. 31.

[4] *Welshman*, 13 Oct. 1843, describes Cawdor lands in the parishes of Cenarth, Penboyr, Llandyfriog, and Cilrhedyn, in the area where Pembrokeshire, Cardiganshire, and Carmarthenshire adjoin one another.

[5] E. H. Stuart-Jones, *The Last Invasion of Britain*, 1950, pp. 97–8, 254–5.

[6] H. M. Vaughan, *The South Wales Squires*, 1926, p. 56, corrected by Glyn Roberts in *The History of Carmarthenshire*, 1939, II, 58.

[7] Hassall, loc. cit.

[8] *Royal Com. Land, Report*, pp. 232, 390; *Royal Com. Land, Evidence*, II, 558; III, 1033; Charles Hassall, *General View of the Agriculture of the County of Carmarthen*, 1794, p. 23.

[9] Hassall, op. cit., p. 50, for lead mines north of Llandovery; Walter Davies, *General View of the Agriculture and Domestic Economy of South Wales*, 1814, I, 79, and II, 408, makes out the profits from lead mines at Rhandir-mwyn and Cil-y-cwm to have been very considerable.

[10] Thomas Nicholas, *Annals and Antiquities of the Counties and County Families of Wales*, 1872, II, 896.

[11] Henry Owen, loc. cit.; *Archaeologia Cambrensis*, 1861, pp. 80–1 (obituary notice).

[12] *Royal Com. Land, Evidence*, II, 579, 621.

[13] J. Roland Phillips, *Memoirs of the Ancient Family of Owen of Orielton*, 1886, p. 81; Edward Laws in N.L.W., MS. 1352 B, folio 398 *et seq.*; for the Orielton estates see the Haverfordwest (Eaton Evans and Williams) Deeds and Documents, 283–375, and the Haverfordwest (Williams and Williams) Deeds and Documents, 25,715 and 25,764 in the National Library of Wales.

[14] Henry Owen, op. cit., pp. 114–15; W. R. Williams, *The Parliamentary History of the Principality of Wales*, 1895, p. 158; *Pembrokeshire Herald*, 2 Jan. 1891, has a notice of a fund opened on behalf of Sir Hugh Owen, described as a 'venerable baronet who in his long life has experienced much variety of fortune'.

[15] *Royal Com. Land, Evidence*, V, 101.

[16] Ibid., III, 710; *Royal Com. Land, Report*, p. 393; Crosswood Deeds and Documents (N.L.W.), II, 678, gives acreage in 1815 as 40,000.

[17] Crosswood Deeds and Documents, II, 676 and 678, give rental in 1814 at £11,000 and the reduced rental in 1815 at £9,000; John Hughes, *A History of the Parliamentary Representation of the County of Cardigan*, 1849, p. 22, reproducing an election address: 'To the Free Burgesses of the Independent Boroughs of Cardigan, Lampeter and Aberystwyth', gives an estimated rental of £10,000 in 1806.

[18] Walter Davies, op. cit., II, 49, gives the number as 3,977,500.

[19] See H. M. Vaughan, 'Some Letters of Thomas Johnes of Hafod', *Y Cymmrodor*, XXXV (1915), 204.

[20] Lewis Morris's letter, dated 24 Feb. 1761, in J. H. Davies, 'Cardiganshire Freeholders in 1760', *West Wales Historical Records*, III (1913), 73–4.

[21] *Royal Com. Land, Evidence*, III, 208.

[22] *Cambrian Register*, I (1795), 144.

[23] Samuel Lewis, *A Topographical Dictionary of Wales*, 1833, sub nom. Llanarthney.

[24] For his will see Francis Green, 'The Stepneys of Prendergast', *West Wales Historical Records*, VII (1917–18), 108–142, especially pp. 122–4.

[25] Obituary quoted in Nicholas, op. cit., I, 289; see also Francis Green, op. cit., p. 137.

[26] Lewis, *Topo. Dict.*, sub nom. Llanelly; *Carmarthenshire Antiquarian Society Transactions*, XXIX (1939), 97, has a lease of Llanelly House, dated 13 May 1776.

[27] Nicholas, op. cit., I, 276.

[28] Lewis, *Topo. Dict.*, list of subscribers.

[29] William Chambers to Home Office, 21 June 1843, H.O. 45/454.

[30] I am indebted for information to Lady Howard-Stepney and Mr. Griffith Thomas of Llanelly. See also D. Bowen, *Hanes Llanelli*, 1857; Arthur Mee, *Llanelly Parish Church*, 1888; John Innes, *Old Llanelly*, 1902; *Bye-Gones relating to Wales and the Border Counties*, 1882, p. 43. The will of Sir John Stepney is recited in An Act to enable William Chambers . . . to grant . . . leases of certain Estates . . . devised by the will of Sir John Stepney, Baronet, 3 Vict., 1840 (copy in Cardiff Public Library). As this act states that William Chambers had no heir it must be assumed that William Chambers, junior, was an illegitimate son. The act has a schedule of the estate. The case of Stepney v Chambers came before the Court of Chancery in 1865.

[31] Cilgwyn MS. 306 (at N.L.W.).

[32] Gruffydd Evans, 'The Story of Newcastle-Emlyn and Adpar', *Y Cymmrodor*, XXXII (1922), 148.

[33] Thomas Lloyd and the Rev. Mr. Turnor, *General View of the Agriculture of the County of Cardigan*, 1794; see Walter Davies, op. cit., II, 158, and *Royal Com. Land, Appendix*, p. 85.

[34] Cilgwyn MS. 296; in 1785, on payment of £1,000, for a thousand years at a pepper corn rent, with a proviso for reconveyance on repayment, and, in 1795, for £2,625.

[35] Gruffydd Evans, op. cit., p. 155, has the unlikely story that the two naval men had in their early days tossed for each other's estates.

[36] Cilgwyn MS. 297.

[37] Cilgwyn MSS. 295, 306.

[38] Col. Love to Home Office, 26 June 1843, H.O. 45/453.

[39] Cilgwyn MS. 297.

[40] Cilgwyn MS. 306.

[41] Petition dated 18 May 1836 and letter, William Philipps, mayor, to Home Office, 28 April 1836, in H.O. 52/31.

[42] *Welshman*, 6 Jan. 1843, and 21 Oct. 1849.

[43] *Welshman*, 5 March 1841.

[44] Controversy in *Welshman*, 14 and 28 April 1843; *Report of the Commissioners of Inquiry for South Wales*, 1844, p. 239.

[45] *Reports of the Commissioners of Inquiry into the State of Education in Wales*, 1847, II, 66, 90.

[46] Burke, *Landed Gentry*, 1937, under FitzWilliams of Cilgwyn.

[47] Home Office to Walter Wilkins, 25 June 1839, H.O. 117/4, shows that the Garter King at Arms did not then think the evidence that the family had borne the surname of De Winton to be sufficient.

[48] H. M. Vaughan, op. cit., p. 130. A little later two branches of the Goring Thomases of Llan-non became Trehernes (Burke, *Landed Gentry*, sub nom.).

[49] Home Office to Col. Love, 22 June 1843, H.O. 41/17; Geo. Rice Trevor to Home Office, 23 June 1843, H.O. 45/454; Edward Laws to Home Office, 26 June 1843, H.O. 45/454; Col. Love to Home Office, 26 June 1843, H.O. 45/453. For Hall's own reports, see later.

[50] Dillwyn Diaries (N.L.W.), 6 and 7 Sept. 1843; Frederick Pollock to Sir James Graham, 3 Nov. 1843, Peel Papers, B.M., Add. MSS. 40,449, folio 210; Sir James Graham to Sir Robert Peel, 18 Nov. 1843, ibid., folio 219.

[51] Earl of Bessborough (ed.), *Lady Charlotte Guest, Extracts from her Journal, 1833-52*, 1950, pp. 131-3, under date 7 May 1842.

[52] Henry Skrine, *Two Successive Tours throughout the whole of Wales*, 1812, p. 270.

[53] Benjamin Heath Malkin, *The Scenery, Antiquities and Biography of South Wales*, 1807, II, 23-4.

[54] *Reports on Education in Wales*, 1847, I, 389.

[55] Skrine, op. cit., p. 269; anon., *The New Estate, or The Young Travellers in Wales and Ireland*, 1831, p. 91; see also Ed. C. Lloyd Hall to Home Office, 23 July 1843, H.O. 45/454.

[56] *Reports on Education in Wales*, 1847, II, 79; the opinion of Col. Powell of Nanteos.

[57] *Royal Com. Land, Evidence*, III, 405.

[58] Cf. E. Davies, 'The Small Landowner, 1780-1832', *Economic History Review*, I (1927-8), 112.

[59] Sir James Graham to Sir Robert Peel, 21 Dec. 1843, Peel Papers, loc. cit., folio 273; see also same to same, 16 Sept. 1843, folio 33: 'The landed proprietors and the magistrates by neglect of their duties have permitted the evils in that district to swell to a dangerous magnitude'.

[60] Glyn Roberts, 'Parliamentary Representation of the Welsh Boroughs', *Bulletin of the Board of Celtic Studies*, IV (1929), 352-60.

[61] Ibid.; *Journal of the House of Commons*, XXI, 90 (19 March 1727).

[62] The parliamentary representation of Carmarthenshire and Carmarthen borough is admirably dealt with in Glyn Roberts, 'Political Affairs from 1536 to 1900', i.e. Chapter One of Sir J. E. Lloyd (ed.), *A History of Carmarthenshire*, Vol. II, 1939.

[63] *Commons Journal*, XVII, 108-10 (23 Feb. 1711).

[64] Ibid., XVIII, 199 (4 July 1715).

[65] Ibid., XXI, 571 (7 March 1730).

⁶⁶ For this belief (which has been generally held) see S. R. Meyrick, *The History and Antiquities of the County of Cardigan*, 1810, p. 137; Lewis, *Topo. Dict.*, under Atpar and Llandyvriog.

⁶⁷ *Reports of Commissioners on Proposed Division of Counties and Boundaries of Boroughs*, 1832, p. 35. For the borough of Adpar see Cilgwyn MS. 261, folio 27, also MS. 296, folios 97, 101 *et seq.*

⁶⁸ Glyn Roberts, op. cit., II, 51; *Cambrian*, 11 June 1831, quoting the *Times*, which accused Sir John Owen of obtaining nearly £3,000 a year for his family in church preferment and in other ways.

⁶⁹ Henry Richard, *Letters and Essays on Wales*, 1884, p. 90.

⁷⁰ *Royal Com. Land, Report*, p. 161, footnote.

⁷¹ R. H. Peckwell, *Cases of Controverted Elections*, 1805.

⁷² Theophilus Jones to Edward Davies, 7 March 1803, speaks of 'a thousand men and women and children besides', of whom he was one: Edwin Davies, *Theophilus Jones, Historian*, 1905, p. 66.

⁷³ Evidence of John Williams in 1831: *Report of the Select Committee on the Pembrokeshire County Election Petition*, 1831. The Carmarthenshire election is fully discussed in Peckwell, op. cit.

⁷⁴ *Carm. Antiq. Soc. Trans.*, IV (1908–9), 67.

⁷⁵ For John Jones, see Glyn Roberts, op. cit., II, 60 *et seq.*; also *Welshman*, 22 April, 6 May, 11 Nov., 18 Nov., 25 Nov. 1842; 7 July (his library), 17 Feb., 18 Aug. 1843; and 2 Aug. 1844 (his estate); *Carm. Antiq. Soc. Trans.*, LXIII (1930), 23. For his attitude towards the Courts of Great Sessions and the Welsh Language, see *First Report of Commissioners on Courts of Common Law*, 1829, pp. 390–2, 427–30; for nationalist opinion, see D. Gwenallt Jones, in *Historical Basis of Welsh Nationalism*, 1950, pp. 99–106.

⁷⁶ *Seren Gomer*, 1819, p. 74.

⁷⁷ The address of the town council of Carmarthen, 20 Oct. 1819, *Carm. Antiq. Soc. Trans.*, XXI (1927–9), 84–5; see also *Seren Gomer*, 1819, pp. 363–5.

⁷⁸ *Efangylydd*, 1831, p. 256.

⁷⁹ Ibid., loc. cit.; *Carmarthen Journal*, 6 May 1831 for decision not to stand.

⁸⁰ For the Carmarthen elections of 1831 see Glyn Roberts, op. cit., II, 67–8; *Seren Gomer*, 29 April 1831; *Cambrian*, 27 Aug. 1831; *Carm. Antiq. Soc. Trans.*, VII (1911–12), 82–4; and especially the dossier on the rioting in H.O. 52/16.

⁸¹ *Welshman*, 27 Dec. 1844.

⁸² For the Pembrokeshire election see *Report of the Select Committee on the Pembrokeshire County Election Petition*, 1831 (a folio volume of 119 pages); Haverfordwest (Williams and Williams) Deeds and Documents, 19479–90 (at National Library of Wales); *Cambrian*, 11 June 1831 (reproducing a lengthy article from the *Times*).

⁸³ *Carmarthen Journal*, 23 Sept. 1831; for Greville's petition, see *Commons Journal*, LXXXVI (1831), pt. 2, pp. 608–9.

⁸⁴ *Carmarthen Journal*, 24 July 1831; *Cambrian*, 24 March 1832.

⁸⁵ Ibid., 29 Oct., 1831; *Carm. Antiq. Soc. Trans.*, XXII (1930–1), 13.

⁸⁶ Haverfordwest Deeds and Documents, as above; Francis Green, 'Harries of Co. Pembroke', *West Wales Hist. Records*, VIII (1917–8), 135, which is very favourable to Harries, says he 'possibly somewhat exceeded his powers' and

was 'sentenced to a fine of over £300'; John Davies, who indexed the Haverfordwest Deeds and Documents, says he was fined £500 and costs. I have been unable to confirm this. See also *Cambrian*, 20 Jan., 11 Aug. 1832.

[87] Haverfordwest Deeds and Documents, as above; Lucas Collection, 172, has a list of 'Subscriptions, in favour of the Inkeepers of Haverfordwest whose houses were opened in the interests of the Blue Party', indicating that a total of £2,300 was collected.

[88] Hansard, *Parliamentary Debates*, Third Series, XLIII (1838), 670–83.

[89] *Diwygiwr*, 1838, p. 91; *Royal Com. Land, Appendix*, p. 188.

[90] Graham to Lord Stanley, 24 Jan. 1838, in C. S. Parker, *The Life and Letters of Sir James Graham*, 1907, I, 260.

[91] *Standard*, 23 Feb. 1838, quoted in Arvel B. Erickson, *The Public Career of Sir James Graham*, 1952, p. 139. The *Standard's* explanation of the transaction, as being due to the admiration of 'influential electors at Pembroke' for Graham, is absurd. See also T. M. Torrens, *The Life and Times of Sir James Graham*, 1863, II, 132.

[92] Erickson, loc. cit.

[93] The election of 1837 is fully dealt with in Hansard, loc. cit.; see also *Welshman*, 23 July 1841; *Royal Com. Land, Report*, p. 161; ibid., *Appendix*, pp. 124, 188.

[94] *Welshman*, 2 July 1841; 29 Oct. 1841; 22 Nov. 1844. Morris made a very brief speech on Wales (in defence of the magistrates) in the debate on the state of the nation, 28 July 1843; Hansard, Third Series, LXX (1843), 1492.

[95] Ibid., 24 June, 1842.

[96] Ibid., 30 Dec. 1842.

NOTES TO CHAPTER II

[1] T. J. Hogg, *Reports upon Certain Boroughs*, 1838, pp. 5–6.

[2] Sidney Webb, *The Evolution of Local Government* (reprinted 1951), p. 12.

[3] *Y Dysgedydd*, 1836, p. 46.

[4] Pembrokeshire Quarter Sessions Records, 1838, in N.L.W.

[5] Geo. Rice Trevor's notes on Petty Sessional Divisions of Carmarthenshire in H.O. 45/454(3).

[6] The mayor of Cardigan to Home Office, 6 June 1838, H.O. 52/38, complains that there was no resident magistrate except himself; ibid., an alderman of Haverfordwest to Home Office, 11 July 1838, complains of inadequate provision of magistrates.

[7] Col. Owen (lord-lieutenant of Pembrokeshire) to Home Office, 4 Oct. 1843, enclosing a letter from J. T. W. James of Pantsaeson, near Cardigan, with regard to the Fishguard rioting, H.O. 45/454(2); Home Office reply, 6 Oct. 1843, H.O. 41/18; Home Office to duke of Wellington, 6 Oct. 1843, H.O. 41/18.

[8] Home Office to lords-lieutenant, 3 Oct. 1843, H.O. 45/454(2) and 41/18.

[9] Geo. Rice Trevor to Home Office, 5 Oct. 1843, H.O. 45/454(2).

[10] Sir John Walsh (lord-lieutenant of Radnorshire) to Home Office, 8 Oct. 1843, H.O. 45/454(2).

[11] *Report of Select Committee on County Rates in England and Wales*, 1835 (206), xiv, 1.

[12] *Commission of Inquiry for South Wales, Evidence*, 1844, p. 113.

[13] Ibid., loc. cit.; see p. 221 for Cardiganshire, where the valuation was made in 1840 from returns supplied by the overseers of the poor in the various parishes, and was not considered to be accurate.

[14] *Welshman*, 27 Oct. 1843, reporting quarter sessions of 20 Oct.

[15] *Commission of Inquiry for South Wales, Evidence*, 1844, pp. 176, 230.

[16] Article in *Atlas*, reproduced *Welshman*, 18 Aug. 1843.

[17] W. Cozens to Home Office, 17 July 1839, H.O. 40/51.

[18] *Times* articles reproduced in *Welshman*, 4 Aug., 11 Aug., 18 Aug. and 22 Sept. 1843. Lengthy extracts from these articles are given in *Royal Com. Land, Appendices*, pp. 201–5.

[19] E. C. Lloyd Hall to Home Office, 15 June 1843, H.O. 45/454.

[20] Ibid., 20 June, 23 June 1843; see also Aliquis (probably Lloyd Hall) in *Welshman*, 7 July 1843. The *Sun* (quoted ibid., 21 July 1843) speaks of the Welsh magistrates as 'ignorant, conceited, proud, . . . accustomed from infancy to perfect submission'.

[21] Geo. H. Ellis, Report to Home Office, 2 Nov. 1843, H.O. 45/454 B.

[22] *Commission of Inquiry for South Wales, Evidence*, 1844, pp. 125–30, 238, 294.

[23] Ibid., *Report*, p. 33.

[24] Ibid., *Evidence*, p. 80.

[25] The case was that of Peter Jones against William Richards and James Mark Child. The third magistrate (who sat in his own case) was W. B. Swann. *Welshman*, 15 March, 29 March, 5 April, 26 April 1844. Lex, ibid., 10 Nov. 1843, quotes instances of magistrates sitting on cases in which they were themselves interested. He states: 'There is no use looking for justice from magistrates'.

[26] *Commission of Inquiry for South Wales, Evidence*, 1844, p. 71.

[27] Ibid., *Report*, p. 31.

[28] Ibid., *Report*, loc. cit.; *Evidence*, pp. 42, 71, 81–2, 131, 196. See *Table of Fees proposed to be taken by Registrars of Borough Courts of Record*, printed copy in H.O. 52/32, and, also, *Parliamentary Papers* XXXIII (1842), no. 570, for itemised fees.

[29] William Cobbett, *Rural Rides*, II, 153–5.

[30] See Caerfallwch in *Seren Gomer*, July 1831, p. 202, and Sept. 1831, p. 275; also *Welshman*, 13 Dec. 1844.

[31] For game laws, see *Royal Com. Land, Report*, pp. 499, 519.

[32] *Carm. Antiq. Soc. Trans.*, LXVI (1938), 134–5.

[33] H.O. 52/2 has a list of convictions for Monmouthshire from 1815 to 1821; the numbers concerned are surprisingly small. The local newspapers give reports of convictions, e.g. *Carm. Journal*, 11 Jan., 1 Feb., 15 Feb. 1839. Pembrokeshire Quarter Sessions Records (in N.L.W.) give numerous instances, e.g. Midsummer 1839, two cases of a fine of £2 for trespassing in pursuit of game and another of £5 for killing a hare.

[34] *Commission of Inquiry for South Wales, Evidence*, 1844, pp. 55, 274.

[35] For a discussion of the Welsh boroughs see S. and B. Webb, *The Manor and the Borough*, 1908, I, 232–60 (Chapter V, 'The Boroughs of Wales').

[36] *Report of Commissioners on the Boundaries of Boroughs*, 1832, p. 183; Lewis, *Topo. Dict.*, sub. nom. Wiston.

[37] S. and B. Webb, op. cit., p. 257, note.

[38] Edward Laws, *Records of an Ancient Borough Bench*, p. 37. (This work was printed but never published, and I am indebted to Mr. A. L. Leach for letting me see what is probably the only copy, which is now in his possession.)

[39] *Carmarthen Journal*, 22 March 1839.

[40] *Report of Commissioners appointed to inquire into Municipal Corporations*, 1835, Appendix, Vol. I, pp. 401–12.

[41] *Commission of Inquiry for South Wales, Evidence*, 1844, p. 207; *Report*, p. 33. These strictures were discussed at the Pembrokeshire Quarter Sessions, 31 Dec. 1844 (see Minute Book in N.L.W.).

[42] For the duel between William Richards and Henry Mannix see the lengthy correspondence in H.O. 52/43; also 52/41 and 52/47. The subject is dealt with in Edward Laws, loc. cit.; also A. L. Leach in *Tenby Observer*, 5 Oct. 1951, and David Williams, ibid., 20 June 1952. The *Gentleman's Magazine*, 1839, p. 558, erred in stating that Richards was killed.

[43] *Report of the Commissioners appointed to inquire into Municipal Corporations not subject to the Municipal Corporations Act*, 1880.

[44] *Cambrian*, 28 May 1831.

[45] *Report . . . Municipal Corporations*, 1835, I, 307; *Report . . . Municipal Corporations*, 1880, pp. 61–2, also ibid., *Evidence*, II, 703–5, 787–9.

[46] *Report*, 1835, Appendix I, p. 279; *Report*, 1880, p. 53; *Evidence*, II, 772–6.

[47] See J. H. Round, *Family Origins and other Studies*, 1930, pp. 73–102 (an essay on 'the Lords of Kemes').

[48] *Report*, 1835, Appendix I, p. 353; *Report*, 1880, p. 79, *Evidence*, II, 765–71.

[49] *Report*, 1835, Appendix I, p. 377; *Report*, 1880, p. 101, *Evidence*, II, 749–53. For St. Clears see the excellent article: T. I. Jeffreys Jones, 'The Court Leet Presentments of the Town, Borough and Liberty of St. Clears, 1719–1889', *Bulletin of the Board of Celtic Studies*, XIII (1948), 28–53. Lord Cawdor claimed to be the lord of the manor of St. Clears; Cawdor to Charles Hassall, 23 Nov. 1807, Haverfordwest (Eaton Evans and Williams) Deeds (N.L.W.), 331.

[50] *Report*, 1835, Appendix I, p. 317; *Report*, 1880, pp. 70–2, *Evidence*, II, 730–4, 782–6.

[51] *Reports on Education in Wales*, 1847, I, 250.

[52] *Report*, 1835, Appendix I, p. 287; *Report*, 1880, pp. 56–9; *Evidence*, II, 715—30; see also Lewis, *Topo. Dict.*, 1833, sub. nom. Laugharne; *Gentleman's Magazine*, 1839, pp. 18–22, 353–9, 599–602 (an admirable account); M. Curtis, *Antiquities of Laugharne*, 1880.

[53] *Report*, 1835, p. 58, Appendix I, pp. 271–6; *Report*, 1880, pp. 50–3; *Evidence*, II, 687–702; H.O. 45/1811, 'Complaints against the corrupt Corporation of Kidwelly'; David Williams, 'The Borough of Kidwelly in the Nineteenth Century', *Bulletin of the Board of Celtic Studies* (forthcoming). Hugh Williams's strictures on Kidwelly should be read in the light of his remarks at the great Rebecca meeting of 27 Sept. 1843, at Allt Cunedda, nearby: 'Its corporation, composed of stern unflinching farmers and able industrious mechanics, was one of the most independent in the kingdom . . . The corporation had withstood all assaults against its privileges and independence, and he (Hugh

Williams) had so far shared, if not led, in its triumph'; reported in *Welshman*, 29 Sept. 1843.

[54] See the very valuable (anonymous) article, 'The Manor of Elvet', *Carm. Antiq. Soc. Trans.* XVI (1922–23), 27–9; see also Elwyn Davies, 'The Black Mountain', ibid., LXIV (1937), 53–64; Lewis, *Topo. Dict.*, sub nom., Abergwili, Llangadock; Daniel E. Jones, *Hanes Plwyfi Llangeler a Phenboyr*, 1899, pp. 69–78; Evan Davies, *Hanes Plwyf Llangynllo*, 1905, pp. 51–66.

[55] *Report of the Commissioners on the best means of establishing an efficient Constabulary Force in the Counties of England and Wales*, 1839.

[56] *Carm. Antiq. Soc. Trans.* XXI (1927–29), 88.

[57] Ibid., X (1914–15), 55; XVII (1923–24), 7; *Bristol Mercury*, 5 Oct. 1818.

[58] *Reports on Education in Wales*, 1847, I, 284.

[59] T. S. Biddulph (of Amroth Castle) to Home Office, 6 July 1839, H.O. 40/51.

[60] *Carmarthen Journal*, 22 March, 5 April 1839; a highway robbery with violence committed on Lord Cawdor's agent when transporting his lordship's rents from Newcastle Emlyn to Carmarthen, 8 Nov. 1838, punished by fourteen years' transportation.

[61] *Report* (1880), *Evidence*, II, 692, as in note 53 above.

[62] *Report of the Select Committee on Inclosures*, 1844, pp. 94 ff., the very remarkable evidence of Thomas Frankland Lewis.

[63] *Carmarthen Journal*, 22 July 1831. For another case of sheep stealing in the parish of Llanddeusant (twenty-seven sheep and lambs killed), with mutilation of sheep, see *Welshman*, 16 June 1843.

[64] Francis Green, 'Pembrokeshire in By-gone Days', *West Wales Historical Records*, IX (1923), 134.

[65] Anon., 'Wreckage rights of Laugharne Lordship', ibid., IV (1914), 175–6.

[66] *Carmarthen Journal*, 22 Nov. 1828.

[67] J. H. Rees (Cilymaenllwyd) to Home Office, 26 Dec. 1833, H.O. 52/23.

[68] Same to same, 11 Dec. 1840, H.O. 52/47. For particularly disgraceful wrecking in North Wales see the correspondence in H.O. 52/4 (1824), and also *Welshman*, 20 Jan., 10 Feb. 1843; for Glamorgan, see H.O. 52/35 (1837). J. Clark, *South Wales Itinerary*, 1843, p. 42, especially commends Gower as being free from wrecking, 'so detestable a practice with the marauders of the neighbouring coasts'.

[69] *Report on a Constabulary Force*, 1839, pp. 56, ff.

[70] Ibid., p. 44.

[71] I am indebted for much information relating to this practice to Mr. Brinley Rees of the University College, Bangor. See also Jonathan Ceredig Davies, *The Folklore of West and Mid Wales*, 1911. There are detailed descriptions in the *Report on a Constabulary Force* already referred to, and in the Home Office papers cited in the following notes.

[72] E. C. Lloyd Hall to Home Office, 15 June 1843, H.O. 45/454. Aliquis (probably Hall) makes the same statement in a letter to the *Welshman*, 7 July 1843.

[73] Morris Lloyd to Officer Commanding, Brecon, 31 March 1837; same to Home Office, 12 April 1837, H.O. 52/35.

[74] D. Saunders Davies and Walter D. Jones to Home Office, 11 May 1837; petition of nineteen persons to Home Office, same date; C. H. Roberts to Home Office, 16 May 1837; Herbert Vaughan to Home Office, 28 May 1837, all in H.O. 52/35; Cardiganshire Assizes, 1837, 72/1.

[75] Herbert Vaughan to Home Office, 23 Oct. 1838, H.O. 40/40. The farmer was John Jones of Parke.

[76] *Carmarthen Journal*, 22 March 1839, account of Carmarthenshire Spring Assizes. The farmer was David Lewis of Maesycrugiau in that parish.

[77] Home Office to Herbert Vaughan, 16 April 1839 (in answer to a letter of 13 April), H.O. 41/13.

[78] *Carmarthen Journal*, 13 March 1840, account of Pembrokeshire Spring Assizes. The farmer concerned was David Morris of Llanfigan.

[79] *Carm. Antiq. Soc. Trans.*, XII (1917–18), 53.

[80] Home Office to Carmarthen magistrates, 27 Dec. 1837, 3 Jan. 1838, H.O. 43/54; David Davies (the victim) to the Mayor, 25 Nov. 1837, and a statement from the magistrates to the Home Office, H.O. 52/35.

[81] *Carmarthen Journal*, 13 Sept. 1839.

[82] E. C. Lloyd Hall to Home Office, 23 June 1843, H.O. 45/454.

[83] Col. Love to Home Office, 23 Sept. 1844; Geo. Rice Trevor to Home Office (incorporating a full report by the Chief Constable), 26 Sept. 1844; same to same, 13 Oct. 1844, H.O. 45/642; Home Office to Col. Love, 28 Sept. 1844; Home Office to Geo. Rice Trevor, 1 Oct. 1844, H.O. 41/18; Edwin Chadwick, Memorandum on the disturbances in Wales, 11 July 1843, H.O. 45/454. For the carrying of Daniel Williams on a wooden horse through the village of Pill, and through the towns of Milford and Hakin, and depositing him in the village of Pill 'stripped naked from the knees upward', 21 Feb. 1848, see *West Wales Historical Records*, VII (1918), 39.

[84] Admiralty to Home Office, 15 July 1843, enclosing a letter from Sir W. Peel, superintendent of Pembroke Dockyard, H.O. 45/454.

[85] *Report on a Constabulary Force*, 1839, p. 101.

[86] Geo. Rice Trevor to Home Office, 7 Aug. 1843, H.O. 45/454. The figures are given inaccurately in *Welshman*, 4 Aug., 11 Aug. 1843, quoting *Times*.

[87] Home Office to Geo. Rice Trevor, 25 Sept. 1843, H.O. 41/18.

[88] Geo. Rice Trevor to Home Office, 29 Sept. 1843, H.O. 45/454.

[89] *Welshman*, 28 July 1843.

[90] 'The Regulations of the Society for Preventing Felony, instituted this 26th day of December 1785' at Llanddewibrefi, N.L.W., MS. 9142D.

[91] For a similar society see *Rules and Regulations of an Association for the prosecuting of felons adopted at a meeting of the several inhabitants of the Parishes of Llanvrechfa, Lower and Upper, Panteague, Lantarnam and Llanthowy held on 30th Day of April, 1819*, Newport, 1819. For similar societies in England see W. E. Tate, *The Parish Chest*, 1951, pp. 169–71.

[92] John Williams to Lord Clive, 17 Oct. 1838, H.O. 52/38.

[93] David Williams, *John Frost*, 1939, pp. 156–7.

[94] Charles Reith, *A Short History of the British Police*, 1948, p. 81.

[95] Pembrokeshire Quarter Sessions Records (N.L.W.), Midsummer 1839; *Carmarthen Journal*, 5 July 1839.

[96] *Welshman*, 9 April, 6 Aug. 1841.

[97] *Welshman*, 25 Nov. 1842, for the parishes of Abergwili, Llanllawddog, Llanpumsaint, Merthyr and Newchurch; ibid., 16 Dec. 1842 for hundred of Elvet.

[98] *Welshman*, 27 Oct. 1843.

[99] For the establishment of the Carmarthenshire police, see especially *Welshman*, 14 July, 28 July, 15 Sept., 20 Oct., 27 Oct. 1843; Geo. Rice Trevor to Home Office, 25 July, H.O. 45/453; same to same, 4 Sept. and 21 Oct., H.O. 45/454.

[100] For the establishment of the Cardiganshire police, see especially *Welshman*, 3 Nov., 10 Nov., 17 Nov., 15 Dec. 1843, 12 Jan., 26 Jan., 9 Feb., 16 Feb., 12 April, 25 Oct. 1844; Minutes of Quarter Sessions, 17 Oct. 1843 in H.O. 45/642; Thomas Jenkins to Home Office, ibid., 21 Oct. 1843; W. E. Powell to Home Office, 9 Nov. 1843, H.O. 45/454; Col. Love to Home Office, 11 Nov. 1843, H.O. 45/453; Home Office to Powell, 13 Nov. 1843, H.O. 41/18; same to Col. Love, ibid., 14 Nov. 1843; Col. Love to Home Office, 16 Nov. 1843, H.O. 45/453; W. E. Powell to Home Office, 17 Nov. 1843, H.O. 45/454; Home Office to Powell, 21 Nov. 1843, H.O. 41/18; Aberystwyth resolutions *re* rural police (majority and minority), 11 Dec. 1843, H.O. 45/453; Col. Love to Home Office, ibid., 12 Dec. 1843; same to same, 3 Jan. and 7 Jan. 1844, H.O. 45/642; Mathew D. Williams to Home Office, ibid., 30 Jan. 1844; Lord Lisburne to same, ibid., 30 Jan. 1844; magistrates memorial (upper Cardiganshire), ibid., 30 Jan. 1844; Col. Love to Home Office, ibid., 19 Oct. 1844.

[101] For the proposals to establish a rural police in Pembrokeshire, see *Welshman*, 1 Dec. 1843, 2 Feb., 29 March, 12 April 1844; Home Office to Col. Owen, Landshipping, 28 Oct. 1843, H.O. 41/18; Col. Owen to Home Office, 2 Nov. 1843, H.O. 45/454; same to same, 3 Jan. 1844, H.O. 45/642; Home Office to Col. Love, 5 Jan., H.O. 41/18; same to Col. Owen, ibid., 5 Jan.; Col. Owen to Col. Love, 10 April, H.O. 45/642; Col. Owen to Home Office, ibid., 10 April; Col. Love to Home Office, ibid., 12 April; Home Office to Col. Love, 12 April, 15 April, H.O. 41/18.

NOTES TO CHAPTER III

[1] Walter Davies, *General View of the Agriculture and Domestic Economy of South Wales*, 1814, I, 119.

[2] *Royal Com. Land, Report*, pp. 549, 574.

[3] Thomas Lloyd and the Rev. Mr. Turnor, *General View of the Agriculture of the County of Cardigan*, 1794, p. 20. For a list of the 952 freeholders in Cardiganshire in 1760, see J. H. Davies, 'Cardiganshire Freeholders in 1760', *West Wales Historical Records*, III (1912), 73–116.

[4] *Report of the Committee on the Employment of Children in Agriculture*, 1867, III, 53; *Royal Com. Land, Report*, p. 551.

[5] Edward Owen, 'The Abbey of Talley', *Archaeologia Cambrensis*, 1894, pp. 96, 202, 206; *Royal Com. Land, Evidence*, V, 78, 397.

[6] *Report of the Royal Commission on Agriculture, 1882, Wales*, p. 7.

[7] *Royal Com. Land, Report*, p. 558.

[8] Ibid., pp. 564–75.

[9] Ibid., p. 143.

[10] Lloyd and Turnor, op. cit.; Charles Hassall, *General View of the Agriculture of the County of Carmarthen*, 1794; Charles Hassall, *General View of the Agriculture of the County of Pembroke*, 1794.

[11] Walter Davies, *South Wales*, I, 171; see *Royal Com. Land, Report*, p. 278.

[12] On the farm of Ffynnon-wen in the parish of Llangynllo. *Royal Com. Land, Evidence, III*, 402–3.

[13] The farm of Penrhos-fach in the parish of Llanrhystyd, belonging to J. A. P. Lloyd Philipps, of Dale Castle. The mansion referred to is Mabws, inherited from the owner's great-grandmother. Haverfordwest (Eaton Evans and Williams) MS. 397, in N.L.W.

[14] Rees Jones, Pwllfein, *Crwth Dyffryn Clettwr*, 1848, pp. 72–5; quoted in full in *Royal Com. Land, Evidence*, III, 1034.

> Cewch ugain punt bob dimau goch,
> A dwy ŵydd dew o gafnau'r moch,
> A dwy iâr ynyd gribgoch lân,
> A llwyth o lo, i gadw'ch tân.

[15] Walter Davies, *South Wales*, II, 166–7.

[16] Hassall, *Carmarthenshire*, p. 48; *Report on Employment of Children in Agriculture*, 1867, III, 49.

[17] *Royal Com. Land, Evidence*, V, 29.

[18] Ibid., loc. cit.

[19] The farm of Cwm-meurig Uchaf in the parish of Gwnnws. Ibid., III, 676. It does not appear that this was a lease for lives.

[20] *Royal Com. Land, Report*, pp. 151, 387; see also p. 286.

[21] Walter Davies, *General View of the Agriculture of and Domestic Economy of North Wales*, 1813, p. 98.

[22] Id., *South Wales*, 1814, I, 166, 171.

[23] T. Rees, *A Topographical and Historical Description of South Wales* [1815], p. 276.

[24] *Commission of Inquiry for South Wales, Evidence*, 1844, p. 208.

[25] Ibid., p. 106. See, however, the statement of William Chambers, junior, p. 130, that there were 'a great many life leases'.

[26] See especially Cilgwyn MS. 306; see also *Commission of Inquiry for South Wales, Evidence*, p. 208.

[27] Lloyd and Turnor, *Cardiganshire*, p. 17.

[28] Letter dated 12 March 1825 in F. Jones, 'An absentee Landlord, 1824–37', *Carm. Antiq. Soc. Trans.* XXIX (1939), 56–9.

[29] Walter Davies, op. cit., I, 121–2.

[30] *Royal Com. Land, Evidence*, II, 645.

[31] For purposes of comparison, see Thomas Campbell Foster, *Letters on the Condition of the People of Ireland*, 1846. The author was the *Times* representative in South Wales during the Rebecca Riots.

[32] *Royal Com. Land, Report*, p. 293.

[33] Ibid., p. 288.

[34] The altitude of land in West Wales, according to percentage, is as follows:

	Up to 500 ft.	500 ft. to 1,000 ft.	Above 1,000 ft.
Cardiganshire ..	32 per cent	44 per cent	24 per cent
Carmarthenshire ..	52 per cent	38 per cent	10 per cent
Pembrokeshire ..	82 per cent	16 per cent	2 per cent

[35] Anon., *A New Description of All Counties of England and Wales*, 1741, p. 219. (This is the fifth edition; the sixth appeared in 1752. See *Carm. Antiq. Soc. Trans.* XIV (1919–21), 23.)

[36] N.L.W. MS. 687 (dated 1805), pp. 129, 136, 137.

[37] T. Rees, op. cit., p. 273.

[38] Mathew Williams (of Llandeilo), *Speculum Terrarum et Coelorum, neu Ddrych y Ddaear a'r Ffurfafen*, 1826. (See *Carm. Antiq. Soc. Trans.* X (1914–15), 56.)

[39] B. H. Malkin, *The Scenery, Antiquities and Biography of South Wales*, 1807, II, 443.

[40] Frank R. Lewis, 'Wales as a Pioneer of Agriculture', *Western Mail* (Agricultural Supplement), 5 July 1938. For the agricultural societies, see Walter Davies, op. cit., II, 487–99.

[41] Walter Davies, op. cit., II, 494.

[42] Thomas Johnes to Arthur Young, 15 April 1799, in H. M. Vaughan, 'Some Letters of Thomas Johnes of Hafod', *Y Cymmrodor*, XXXV (1925), 201. Its secretary was the Rev. David Turnor, collaborator with Thomas Lloyd of Cilgwyn in 1794 Report.

[43] For an admirable brief discussion of his work see Dafydd Jenkins, *Thomas Johnes o'r Hafod*, 1948. Elizabeth Inglis Jones, *Peacocks in Paradise*, 1950, deals with the same subject.

[44] F. Jones, 'Some Farmers of Bygone Pembrokeshire', *Cymmrodorion Transactions*, 1943–4, p. 143. This article contains valuable information on the whole subject under discussion.

[45] *The Rules, Orders and Premiums of the Society for the encouragement of Agriculture and Manufactures in the County of Carmarthen for the year 1793*, 1793. (In N.L.W.)

[46] Lloyd and Turnor, op. cit., p. 7. Walter Davies, op. cit., II, 363, speaks of a piece of land in this area, which, according to tradition, had borne a hundred crops of barley in a hundred years, and gives his authority. See, also, ibid., pp. 357–8; *Royal Com. Land, Report*, p. 490; Clare Sewell Read, 'On the farming of South Wales', *Journal of the Royal Agricultural Society of England*, X (1849), 122–65.

[47] Arthur Young, *Tours in England and Wales* (reprint), 1932, pp. 1–16.

[48] Charles Hassall, *Carmarthenshire*, p. 40.

[49] Edward Williams (Iolo Morganwg), 'Journal of an Excursion into Carmarthenshire in June 1796', *Carm. Antiq. Soc. Trans.*, XIV (1919–21), 19–22. (MS. in N.L.W. The writer is referring particularly to Brechfa.) For the assistance given by him to Walter Davies, see *Bye-Gones relating to Wales and the Border Counties*, 1892, pp. 258, 280–1, 295, 326.

[50] David Williams, 'The Acreage Returns of 1801 for Wales', *Bulletin of the Board of Celtic Studies*, XIV (1950), 54–68, and 139–54.

[51] K. G. Davies and G. E. Fussell, 'Worcestershire in the Acreage Returns for 1801', *Transactions of the Worcestershire Archaeological Society*, 1950, p. 18, shows that no further returns were called for because these were 'so extremely erroneous as well as defective' (quotation from Minute Book of the Board of Agriculture).

[52] Walter Davies, op. cit., II, 305–83 (section on 'Courses of Crops').

[53] Lewis, *Topo. Dict.*, 1833. (See the general articles on Cardiganshire and Carmarthenshire. The article on Pembrokeshire is more favourable. See also under St. Ishmaels (Carms.) for the Norfolk system.)

[54] Clare Sewell Read, *ut supra*.

[55] William Williams (M.P. for Coventry, a native of Carmarthenshire and the originator of the education commission of 1846) in a speech to the Derllys Agricultural Society, *Welshman*, 5 Nov. 1841.

[56] George Owen, *The Description of Pembrokeshire*, 1892, II, 365–6.

[57] F. J. Fisher, 'The Development of the London Food Market', *Economic History Review*, V (1935), 54.

[58] John Aubrey, *The Natural History of Wiltshire*, 1685, quoted in *Cardiff Naturalists Society Transactions*, LXIV (1931). See G. E. Fussell, 'Pioneer Farming in the late Stuart Age', *Journal of the Royal Agricultural Society of England*, C (1940), 4, who seems to doubt the accuracy of this statement.

[59] Francis Jones, 'The Mathry Tithe Suit', *Journal of the Historical Society of the Church in Wales*, II (1950), 100.

[60] Lloyd and Turnor, *Cardiganshire*, p. 11; Hassall, *Pembrokeshire*, p. 17.

[61] David Williams, op. cit., pp. 149–50. The incumbent was the rector of Burton in south Pembrokeshire.

[62] Walter Davies, op. cit., I, 519.

[63] Clare Sewell Read, *ut supra*.

[64] Walter Davies, op. cit., I, 505. Compare Thomas Pennant, *Tours in Wales*, 1883, I, 22; III, 405, for North Wales.

[65] Lloyd and Turnor, *Cardiganshire*, pp. 28, 31; Arthur Aikin, *Journal of a Tour through North Wales*, 1797, p. 49, says of the Rheidol Valley: 'Much ground has lately been broken up for the culture of potatoes'.

[66] Walter Davies, loc. cit.

[67] W. H. R. Curtler, *A Short History of English Agriculture*, 1909, p. 277. See Hubert Hall, 'The Foreign Aspect of Welsh Records', *Y Cymmrodor*, XXII (1910), 21, for reference to documentary material relating to Wales.

[68] Lloyd and Turnor, *Cardiganshire*, p. 30.

[69] *Commission of Inquiry for South Wales, Evidence*, 1844, p. 339.

[70] Hassall, *Pembrokeshire*, p. 18.

[71] Walter Davies, op. cit., I, 187–201.

[72] Clare Sewell Read, *ut supra*.

[73] Walter Davies, op. cit., I, 439–45. It is not clear when they were introduced.

[74] *Commission of Inquiry for South Wales, Evidence*, 1844, p. 295. See also Lewis, *Topo. Dict.*, article on Cardiganshire.

[75] George Owen, op. cit., I, 70–1.

[76] Walter Davies, op. cit., II, 169.

[77] Arthur Young, op. cit., p. 5.

[78] Ibid., p. 8.

[79] Francis Green, 'Dewisland Coasters in 1751', *West Wales Historical Records*, VIII (1919–20), 159. See also Lewis, *Topo. Dict.*, sub. Llandysilio Gogo, Solva.

[80] *Royal Com. Land, Report*, p. 604.

[81] See Lewis, *Topo. Dict.*, articles: Pembrokeshire, Cardiganshire, Carmarthenshire, Ludchurch, Narberth, Carew, Llandebie, Llangadock, Llangathen, Llangendeirn, Llanfihangel Aberbythic, Lampeter Velfrey, Lamphey, Lawrenny, Roboston Wathen.

[82] William Day's report on the state of South Wales, 9 July 1843, H.O. 45/1611.

[83] *Commission of Inquiry for South Wales, Evidence*, 1844, p. 30.

[84] A correspondent in *Welshman*, 26 April 1844, describes this as a well-known fact.

[85] Lloyd and Turnor, *Cardiganshire*, pp. 8, 34; Walter Davies, op. cit., II, 212; Lewis., *Topo. Dict*, article on Cardiganshire.

[86] 'A'i drwyn fewn llathen at gynffon llo', Ab Owen, *Gwaith Glan y Gors*, 1905, t. 51.

[87] As in note 85.

[88] *Commission of Inquiry for South Wales, Evidence*, 1844, p. 381.

[89] Lewis, *Topo. Dict.*, loc. cit.

[90] Elwyn Davies, 'Seasonal movements of Sheep in Wales', *Journal of the Manchester Geographical Society*, 1935; 'Sheep Farming in Upland Wales', *Geography*, 1935; 'The Patterns of Transhumance in Europe', ibid., 1941.

[91] Hassall, *Pembrokeshire*, p. 20; cf. J. H. Clapham, *An Economic History of Modern Britain*, 1926, I, 26. See Lewis, *Topo. Dict.*, article on Carmarthenshire, for intermixture.

[92] Walter Davies, op. cit., II, 482.

[93] Young, op. cit., p. 2.

[94] List of Crown Manors in Wales, *Parl. Accounts and Papers*, XXXV, 1837. (Crown rights in Pembrokeshire seem to have been confined to the land of the ancient lordship of Pembroke.)

[95] Crosswood Deeds and Documents, II, 1068, folio 11.

[96] *Royal Com. Land, Report*, p. 198.

[97] Letter in *Welshman*, 15 Nov. 1844.

[98] *Report on Commons Inclosure*, 1844, p. 96. Evidence of Sir Thomas Frankland Lewis.

[99] Return of copies of all Surveys and Valuations of Land belonging to the Crown adjoining the Hafod estate in Cardiganshire, *Parl. Accounts and Papers*, XLV, 1845. See also *Royal Com. Land, Report*, pp. 201–2.

[100] *Report on Commons Inclosure*, p. 109.

[101] See R. Flenley (ed.), *A Calendar of the Register of the Council of Wales*, 1916, pp. 105–7, 112–3, 121.

[102] Lewis, *Topo. Dict.*, article on Pembrokeshire.

[103] *Welshman*, 6 Dec. 1844.

[104] *Report on Commons Inclosure*, pp. 205, 333.

[105] Ibid., p. 212.

[106] Ibid., p. 100.

[107] Ibid., loc. cit., p. 143. See Chapter II, note 62, above.

[108] Ibid., p. 100, case brought in 1842 before Thomas Frankland Lewis. See ibid., p. 137, for fear of retaliation.

[109] Returns of writs of intrusion and other process issued since 1 Jan. 1820, *Parl. Accounts and Papers*, XLIII, 1836; F. Green, 'Fishguard Manor', *West Wales Historical Records*, VIII (1919–20), 20. Fenton, the historian, died in Nov. 1821. The purchase was made by Mr. Hamlet of Cavendish Square on 20 Nov. 1823 for £1,100. The riot occurred on 27 and 30 Aug. 1824.

[110] See *Parl. Accounts and Papers*, XLIII, 1836, *ut supra*, for all sales since 1 Jan. 1820. See also Cambrensis, *A Letter to the Chancellor of the Exchequer on the Abuses stated in the Petition of Landowners and others connected with the Principality of Wales*, 1838, especially pp. 48–9.

[111] See the very important set of documents printed in Schedule of Papers of Sale by the Crown to Mr. James Watt, *Parl. Accounts and Papers*, XXX, 1839. See also *Report on Commons Inclosure*, 96–9; *Royal Com. Land, Report*, 591. It was denied on behalf of Watt that he had oppressed encroachers; only three were actually ejected. For another enclosure dispute at Rhayader, see *Report of Commissioners on the best means of establishing an efficient Constabulary Force in the Counties of England and Wales*, XIX, 1839, p. 45.

[112] Bronwydd MS. 3955, letter dated 20 Oct. 1833, and case for opinion of Counsel, 24 Jan. 1834 (kindly drawn to my attention by Dr. B. G. Charles).

[113] *Report on Commons Inclosure*, p. 96.

[114] *Royal Com. Land, Evidence*, V, 393.

[115] *Seren Gomer*, 1818, pp. 280, 343.

[116] *Report on Commons Inclosure*, p. 228.

[117] Ibid., p. 211.

[118] Ibid., loc. cit.

[119] Ibid., p. 220.

[120] *Welshman*, 28 July 1843, evidence of John Jones against William, Henry and Mathew Morgan. The informer's wife attributed his action to revenge.

[121] *Welshman*, 29 Dec. 1843.

[122] Assize Indictments, P.R.O. 71/8, 1845. Bronwydd MS. 6814, 14 June 1843, relates to objection to encroachment by commoners. The statement in *Royal Com. Land, Report*, p. 577: 'No instance has come to our notice of any commoner or tenant farmer (as such) taking active steps against the builder of a tŷ un-nos' is strange.

[123] Walter Davies, op. cit., I, 221. Clapham, op. cit., I, 26, accepts this statement at its face value.

[124] Richard Fenton, *A Historical Tour through Pembrokeshire*, 1811, pp. 305–6.

[125] For a list of acts, see Ivor Bowen, *The Great Enclosures of Common Lands in Wales*, 1914; Enclosure Acts since 1800, *Parl. Accounts and Papers*, XLVIII, 1843.

[126] *Report on Commons Inclosure*, p. 222; *Report of Commissioners appointed to inquire into Municipal Corporations not subject to the Municipal Corporations Act*, 1880, II, 693.

[127] For particulars relating to this Act see Pembrokeshire Quarter Sessions Records (N.L.W.), Letters to Clerk of Peace, 1836–8; also *Carmarthen Journal*, 10 July 1840.

[128] *Parl. Accounts and Papers*, XLVIII, 1843, as above. (Cards., 22,165 acres; Carms., 32,255 acres; Pembs., 10,773 acres.)

[129] *Report on Commons Inclosure*, p. 102.

[130] Walter Davies, op. cit., II, 87.

[131] *Report on Commons Inclosure*, p. 208. The extent of the enclosure was only 83 acres.

[132] Ibid., pp. 209, 269. The acreage was 1,962.

[133] Ibid., pp. 335–8, 435–40; *Royal Com. Land, Evidence*, III, 823–30, 1043–52; ibid., *Report*, pp. 221–5; ibid., *Appendices*, pp. 455–6; John Lloyd, *The Great Forest of Brecknock*, 1905.

[134] The Cwmgwili MSS. have a letter, 28 March 1789, relating to an enclosure riot at Carmarthen, *Carm. Antiq. Soc. Trans.*, XXVI (1935–36), 65. In Nov. 1826, a riot at Cwrt Henry (Carmarthenshire) was caused by the closing of pathways, *Seren Gomer*, 1827, pp. 31, 81. Neither of these, nor the Fishguard riot noticed above, was the result of an act of parliament.

[135] *Seren Gomer*, 1820, p. 191; *Royal Com. Land, Evidence*, p. 186. Haverfordwest (Williams and Williams) Deeds and Documents, 27159, gives details of this enclosure, but I have been unable to find any further reference to the riot.

[136] David Williams, ' "Rhyfel y Sais Bach", An Enclosure Riot on Mynydd Bach', *Ceredigion*, II (1952), 39–52.

[137] Ivor Bowen, op. cit., p. 41.

[138] The letter of David Gower, carpenter, Graig Capel, Pembrey, 13 Dec. 1843, *Welshman*, 22 Dec. 1843. The style makes me think that the letter was written by Hugh Williams.

[139] *Commission of Inquiry for South Wales, Evidence*, pp. 76, 224.

[140] The numbers employed in 1841 in the three shires (including the boroughs) were:

	Cards.	Carms.	Pembs.
Bootmakers	675	1,344	1,054
Tailors	582	839	759

[141] For 'customer weavers' in Wales, see J. H. Clapham, op. cit., pp. 160–1; also Young, op. cit., p. 14.

[142] *Royal Com. Land, Report*, p. 46; Anon. (Sir D. Lleufer Thomas), *Memorandum on the Woollen Industries of Wales*, n.d. (about 1900).

[143] *Report of the Commission on the Boundaries of Boroughs*, 1832, p. 149.

[144] *Census Abstract of Answers and Returns*, 1821, p. 477.

[145] Lewis, *Topo. Dict.*, sub Cardiganshire.

[146] *Reports on Education in Wales*, 1847, I, 431; the change in taste was the introduction of 'Jim Crow' hats.

[147] Ibid., loc. cit.

[148] *Report of the Commissioners into Municipal Corporations*, 1835, I, 234, quoting Crompton and Jarvis, *Exchequer Reports*, 1830–2, p. 587; *Carmarthen Journal*, 18 March 1831.

[149] W. Matthews, *The Miscellaneous Companions*, 1786, I, 210; Malkin, op. cit. (1807), II, 298; Fenton, op. cit. (1811), p. 224; Walter Davies, op. cit. (1814), II, 447; James Dugdale, *British Traveller*, 1814, p. 718; 'Christopher Cobbe-Webbe', *Haverfordwest and its Story*, 1882, p. 165.

[150] T. A. Welton, 'On the distribution of population in England and Wales, 1801–1891', *Journal of the Royal Statistical Society*, LXIII (1900), 546.

[161] *Universal British Directory of Trade*, n.d. (probably 1794); Pigot and Company, *National and Commercial Directories*, 1829; *Welshman*, 14 and 21 Oct. 1842, for Irish Mail.

[162] Welton, loc. cit.; S. and B. Webb, *The Manor and the Borough*, 1908, I, 258.

[153] The story of the curate of St. Mary's, Haverfordwest, who preached one of Spurgeon's sermons without editing it, telling his congregation: 'This night thousands of young men and women are walking the streets of this great metropolis', if not authentic is *ben trovato*.

[154] *Report of the Commissioners on the Boundaries of Boroughs*, 1832, p. 149.

[155] Ibid., p. 167.

[156] Lewis, *Topo. Dict.*, sub nom.

[157] Messrs. Taylor and Co., *Welshman*, 21 Jan. 1842.

[158] J. E. Lloyd (ed.), *History of Carmarthenshire*, 1939, II, 325, 331.

[159] Malkin, op. cit., II, 166; Lewis, *Topo. Dict.*, sub nom. Manerdivy.

NOTES TO CHAPTER IV

[1] For the subject in general see J. H. Marshall, 'The Population of England and Wales from the Industrial Revolution to the World War', *Economic History Review*, V (1935), 65–78.

[2] David Williams, 'A note on the Population of Wales, 1536–1801', *Bulletin of the Board of Celtic Studies*, VIII (1937), 359–63, analyses the figures available.

[3] The census tables for the three shires are as follows:

	Acreage	Estimated population in			
		1750	1801	1811	1821
Cardiganshire ..	440,746	32,000	42,956	50,260	57,784
Carmarthenshire ..	588,472	62,000	67,317	77,217	90,239
Pembrokeshire ..	395,446	44,800	56,280	60,615	73,788

	Acreage	Estimated population in			
		1831	1841	1851	—
Cardiganshire ..	440,746	64,780	68,766	70,796	—
Carmarthenshire ..	588,472	100,740	106,326	110,632	—
Pembrokeshire ..	395,446	81,425	88,044	94,140	—

[4] Census Abstract of Answers and Returns, 1841: Cardiganshire, p. 411; Carmarthenshire, p. 415; Pembrokeshire, p. 450. See *Royal Com. Land, Report*, p. 52; David Williams, 'Some Figures relating to Emigration from Wales', *Bulletin of the Board of Celtic Studies*, VII (1935), 396–415.

[5] Census, 1851, Population Tables, Welsh Division, pp. 26–40.

[6] *Royal Com. Land, Evidence*, III, 66.

[7] For purposes of comparison, see the very remarkable study of the subject in K. H. Connell, *The Population of Ireland*, 1950.

[8] Dr. Perrot Williams, in *Philosophical Transactions* of 1722, quoted, Connell, op. cit., p. 211. Lady Mary Wortley Montagu had drawn attention to the practice in Turkey only five years previously, in 1717.

[9] *Commission of Inquiry for South Wales, Evidence*, p. 234.

[10] Advertisement in *Welshman*, 4 March 1842: 'Medical Apprentice Wanted. Wanted, by a medical man in extensive practice at Cardigan, a respectable and well-educated youth as an apprentice'.

[11] Census, Occupations, 1851. These figures show a decrease in Cardiganshire and Carmarthenshire, as compared with 1841 (Cardiganshire 49; Carmarthenshire 64; Pembrokeshire 48).

[12] E.g. at Laugharne, *Carmarthen Journal*, 10 Jan. 1840.

[13] *Commission of Inquiry for South Wales, Evidence*, p. 107.

[14] The census figures for 1841 are as follows:

	Male	Female
Cardiganshire ..	32,215	36,551
Carmarthenshire ..	50,676	55,650
Pembrokeshire ..	40,250	47,794

[15] It should be pointed out that the percentage of early marriages was, nevertheless, low as compared with rural England. Percentage of persons marrying in the three years ending 30 June 1841 who were under 21 years of age: Women—South Wales 8·07 per cent; North Wales 7·89 per cent; Bedfordshire 25·19 per cent; Men—South Wales 2·85 per cent; North Wales 3·16 per cent; Bedfordshire 11·86 per cent. *Fourth Annual Report of the Registrar General of Births, Marriages and Deaths*, XIX, 1842.

[16] John Ballinger, 'Local History from a Printer's File', *Welsh Wales Historical Records*, X (1924), 164–70. B. H. Malkin, *The Scenery, Antiquities and Biography of South Wales*, 1807, II, 40, seems to confirm that the practice was confined to West Wales. In addition to the references in Ballinger, see *Education Reports*, 1847, I, 8, 217, 284, 422; *Royal Com. Land, Evidence*, III, 1035; ibid., *Appendices*, p. 201.

[17] See R. N. Salaman, *The History and Social Influence of the Potato*, 1949; (especially Chapter XXII, 'The Potato in Wales'); Connell, op. cit.; id., 'The History of the Potato', *Economic History Review*, III (1951), 388–95.

[18] Walter Davies, op. cit., I, 504–6, 509.

[19] Connell and Salaman, loc. cit.

[20] G. I. Lewis, An investigation of changes in population density and distribution, together with changes in agricultural practice, in Pembrokeshire during the period 1831–1931. (An unpublished dissertation submitted for the M.A. degree of the University of Birmingham in 1937; a very remarkable study.)

[21] *Royal Com. Land, Evidence*, II, 1028–9, 1031.

[22] Thomas John Masleni, A sketch of a tour and of Scenery in Wales, N.L.W., MS. 65.

[23] Catherine Sinclair, *Hill and Valley, or Wales and the Welsh*, 1839, p. 264.

[24] T. Cullum, unpublished tour in South Wales (1811), N.L.W., MS. 5446; Walter Davies, op. cit., I, 144; Lewis, *Topo. Dict.*, articles on Cardiganshire, Carmarthenshire and Pembrokeshire.

[25] *Royal Com. Land, Report*, p. 294.

[26] Cullum, loc. cit.

[27] *Reports on Education in Wales*, 1847, I, 243–4; *Report on Employment of Children in Agriculture*, 1867, III, 48.

[28] Young, op. cit., p. 2.

[29] Cullum, loc. cit.

[30] Captain Jenkin Jones's Diary, N.L.W., MS. 785, printed in *West Wales Hist. Records*, I (1911), 125–6.

[31] *Commission of Inquiry for South Wales, Evidence*, p. 113.

[32] Ibid., p. 234.

[33] *Reports on Education in Wales*, 1847, I, 217.

[34] Thomas Jones, C.H., *Rhymney Memories*, 1938, p. 92; *Report on Employment of Children in Agriculture*, 1867, III, 47; *Royal Commission on Labour, The Agricultural Labourer*, 1894, II, 47 (report by Lleufer Thomas).

[35] Anon. MS. tour (1801), N.L.W. MS. 1340.

[36] Ibid.; *Report on Employment of Children in Agriculture*, 1867, III, 47.

[37] *Reports on Education in Wales*, 1847, I, 241.

[38] Evan Davies, *Hanes Plwyf Llangynllo*, 1905, p. 33 (extract from parish register dated 17 May 1848).

[39] Malkin, op. cit., II, 32; *Reports on Education in Wales*, 1847, I, 229 (the evidence of the vicar of Llandeilo); *Royal Com. Land, Report*, p. 611.

[40] *Report on Employment of Children in Agriculture*, 1867, III, 53.

[41] Malkin, op. cit., II, 469.

[42] Ibid., II, 240.

[43] Lewis, *Topo. Dict.*, sub nom. Carmarthen. (The Act was 32 Geo. III, c. civ.)

[44] Ibid., sub nom. Aberystwyth.

[45] *Copies of Bye Laws made in several Municipal Boroughs under the Act, 5 and 6 William IV, c. 76*, 1836.

[46] *Reports on Education in Wales*, 1847, II, 56, 147.

[47] H.O. 45/1811, 'Complaints against the corrupt Corporation of Kidwelly'.

[48] Sir Christopher Sykes, unpublished journal, 1796, N.L.W., MS. 2258; G. Lipscomb, *Journey into South Wales*, 1802, pp. 111–2, 181; *Report of Special Assistant Poor Law Commissioner on Employment of Women and Children in Agriculture*, 1843, p. 3; *Report on Employment of Children in Agriculture*, 1867, III, 40–1, 51.

[49] N.L.W., MS. 1340 (1801); N.L.W., MS. 6716 (1828), both anonymous.

[50] Sykes and Lipscom, as above; *Commission of Inquiry for South Wales, Evidence*, p. 239.

[51] Henry Owen (ed.), *The Description of Pembrokeshire by George Owen of Henllys*, 1892, p. 43.

[52] Young, op. cit., p. 2; contrast pp. 5, 9, 14, 19.

[53] Thomas Campbell Foster, *Letters on the Condition of the people of Ireland*, p. 478.

[54] Walter Davies, op. cit., II, 291.

[55] *Commission of Inquiry for South Wales, Evidence*, p. 293.

[56] Ibid., p. 239; see also *Royal Com. Land, Evidence*, II, 567; ibid., *Report*, p. 633.

[57] *Report on Employment of Children in Agriculture*, 1867, III, 14, 38–9, 52, (quoting *Sixth Report of Medical Officer of Health to Privy Council*, 1864).

[58] Clare Sewell Read, loc. cit.

[59] List given in *Carm. Antiq. Soc. Trans.*, XXII (1930), 61.

[60] *Reports on Education in Wales*, 1847, I, 21, 237, 282.

[61] See lengthy memorandum on teetotalism by Thomas Yates, incorporated in Edwin Chadwick, Memorandum on Disturbances in Wales, 11 July 1843, H.O. 45/454.

[62] *Reports on Education in Wales*, 1847, II, 162.

[63] *Commission of Inquiry for South Wales, Evidence*, p. 360.

[64] *Reports on Education in Wales*, 1847, I. 234.

[65] *Royal Commission on Agriculture, Wales*, 1882, p. 6. Total number of farms—Cards. 5,897, Carms. 8,264, Pembs. 5,999; under fifty acres—Cards. 3,973, Carms. 5,120, Pembs. 4,222. Percentage under fifty acres—65 per cent.

[66] Article in *Morning Herald*, reproduced in *Welshman*, 22 Dec. 1843.

[67] *Report on the Employment of Children in Agriculture*, 1867, III, 16, 49.

[68] Walter Davies, op. cit., I,162.

[69] Isaiah, V, 8.

[70] David Williams, 'The Acreage Returns of 1801 for Wales', *Bulletin of the Board of Celtic Studies*, XIV (1950–51), 54–68, 139–54.

[71] *Y Diwygiwr*, 1840, p. 239.

[72] See above, Chapter II, note 75.

[73] *Commission of Inquiry for South Wales, Evidence*, p. 110. Two such letters are reproduced in H. Tobit Evans, *Rebecca and her Daughters*, 1910, pp. 198–9.

[74] At Cwm Ifor, 20 July 1843, and Pen Das Eithin, 30 Oct. 1843.

[75] Crosswood Deeds and Documents, II, 676, 678.

[76] Ffynnone, 20 per cent from Michaelmas 1816, *Seren Gomer*, 1821, p. 60; Falcondale, 25 per cent, ibid., 1822, p. 69; Llysnewydd, 40 to 50 per cent, ibid, 1823, p. 120. For the period of rioting see, e.g., *Welshman*, 11 Aug. 1843, reduction of 20 per cent on Cawdor estates. Instances are too numerous to detail.

[77] William Day to George Cornewall Lewis, 9 July 1843, H.O. 45/1611; Menippus in *Welshman*, 28 July 1843.

[78] Detailed figures are given in B.M. Add. MSS. 40,597 (Peel Correspondence) from which the following are drawn:

	Cards.	Carms.	Pembs.
Gross rental, 1814–15 ..	£126,399	£240,714	£181,057
,, ,, 1842–43 ..	£159,949	£315,761	£266,865

[79] *Royal Com. Land, Report*, p. 372.

[80] *Welshman*, 11 Aug., 8 Sept. 1843, reproducing *Times* articles.

[81] *Efangylydd*, 1832, p. 222–4.

[82] *Royal Com. Land, Evidence*, III, 405.

[83] *Welshman*, 3 Feb. 1843; see a previous letter, ibid., 30 Dec. 1842.

[84] J. Lloyd Davies to Home Office, 17 June 1843, H.O. 45/454.

[85] In translation in G. R. Trevor to Home Office, 23 Sept. 1843, H.O. 45/454, and in *Welshman*, 29 Sept. 1843.

[86] Census figures for 1851 reproduced in *Royal Com. Land, Appendices*, pp. 276–8. See also A. W. Ashby and Ifor L. Evans, *The Agriculture of Wales and Monmouthshire*, 1944, p. 85.

	Cards.	Carms.	Pembs.
Farmers	4,551	4,042	2,464
Farmers' sons, brothers, etc. ..	2,529	2,223	1,185
Labourers	5,885	6,190	5,604

[87] Francis Green, 'Pembrokeshire in By-gone Days', *West Wales Historical Records*, IX (1920–23), 105.

[88] Ibid.; *Carm. Antiq. Soc. Trans.*, VIII (1912–13), 27–32; *Royal Com. Land, Evidence*, III, 1,035.

[89] See the table of wages from 1784 to 1850 in ibid., V, 31.

[90] Ibid., loc. cit., and III, 403.

[91] Ibid., III, 1,035 (account book of Ffynnon-wen, in the parish of Llangynllo, Cards., 1809).

[92] The Pembrokeshire hiring fairs were as follows: Maenclochog, 16 Sept.; Llanboidy, 18 Sept.; Henfeddau (near Llanfyrnach), 27 Sept. and 27 Oct.; St. Davids, first Tuesday in Oct.; Haverfordwest, 5 Oct.; Fishguard, 8 and 9 Oct.; Pembroke, 10 and 29 Oct.; Mathry, 11 Oct.; Herbrandston, 12 Oct.; Little Haven, 1 Nov.; *Royal Commission on Labour*, 1893, II, 61.

[93] See the very remarkable evidence of Miss Gwenllian Morgan, in *Royal Com. Land, Evidence*, III, 797–80.

[94] Ibid., *Appendices*, pp. 72–3.

[95] *Royal Commission on Labour*, loc. cit.

[96] Ibid., p. 181; W. D. Jones to Home Office, Aug. 1843, H.O. 45/454.

[97] *Commission of Inquiry for South Wales, Evidence*, p. 446; *Report on Employment of Children in Agriculture*, 1867, III, 37, 108; *Royal Commission on Labour*, II, 32; *Royal Com. Land, Evidence*, III, 65; ibid., *Report*, pp. 611, 639.

[98] *Report on Employment of Children in Agriculture*, 1867, III, 39–40.

[99] Lloyd and Turnor, *Cardiganshire*, p. 14; Hassall, *Carmarthenshire*, p. 24; Hassall, *Pembrokeshire*, p. 25.

[100] Walter Davies, op. cit., II, 284.

[101] Cullum, loc. cit.

[102] These figures are admirably tabulated in *Royal Com. Land, Appendices*, pp. 47–51.

[103] *Commission of Inquiry for South Wales, Evidence*, p. 239.

[104] *Report of Commissioners on Employment of Children in Mines, Appendix*, 1842, II, 704, 706.

[105] W. O. Henderson, 'Trade Cycles in the Nineteenth Century', *History*, XVIII (1933), 147–53; M. Dorothy George, *England in Transition*, 1931.

[106] J. H. Davies, 'A Bibliography of Welsh Ballads printed in the Eighteenth Century', *Cymmrodorion Transactions*, 1906–7, Nos. 520, 523 (1762, drought); No. 332 (1782, wet); No. 651 (1799, wet).

[107] *Welshman*, 10 Dec. 1841, has an analysis of the weather, year by year, for each summer from 1816 to 1841.

[108] Ibid., loc. cit.

[109] C. E. P. Brooks, 'Historical Climatology of England and Wales', *Journal of the Meteorological Society*, 1928, p. 315.

[110] *Commission of Inquiry for South Wales, Evidence*, p. 135.

[111] *Welshman*, loc. cit.

[112] Ibid., loc. cit.

[113] 20 Sept., 23 Sept. 1818, diary in *Carm. Antiq. Soc. Trans.* XX (1926–27), 11–12.

[114] For prices, see Young, op. cit., pp. 2, 9, 15 (1776); diary of David Davies, Llechdwni, *Carm. Antiq. Soc. Trans.* XXVI (1935–36), 60–2 (1792); Hassall, *Carms.*, p. 45, *Pembs.*, p. 29 (1794); Theophilus Jones, *Letters*, 1905, p. 129 (1796); *Royal Com. Land, Appendices*, p. 89 (1797); *Carm. Antiq. Soc. Trans.* VII (1911–12), 74 (1802); *Cambrian*, 11 Feb. 1804; *Carm. Antiq. Soc. Trans.* XXII (1930), 35–7 (1815); *Royal Com. Land, Evidence*, III, 403 (1832); ibid., p. 98 (about 1840); ibid., p. 759 (table for various dates, 1757 to 1891); and weekly in newspapers.

[115] J. Evans, *Tour through South Wales*, 1804, p. 280.

[116] *Royal Com. Land, Appendices*, p. 23, digest of 'Replies as to Agricultural Distress, 1816'.

[117] Ibid., p. 24.

[118] Ibid., p. 26, digest of 'Report of Select Committee on Agriculture, 1821'.

[119] Ibid., p. 25, digest of 'Report of Committee on petitions complaining of Agricultural Distress, 1820'.

[120] For this subject see F. Green, 'Early Banks in West Wales', *West Wales Historical Records*, VI (1916), 129–64.

[121] *Royal Com. Land, Appendices*, p. 22, digest of 'Replies as to Agricultural Distress, 1816'.

[122] For this, see *National Library of Wales Journal*, III (1943), p. 35.

[123] Green, op. cit., p. 137.

[124] Ibid., p. 158; Return of Country Banks bankrupt since Jan. 1816, *H. of C. Accounts and Papers*, XXII, 1826.

[125] *H. of C. Report on Bank of England Charter*, 1831–32, Appendix 101, gives figures of bankruptcies from 1780 to 1830, showing that thirty-seven became bankrupt in 1825 and forty-three in 1826.

[126] Green, op. cit., p. 161.

[127] Anon. ('Christopher Cobbe-Webbe, Gentleman'), *Haverfordwest and its Story*, 1882, p. 138.

[128] Green, op. cit., p. 150; W. Spurrell, *Carmarthen and its Neighbourhood*, 1879, p. 142.

[129] *Commission of Inquiry for South Wales, Evidence*, p. 280.

[130] Green, op. cit., p. 152.

[131] Managers of Haverfordwest Savings Bank to Home Office, 4 March 1826, H.O. 40/19 (asks for advice in consequence of the failure of Phillips's bank).

[132] Brechfa Turnpike Trust Minute Book, folio 80, under date 26 April 1832. The trust lost £86 17s. 3d. through the failure of Messrs. Waters, Jones and Co. (see also folio 113).

[133] L. W. Dillwyn, Diary (N.L.W.), under date 16 Feb. 1826.

[134] William Day to George Cornewall Lewis, 9 July 1843, H.O. 45/1611.

[135] A letter from William Augustus Miles (dated Dec. 1837) in *Journal of the Royal Statistical Society*, I (1839), 105–6.

[136] For this aspect of emigration, see G. D. Owen, 'The Poor Law System in Carmarthenshire', *Cymmrodorion Transactions*, 1941, p. 77; T. I. Jeffreys Jones, 'The Parish Vestries and the Problem of Poverty', *Bulletin of the Board of Celtic Studies*, XIV (1951), 228; *Carm. Antiq. Soc. Trans.*, III (1907–8), 63; D. E. Jones, *Hanes Plwyfi Llangeler a Phenboyr*, 1899, pp. 354–5.

[137] *Welshman*, 15 April 1842.

[138] *Carmarthen Journal*, 5 June 1840.

[139] Ibid., 20 March 1840; see also ibid., 5 April 1839, and J. Ballinger, 'Local History from a Printer's File', *West Wales Historical Records*, IX (1920–3), 212–3.

[140] *Welshman*, 19 March 1841, 21 May 1841, 29 April 1842.

[141] *Carmarthen Journal*, 5 June 1840.

[142] Henderson, op. cit., p. 150.

[143] *Commission of Inquiry for South Wales, Evidence*, pp. 5, 55, 187, 204, 219, 234, 295–6, 309, 444, 462.

[144] Ibid., p. 187.

[145] *Welshman*, 30 Sept. 1842; W. Day to G. C. Lewis, 9 July 1843, H.O. 45/1611.

[146] Prize essay in *Atlas* on causes of prevailing distress, summarised in *Welshman*, 24 May 1844.

[147] *Welshman*, 8 Oct. 1841.

[148] Ibid., 3 Feb., 24 Feb. 1843; *Diwygiwr*, 1843, pp. 347–8.

[149] *Welshman*, 23 June 1843.

[150] Edwin Chadwick, Memorandum on the disturbances in Wales, 11 July 1843, H.O. 45/454 (in his own hand). Characteristically Chadwick attributed the failure of Messrs. Harford and Davies (Ebbw Vale Company) to the payment of excessive wages. Col. Love to Home Office, 26 Aug. 1843; H.O. 45/453. See also *Ninth Annual Report of the Poor Law Commissioners*, XXI, 1843.

[151] Ibid., loc. cit.

[152] W. Day to G. C. Lewis, 9 July 1843, H.O. 45/1611.

[153] *Commission of Inquiry for South Wales, Evidence*, p. 204.

[154] Tenby MS. on the Rebecca Riots.

[155] W. Day, as above.

[156] *Diwygiwr*, loc. cit.; Geo. Rice Trevor to Home Office, 11 July 1843, H.O. 45/454.

[157] *Welshman*, 23 Dec. 1842.

[158] *Commission of Inquiry for South Wales, Evidence*, p. 281.

[159] E. C. Lloyd Hall to Home Office, 23 July 1843, H.O. 45/454.

[160] *Welshman*, 1 Sept. 1843.

NOTES TO CHAPTER V

[1] *Times*, 28 June 1843, quoted *Royal Com. Land, Appendices*, p. 201. (Cf. *Times*, 18 Aug. 1843, quoted ibid., p. 202: 'It is difficult to stuff the head of the Welsh farmer, who speaks and reads only Welsh, with the political crotchets of Chartism.')

[2] *Reports on Education in Wales*, 1847, I, 287, the evidence of the Rev. David Lloyd, classical tutor at the Presbyterian Academy, Carmarthen.

³ For the traditional story of a coachload of Oxford scholars, who had become lost in the lanes of Cardiganshire, receiving replies to their enquiries from roadmen in Latin, Greek and Hebrew, see A. T. Fryer, 'Edward Richard of Ystrad Meurig', *West Wales Historical Records*, VIII (1919–20), 67.

⁴ Lewis, *Topo. Dict.*, sub nom. Llandowror, Llanddewi Velfrey, St. Mary's (i.e. Maenclochog), and Newport. The figures given are twenty-nine in South Wales and nine in North Wales. *Commission of Inquiry for South Wales, Evidence*, p. 102, gives number as thirty-three in South Wales, and states that they circulated every three years. See also *Reports on Education in Wales*, 1847, I, 11–12.

⁵ Ibid., I, 32.

⁶ Ibid., I, 425, at Cater's Hook.

⁷ It should be noted that Pembrokeshire parishes are smaller and more numerous than those of Carmarthenshire.

⁸ Ibid., I, 217.

⁹ Sir Thomas Phillips, *Wales, the Language, Social Condition, Moral Character, and Religious Opinions of the People, considered in their relation to Education*, 1849, pp. 353–66.

¹⁰ *Parliamentary Paper*, 1839 (3), XXX, 469, gives the number of stamps issued for three years ending 5 Jan. 1839, and the advertisement duty paid. See also *Carm. Journal*, 1 March 1839, *Cambrian*, 17 Aug. 1839, *Welshman*, 5 March 1841, 3 June 1842, 20 Jan. 1843, for return of stamps issued at various dates. Newspapers (e.g. *Welshman*, loc. cit.) accused each other of applying for more stamps than was necessary in order to give a false impression of the extent of their circulation.

¹¹ *Carm. Antiq. Soc. Trans.*, XXI (1927–29), 20; XXII (1930), 28. Strangely enough, Palmer ended his life as H.M. Treasurer in Dominica, in the Leeward Islands.

¹² Ibid., XI (1916–17), 9–10; *Shrewsbury Chronicle*, 1 Dec. 1837.

¹³ *Reports on Education in Wales*, 1847, I, 43, 50; II, 12.

¹⁴ Ibid., I, 3–4.

¹⁵ Anon. to Home Office, received 4 Oct. 1843, H.O. 45/454.

¹⁶ *Census of Great Britain, 1851. Religious Worship, England and Wales, Report and Tables*, 1853, pp. 122–5. The percentage has been calculated by taking all the worshippers at all the services enumerated in the three shires. For an analysis on a different basis, see Henry Richard, *Letters and Essays on Wales*, 1884, pp. 16–25.

¹⁷ *Welshman*, 22 Feb. 1844. Population of parish of St. Peter's in 1841, 9,526 persons; seating accommodation at St. Peter's, at Llan-llwch (outside the town) and at St. David's (consecrated only on 3 Feb. 1841), 2,262.

¹⁸ For a remarkable character sketch of Brutus, see *Red Dragon*, III (1883), 385–405.

¹⁹ *Efangylydd*, 1830, p. 96; 1831, pp. 257, 319; 1832, p. 223.

²⁰ Ibid., 1833, p. 317.

²¹ For the subject matter of this paragraph, see R. Ifor Parry, 'Cefndir Gwleidyddol yr Annibynwyr Cymraeg', *Y Cofiadur*, XIX (1949), 3–19.

²² *Seren Gomer*, 1833, pp. 187–9.

²³ See, e.g., W. E. Tate, *The Parish Chest*, 1951, pp. 23–4.

[24] For Ebenezer Morris see Arthur Mee, *Llanelly Parish Church*, 1888, and John Innes, *Old Llanelly*, 1902. He was the great-grandfather of C. A. H. Green, second Archbishop of Wales.

[25] *Cambrian*, 28 July 1832.

[26] For a full account see *Shrewsbury Chronicle*, 4 Jan. 1839; *Carmarthen Journal*, 1 Feb. 1839.

[27] *Carnarvonshire and Denbigh Herald*, 29 Dec. 1838.

[28] *Carmarthen Journal*, 1 March, 3 May 1839. Hansard, 3rd series, XLVII (1839), 522–48, which concerns this affair, states the costs were under £30.

[29] Hansard, loc. cit.

[30] John Jones, M.P., and Rees Goring Thomas attended the vicar's second wedding, *Carmarthen Journal*, 29 Nov. 1839.

[31] *Cambrian*, 8 June 1839.

[32] Ibid., 29 June 1839; *Carmarthen Journal*, 28 June 1839.

[33] Ibid., 29 Nov., 6 Dec., 20 Dec. 1839.

[34] *Welshman*, 1 Jan. 1841.

[35] *Carmarthen Journal*, 1 May 1840.

[36] *Welshman*, 19 May, 21 July, 15 Sept. 1843.

[37] As at Meidrim; *Welshman*, 28 May 1841.

[38] Ibid., 12 Feb. 1841, 4 Feb. 1842, 9 Aug. 1844.

[39] Ibid., 19 Feb. 1841.

[40] *Carmarthen Journal*, 8 Nov. 1839.

[41] *Welshman*, 27 Jan. 1843; *Commission of Inquiry for South Wales, Evidence*, p. 204. See ibid., p. 215, for another case.

[42] Arvel B. Erickson, *The Public Career of Sir James Graham*, 1952, p. 135, quoting Hansard, 3rd series, XXXVIII, 1031.

[43] Walter Davies, *North Wales*, 1813, p. 96, strongly denies this. It should be noted that he was himself a rector.

[44] *Commission of Inquiry for South Wales, Report*, p. 37; see Erasmus Saunders, *A View of the State of Religion in the Diocese of St. David's*, 1721 (reprinted 1949), pp. 63–73.

[45] *Carmarthen Journal*, 4 Oct. 1839; 28 Feb. 1840.

[46] Advertisements of livings of Aber-nant, Conwil, Conwil Elfed, and of Hayscastle, *Welshman*, 10 Dec. 1841.

[47] *Carmarthen Journal*, 6 March 1840.

[48] *Welshman*, 24 Feb. 1843.

[49] Ibid., 15 Sept. 1843.

[50] Ibid., 8 Sept. 1843; Lewis, *Topo. Dict.*, sub nom. Llangendeirn.

[51] *Welshman*, 15 Sept. 1843; ibid., 27 Oct. 1843, reproducing *Times* article; ibid., 5 April 1844, which quotes William Williams, M.P., that he had verified the accuracy of the statement.

[52] Ibid., 27 May 1842.

[53] Ibid., 4 Aug. 1843. See also *Commission of Inquiry for South Wales, Report*, p. 26.

[54] Letter dated 1828 in J. Innes, *Old Llanelly*, 1902, p. 142.

[55] William Chambers, junior, to Rees Goring Thomas, 2 Sept. 1843, *Carmarthen Antiquary*, I (1943–44), 21.

[56] *Commission of Inquiry for South Wales, Evidence*, p. 360 (evidence of sole woman witness).

[57] Francis Jones, 'The Mathry Tithe Suit', *Journal of the Hist. Soc. of Church in Wales*, II (1950), 97–102.

[58] Haverfordwest (Williams and Williams) Deeds and Documents, 15,400; for tithe of milk see Tate, op. cit., p. 136.

[59] *Commission of Inquiry for South Wales, Evidence*, pp. 254, 256, 259.

[60] Haverfordwest (Williams and Williams) Deeds and Documents, 15,396.

[61] Charles Hassall, *Pembrokeshire*, 1794, p. 43.

[62] 1 and 2 William IV, c. 50. An Act for extinguishing Tithes, and customary Payments in lieu of Tithes, within the Parish of Llanelly, in the county of Carmarthen, and for making Compensation in lieu thereof; see *Commons Journals*, LXXXVI (1831), 568. Resolution of parishioners of Llanelly, 17 Aug. 1843, *Carmarthen Antiquary*, I (1943–44), 26; R. Goring Thomas to William Chambers, junior, 23 Aug. 1843, ibid., p. 27; same to same, ibid., p. 32. *Welshman*, 15 Dec. 1843; *Commission of Inquiry for South Wales, Evidence*, pp. 129, 356; J. L. Bowen, *The History of Llanelly*, 1886, p. 32.

[63] Arvel B. Erickson, op. cit., p. 130, quoting Hansard, 3rd series, XXIX, 926.

[64] Home Office to lords-lieutenant, 15 Sept. 1843, H.O. 45/454.

[65] E.g. E. C. Lloyd Hall, *Commission of Inquiry for South Wales, Evidence*, p. 241; J. Lloyd Davies, M.P., ibid., p. 6.

[66] Ibid., p. 210.

[67] *Times* article reproduced *Welshman*, 27 Oct. 1843.

[68] Tithe Commissioners' Report, reproduced *Welshman*, 31 March 1843.

[69] *Times* article, reproduced *Welshman*, 27 Oct. 1843.

[70] *Welshman*, 29 Dec. 1843.

[71] Tithe Commissioners' Report, reproduced *Welshman*, 10 May 1844. See also Home Office to lords-lieutenant, as above.

[72] *Welshman*, 29 Dec. 1843.

[73] *Commission of Inquiry for South Wales, Report*, p. 26.

[74] Ibid., pp. 58, 225, 235–7, 248–53; William Day to G. C. Lewis, 9 July 1843, H.O. 45/1611; N.L.W., MS. 3294E (the Rebecca letter).

[75] *Commission of Inquiry for South Wales, Evidence*, pp. 75–6, 148–9; *Welshman*, 1 Sept., 1 Dec., 8 Dec., 15 Dec. 1843.

[76] *Welshman*, 6 Oct., 17 Nov. 1843.

[77] Ibid., 25 Aug. 1843.

[78] *Commission of Inquiry for South Wales, Evidence*, p. 280.

[79] Ibid., p. 281.

[80] For West Wales, see Geraint Dyfnallt Owen, 'The Poor Law System in Carmarthenshire during the eighteenth and early nineteenth centuries', *Cymmrodorion Transactions*, 1941, 71–86; T. I. Jeffreys Jones, 'The Parish Vestries and the Problem of Poverty, 1783–1833', *Bulletin of the Board of Celtic Studies*, XIV (1951), 222–35.

[81] Tate, op. cit., p. 21. For tables of expenditure on poor relief in the three shires from 1750 onwards, see *Parliamentary Accounts and Papers*, XL, 1846, and XLV, 1849.

[82] S. and B. Webb, *English Poor Law History, Part II, The Last Hundred Years*, 1927, pp. 40, 43, 102, 105.

83 S. E. Finer, *The Life and Times of Sir Edwin Chadwick*, 1952. Finer's method is to prejudice the issue by introducing a derogatory epithet every time Lewis's name is mentioned: 'that little-known pompous mediocrity', 'that very dull man', 'pontifical, unctuous, mediocre', 'disdainful', 'Pecksniff-like', 'mixture of Polonius and Pecksniff', 'self-opinionated, vain, long-winded', 'tired old man, crushed down by the burden of popular hatred'.

84 See numerous extracts from him in Walter Davies, op. cit.; also his evidence in *Report on Commons Inclosure*, quoted earlier.

85 He figured in the Andover Enquiry in 1846. Sir George Nicholls (one of the three Poor Law Commissioners) said of him: 'a very good man; he is a Welshman and a very good specimen of the Principality'; *Report of Select Committee on the Andover Union*, 1846, p. 1150. His assistant was David Jones.

86 Dillwyn Diaries (N.L.W.), 9 May 1834.

87 Quoted by H. L. Beales, 'The New Poor Law', *History*, XV (1931), 311; for the same opinion see Report of Edward Senior, in Report on public opinion, submitted by the Poor Law Commissioners to Lord John Russell, 28 Dec. 1838, H.O. 73/54.

88 *Royal Com. Land, Appendices*, p. 378.

89 *Carmarthen Journal*, 1 March 1839; *Welshman*, 5 March 1841.

90 This general impression is gained from reading the papers in H.O. 73/54.

91 *Commission of Inquiry for South Wales*, p. 233. See ibid., p. 285, for payment of guardians. The guardians of the Carmarthen union elected in 1843 comprised twenty farmers, one butcher, two innkeepers, one printer, one banker, one merchant, six gentlemen; *Welshman*, 31 March 1843.

92 William Day to Lefevre, 15 Aug. 1839, H.O. 45/1611; *Tenth Annual Report of Poor Law Commissioners*, 1844; William Day in *Report of Select Committee on Andover Union*, 1846, p. 1,254.

93 Report of Edward Senior as in note 87. The guardians of Tregaron union unanimously resolved that the building of a workhouse was not necessary, *Carm. Journal*, 22 March 1839.

94 Home Office to J. S. Biddulph, Amroth Castle, 24 Jan. 1839, H.O. 43/56, offers reward of £50 and implies that the Guardians offered another £50; same to same, 31 Jan., raises reward to £100. See also Poor Law Commissioners to Home Office, 26 Jan. 1839, H.O. 73/55. *Carmarthen Journal*, 1 Feb., 8 Feb. 1839, states that the Guardians offered £100, the directors of the Norwich Fire Office £50, and the Home Office £150.

95 *Seventh Annual Report of the Poor Law Commissioners*, 1841, p. 251.

96 *Parliamentary Accounts and Papers*, XLVIII, 1843.

97 The information in this paragraph is extracted from *Second Annual Report of the Poor Law Commissioners*, 1836.

98 Report on public opinion, as in note 87; see William Day to Geo. Cornewall Lewis, 9 July 1843, H.O. 45/1611, for opinion that objections came from ratepayers not from paupers.

99 *Parliamentary Accounts and Papers*, XLV, 1843.

100 William Day, *An Inquiry into the Poor Laws and Surplus Labour*, 1833.

101 Duties of Assistant Poor Law Commissioners, 10 June, 1840, H.O. 73/56.

102 J. Jarvis, postmaster of Welshpool, to Lt.-Col. Moberly (of the Post Office), 27 April 1837, H.O. 52/35.

[103] *Parl. Accounts and Papers*, XLV, 1849, give figures. See, however, *Welshman*, 28 April 1843, for a reduction in Carmarthen union from an average of £14,566 before the union was formed to £12,785 in 1842–43.

[104] *Tenth Annual Report of Poor Law Commissioners*, 1844, pp. 21–5.

[105] *Commission of Inquiry for South Wales, Evidence*, pp. 227, 279.

[106] Ibid., pp. 134, 448–52; see also instructions as in note 101 above.

[107] Both Cardigan and Aberaeron unions were in debt to the extent of nearly £1,000 in Sept. 1843: G. W. Griffith, chairman, Cardigan union to Chadwick, 9 Sept. 1843, H.O. 45/454; Robert Weale, Assistant Poor Law Commissioner, to Sir Edmund Head, ibid., 14 Sept. 1843; Home Office to Poor Law Commissioners, ibid., 20 Sept. 1843; Home Office to Col. Powell, 25 Sept. 1843, H.O. 41/18.

[108] *Commission of Inquiry for South Wales, Evidence*, pp. 106–7, 463; *Times* articles reproduced in *Welshman*, 4 Aug., 11 Aug. 1843.

[109] Orders of Poor Law Commission, Carmarthen Union, 24 Jan. 1839, H.O. 73/55.

[110] *Carm. Journal*, 28 June 1839; *Cambrian*, 6 July 1839.

[111] William Day to Poor Law Commission, 22 Jan. 1844, printed in William Day, *Correspondence with the Poor Law Commissioners*, 1844, appendix.

[112] *Welshman*, 26 Jan. 1844.

[113] *Y Diwygiwr*, 1843, p. 223.

[114] *Welshman*, 1 Dec. 1843.

[115] Sir James Graham in House of Commons, 10 Feb. 1844; debate reported in *Welshman*, 16 Feb. 1844.

[116] *Reports on Education in Wales*, 1847, I, 237; the vicars of Llandisilio, ibid., p. 254, and of Bleddfa, ibid., II, 61, were of the same opinion, but I can find no others in South Wales. Symons, ibid., II, 57, reports '(The want of chastity) is also said to be much increased by night prayer-meetings and the intercourse which ensues in returning home', but Lingen makes no such comment.

[117] For England, see Tate, op. cit., pp. 213–4.

[118] Albert Leffingwell, *Illegitimacy, A Study in Morals*, 1892; *Report of Royal Commission on Labour*, 1893, p. 40 (by Daniel Lleufer Thomas).

[119] *Report of Commission for enquiring into Poor Laws*, 1834, p. 350.

[120] *Seren Gomer*, 1843, pp. 230–1.

[121] *Commission of Inquiry for South Wales, Report*, p. 30, *Evidence*, pp. 56, 80, 81, 103, 115, 149, 150, 166, 177, 203, 212, 229, 243, 277, 331, 348.

[122] Debate in House of Commons as in note 115 above; also *Welshman*, 1 March 1844.

[123] *Tenth Annual Report of the Poor Law Commissioners*, 1844, produced after the Rebecca Riots had taken place.

[124] *Welshman*, 28 July, 18 Aug. 1843, for an old man who had formerly been a prosperous farmer. *Commission of Inquiry for South Wales, Evidence*, p. 350.

[125] William Day, *Correspondence with the Poor Law Commissioners*, 1844; see also the evidence of Sir Richard Philipps, *Commission of Inquiry for South Wales, Evidence*, p. 154.

[126] Ibid., pp. 272, 342.

[127] *Times* article reproduced *Welshman*, 30 June 1843.

[128] *Commission of Inquiry for South Wales, Evidence*, p. 219. Day also makes this point: W. Day to Geo. Cornewall Lewis, 9 July 1843, H.O.45/1 611.

[129] T. C. Foster, *Letters on the Condition of the People of Ireland*, 1846, p. 478.

[130] *Commission of Inquiry for South Wales, Evidence*, p. 234.

[131] Ibid., p. 343.

[132] William Day to Poor Law Commissioners, 22 Jan. 1844, in William Day, *Andover Union, Extracts from the Report*, 1847; also *Report of Select Committee on Andover Union*, 1846, p. 1,237.

[133] *Reports on Education in Wales*, I, 290, is severe on that of Carmarthen workhouse, but favourably notices that of Narberth workhouse.

[134] William Day, *A Letter to Lord Viscount Courtenay*, 1847.

[135] Geo. Rice Trevor to Home Office, 4 July 1843, H.O. 45/454.

[136] *Welshman*, 4 Aug., 11 Aug., 1 Sept., 8 Sept., 17 Nov. 1843.

[137] Edwin Chadwick, Report on Disturbances in Wales, 11 July 1843, H.O. 45/454.

[138] Memorandum on state of South Wales submitted by William Day to Geo. Cornewall Lewis, 9 July 1843, H.O. 45/1611 (nine foolscap pages in small handwriting).

[139] The affair is dealt with in S. E. Finer, op. cit., pp. 253–5, but Finer seems to have missed the large dossier, 'The Dismissal of Mr. Day', H.O. 45/1611. See also William Day, *Correspondence with Poor Law Commissioners*, 1844; ibid., *A Letter to Lord Viscount Courtenay*, 1847; ibid., *Andover Union. Extracts from the Report*, 1847; also *Report of the Select Committee on the Andover Union*, 1846.

[140] *Cambrian*, 15 Nov. 1839. This subject is more fully dealt with in my *John Frost. A Study in Chartism*, 1939.

[141] *The Garthe Estate. Particulars of Sale*, 13 Oct. 1869, copy in my possession through the courtesy of Caleb Rees, Esq., H.M.I.

[142] An acquaintance of his youth, Edward Davies, Dolcaradog (who is admittedly unreliable) records Hugh Williams as saying: 'Who would have thought that the old devil would live so long?' Edward Davies to (Sir) Daniel Lleufer Thomas, 13 March 1896 (in my possession). See also a twenty-nine paged MS. by Edward Davies entitled 'Who was Rebecca?', 15 Jan. 1901, N.L.W., MS. 2114C. This is printed in *Welsh Gazette*, 24 Jan. 1901. See also ibid., 15 Nov., 22 Nov., 6 Dec., 13 Dec., 20 Dec. 1900, 3 Jan., 31 Jan. 1901.

[143] An illegitimate child, Eleanor Margaret Anne, daughter of Mary Jenkins, born 16 Nov. 1847, was baptised on 1 July 1849, her father being given as Hugh Williams, Gardde, Solicitor. Parish Register of St. Clears, through the courtesy of the vicar. Williams was known locally as 'Hugh Williams of the hundred bastards' (information from his grandson).

[144] W. J. Linton, *Memories*, 1895, p. 91.

[145] Sir James Graham to Sir Robert Peel, 25 June 1843, B.M. Add. MS. 40,448, folio 363.

[146] Linton, op. cit. See *Y Bywgraffiadur Cymreig*, 1953, sub nom. Thomas Powell.

[147] Lovett Collection in Birmingham Public Library, I, 48.

[148] Ibid., I, 250; *Carm. Journal*, 21 Sept. 1838.

[149] *Silurian*, 19 Jan. 1839.

[150] Place Collection in British Museum, set 56, V, 135.

[151] *Silurian*, 16 Feb. 1839. See also *Charter*, 24 Feb. 1839 (meetings at Narberth, Llanfihangel Abercowin, etc.). For Chartism in West Wales, see Home Office to W. Melvin, 4 May 1839, H.O. 41/13 (Aberystwyth); J. R. L.

Lloyd to Home Office, 8 May 1839, H.O. 40/46 (Adpar); J. H. Allen to Home Office, 18 July 1839, H.O. 40/51 (Narberth); W. B. Swann to Lord Dynevor, 20 July 1839, H.O. 40/51 (two Birmingham Chartists reported in the neighbourhood of Efailwen); Magistrates at Narberth to Home Office, 1 Aug. 1839, H.O. 40/51 (the outbreak not due to Chartist meetings); *Carm. Journal*, 21 Nov. 1839 (Chartists at Cenarth 'nine to ten months previously').

[152] F. Povey, Welshpool, to Robert Hartwell, at National Convention, 19 July 1839, B.M. Add. MSS. 34,245 B. 49. Williams acted as solicitor instructing the counsel, Yardley; Edward Hamer, *A Brief Account of the Chartist Outbreak at Llanidloes*, 1867, p. 29.

[153] Hugh Williams, *National Songs and Poetical Pieces*, 1839 (but published in 1840), p. 59, and as a broadsheet; *Monmouthshire Merlin*, 9 Nov. 1839.

[154] *Welshman*, 5 Nov., 19 Nov. 1841.

[155] *Y Diwygiwr*, 1838, p. 372.

[156] *Welshman*, 29 Jan., 5 Feb., 12 Feb. 1841.

[157] Col. Love to Home Office, 26 July 1843, H.O. 45/453. See same to same, ibid., 20 July, for arrival of discharged men from Merthyr in Cardigan neighbourhood. Lloyd Hall to Home Office, 21 June 1843, H.O. 45/454, speaks of workmen coming home in hundreds from ironworks.

[158] *Commission of Inquiry for South Wales, Evidence*, p. 74.

[159] *Reports on Education in Wales*, 1847, II, 90; Jellinger Cookson Symons, *Rough Types of English Life*, 1860, p. 27.

[160] Harriet Martineau, *A History of the Peace*, 1858, pp. 636–8.

[161] *English Chartist Circular*, No. 18.

[162] *The Poor Man's Guardian*, 2 Sept., 9 Sept., 16 Sept. 1843. I have to thank Dr. Caradog Morris for drawing my attention to this.

[163] Letter from a Pembrey collier in *Welshman*, 28 July 1843.

[164] Report of Chartist meeting, 2 July 1843, H.O. 45/453.

[165] Ibid., Col. Love to Home Office, 6 July 1843.

[166] Ibid., report of Chartist meeting, 6 Aug. 1843.

[167] Ibid., report of Chartist meeting, 19 Aug. 1843.

[168] Home Office to Col. Love, 19 Sept. 1843, H.O. 79/4.

[169] Ibid., Home Office to Postmaster-General, 18 Sept. 1843. The order was cancelled on 6 Oct.

[170] Reports of Chartist meetings, 24 Sept., 25 Sept. 1843, H.O. 45/453.

[171] Ibid., report of Chartist meeting 2 Sept. 1843 (this is certainly a mistake for 2 Oct.).

[172] Ibid., Col. Love to Home Office, 8 Oct. 1843.

[173] Ibid., reports of Chartist meetings, 29 Oct., 30 Oct. 1843.

[174] Ibid., reports of Chartist meetings, 5 Nov. 1843, and an undated meeting, the report of which was enclosed in Col. Love to Home Office, 18 Nov. 1843.

[175] Lord Bute to Home Office, 5 Nov. 1843, H.O. 45/454.

[176] Undated report, as in note 174, and copy of letters left at levels enclosed in Col. Love to Home Office, 21 Nov. 1843, H.O. 45/453.

[177] R. Ifor Parry, 'Yr Annibynwyr Cymraeg a Threth yr Ŷd', *Cofiadur*, XIX (1949), 20–61.

[178] *Carm. Journal*, 25 Dec. 1840; *Welshman*, 8 Jan. 1841.

[179] Ibid., 14 Oct. 1842.

[180] Ibid., 21 Oct. 1842.

[181] Ibid., 19 May 1843.

[182] *Seren Gomer*, 1842, p. 59; *Y Diwygiwr*, 1843, pp. 93–4.

[183] Col. Love to Home Office, 6 Jan. 1846, H.O. 45/1431.

[184] Home Office to Postmaster-General, 19 Aug. 1842, H.O. 79/4, cancelled 25 Aug.

[185] Home Office to Col. Love, 10 Jan. 1844, H.O. 41/18, in reply to Col. Love to Home Office, 7 Jan. 1844, H.O. 45/642 (which is endorsed with the reply in Sir James Graham's own handwriting).

[186] *Welshman*, 7 April, 21 April, 5 May, 26 May 1843.

[187] *Yr Amserau*, 20 Sept. 1843; *Y Cronicl*, 1843, p. 96.

[188] Owen Thomas a J. Machreth Rees, *Cofiant y Parch. John Thomas*, 1898, pp. 96–7; R. T. Jenkins, *Hanes Cymru yn y Bedwaredd Ganrif ar Bymtheg*, 1933, p. 140.

[189] *Welshman*, 29 Sept. 1843.

[190] D. Tyssil Evans, *The Life and Ministry of the Rev. Caleb Morris*, 1902, p. 245.

[191] Christina Phelps, *The Anglo-American Peace Movement*, 1930, pp. 83–4.

[192] *Y Diwygiwr*, 1843, pp. 63–4, 223, 288, 379; *Yr Haul*, 1843, 252, 319.

[193] *Welshman*, 4 Aug., 11 Aug., 18 Aug., 29 Sept. 1843, quoting *Times*.

[194] Blackwood's and anon., *A Journey in the Disturbed Districts*, quoted *Welshman*, 10 Nov., 8 Dec. 1843.

[195] William Spurrell, *Carmarthen and its Neighbourhood*, 1879, p. 148.

[196] John Connop Thirlwall, *Connop Thirlwall*, 1936, pp. 136, 140–2.

[197] *Welshman*, 6 Oct. 1843.

[198] Ibid., 3 Nov., 24 Nov. 1843.

[199] Ibid., 19 April 1844. I have not been able to trace Walter Anthony the Socialist. (The father of Hugh Williams's second wife was named Peter Anthony.)

[200] Walter Davies, *South Wales*, II, 466.

[201] See Arthur Mee (ed.), *Carmarthenshire Notes*, I (1889), 18 ff.

[202] Pembrokeshire Quarter Sessions Records, Easter 1843, has the composition of the Loyal Welsh Lodge of Freemasons, No. 525 (at Pembroke Dock), namely eight shipwrights, two surgeons, two solicitors, two clerks, together with a sergeant of the Royal Artillery, a printer, a jeweller, an engineer, a mercer, a druggist, an agent, a tailor, a cashier and a baker. The lodge was required to make a declaration under an act (39 George III) for the suppression of societies established for seditious and treasonable practices. For the revival of Freemasonry in Pembrokeshire, see *Carmarthen Journal*, 3 Feb., 11 Dec. 1840; *Welshman*, 7 Jan. 1842; for Carmarthenshire, see Spurrell, op. cit., p. 136; *Carm. Antiq. Soc. Trans.*, VI (1910–11), 52–3; W. Davies, *Llandilo Vawr and its Neighbourhood*, 1858, p. 21.

[203] *Welshman*, 4 June 1841.

[204] *Welshman*, 2 July 1841.

[205] *Carmarthen Journal*, 20 Feb. 1840.

[206] Arvel B. Erickson, *The Public Career of Sir James Graham*, 1952, p. 173.

[207] R. T. Jenkins, *Hanes Cymru yn y Bedwaredd Ganrif ar Bymtheg*, 1933, p. 125.

[208] *Carm. Antiq. Soc. Trans.*, IV (1908–9), 11.

[209] *Reports on Education in Wales*, 1847, I, 473.

[210] *Carmarthen Antiquary*, loc. cit., document 40; *Welshman*, 22 Sept. 1843.

[211] Ibid., 29 Sept. 1843.

[212] Ibid., 22 Dec. 1843; meeting of 4 Dec.

NOTES TO CHAPTER VI

[1] See E. A. Pratt, *A History of Inland Transport and Communication in England*, 1912; S. and B. Webb, *The Story of the King's Highway*, 1913; W. T. Jackman, *The Development of Transport in Modern England*, 1916.

[2] William Rees, *South Wales and the March, 1284–1415*, 1924, p. 236.

[3] For numerous cases of indictment, see Haverfordwest MSS. 19476, 27402–14, in N.L.W.

[4] John Ogilby, *Britannia*, (1675), gives the coastal route, and not the Brecon route, as the main road to St. David's.

[5] Jackman, op. cit., p. 61.

[6] Ibid., p. 70.

[7] Ibid., loc. cit., Pratt, op. cit., pp. 78–80; Mark Searle, *Turnpikes and Tollbars*, n.d., p. 773.

[8] For a discussion of turnpike acts, see S. and B. Webb, op. cit., chapter VII.

[9] *Commons Journal*, XXIX (1761–64), 409, 444, 448, 452, 528.

[10] 3 Geo. III c. 34 (P.R.O., C 65/767). Turnpike acts are listed as Public Acts. Up to 37 Geo. III these are numbered in Arabic numerals. After this year, Public Acts are divided into Public General Acts, with an Arabic numeral, and Public Local Acts, which include turnpike acts, with a Roman numeral. There are printed copies of all the Main Turnpike Trust Acts, namely: 3 Geo. III c. 34; 24 Geo. III c. 33; 43 Geo. III c. xxx; 52 Geo. III c. cli; 9 Geo. IV c. lxxvi; 3 Wm. IV c. xlv, in the Carmarthen County Hall, and of the original act in N.L.W.

[11] *Commons Journal*, XXX (1765–66), pp. 117, 162, 202; 5 Geo. III c. 76 (P.R.O., C 65/800); printed copy in Carmarthen County Hall. The renewal act, 19 Geo. III c. 103, refers to the Kidwelly district only. This was renewed 42 Geo. III c. lvi; 5 Geo. IV c. ii (printed copy in N.L.W.); and 1 Wm. IV c. lxv. The renewal act 26 Geo. III c. 150 refers to the Llandeilo district only. This was renewed 47 Geo. III c. lxxxix and 9 Geo. IV c. lxxxi.

[12] 10 Geo. III c. 55 (P.R.O., C 65/887). This was renewed by 31 Geo. III c. 97; 52 Geo. III c. xl; 3–4 Wm. IV c. xxxvii; 5–6 Wm. IV c. xxi. Printed copies of 10 Geo. III, 31 Geo. III and 3–4 Wm. IV in N.L.W. The Order Book of the Aberystwyth District from the start is in N.L.W. The first meeting of the trust was held on 4 May 1770. At the next meeting parishes were asked to supply lists of inhabitants liable to statute duty, distinguishing those who kept a team of horses. In 1771 there were already five adjournments, presumably because of insufficient attendance.

[13] *Commons Journal*, XXXIII (1770–72), 130, 274; 11 Geo. III c. 116 (P.R.O., C 65/919). Its original name was the Pembrokeshire Trust, and it was called the Tavernspite Trust only from 1809 onwards. A MS. 'Interest Account with Subscribers to the Pembrokeshire Turnpike Trust', 2 vols., is among the Pembrokeshire Records in N.L.W. This act was renewed 30 Geo. III c. 91; 48 Geo. III c. cxxxix; 9 Geo. IV c. cvi (printed copies of last two in N.L.W.).

[14] *Commons Journal*, XXXIV (1772–74), 91, 222, 224, 300, 304, 305, 309, 344; 13 Geo. III c. lll.

[15] Walter Davies, *South Wales*, II, 392; Lewis, *Topo. Dict.*, sub nom. Llandovery; J. F. Jones, 'Some Fords and Bridges near Llandovery', *Carm. Antiq. Soc. Trans.*, LXII (1936), 46–8; *History of Carmarthenshire*, II, 356. The bridge

is called the Dolauhirion Bridge, and is now scheduled as an Ancient Monument.

[16] *Commons Journal*, XLIII (1788), 158, 355; 28 Geo. III c. 102. This was renewed 48 Geo. III c. cxiv and 11 Geo. IV c. xxxv.

[17] *Commons Journal*, XLVI (1791), 231; 31 Geo. III c. 109. This was renewed 48 Geo. III c. cxlvii; 10 Geo. IV c. cxxxiv.

[18] *Commons Journal*, XLI (1786), 606; petition from the parishes of Conwil Gaio, Llansawel, Llan-y-crwys, Llanybyther and Talley. No one, however, appeared in the house of commons to support this petition.

[19] *Commons Journal*, XXXVII (1778–80), 58; 19 Geo. III c. 102. Renewed 35 Geo. III c. 143; 53 Geo. III c. lxiv; 1 Wm. IV c. lix. This is sometimes called the Llandovery and Llangadog Trust and sometimes the Llandeilo and Llangadog Trust. (Printed copy of 53 Geo. III c. lxiv in N.L.W.)

[20] *Commons Journal*, XXXIX (1783–84), 928; 24 Geo. III c. 66. Printed copy in Carmarthen County Hall. The Llandeilo Rwnws Order Book is in Carmarthen County Hall. The bridge is called Llandilo yr Ynys on the Ordnance Survey Map.

[21] Geo. H. Ellis to Home Office, 2 Nov. 1843, H.O. 45/454 B. *Commission of Inquiry for South Wales, Report*, p. 5, *Evidence*, p. 45. The principal talley-holders were John Vaughan of Golden Grove and Thomas Jones, father of John Jones. In time John Jones acquired all the tallies.

[22] It derived its name from the ancient commotes of Kidwelly, Iscennen and Carnwyllon.

[23] *Commons Journal*, XLVII (1792), 512, 567, 722, 735, 744; 32 Geo. III c. 156. Renewed 41 Geo. III c. y; 51 Geo. III c. xii; 52 Geo. III c. clii; 2 Wm. IV c. cii. Printed copies of all acts in Carmarthen County Hall; also of 32 Geo. III c. 156 in Cardiff Public Library, and of 32 Geo. III c. 156 and 41 Geo. III c. v in N.L.W.

[24] *Commission of Inquiry for South Wales, Evidence*, p. 46.

[25] *Commons Journal*, LXIV (1809), 98; 49 Geo. III c. lxxxvii; renewed 11 Geo. IV c. xxvii.

[26] *Commons Journal*, LXXXV (1830), 61, 120.

[27] Ibid., XLVI (1791), 174, 191; (the witness examined by the committee of the house of commons was Charles Hassall); 31 Geo. III c. 102; renewed 51 Geo. III c. lxv; 2–3 Wm. IV c. liv.

[28] *Commons Journal*, XLIII (1788), 186; 28 Geo. III c. 109; renewed 49 Geo. III c. cxlvi.

[29] *Commons Journal*, LXIV (1809), 73; 49 Geo. III c. xv; renewed 1 Wm. IV c. lviii (copy of renewal act in Cardiff Public Library).

[30] *Commons Journal*, LXIV (1809), 26; 49 Geo. III c. cxlvi; renewed 11 Geo. IV c. xxix, creating the Carmarthen–Lampeter section into the Carmarthen and Tivyside District of Roads (copy of renewal act in Carmarthen County Hall and in N.L.W.).

[31] *Commons Journal*, LVIII (1802–3), 172; 43 Geo. III c. xxxi, renewed 5 Geo. IV c. lxxiv and 5 Wm. IV c. iii. Copies of renewal acts in Carmarthen County Hall.

[32] *Commons Journal*, LXVII (1812), 62; 52 Geo. III c. xl.

[33] *Commons Journal*, LXXXIV (1829), 31; 10 Geo. IV c. iv. See Memorial of Freeholders in Co. Radnor to Home Office, 30 April 1845, H.O. 45/454.

[34] *Commons Journal*, XLV (1790), 59.

[35] Ibid., p. 265; petition of the parishes of Llanwinio, Cilrhedyn, Clydau, Llanfyrnach, Llanboidy, Eglwys Fair a Churig, Llanglydwen, Cilmaenllwyd, Llandisilio, Mynachlog-ddu, Llangolman, Llandeilo, Maenclochog, Llan-y-cefn, Egremont, Llawhaden, Bletherston, New Moat, Henry's Moat, Llysyfrân, Walton East, Clarbeston, Wiston and Rudbaxton.

[36] Ibid., XLVI (1791), 178, 189, 231; 31 Geo. III c. 106 and 126, renewed 52 Geo. III c. xli.

[37] *Commons Journal*, LXII (1812), 175; 52 Geo. III c. lxxxvii.

[38] See e.g. Evan Davies, *Hanes Plwyf Llangynllo*, 1905, p. 28.

[39] S. and B. Webb, op. cit., p. 85.

[40] See the quarterly reports of the various county treasurers published in the weekly newspapers; also reports of surveyors to quarter sessions in Pembrokeshire Quarter Sessions Records in N.L.W. *Report of Select Committee on County Rates*, 1835, gives expenditure in Carmarthenshire on bridges: 1816, £696 13s. 4d.; 1822, £1,098 4s. 7d.; 1832, £2,320 2s. 11d. *Commission of Inquiry for South Wales, Evidence*, p. 269, gives expenditure in Cardiganshire on bridges: 1820, £239 8s. 6d.; 1830, £321 15s.; 1840, £825 15s. 8d. Brecknockshire had a unique act (1821), giving quarter sessions responsibility for all bridges. This constituted the chief expenditure from county stock. Ibid., pp. 334, 337, 338.

[41] Ibid., p. 129. Provision for this bridge was made in 1 Wm. IV c. lviii. The 'Chain Bridge', as it was called, resembled Telford's bridge across the Menai Straits. It was replaced by a stone bridge in 1883, but this is still called the 'Chain Bridge'; J. F. Jones, loc. cit.

[42] *Commission of Inquiry for South Wales, Evidence*, p. 129.

[43] Carmarthen Quarter Sessions, reported *Welshman*, 6 Jan. 1843.

[44] Ibid., 1 Jan., 25 Feb., 11 March, 25 March, 1 July 1842; 17 March, 30 June 1843; *Commission of Inquiry for South Wales, Evidence*, pp. 119, 129. *Carm. Antiq. Soc. Trans.*, V (1909–10), 39, gives total cost as £22,000.

[45] The Main Trust contributed £800 to building a new bridge near Abermarlais, hitherto chargeable to the neighbouring parishes. Main Trust Order Book, 3 Jan. 1816 (Carmarthen County Hall).

[46] *Commission of Inquiry for South Wales, Evidence*, p. 89.

[47] *Commons Journal*, LXXXVIII (1833), 199, 531; 3 and 4 Wm. IV c. cii.

[48] *Commission of Inquiry for South Wales, Evidence*, pp. 24, 362, 363; Kidwelly Order Book, 14 March 1837, in Carmarthen County Hall.

[49] Form of Award in the Matter of the Turnpike Trusts, covering letter from Thomas Frankland Lewis, William Cripps and George Kettilby Rickards, dated 13 Jan. 1845, H.O. 45/454 B.

[50] Geo. Rice Trevor to Home Office, 19 Sept. 1843, H.O. 45/454 (2); *Commission of Inquiry for South Wales, Evidence*, pp. 122, 329.

[51] Ibid., p. 379. (The witness was Thomas Bullin.) S. and B. Webb, op. cit., p. 218.

[52] Form of award, as above. It may be noticed that Lord Cawdor had no money in the Kidwelly Trust, and opposed its renewal act in 1833; *Commission of Inquiry for South Wales, Evidence*, p. 26.

[53] Brechfa Minute Book, in Carmarthen County Museum, several entries.

[54] *Welshman*, 1 Jan., 5 Nov. 1841, sale of Kidwelly tally, bearing interest at 5 per cent, by private contract. There are several transfers of tallies in Haverfordwest MSS. 19061–3, and in Crosswood Deeds and Documents, I, 1369, 1503, II, 1211.

[55] *Commission of Inquiry for South Wales, Evidence*, pp. 136, 187. (There are several requests for payment in Carmarthen County Hall, Miscellaneous MSS.).

[56] Ibid., p. 156.

[57] See Fishguard Trust below. It is noticeable that the answer to a query on this in *Report of Commissioners for enquiring into the state of roads in England and Wales*, 1840 (280), xxvii, by the Fishguard Trust is that they were unable to answer as 'in the time of former clerks the books were kept imperfectly'. It is likely that similar evasive replies from Brechfa and from Llandovery and Lampeter cover the same practice. For this practice, see Pratt, op. cit., p. 314.

[58] Form of award, as above. Albany Chapel was one of the few tally-holders of the Cardigan Trust who refused to agree to a reduction of interest from 5 to $3\frac{1}{2}$ per cent; *Commission of Inquiry for South Wales, Evidence*, p. 244.

[59] Ibid., p. 10; Form of Award, as above. See *Hansard*, XLV, 5 March 1839, for small investors. One of the most important trustees of the Whitland Trust was Nathaniel Rowland of Parke, son of the Methodist revivalist, the Rev. Daniel Rowland.

[60] *Commission of Inquiry for South Wales, Evidence*, p. 158, payment of £75 regularly by Tavernspite Trust, in addition to interest on £8,000.

[61] Brechfa Minute Book.

[62] Ibid., 26 April 1832, 4 June 1836, 30 May 1837. *Commission of Inquiry for South Wales, Evidence*, p. 70, for imprisonment of clerk.

[63] Fishguard Trust Order Book, N.L.W., MS. 7453 D.

[64] Ibid., under date 26 Nov. 1813.

[65] Haverfordwest (Williams and Williams) Deeds and Documents, 19068, statement for opinion of counsel.

[66] *Commission of Inquiry for South Wales, Report*, p. 10; *Evidence*, pp. 155, 162, 178, 181, 187. For stormy meetings relating to this trust, when much dirty linen was washed, see *Welshman*, 8 Sept., 22 Sept. 1843.

[67] Form of award, as above.

[68] G. H. Ellis, Report to Home Office, 2 Nov. 1843, H.O. 45/454 B.

[69] Carmarthen County Hall, Miscellaneous MSS.; *Commission of Inquiry for South Wales, Evidence*, p. 14.

[70] Fishguard Trust Order Book.

[71] *Commission of Inquiry for South Wales, Report*, p. 8; *Evidence*, p. 136.

[72] Ibid., pp. 141, 360.

[73] Ibid., pp. 286, 290, 291, 295, 317.

[74] G. H. Ellis, loc. cit.

[75] Kidwelly Order Book, 1835–45, in Carmarthen County Hall; *Commission of Inquiry for South Wales, Evidence*, pp. 14, 127.

[76] The Carmarthen and Newcastle Act, 5 Geo. IV c. lxxxiv, did give power to increase tolls by one-half.

[77] Cardigan District Order Book in N.L.W.; *Commission of Inquiry for South Wales, Evidence*, p. 242.

[78] Ibid., pp. 330, 334, 335.

[79] Cardiganshire, 31 Geo. III c. 97; (see Order Book, 3 Sept. 1811); Main Trust, 52 Geo. III c. cli; Kidwelly Trust, 5 Geo. IV c. ii.

[80] *Commons Journal*, XLI (1786), 606, petition against omission of exemption on lime in renewal of that part of 5 Geo. III c. 76 relating to the Llandeilo and Llandybie Trust.

[81] *Commission of Inquiry for South Wales, Evidence*, pp. 23, 68, 120, 154.

[82] Ibid., pp. 97, 108.

[83] G. H. Ellis, loc. cit.

[84] *Report of the Select Committee on Turnpike Trusts*, 1836 (547), xix, 335; see Jackman, op. cit., II, 682, for a contemporary description.

[85] His name is given as Bullen in the *Commission of Inquiry for South Wales, Evidence*, up to p. 194, but Bullin usually from then on and in most MS. sources. Slater's *Directory, Wales*, 1850, gives him as 'Bullen, Thomas, farmer of tolls, Wellington Row'. His evidence before the above commission is given pp. 376–82.

[86] Correspondence in Carmarthen County Hall, Miscellaneous MSS.

[87] Bullin took the gates of the following trusts *en bloc*: 1836, Aberystwyth; 1837–41, Kidwelly, including Loughor Bridge; 1837–42, Bridgend (Glamorgan); 1838, Newcastle, Cardigan, Milford, Whitland; 1838–41, Tavernspite; 1838–43, Main Trust. Minor takings are too numerous to give in detail.

[88] *Commission of Inquiry for South Wales, Evidence*, p. 8.

[89] Ibid., pp. 124, 243.

[90] Ibid., p. 376.

[91] Ibid., pp. 15, 25, 46, 48, 137, 141, 151, 152, 355, 358 ('the man who caused all the row in this country'); *Welshman*, 15 Dec. 1843, 12 April 1844. Kidwelly Order Book in Carmarthen County Hall. Lewis is described as of Swansea; *Carmarthen Journal*, 12 April 1844. The two gates at Porth-y-rhyd were on the road of the Three Commotts Trust; Lewis added a chain where the Kidwelly road intersected it; *Commission of Inquiry for South Wales*, p. 25. He is said to have held £6,000 worth of gates; ibid., p. 151.

[92] *Commission of Inquiry for South Wales, Evidence*, p. 50.

[93] Among celebrated toll-gate keepers was Twm o'r Nant, who kept the Walk Gate at Llandeilo; W. Davies, *Llandilo Fawr and its Neighbourhood*, 1858, p. 41.

[94] *Commission of Inquiry for South Wales, Evidence*, p. 29.

[95] Ibid., pp. 127, 380.

[96] Ibid., p. 86.

[97] Ibid., p. 16. It cost £200; some cost as little as £15.

[98] *Welshman*, 21 Jan., 6 May, 13 May, 17 June 1842.

[99] *Commission of Inquiry for South Wales, Evidence*, p. 28.

[100] Ibid., p. 125; also W. Chambers's statement of grievances, ibid., pp. 465–6.

[101] Ibid., p. 287.

[102] Ibid., p. 379.

[103] S. and B. Webb, op. cit., p. 176.

[104] *Report of Select Committee on Turnpike Returns*, 1833 (703), XV, 409–641; *Report of Select Committee on Turnpike Trusts and Tolls*, 1836 (547), XIX, 315; *Report of Commissioners for enquiry into state of Roads in England and Wales*, 1840 (280), XXVII; see also *Hansard*, XLV, 5 March 1839.

[105] Twelve, if the Towy Bridge Trust is counted separately. Occasionally, as in *Report on Roads* (1840), as above, the Carmarthen and Newcastle and the Carmarthen and Tivyside Trusts are given separately.

[106] Anon., 'Turnpike roads of England and Wales', *Journal of the Royal Statistical Society*, I (1839), 542–5; *Report on Roads* (1840), as above.

[107] E.g. D. E. Jones, *Hanes Plwyfi Llangeler a Phenboyr*, 1899, p. 326.

[108] *Report on Roads* (1840), as above. Average mileages in 1812, 1813, and 1814: turnpike roads—Cardiganshire 141, Carmarthenshire 356, Pembrokeshire 136, total 633; other highways using wheeled carriages—Cardiganshire 687, Carmarthenshire 1,158, Pembrokeshire 1,019, total 2,864. Therefore the trusts accounted for 633 out of 3,497 miles.

[109] Ibid., p. 607, gives proportion as one to five for the country as a whole in 1818. See S. and B. Webb, op. cit., p. 193.

[110] *Commission of Inquiry for South Wales, Evidence*, p. 240.

[111] *Report on Roads* (1840), as above.

[112] *Welshman*, 22 Sept. 1843, *re* Carmarthen and Newcastle Emlyn Trust.

[113] *Abstract of Income and Expenditure of Turnpike Trusts*, 1836, XLVII; see also *Report on Roads* (1840), as above.

[114] Pratt, op. cit., p. 312.

[115] *Commission of Inquiry for South Wales, Evidence*, pp. 172, 312, 313; Tavernspite Trust accounts in Pembrokeshire Quarter Sessions Records, parish contribution, 31 Dec. 1842 to 31 Dec. 1843, £616.

[116] Jackman, op. cit., p. 614. Jackman, in his standard work on transport, makes only this one footnote reference to the Rebecca Riots, and seems to attribute them to this act.

[117] Richard Ayton, *Voyage around Great Britain*, 1814, p. 110.

[118] E. H. Stuart-Jones in *Western Mail*, 22 June 1950.

[119] Walter Davies, *South Wales*, II, 369.

[120] *South Wales Association for Improvement of Roads. Abstract of Proceedings*, 1792. (Copy in Cardiff Public Library.)

[121] S. and B. Webb, op. cit., chapter VIII.

[122] *Commission of Inquiry for South Wales, Evidence*, pp. 164–5, the evidence of Henry Leach, who carried out an investigation at the request of the postmaster-general in 1818.

[123] Ibid., p. 158.

[124] *Report of the Select Committee on Milford Haven Communication*, 1827 (258), III, 551; Second Report, 1827 (472), III, 649 (with Telford's report as an appendix). For the whole subject see the admirable 'Open Letter from Lord Cawdor to Sir Robert Peel', reprinted in *Welshman*, 15 July 1842.

[125] The epithets are those of S. and B. Webb, op. cit., chapter VI.

[126] *Commission of Inquiry for South Wales, Evidence*, p. 158.

[127] Various letters in Carmarthen County Hall, Miscellaneous MSS., especially Macadam to Stacey, 15 July 1836.

[128] *Commission of Inquiry for South Wales, Appendix*, pp. 441–2, memorial of magistrates.

[129] Main Trust Order Book, 29 Jan. 1842.

[130] Memorial of Magistrates, as above.

[131] The figure is for 1850: 'Estimated amount of toll which mail coaches would be liable to pay if not exempted by general turnpike acts', *Parliamentary Accounts and Papers*, XLIX, 1850.

[132] G. H. Ellis, loc. cit.

[133] Ibid.; *Commission of Inquiry for South Wales, Evidence*, pp. 83, 88, 351, 360. The accusation in respect of the Kidwelly Trust was vigorously denied; Kidwelly Trust Order Book, 13 March 1843, in Carmarthen County Hall.

[134] *Times* articles reproduced *Welshman*, 4 Aug., 11 Aug. 1843.

[135] G. H. Ellis, loc. cit.

[136] Ibid., loc. cit.

[137] *Commission of Inquiry for South Wales, Evidence*, p. 54.

[138] *Welshman*, 11 Aug. 1843.

[139] *Commission of Inquiry for South Wales, Evidence*, pp. 201, 214, 228, 273.

NOTES TO CHAPTER VII

[1] Home Office to J. R. Lewes Lloyd, 24 April 1839, H.O. 41/13; J. R. Lewes Lloyd to Home Office, 8 May 1839, H.O. 40/46.

[2] *Carmarthen Journal*, 18 Jan., 23 Aug. 1829; *Commission of Inquiry for South Wales, Report*, p. 35, *Evidence*, pp. 4, 8, 206, 377. The leading trustee was Nathaniel Rowland.

[3] J. M. Child and W. B. Swann to Home Office, 14 June, 18 June, 21 June 1839, H.O. 40/51; *Carmarthen Journal*, 21 June 1839.

[4] Home Office to J. M. Child and W. B. Swann, 17 June, 24 June, 2 July 1839, H.O. 41/14; Child to Home Office, 29 June 1839, H.O. 40/46; Ben Thomas to Home Office, 11 July 1839, H.O. 40/51.

[5] *Carmarthen Journal*, 12 July 1839; *Cambrian*, 13 July 1839; T. Shrapnel Biddulph and W. B. Swann to Home Office, 4 July, 6 July 1839, H.O. 40/51; Home Office to W. B. Swann, 9 July 1839, H.O. 41/14.

[6] T. Shrapnel Biddulph, loc. cit.; Lord Dynevor to Home Office, 8 July 1839, H.O. 40/51.

[7] *Commission of Inquiry for South Wales, Report*, p. 11; *Carmarthen Journal*, 20 March 1840; J. H. Allen to Home Office, 21 Nov. 1840, H.O. 52/44; *Welshman*, 22 Sept., 6 Oct. 1843. The constables were John Mends and Henry Rees, and the farmers William Philip and Daniel Luke.

[8] W. Cozens to Home Office, 17 July 1839 (an error for 18 July), H.O. 40/51; *Cambrian*, 27 July 1839; G. R. Trevor to Home Office, 27 Dec. 1842, H.O. 45/265.

[9] J. Thomas to Home Office, 19 July 1839, H.O. 52/43; W. B. Swann to Lord Dynevor, 20 July 1839, H.O. 40/51; W. B. Swann to Home Office, 22 July 1839, H.O. 40/51.

[10] *Carmarthen Journal*, 26 July 1839.

[11] *Commission of Inquiry for South Wales, Evidence*, p. 4; *Welshman*, 10 Feb. 1843.

[12] G. H. Ellis to Home Office, 2 Nov. 1843, H.O. 45/454.

[13] G. R. Trevor to Home Office, 27 Dec. 1843, H.O. 45/265.

[14] *Commission of Inquiry for South Wales, Evidence,* pp. 160, 377, 463; Resolutions of the magistrates meeting at the Blue Boar, 23 July 1839, H.O. 45/51; *Carmarthen Journal,* 26 July, 23 Aug., 4 Oct. 1839; J. H. Allen to Home Office, 2 Aug. 1839, H.O. 40/51; *Welshman,* 16 Feb. 1844.

[15] See G. Kitson Clark, 'Hunger and Politics in 1842', *Journal of Modern History,* XXV (1953), 355–74.

[16] *Welshman,* 19 Aug. 1842.

[17] Ibid., 26 Aug. 1842.

[18] William Day, Memorandum on State of South Wales, 9 July 1843, H.O. 45/1611.

[19] *Welshman,* 21 Oct., 18 Nov. 1842.

[20] *Reports on Education in Wales,* 1847, I, 245.

[21] *Welshman,* 30 Sept., 7 Oct. 1842, 24 Feb. 1843; Main Trust Order Book, under date 8 Feb. 1843; G. H. Ellis, loc. cit.

[22] Timothy Powell to Lord Dynevor, 26 Nov. 1842, H.O. 45/265; G. R. Trevor to Home Office, 27 Dec. 1842, H.O. 45/265.

[23] Report of Police Inspector Geo. Martin, 2 Jan. 1843, H.O. 45/454.

[24] Timothy Powell and G. R. Trevor, loc. cit.; Lord Dynevor to Home Office, 30 Nov. 1842, H.O. 45/265.

[25] Timothy Powell to Home Office, 13 Dec. 1842, H.O. 45/265.

[26] *Welshman,* 17 March 1843.

[27] Geo. Martin to Geo. Rice Trevor, 21 Dec. 1842, H.O. 45/265.

[28] This is dated 7 April 1843 in H. Tobit Evans, *Rebecca and her Daughters,* 1910, p. 41, when Pwll-trap was destroyed for the fourth time, but as it is given in the *Welshman* for 6 Jan. 1843, it must have been on an earlier occasion.

[29] Both are in H.O. 45/265, one enclosed in Lord Dynevor's letter to the Home Office of 30 Dec., and the other in Timothy Powell's letter of 31 Dec. They are dated 'Dec. 16th 1842', but they must be later than the arrival of Martin at St. Clears on 20 Dec.

[30] This is a reference to 'Brad y Cyllyll Hirion', the treachery of the long knives, an eponymous incident in the wars between the English and the Welsh associated with the derivation of the name Saxon from seax, a knife. The education reports which appeared four years later were, by analogy, called 'Brad y Llyfrau Gleision', the treachery of the blue books.

[31] Timothy Powell to Home Office, 31 Dec. 1842, H.O. 45/265.

[32] Inspector Martin's report, 2 Jan. 1843, H.O. 45/454.

[33] G. R. Trevor to Home Office, 6 Jan. 1843, H.O. 45/454.

[34] Home Office to Lord Dynevor, 16 Jan., 20 Jan. 1843, H.O. 41/17.

[35] Lord Dynevor to Home Office, 15 Jan. 1843, H.O. 45/454.

[36] *Welshman,* 20 Jan. 1843.

[37] Home Office to Admiralty, 21 Jan. 1843, H.O. 45/454.

[38] Sir John Owen to Home Office, 23 Jan. 1843, H.O. 45/454.

[39] Lieut. Bryant to Major Bowling, 27 Jan., and Major Bowling to Sir John Owen, 29 Jan. 1843, H.O. 45/454.

[40] Major Bowling to Sir John Owen, 14 Feb.; Timothy Powell to Lord Dynevor, 17 Feb.; Sir John Owen to Home Office, 17 Feb.; Geo. Rice Trevor to Home Office, 17 Feb. 1843, H.O. 45/454; Home Office to Sir John Owen, 17 Feb. 1843, H.O. 41/17.

[41] *Welshman*, 3 Feb. 1843. The clerk of the Union denied that any threatening letters had been received, ibid., 10 Feb. 1843, as did Wiliam Day, loc. cit.

[42] *Welshman*, 3 Feb. 1843.

[43] G. H. Ellis, loc. cit.; Haverfordwest Deeds and Documents (N.L.W.), MS. 19130.

[44] The mansion (accent on the last syllable) has given its name to a celebrated breed of dogs. For William Edwardes's criticisms at a meeting held at Wolf's Castle, 8 Sept., 22 Sept., 6 Oct. 1843.

[45] *Illustrated London News*, 11 Feb. 1843, quoted Searle, op. cit., p. 775.

[46] *Welshman*, 13 Oct. 1843. See Brown, *History of Haverfordwest*, p. 104. Willis Bund thought that Edwardes 'was the originator of the whole business'; letter to Miss Gwladys Tobit Evans (Mrs. H. J. Huws) quoted in her letter to H. M. Vaughan, 18 Nov. 1910. The Rev. D. Gerwyn Stephens tells me that the tradition persists in the Haverfordwest neighbourhood.

[47] *Welshman*, 10 Feb. 1843.

[48] Ibid., 17 Feb., 24 Feb., 17 March 1843. Francis Green, 'Rebecca in West Wales', *West Wales Historical Records*, VII (1918), 27–33, gives extracts from the brief for the prosecution and from the depositions. The accused men were Thomas Howells of Llwyndrissy and David Howell, Bower Hill, in the parish of Lampeter Velfrey. The pig dealer was Lewis Griffiths of Pentypark Mill in the parish of Wiston. The action was brought at the instance of Nathaniel Rowland, son of the revivalist, Daniel Rowland. H. Leach to Home Office, 8 April 1843, H.O. 45/454, speaks of the hostile feeling against the chief witness and states that only very large rewards would produce information.

[49] *Welshman*, 10 March, 17 March 1843; F. Green, op. cit., p. 30.

[50] The incidents took place on 13 and 17 July. *Welshman*, 11 Aug., 20 Oct. 1843. There are some eight papers relating to the Colby affair in H.O. 45/454, and four in H.O. 41/18. See also Haverfordwest Deeds and Documents (N.L.W.), MSS. 19064–7; also Calendar of Prisoners, Pembrokeshire Quarter Sessions, 17 Oct. 1843 (N.L.W.). Thomas Frederick Colby of Pantyderi (a branch of the Colbys of Ffynone) was director of the Ordnance Survey. He gets nine columns in D.N.B. His bust is in the University College of Wales, Aberystwyth.

[51] *Welshman*, 3 March 1843.

[52] Ibid., 12 May 1843, 'one night last week'.

[53] Ibid., 3 March, 14 April, 21 April 1843; J. Lloyd Davies, Alltyrodyn, to Home Office, 21 April 1843, H.O. 45/454.

[54] *Welshman*, 12 May 1843 (the date was 5 May).

[55] Memoranda concerning the Rebecca Riots, compiled by Alcwyn Evans, 1893, in Tenby Museum. This comprises, almost exclusively, excerpts from the *Welshman*, but it has some additional information. The tithe award of 1845 (Crosswood Deeds and Documents, IV, 18, in N.L.W.), gives John Bowen as the owner and occupier of Plasyparke (two hundred and sixty-six acres) and of Clunblewog (three hundred and fifty-six acres), and the owner of Gelli (sixty-eight acres) and of Cwmlleiniogau-isaf (forty-two acres) occupied by his son, Michael Bowen, as well as of other property. John Bowen died in Sept. 1845, aged 79, and was buried in Pen-y-bont churchyard. Michael Bowen died at the early age of 37 on 14 June 1854. He was therefore 26 at the time of the

Rebecca Riots. His wife lived for another forty-one years, and died on 13 Sept. 1895, aged 77. Both are buried in Pen-y-bont churchyard. I am indebted for information to my former student, Miss Muriel Bowen Evans, a relative of Michael Bowen. The tradition in the family is that he was an unwilling rioter.

[56] *Welshman*, 2 June 1843; (*Welshman*, 22 Dec. 1843, records the arrest of four people engaged in the riot on information supplied by one Benjamin Evans, but he later claimed that a statement had been extracted from him while intoxicated); *Commission of Inquiry for South Wales, Evidence*, p. 66; mayor of Carmarthen to Home Office, 27 May 1843, has the depositions of the gate-keeper and others.

[57] Penllwyni, 12 June; Llandeilo Rwnws, 13 June; *Welshman*, 16 June 1843.

[58] E. C. Ll. Hall to Home Office, 15 June 1843, H.O. 45/454; *Welshman*, loc. cit.

[59] J. Lloyd Davies to Home Office, 17 June; Lloyd Hall to Home Office, 21 June, H.O. 45/454.

[60] J. Lloyd Davies, loc. cit.

[61] The prisoner was David Evans of Pen-lan; the barristers, Chilton, Q.C., and E. Vaughan Williams. A lengthy, three-paged report of the riot, made by a special constable to a magistrate, was sent by Geo. Rice Trevor to the Home Office, 30 June, and by Col. Love, 1 July, H.O. 45/454. The indictment against David Evans 'and twenty others unknown', is in Assizes 71/8, and the depositions of witnesses in Assizes 72/1, in P.R.O.

[62] *Welshman*, 3 Feb., 17 Feb. 1843.

[63] Ibid., 19 May 1843; J. Lloyd Davies to Home Office, 21 April 1843, H.O. 45/454.

[64] *Welshman*, 14 July 1843.

[65] Ibid., 30 June 1843.

[66] Ibid., 10 Feb. 1843.

[67] Ibid., ?1 March, 21 April 1843; Home Office to Lord Cawdor, 13 April 1843, H.O.l41/17.

[68] J. Lloyd Davies, loc. cit.; *Welshman*, 4 March, 5 May 1843.

[69] Home Office to War Office, 16 June 1843, H.O. 41/17; War Office to Home Office, same date, H.O. 45/454; Home Office to Lord Dynevor, 19 June 1843, H.O. 41/17.

[70] N.L.W., MS. 3294 E, dated 16 June 1843.

[71] Dated 19 June 1843, enclosed in Lloyd Hall to Home Office, 20 June 1843, H.O. 45/454.

[72] Dated 19 June 1843, enclosed in Lord Dynevor to Home Office, 27 June 1843, H.O. 45/454.

[73] F. Green, op. cit., p. 31; *Welshman*, 17 March 1843; J. Lloyd Davies to Home Office, 17 June 1843, H.O. 45/454; *Commission of Inquiry for South Wales, Evidence*, p. 255.

[74] J. Lloyd Davies to Home Office, 14 June 1843, H.O. 45/454.

[75] Anon., 'Hanes Becca a'i Phlant', *Tarian y Gweithiwr*, 2 Sept. 1886. This is a third of a series of a dozen well-informed brief articles on the riots by one who was present at some incidents, including the march on Carmarthen.

[76] Dated 16 June 1843, enclosed in Lloyd Hall to Home Office, 20 June 1843, H.O. 45/454.

[77] Tenby MS.

[78] *Welshman*, 9 June 1843.

[79] Mayor of Carmarthen to Home Office, 12 June 1843, H.O. 45/454 has all the depositions; *Welshman*, 16 June 1843; *Commission of Inquiry for South Wales, Evidence*, pp. 60, 145.

[80] Col. Love to Home Office, 6 July 1843, H.O. 45/453; *Welshman*, 14 July, 21 July 1843, 5 Jan., 19 March 1844.

[81] J. Lloyd Davies, loc. cit.

[82] E. D. Jones, ' A File of Rebecca Papers', *Carmarthen Antiquary*, I (1943), 31, document 18; Tenby MS. under 14 June 1843.

[83] J. Lloyd Davies to Home Office, 17 June 1843, H.O. 45/454.

[84] Mayor of Carmarthen to Home Office, 27 May 1843, H.O. 45/454.

[85] Same to same, 12 June 1843, H.O. 45/454.

[86] J. Lloyd Davies, loc. cit.

[87] Mayor of Carmarthen to Home Office, 17 June 1843, H.O. 45/454.

[88] Tenby MS., loc. cit.

[89] *Welshman*, 30 June 1843 (report of petty sessions); 22 March 1844 (report of assizes).

[90] J. Lloyd Davies to Home Office, 19 June 1843, H.O. 45/454.

[91] Lloyd Hall to Home Office, 15 June 1843, H.O. 45/454.

[92] Letter dated 17 June and signed Becca, addressed to 'John Wood, Esq., Cwm, Mydrim', enclosed in John Wood to mayor of Carmarthen, 21 June 1843, H.O. 45/454.

[93] *Welshman*, 22 March 1844, evidence of James Lewis at the assizes.

[94] Ibid., evidence of Thomas Davies.

[95] *Welshman*, 23 June 1843 (four days after the riot) gives three hundred on horseback and 'some hundreds' on foot. One witness at the trial gave 'about three hundred and fifty' on horseback and 'a couple of thousand' on foot; he says that the procession took a quarter of an hour to pass where he was standing. Another witness gave three to five hundred horsemen and one thousand five hundred to one thousand eight hundred on foot. A third, an inspector of police, had counted three hundred and ten horsemen. *Welshman*, 22 March 1844. Alcwyn Evans gives five hundred on horseback and four thousand on foot, Tenby MS. Mayor of Carmarthen to Home Office, 20 June 1843, H.O. 45/454, gives 'a mob of between four thousand and five thousand'. *Tarian y Gweithiwr*, 9 Sept. 1886 (the reminiscences of a participant) gives five hundred horses and three thousand foot.

[96] See, e.g., my *History of Modern Wales*, 1950, p. 209.

[97] *Welshman*, 23 June 1843.

[98] Ibid., 7 July 1843. She worked at Cilgwyn-uchaf in the parish of New-church. She was pert at her trial; she was glad she had done nothing to hang herself, at all events.

[99] William Chambers to Home Office, 21 June 1843, H.O. 45/454.

[100] T. Charles Morris, the banker.

[101] *Welshman*, 21 July 1843.

[102] This account has been constructed from *Welshman*, 23 June, 6 Oct. 1843, 22 March 1844, and Alcwyn Evans, loc. cit.

NOTES TO CHAPTER VIII

[1] See the two admirable (unpublished) dissertations: N. Gash, Unrest in Rural England, with special reference to Berkshire, 1830, Oxford (B.Litt.), 1935; A. M. Colson, The Revolt of the Hampshire Agricultural Labourers and its causes, London (M.A.), 1937.

[2] It is strange that no writer on the riots has hitherto identified the *Times*'s representative. D. Lleufer Thomas, *The Welsh Land Commission, A Digest of its Report*, 1896, p. 55, states: 'I have been at some pains to discover the identity of this correspondent and have come to the conclusion—though not wholly satisfied on the point—that he was John Forster, the friend and biographer of Dickens'. The identity of Thomas Campbell Foster presents no difficulty to anyone who has read the local newspapers for 1843. *D.N.B.* has a brief Life, but does not mention his visit to Wales.

[3] For an analysis, see *Royal Com. Land, Appendices*, pp. 201–5.

[4] *Commission of Inquiry for South Wales, Evidence*, p. 41.

[5] *Welshman*, 8 Sept. 1843.

[6] *Commission of Inquiry for South Wales, Evidence*, pp. 105, 378.

[7] Peel to Graham, 1 Sept. 1843, Peel Correspondence, B.M. MS. 40,449, folio 11.

[8] *Welshman*, 17 Nov., 24 Nov., 1 Dec. 1843, 15 March 1844. Among the subscribers were William Williams, M.P. (for Coventry), Hugh Williams, E. C. Lloyd Hall, William Edwardes of Sealyham and the editor of the *Welshman*.

[9] Ibid., 19 July 1844.

[10] Thomas Campbell Foster, *Letters on the Condition of the People of Ireland*, 1846. It would appear from this (pp. 632 and 716) that he had conducted similar investigations in Scotland also.

[11] Home Office to Col. Love, 22 June, 29 June 1843, H.O. 41/17; G. R. Trevor to Home Office, 23 June; Edward Laws to Home Office, 26 June 1843, H.O. 45/454; Col. Love to Home Office, 26 June, 1 July 1843, H.O. 45/453.

[12] Lloyd Hall to Home Office, 20 June 1843, H.O. 45/454.

[13] Col. Love to Home Office, loc. cit.

[14] W. J. Linton, *James Watson, a Memoir*, 1879, p. 51; id., *Memories*, 1895, pp. 89–91.

[15] The writer was Edward Davies of Dolcaradog, Machynlleth. He wrote under the pen name of 'Gordofig'. His opponent, whom I have been unable to identify, wrote as 'Hywel', and also knew Hugh Williams. Hywel's letters are pungent and incisive, in contrast to those of Gordofig which are incoherent. The letters appeared in *Welsh Gazette*, 15 Nov., 22 Nov., 6 Dec., 13 Dec., 20 Dec. 1900, 3 Jan., 24 Jan., 31 Jan. 1901. There is a memorandum from Edward Davies to Richard Williams on the subject in a letter from Richard Williams to D. Lleufer Thomas, 3 Oct. 1894, in my possession. See also Richard Williams to D. Lleufer Thomas, 3 March 1896, and D. Lleufer Thomas to Richard Morgan, 11 March 1896 in N.L.W., MS. 6244 B. Edward Davies's twenty-nine paged quarto manuscript (much of it incoherent), N.L.W., MS. 2114, is his letter to the *Welsh Gazette*, 24 Jan. 1901. See, also, *Montgomeryshire Collections*, xxviii (1894), 142–4.

[16] Home Office to Post Office, 6 Oct., 10 Oct., 13 Oct., 16 Oct. 1843, H.O. 79/4. Home Office to Col. Love, 10 July 1843, H.O. 41/17, asks him to obtain information of Hugh Williams's movements.

[17] Geo. Eyre Evans in *Carm. Antiq. Soc. Trans.*, XXII! (1932), 64.

[18] Information from Librarian, Law Society's Hall, Chancery Lane, London, 3 Nov. 1939, 28 March 1951.

[19] Home Office to War Office, 19 June 1843, H.O. 41/17.

[20] *D.N.B.*; H.O. 52/16, 52/23 and 52/25 has some material on his service in the industrial districts; H.O. 45/1126 has letters which refer to his service at Waterloo and in Bradford. See especially Love's report to Home Office on the grievances of the farmers, 26 June 1843, H.O. 45/453.

[21] Col. Love to Home Office, 23 June 1843, H.O. 45/453.

[22] Home Office to War Office, 22 June; Home Office to Col. Love, 22 June, H.O. 41/17; Admiralty to Home Office, 22 June, 23 June 1843, H.O. 45/454.

[23] *Welshman*, 30 June 1843.

[24] Home Office to Col. Powell, 21 June 1843, H.O. 41/17.

[25] Geo. Rice Trevor to Home Office, 24 June 1843, H.O. 45/454.

[26] Home Office to Col. Love, 24 June, 27 June 1843, H.O. 41/17; Col. Love to Home Office, 25 June 1843, H.O. 45/453; Geo. Rice Trevor to Home Office, 25 June, 30 June 1843, H.O. 45/454.

[27] Geo. Rice Trevor to Home Office, 28 June 1843, H.O. 45/454.

[28] Col. Love to Home Office, 11 July 1843, H.O. 45/453; Home Office to War Office, 15 July 1843, H.O. 41/17.

[29] Geo. Rice Trevor to Home Office, 25 June 1843, E. Lloyd Williams to Home Office, 26 June 1843, H.O. 45/454.

[30] E. Laws to Home Office, 26 June 1843, H.O. 45/454.

[31] Ibid., loc. cit.

[32] Home Office to War Office, Home Office to Col. Love, 10 July 1843, H.O. 41/17; War Office to Home Office, same date, H.O. 45/454.

[33] War Office to Home Office, 12 July 1843, H.O. 45/454.

[34] Col. Love to Home Office, 11 July 1843, H.O. 45/453.

[35] Geo. R. Trevor to Home Office, 22 June 1843, H.O. 45/454; *Welshman*, 23 June 1843. The gates, this time, were the Mermaid and Maeswholand (on the old road to Llanddowror).

[36] *Welshman*, loc. cit.

[37] Henhafod, Adpar, Aberceri.

[38] Lloyd Hall to Home Office, 21 June 1843, H.O. 45/454.

[39] Same to same, 22 June 1843, H.O. 45/454.

[40] Mayor of Cardigan to Home Office, Lt.-Col. Vaughan (of Llangoedmor) to Home Office, 24 June 1843, H.O. 45/454; *Welshman*, 30 June 1843.

[41] Ibid., 18 Aug., 25 Aug., 30 Dec. 1843. The farmer was William Davies of Pant-y-fen.

[42] Geo. Rice Trevor to Home Office, 2 July 1843, H.O. 45/454.

[43] Tenby MS., 27 June 1843.

[44] The account in the *Standard*, 29 June 1843, is reproduced in *Welshman*, 7 July 1843, and in Tobit Evans, op. cit., pp. 80–1, Col. Love to Home Office, 1 July 1843, H.O. 45/453, complained of such rumours.

[45] *Welshman*, 23 June 1843.

⁴⁶ Copy in Lloyd Hall to Home Office, 21 June 1843, H.O. 45/454, printed by William Jones, Printer, Columbian Press Office, Newcastle Emlyn, and dated 20 June 1843; reproduced by Tobit Evans, op. cit., pp. 69–71.

⁴⁷ Copy enclosed in Lloyd Hall to Home Office, 23 June 1843, H.O. 45/454; reproduced (with inaccuracies) in Tobit Evans, op. cit., pp. 75–6.

⁴⁸ Geo. R. Trevor to Home Office, 23 June, 2 July 1843, H.O. 45/454.

⁴⁹ Bwlchydomen, Nant-y-clawdd and Felindre.

⁵⁰ Minutes of meeting at Newcastle Emlyn, 30 June 1843 (in the handwriting of Lloyd Hall, signed R. Goring Thomas), in H.O. 45/454, and copy of printed handbill in H.O. 45/453; Col. Love to Home Office, 1 July 1843, H.O. 45/453; Lloyd Hall to Home Office, 1 July 1843, Geo. Rice Trevor to Home Office, 4 July 1843, H.O. 45/454. *Welshman*, 7 July, 11 Aug., 15 Sept., 22 Sept. 1843 (letter from Lloyd Hall); *Carmarthen Antiquary*, document 2.

⁵¹ 'Gyd Wladwyr a Chyd Gristionogion'. Copy sent by Lloyd Hall to Home Office, 30 June 1843; English version in *Carmarthen Journal*, 30 June 1843, enclosed in Geo. Rice Trevor to Home Office, 2 July 1843, H.O. 45/454.

⁵² Copy with letter E. Ll. Williams to Home Office, 9 July 1843, H.O. 45/454, a very garbled version in Tobit Evans, op. cit., pp. 88–91.

⁵³ *Welshman*, 30 June 1843; Home Office to lords-lieutenant (three shires), 27 June 1843, H.O. 41/17; Cardiganshire Quarter Sessions Order Book (N.L.W.), 27 June 1843; Proclamation 'To the Inhabitants of County Carmarthen', 28 June 1843, copy in H.O. 45/453 and in Tobit Evans, op. cit., pp. 78–9; Col. Owen (Pembs.) to Home Office, 28 June, 1 July 1843, H.O. 45/454; ibid., Col. Powell (Cards.) to Home Office, 29 June 1843; Col. Love to Home Office, 30 June 1843, H.O. 45/453; Clerk of Peace, Cards., to Home Office, 1 July 1843, H.O. 45/454; Home Office to Geo. Rice Trevor, and to Clerk of the Peace, Cards., 4 July 1843, H.O. 41/17 (refusal to alter law); Geo. Rice Trevor to Home Office, 10 July 1843, H.O. 45/454 (regrets this decision).

⁵⁴ Home Office to Geo. Rice Trevor, 13 July 1843, H.O. 41/17.

⁵⁵ Lloyd Hall to Home Office, 21 June 1843, H.O. 45/454; ibid., report of Sir William Pell (Pembroke Dock) in Admiralty to Home Office, 15 July 1843; Col. Love to Home Office, 20 July, 22 July 1843, H.O. 45/453.

⁵⁶ *Welshman*, 28 July, 11 Aug. 1843; Col. Love to Home Office, 9 Aug. 1843, H.O. 45/453.

⁵⁷ *Welshman*, 7 July 1843.

⁵⁸ It would appear that there was a gate at Bolgoed and a bar at the same spot on a side road to Goppa Fach.

⁵⁹ *Welshman*, 28 July 1843, says he lived at Lletty, but ibid., 11 Aug. 1843, gives Cwm Scer, Llangyfelach, as his home.

⁶⁰ The first Ordnance Survey (1 in.) has both Cwm Cile Fawr and Cwm Cile Fach. The indictments speak of Morgan Morgan as a labourer (Assizes, 1843, 71/7), but Col. Love to Home Office, 23 July 1843, H.O. 45/453, calls him 'a respectable farmer'. He must have been a freeholder to have had rights of common. His great-grandson, Emeritus Professor Morgan Watkin, assures me that he was a man of property, owning farms in the Amman Valley, in addition to Cwm Cile. The graves of the family in the neighbouring graveyard of Salem Baptist Chapel indicate a yeoman status. The farmer who led the party which destroyed John Jones's hovel was Jenkins, Cynghordy.

[61] J. Davies, postmaster, Swansea, to G.P.O., 24 July 1843, copy in H.O. 45/454.

[62] The family tradition is that he only wanted to change his clothes before going with the policemen, that Napier tried to follow him but that the mother objected to his going upstairs without taking off his dirty boots, and that Napier fired at her. All this is highly improbable.

[63] Home Office to Swansea magistrates, 27 July, 28 July 1843 (two letters), H.O. 41/18.

[64] Ibid., loc. cit.; Col. Love to Home Office, 30 July 1843, H.O. 45/453.

[65] For this account I have relied mainly on indictment and depositions at Glamorgan Assizes, wrongly placed in Assizes 71/7 (there is another copy in 72/1), indictment in Assizes 71/8, and roll and indictment, Special Assizes, 73/2. Newspaper accounts are confused in details; *Welshman*, 14 July, 28 July, 4 Aug., 11 Aug., 3 Nov. 1843, 8 March 1844. The account in Tobit Evans, op. cit., pp. 104–9, is identical with that of Alcwyn Evans in Tenby MS. apart from the usual numerous verbal inaccuracies. Both give the wrong dates. At the time of the trial, Morgan Morgan was aged 57, his wife, Esther, 63, Margaret Morgan, 25, Rees Morgan, 23, and John Morgan, 21. I am indebted to Emeritus Professor Morgan Watkin for the family traditions; he was present, as a child, at Mathew Morgan's funeral.

[66] Lloyd Hall to Home Office, 9 July 1843, H.O. 45/454.

[67] Tenby MS.; Geo. Rice Trevor to Home Office, 11 July 1843, H.O. 45/454. The lessee was William Lewis, who was fined £50 for erecting an illegal bar at Porth-y-rhyd.

[68] The farmer was David Evans of Pen-lan. *Welshman*, 19 July 1844; Col. Love to Home Office, 27 July 1844, H.O. 45/642.

[69] The Aberceri gate at Newcastle Emlyn, Lloyd Hall to Home Office, H.O. 45/454.

[70] The name is variously given as Poundfald, Pumfold, Pumpfald, Pumfag, Pumfrey. Clerk to Magistrates, Swansea, to Home Office, 15 July 1843, H.O. 45/454; ibid., Thomas Penrice, Kilvrough, to Home Office, 4 Sept. 1843.

[71] C. A. Prichard to Home Office, 22 July 1843, H.O. 45/454.

[72] *Welshman*, 28 July 1843.

[73] Pompren (15 July) two miles from Llangadog, and Waunystradfeiris (19 July) near Llangadog; *Welshman*, loc. cit.

[74] Abergwili (24 July), Croeslwyd (25 July), Pen-y-garn (31 July).

[75] Lloyd Hall to Home Office, 21 June 1843; Geo. Rice Trevor to Home Office, 23 June 1843, H.O. 45/454.

[76] Ibid., William Chambers, senior, to Home Office, 25 June 1843.

[77] Ibid., Henry Leach to Home Office, 25 June 1843.

[78] Ibid., Col. Owen to Home Office, 28 June 1843.

[79] Col. Love to Home Office, 1 July 1843, H.O. 45/453. See also *Welshman*, 30 June 1843.

[80] William Day to G. C. Lewis, 9 July 1843, H.O. 45/1611.

[81] *West Wales Historical Records*, V (1915), 291–2.

[82] Col. Vaughan, Llangoedmor, to Home Office, 24 June 1843, H.O. 45/454.

[83] He was of Castell Maelgwyn, and was the nephew of Admiral Sir Erasmus Gower. He paid a rent of £55 a year for the weir.

[84] Copy of handbill in *West Wales Historical Records*, X (1924), 161. He apparently employed ninety day labourers.

[85] D. Prothero to E. C. Lloyd Hall, 27 July 1843, H.O. 45/454; ibid., copy of Lloyd Hall's address; ibid., 'A Friend of Peace and Good Order' writes to Lloyd Hall, 25 Aug., complaining that fish could not go further than Felingigfran to spawn. He also complained that the vicar of Eglwyswrw (D. Prothero) fed his sheep in the churchyard where grass grew from the putrefaction of human bodies, and sold them at Cardigan, thereby proving himself a cannibal; *Welshman*, 4 Aug. 1843.

[86] Original letter from John James, Velingigvran, 12 Sept. 1843, inserted in Tenby MS. He had been warned of a gathering in the parish of Meline, and feared that all his property, if not also his life, was imperilled.

[87] Lloyd Hall to Home Office, 14 Sept. 1843, H.O. 45/454; *Welshman*, 15 Sept., 22 Sept., 29 Dec. 1843, 26 Jan., 2 Feb. 1844; *Commission of Inquiry for South Wales, Evidence*, p. 44.

[88] Ibid., p. 38; N.L.W., MS. 1398 B. (See also Slebech MS. 2980, in N.L.W., dated 6 June 1835, for this weir.) The fishery both on the Teify and at Blackpool still remains a matter of controversy.

[89] Col. Love to Home Office, 22 July 1843, H.O. 45/453; *Welshman*, 28 July 1843. The attack was intended both on Porth-y-rhyd and on the house of a Mr. Thomas, Cwm Mawr. I have not found the reason for this. Men from Pontyberem and Gors-las were to join. Thomas's son guided the troops on this occasion (and had probably given the warning). As a result a threatening notice was pinned on the door of Cwm Mawr on the night of 25 July telling Thomas to dismiss his workmen, and saying that his son was a marked man. (Tenby MS.). The dispute was probably an industrial one. The gate destroyed was at Bethania.

[90] Geo. Rice Trevor to Home Office, 22 July 1843, H.O. 45/454; *Welshman*, 28 July 1843; the resolutions (with the usual inaccuracies) are reproduced in Tobit Evans, op. cit., pp. 96–7. The Cwm Ifor schoolroom figures in *Reports on Education in Wales*, 1847, I Appendix, pp. 6, 230, but is there stated to have been opened in 1846.

[91] Home Office to Geo. Rice Trevor, 27 July 1843, H.O. 41/17.

[92] Pembrokeshire Quarter Sessions, Michaelmas 1843 (in N.L.W.), for example, has ten such cases relating to the Narberth gates alone. The usual fine was £1 for passing with a cart, and £2 for doing so with a carriage.

[93] Col. Vaughan to Home Office, 20 July 1843, H.O. 45/454; ibid., Lloyd Hall to Home Office, 21 July 1843, has a notice served on a shoemaker.

[94] Ibid., Geo. Rice Trevor to Home Office, 7 Aug. 1843.

[95] Ibid., Lloyd Hall to Home Office, 15 July 1843.

[96] 'Rhybyddeg Syr R. M. Rolfe ym Mrawdlys Aberteifi, Gorphenhaf 27ain 1843', broadside in N.L.W. *Welshman*, 28 July 1843, has his address to the Pembrokeshire grand jury.

[97] Lloyd Hall to Home Office, 8 July 1844, H.O. 45/454; Dillwyn Diaries (N.L.W.), 24 July, 25 July, 26 July, 4 Aug., 10 Aug. 1843.

[98] Printed notice of Cardigan Trust in Lloyd Hall to Home Office, 21 July 1843, H.O. 45/454.

[99] Main Trust Miscellaneous MSS., Carmarthen County Hall, has a number of petitions relating to July and August.

[100] Col. Love to Home Office, 12 July 1843, H.O. 45/ 454.

[101] Ibid., Geo. Rice Trevor to Home Office, 12 July 1843, transmits petition of sixteen magistrates.

[102] For this enquiry, see my 'A Report on the Turnpike Trusts', *National Library of Wales Journal*, VIII (1953), 171–5, and the references therein.

[103] *Welshman*, 4 Aug., 11 Aug., 25 Aug. 1843.

[104] Ibid., 4 Aug. 1843.

[105] Ibid., 18 Aug. 1843; Col. Vaughan to Col. Powell, 8 Aug. 1843, H.O. 45/454; ibid., Lloyd Hall to Home Office, 12 Aug. 1843, G. S. Wigley to Home Office, 24 Aug. 1843.

[106] Lloyd Hall, loc. cit.; ibid., A. L. Gwynne to Home Office, 12 Aug. 1843.

[107] Depositions of gate-keeper in *Carmarthen Antiquary*, loc. cit., document 3, (copy, also, in H.O. 45/454). William Chambers to Home Office, 5 Aug. 1843, H.O. 45/454; ibid., Clerk of Magistrates, Llanelly, to Home Office, 31 Aug. 1843; Home Office to Clerk of Magistrates, 7 Sept. 1843, *Carmarthen Antiquary*, loc. cit., document 22 (copy in H.O. 41/18); Geo. Rice Trevor to William Chambers, 16 Aug., 18 Aug. 1843, *Carm. Antiq. Soc. Trans.*, LVI (1932), letters 6, 8. *Welshman*, 11 Aug., 18 Aug. 1843, 5 Jan. 1844; indictment for perjury, Assizes 71/7.

[108] *Welshman*, 4 Aug. 1843.

[109] Ibid., 11 Aug. 1843; Col. Love to Home Office, 3 Aug. 1843, H.O. 45/453; Assizes 71/7 and 72/1. I have not found the verdict in this case.

[110] *Welshman*, 4 Aug. 1843; 5 Jan., 23 March, 30 Aug. 1844.

[111] Tenby MS.; balance sheet of Pembroke Ferry Trust, in Pembrokeshire Quarter Sessions Records, Easter 1844, has entry of £12 3s. to replace demolished gate at Burton.

[112] Tenby MS.; Tobit Evans, op. cit., p. 130, with verbal differences.

[113] *Welshman*, 26 Jan. 1844.

[114] Tenby MS.; *Welshman*, 25 Aug. 1843.

[115] Ibid., 27 Oct. 1843.

[116] Geo. Rice Trevor to Home Office, 11 Aug. 1843, H.O. 45/454; *Welshman*, 11 Aug. 1843. It was here that Twm o'r Nant had collected tolls; William Davies, *Llandilo Fawr and its neighbourhood*, 1848, p. 41.

[117] Geo. Rice Trevor, loc. cit.; *Welshman*, loc. cit. William Davies of Pant-y-fen was suspected, as on 26 June.

[118] *Welshman*, loc. cit.

[119] Ibid., 18 Aug. 1843; Col. Owen to Home Office, 16 Aug. 1843, H.O. 45/454.

[120] Tenby MS.

[121] *Welshman*, 25 Aug. 1843.

[122] Tenby MS.

[123] Ibid.

[124] Ibid.; *Welshman*, 25 Aug., 1 Sept., 8 Sept., 8 Dec. 1843, 5 Jan. 1844.

[125] Ibid., 1 Sept., 8 Sept., 15 March 1844; mayor of Haverfordwest to officer commanding marines, and to officer commanding yeomanry, 24 Aug. 1843, H.O. 45/453; ibid., Major Bowling to Lieut. Parry, 24 August 1843; ibid., J. H. Peel to officer commanding marines, 27 Aug. 1843; W. Philipps (Picton Castle) to Home Office, 28 Aug. 1843, H.O. 45/454; Home Office to mayor of Haverfordwest, 31 Aug. 1843, H.O. 41/18; Assizes, 72/1 (depositions taken

by magistrates); Haverfordwest (Williams and Williams) Deeds and Documents (N.L.W.), MS. 19130 (brief for the prosecution). Lloyd Hall's retainer was seven guineas together with 5s. for his clerk, in addition to two guineas and 2s. 6d. for his clerk for each consultation. The horse that was killed belonged to John Jenkins of Longhook in the parish of Puncheston.

[126] *Welshman*, 1 Sept. 1843.

NOTES TO CHAPTER IX

[1] Letter dated 16 June 1843, N.L.W., MS. 3294 E.

[2] Letters dated 19 June, 5 Aug. 1843, *Commission of Inquiry for South Wales, Evidence*, pp. 254–5.

[3] S. R. P. Wagner, Manareifed, Newcastle Emlyn, to Home Office, 26 Aug. 1843, H.O. 45/454, enclosing two anonymous letters, 3 August, to himself and to his agent.

[4] Notice dated 3 Aug. 1843, signed Charlotte and Lidia; letter, undated, signed Lady Rebecca, in the possession of Sir Grismond Philipps.

[5] Letter to T. Jones, Penrhiw, Henfynyw, Aberaeron, postmarks: Carmarthen 9 Aug. 1843, Lampeter 11 Aug. 1843, in H.O. 45/454.

[6] Notices in Welsh posted on door of public house in Pen-boyr, copies of translation sent by Geo. Rice Trevor to Home Office, 23 Sept. 1843, in H.O. 45/454, and by Col. Love, 24 Sept. 1843, in H.O. 45/453; *Welshman*, 29 Sept. 1843.

[7] Copy of letter addressed to Charles Morgan, Esqʳ, Havodneathin, Carmarthenshire, postmarks: Carmarthen 7 Oct. 1843, Llandilo 8 Oct. 1843, in N.L.W., MS. 3294 E, as above, signed 'F . . G . . R . . S . . M . . J . . B . . L . . Rebecca'.

[8] Letter to F. Kynaston, St. Clears, dated 13 Oct. 1843, Tenby MS.

[9] Ibid., letters to Miss Yelverton and George Wood.

[10] Ibid., letter to Thomas William, Forge, Henllan Amgoed.

[11] Letter to Evans, Solicitor, Newcastle Emlyn, postmark: Cardigan, 20 Sept. 1843, in Lloyd Hall to Home Office, 21 Sept. 1843, H.O. 45/454. Lloyd Hall asserted that the woman, Mrs. Jones, Blaenbedw, was quite able to pay her debts but obstinately refused to do so.

[12] Letter to John Williams, Solicitor, signed 'B.J.G.J.O. Rebecca', in *Welshman*, 29 Sept. 1843.

[13] Indictment of John Jones, Llandingat, for letter sent to Thomas Williams, Auctioneer, Llandovery, 7 Oct. 1843, in Assizes 71/7; *Welshman*, 29 Dec. 1843. (The prisoner was acquitted.)

[14] Indictment of David Jones, Llandingat, for letter dated 14 Oct. 1843, Assizes, 71/7; *Welshman*, loc. cit. I can make no sense of the letter threatening to kill John Trewartha in the indictment of John Hughes and Morgan Walters of Llanfair-ar-y-bryn; Assizes 71/7 and *Welshman*, loc. cit.

[15] Letter to Benjamin Evans, Penyrherber, 15 Oct. 1843; indictment of Bridget Williams, Cenarth, Assizes 71/7; *Welshman*, loc. cit.; (ibid., 5 Jan. 1844, gives sentence as three months).

[16] Letter to Mrs. Sarah Jones, Penrallt-ddu, Llangeler, in Lloyd Hall to Home Office, 12 Sept. 1843, H.O. 45/454.

[17] Indictment of Martha John and William Evans, for letter dated 26 Oct. 1843, Assizes 71/7. The farmer was George Protheroe; *Drysorfa Gynnulleidfaol, Ionawr* 1844.

[18] Anon. letter, 26 Aug. 1843, *Carmarthen Antiquary*, loc. cit., document 13.

[19] Letter sent by clerk of magistrates, Swansea, to Home Office, 25 July 1843, H.O. 45/454.

[20] Examination of Walter David Jones, M.D., Llan-cych, 5 Aug. 1843; handbill (in Welsh) issued by W. D. Jones; W. D. Jones to Home Office, 7 Aug., 19 Sept. 1843, in H.O. 45/454; Col. Love to Home Office, 8 Aug., 12 Aug. 1843, H.O. 45/453; Home Office to Col. Powell, 8 Aug., to G. R. Trevor, 9 Aug., to W. D. Jones, 10 Aug., to Col. Love, 10 Aug. 1843, all in H.O. 41/18; *Commission of Inquiry for South Wales, Evidence,* p. 224.

[21] The incident took place on the night of 29 Aug. 1843. Home Office to Geo. Rice Trevor, 5 Sept. 1843, H.O. 41/18; Geo. Rice Trevor to Home Office, 7 Sept. 1843, H.O. 45/454; Col. Love to Home Office, 13 Sept. 1843, H.O. 45/453; *Welshman,* 1 Sept., 15 Sept. 1843.

[22] Geo. Rice Trevor to Home Office, 13 Sept. 1843, H.O. 45/454; Home Office to Geo. Rice Trevor, 16 Sept. 1843, H.O. 41/18; *Welshman,* 15 Sept. 1843. Edward Adams later changed his name to Edward Abadam.

[23] The incident took place on 21 Sept. 1843. Lloyd Hall to Home Office, 22 Sept., 30 Sept., Capt. J. R. L. Lloyd to Home Office, 25 Sept., Geo. Rice Trevor to Home Office, 1 Oct. 1843, all in H.O. 45/454; Col. Love to Home Office, 23 Sept. 1843, H.O. 45/453; Home Office to Col. Love, 25 Sept., to Capt. Lloyd, 25 Sept., 30 Sept. 1843, H.O. 41/18; *Welshman,* 22 Sept., 29 Sept. 1843. Strange to say, Capt. Lloyd attended the Tre-lech Rebecca meeting on 25 Sept. at which Hugh Williams spoke. According to the writer of reminiscences in *Tarian y Gweithiwr,* 7 Oct. 1866, Rebecca had nothing to do with the incendiarism at Dôl-haidd.

[24] Tenby MS., 23 July 1843.

[25] This occurred on 4 Aug. 1843. Col. Vaughan to Home Office, 8 Aug., Lloyd Hall to Home Office, 12 and 13 Aug., G. S. Wigley to Home Office, 24 Aug., Col. Powell to Home Office, 6 Sept. 1843, all in H.O. 45/454.

[26] Lloyd Hall to Home Office, 26 Aug. 1843, H.O. 45/454.

[27] Tenby MS., 21 Sept. 1843.

[28] Ibid.

[29] *Welshman,* 27 Oct. 1843.

[30] Ibid. The farm was Gwar-y-graig, belonging to Mrs. Nichols, formerly a Davies of Maesycrugiau.

[31] Lloyd Hall to Home Office, 29 July 1843, H.O. 45/454.

[32] Depositions in *West Wales Historical Records,* VII (1917), 33–7; *Welshman,* 22 Dec. 1843. The farmer was Young of High Toch; the shoemaker, William Narbet of Robeston Wathan. The pound-keeper bore the delightful Pembrokeshire name of Merryman.

[33] Tenby MS.

[34] Ibid. The farm was Ffos-grech, Llanfynydd.

[35] The incident took place on the night of 8 Oct. 1843. *Welshman,* 20 Oct. 1843, 5 Jan. 1844; Tenby MS. The bailiffs' nicknames were Ballcourt and John my Maid.

[36] Lloyd Hall to Home Office, 15 Oct. 1843, H.O. 45/454.

[37] Tenby MS.

[38] Geo. Rice Trevor to Home Office, 24 Aug., 30 Aug. 1843, H.O. 45/454; Col. Love to Home Office, 30 Aug. 1843 (enclosing handbill relating to award), H.O. 45/453; Home Office to Geo. Rice Trevor, 26 Aug. 1843, H.O. 41/18; Rees Goring Thomas to William Chambers, 29 Aug., H. R. Edwards to William Chambers, 29 Aug., William Chambers to Rees Goring Thomas, 31 Aug. 1843, *Carmarthen Antiquary*, loc. cit., documents 14, 15, 19; *Welshman*, 1 Sept. 1843. Tobit Evans, op. cit., pp. 149–52, has a fuller account of this incident than Tenby MS. A grandfather clock, formerly the property of John Edwards, which still has shot marks in it, may be seen in Mount Farm, Sylen, Five Roads, Llanelly. I am indebted for information to Mr. D. J. Daniel, Llandre, Five Roads, Llanelly, whose grandmother, a niece of John Edwards, was at Gelliwernen on the night of the attack.

[39] *Welshman*, 4 Aug. 1843; Tenby MS.

[40] *Welshman*, 4 Aug., 8 Dec., 29 Dec. 1843. The accused men were Isaac, Daniel and Thomas Mainwaring and John Powell. See, also, Gomer M. Roberts, *Hanes Plwyf Llandebie*, 1939, p. 191. Tobit Evans, op. cit., p. 148, describes a riot at Crugebolion Common in the parish of Tre-lech, but I have not found any other reference to this. It is not mentioned in Tenby MS.

[41] *Welshman*, 15 Sept. 1843; Lloyd Hall to Home Office, 7 Sept. 1843, H.O. 45/454; several letters from Miss Jane Walters to Home Office in H.O. 45/454 and 45/642, and replies in H.O. 41/18.

[42] *Welshman*, 22 March 1844.

[43] Lloyd Hall to Home Office, 14 Sept. 1843, H.O. 45/454.

[44] Same to same, 7 Oct. 1843, H.O. 45/642.

[45] *Tarian y Gweithiwr*, loc. cit.

[46] W. J. Linton, *Memories*, 1895, p. 89.

[47] John Johnes, *An Address to the Inhabitants of Conwil Gaio*, Llandovery, 1843. This is reproduced, but with some errors, in Tobit Evans, op. cit., pp. 134–9.

[48] Tenby MS.; Christina Phelps, *The Anglo-American Peace Movement*, 1930, pp. 83–4. Tobit Evans, op. cit., pp. 157–8, prints this address, which I have not seen otherwise.

[49] *Tarian y Gweithiwr*, 21 Oct. 1886.

[50] Lloyd Hall to Home Office, 24 Aug., 26 Aug. 1843; W. D. Jones to Home Office, 19 Sept. 1843, H.O. 45/454; W. Edwardes, Sealyham, at Wolfs' Castle meeting, *Welshman*, 8 Sept. 1843.

[51] Lloyd Hall, loc. cit.

[52] Col. Love to Home Office, 23 Sept. 1844; H.O. 45/642.

[53] *Welshman*, 4 Aug., 11 Aug. 1843.

[54] *Welshman*, 11 Aug. 1843, reproducing lengthy article in the *Times*. This is printed in Tobit Evans, op. cit., pp. 117–25, but is very garbled. It is interesting to note that some of the rules are identical with those suggested in a letter to the *Welshman*, 3 Feb. 1843.

[55] *Welshman*, 11 Aug., 18 Aug. 1843, reproducing article in *Times*.

[56] Ibid., 25 Aug. 1843.

[57] Ibid., 18 Aug. 1843.

[58] Ibid., 25 Aug. 1843.

⁵⁹ Ibid., 18 Aug. 1843. Both Tenby MS. and Tobit Evans, op. cit., pp. 144–6, wrongly date this meeting a week later, and this date has been accepted by W. Lloyd Davies, 'Notes on Hugh Williams and the Rebecca Riots', *Bulletin of the Board of Celtic Studies*, XI (1944), 166.

⁶⁰ *Welshman*, 1 Sept. (gives number present as three thousand), 6 Oct. 1843, 8 March, 7 June 1844; *Carmarthen Antiquary*, loc. cit., document 7 (the resolutions); ibid., document 20, Geo. Rice Trevor to William Chambers, 6 Sept. 1843; Address to Inhabitants of Llanelly by William Chambers, 9 Sept. 1843, in H.O. 45/454; ibid., Resolutions (sent by Geo. Rice Trevor); *Hanes Cyfarfod Cyhoeddus gynnaliwyd ar Fynydd Selen, yn mhlwyf Llanelly* [sic] *ar ddydd Gwener, y 25ain o Awst 1843, i'r dyben i ddanfon Deiseb at ei Mawrhydi i ysgafnhau Beichiau y Wlad* (eight-paged pamphlet printed by John Thomas, Priory Street, Carmarthen; this says the crowd started at two thousand but increased to four thousand); *Yr Amserau*, 6 Sept. 1843 (the second number of this weekly); W. J. Linton, loc. cit. Stephan Evans won the prize for an essay 'Hanes Pontyberem' at the Llanelly eisteddfod in 1856; it is printed in *Detholiad o'r Cyfansoddiadau Buddugol yn Eisteddfod Llanelli*, 1857.

⁶¹ *Welshman*, 1 Sept. 1843.

⁶² Lloyd Hall to Home Office, 1 Sept., 8 Sept. 1843, H.O. 45/454. (There seem to have been two meetings presided over by Ed. Lloyd Williams, at the Gogerddan Arms on 30 Aug. and on the beach on 6 Sept.).

⁶³ *Welshman*, 8 Sept. 1843. (The resolutions are reproduced in Tobit Evans, op. cit., pp. 164–6. Readers who, like the writer, have been puzzled by 'The D.V.J. Tax' (ibid., p. 166) will be relieved to know that this is a mis-copying of 'The Dog Tax'.)

⁶⁴ I am greatly indebted to R. C. Sharman, Esq., Archivist, State Library of Tasmania, Hobart, for looking up police records for me. These are remarkably full on all the transported Rebeccaites. See, also, Beili Glas (D. Rhys Phillips), 'Echo of the Rebecca Riots', *Western Mail*, 22 Dec. 1921. Beili Glas had written to the Agent General for Tasmania, 18 Aug., 7 Oct. 1897, but he was confused through thinking that Shoni's name was John Thomas. *Welshman*, 9 Feb. 1844, has some biographical material on both men. *Welshman*, 2 Feb. 1844, states that Col. Wood, M.P. (Brecknockshire), intervened for Shoni because he had acted as a special constable in Brecon during an election. *Cardiff Naturalist Society Transactions*, XXIV (1891–2), 21–6, has some details. See also *Carmarthen Antiquary*, loc. cit., document 61.

⁶⁵ James Brown to William Chambers, junior, Jan. 1844, *Carmarthen Antiquary*, loc. cit., document 63.

⁶⁶ *Western Mail*, 2 Feb. 1942.

⁶⁷ *Welshman*, 10 March 1843.

⁶⁸ *Cambrian*, 13 May 1843; *Welshman*, 26 May 1843.

⁶⁹ References as for Shoni. See also *Carmarthen Journal*, 15 Aug. 1890; *South Wales Daily News*, 26 May 1928. Geo. Rice Trevor to Home Office, 3 Oct. 1843, H.O. 45/454, and reply, 5 Oct. 1843, H.O. 41/18, show that enquiries were made to find whether Dai had taken part in Chartist proceedings; the Home Office had no knowledge that he had done so.

⁷⁰ *Western Mail*, 10 July 1933.

⁷¹ Ibid., 10 Dec. 1926.

⁷² *Welshman*, 8 Dec. 1843, copy of indictment.

[73] *Carmarthen Antiquary*, loc. cit., document 61.

[74] *Welshman*, 8 Dec., 29 Dec. 1843.

[75] *Carmarthen Antiquary*, loc. cit., documents 16, 23, 72; Col. Love to Home Office, 31 Aug. 1843, H.O. 45/453; G. R. Trevor to Home Office, 31 Aug. 1843, J. H. Rees, Cilymaenllwyd to Home Office, 31 Aug. 1843, H.O. 45/454; *Welshman*, 8 Dec. 1843. The house was Gelli-glyd.

[76] *Carmarthen Antiquary*, loc. cit., documents 21, 52, 53 and 54; Col. Love to Home Office, 13 Sept. 1843, H.O. 45/453. The harbour-master was John P. Luckcraft.

[77] Newspaper reports of this riot are confused (as are Tenby MS. and Tobit Evans, op. cit., pp. 167–70, which are identical but for slight verbal differences). The account in the text of the riot and of the trial is based mainly on assize records and official letters: Assize, Indictments, 71/7; Depositions, 72/1; Roll and Indictments, 73/2; Col. Love to Home Office, 7 Sept., 8 Sept., 13 Sept. 1843; Lord James Stuart to Col. Love, 10 Sept. 1843; Geo. Rice Trevor to Home Office, 7 Sept.; J. Attwood to Home Office, 7 Sept., 13 Sept.; Lord James Stuart to Home Office, 12 Sept.; Bute to Home Office, 12 Sept., 27 Dec.; J. T. Jenkins to Geo. Maule, 12 Sept.; Sir James Graham to Bute (draft, also, in Glamorgan Constabulary Day Book), 11 Sept.; Sir James Graham to Maule, 12 Sept. 1843, all in H.O. 45/454; Home Office to Bute, 11 Sept., 20 Sept., 16 Dec. 1843; Home Office to Attwood, 12 Sept.; Home Office to Col. Love, 12 Sept. 1843, all in H.O. 41/18; Dillwyn Diaries (N.L.W.), 6 Sept., 7 Sept. 1843; *Carmarthen Antiquary*, loc. cit., documents 26, 33, 34; *Welshman*, 8 Sept., 15 Sept., 22 Sept., 13 Oct., 20 Oct., 3 Nov., 10 Nov., 24 Nov. 1843, 19 Jan., 26 Jan., 2 Feb., 5 April 1844; *Beccayddiaeth*, Medi 1843 (an apologia in pamphlet form for William Chambers, junior); *Beccayddiaeth*, *Can Newydd yn rhoddi hanes y personau a ddaliwyd*, 1843.

[78] R. J. Nevill, according to Col. Love to Home Office, 7 Sept., H.O. 45/453; William Chambers, junior, according to *Welshman*, 15 Sept. 1843.

[79] Family entries in Welsh Book of Common Prayer in the possession of Mrs. Hughes, Tŷ-isha, Tumble, kindly shown me through the courtesy of the Rev. J. S. Williams. John Hughes's father was Morgan Hugh, born at Clyngwernen, 30 May 1795; his mother, Mary Hugh, was born at Tynyrheol in the parish of Llanelly, 4 June 1796. John Hughes himself was born on 7 Jan. 1819 at Tŷ-isha. There were six younger brothers and sisters. The portrait of John Hughes in Tasmania was lent me by Mrs. Hughes. See letter by D. Ll. G. in *Western Mail*, 24 Dec. 1921. Convict Indents, Vol. 28 (State Library of Tasmania) give his father's name as James, although they agree in all other particulars.

[80] Convict Indents, loc. cit., give his wife's name as Susannah, and name two brothers and five sisters. His parents seem to have been dead.

[81] Ibid. His mother's name is given as Letitia Davis; he had a brother and sisters.

[82] *Carm. Antiq. Soc. Trans.*, loc. cit., letters 16, 17.

[83] *D.N.B.*; Rosamond and Florence Davenport-Hill, *The Recorder of Birmingham. A Memoir of Matthew Davenport Hill*, 1878. (He was the brother of Sir Rowland Hill, of penny postage fame.)

[84] J. Homfray, high sheriff, to Home Office, 9 Oct. 1843, H.O. 45/454. Three jurymen refused to appear and were fined £10, *Welshman*, 3 Nov. 1843.

[85] R. and F. Davenport-Hill, op. cit., p. 223.

[86] Sir James Graham approved the sentence. Sir James Graham to Sir Robert Peel, 31 Oct. 1843, Peel Papers (B.M.), 40,449, folio 172.

[87] 'To the Public generally and to our Neighbours in particular', issued from Cardiff Gaol, 1 Nov. 1843, with the signature of John Hughes and David Jones and the mark of John Hugh, printed in *West Wales Historical Records*, X (1924), 163. The version given in Tobit Evans, op. cit., pp. 206–7, must be a free translation of the Welsh broadside (with strange errors) and not the original English broadside. E. Lewis Evans, *Hanes Pontarddulais*, 1949, p. 48, says that no-one of the prisoners' friends believed the letter to be genuine. This is strange, if true, as two of the prisoners had themselves pleaded guilty.

[88] Earl of Bessborough (ed.), *The Diaries of Lady Charlotte Guest*, 1950, p. 157.

[89] Sir James Graham to Sir Robert Peel, 18 Nov. 1843, Peel Papers, loc. cit., folio 219; Treasury to Home Office, 14 Dec. 1843, H.O. 45/454.

[90] Sir Frederick Pollock to Sir James Graham, 3 Nov. 1843, Peel Papers, loc. cit., folio 210. His son, John Talbot Dillwyn-Llewelyn, became a baronet in 1890.

[91] *Welshman*, 12 Jan. 1844; *Carmarthen Antiquary*, document 55 (evidently notes taken on examination of Shoni) implies that the murderer was Jac y Crydd, shoemaker of Llangennech. Dull is Anglo-Welsh for stupid.

[92] *Welshman*, 15 Sept., 22 Sept., 6 Oct., 17 Nov. 1843; Col. Love to Home Office, 10 Sept., 12 Sept. 1843, H.O. 45/453; Geo. Rice Trevor to Home Office, 10 Sept. 1843, H.O. 45/454; *Carm. Antiq. Soc. Trans.*, loc. cit., letter 13; *Carmarthen Antiquary*, documents 30, 31, 32.

[93] Pont Rhys Bwdwr (Rotten Rees's Bridge); one wonders who Rhys may have been.

[94] The farm was Cynheidre, and the creditor John Bonnel of Felinfoel.

[95] *Welshman*, 8 Dec., 29 Dec. 1843; *Carmarthen Antiquary*, loc. cit., documents 44, 46, 48.

[96] The Stag and Pheasant is now the Five Roads Inn, still known locally as the 'Stack'. Information kindly supplied by D. J. Daniel, Esq., Llandre, Five Roads, Llanelly.

[97] *Carmarthen Antiquary*, loc. cit., documents 48, 50, and 57. Document 50 states that the landlord of the Stag and Pheasant identified Thomas Phillips as the only person who offered £5, but he had got his information from Dai Cilferi. (This is omitted in the printed summary of the document in the *Carmarthen Antiquary*.)

[98] Ibid., documents 59, 61.

[99] Ibid., document 45. (This has an important phrase omitted, an omission which makes nonsense of the account. See *Reports on Education in Wales*, 1847, I, 16.)

[100] Ibid., document 58.

[101] *Welshman*, 8 Dec., 29 Dec. 1843, 15 March, 29 March 1844. The farmer was Thomas Thomas; his home is given as both Llwynypiod and Bremenda.

[102] Ibid., 15 Sept. 1843; *Carmarthen Antiquary*, loc. cit., document 61; Col. Love to Home Office, 11 Sept. 1843, H.O. 45/453; Geo. Rice Trevor to Home Office, 11 Sept. 1843, H.O. 45/454.

[103] *Carmarthen Antiquary*, loc. cit., document 57 (evidence of Dai).

[104] Col. Love to Home Office, 30 Sept. 1843, H.O. 45/453; *Commission of Inquiry for South Wales, Evidence,* p. 130.

[105] *Welshman,* 12 Jan., 19 Jan. 1844 (confessions of Shoni and Dai).

[106] Tenby MS. See also *Commission of Inquiry for South Wales, Evidence,* loc. cit.

[107] *Carmarthen Antiquary,* loc. cit., document 59.

[108] *Welshman,* 8 Dec. 1843.

[109] *Carmarthen Antiquary,* loc. cit., documents 35 and 46; *Welshman,* 6 Oct., 8 Dec. 1843. The authorities had heard a rumour of this attack, Geo. Rice Trevor, 23 Sept. 1843, *Carm. Antiq. Soc. Trans.,* loc. cit., letter 18. In the indictment the works are called the Coalbrook Works. The owner was a man named Newman, and Slocombe lived in his house. The rioters stated that they had no quarrel with Newman, yet Newman was prosecuted two years later for contravening the Truck Act (Col. Love to Home Office, 8 Aug. 1845, H.O. 45/1126). *Carmarthen Antiquary,* loc. cit., document 56, shows that a shopkeeper, named John Williams, tried to hire Dai and the others to terrify a Mr. McDougall from opening a company shop at Trimsaran as this would interfere with his customers.

[110] *Carmarthen Antiquary,* loc. cit., document 35.

[111] Ibid., document 62.

[112] Ibid., loc. cit. (His depositions came later, 12 Dec. 1843, document 45.)

[113] *Welshman,* 6 Oct. 1843; Geo. Rice Trevor to Home Office, 1 Oct., 3 Oct. 1843, H.O. 45/454.

[114] *Carmarthen Antiquary,* loc. cit., document 45.

[115] Letter dated 31 Oct. 1843, in John Innes, *Old Llanelly,* 1902, p. 141.

[116] *Carmarthen Antiquary,* loc. cit., document 61. This is undated, but the statement was taken by the police officer who arrested Dai and Shoni, and was therefore taken before they were placed in Carmarthen Gaol.

[117] Ibid., documents 72, 73, 74.

[118] *Welshman,* 29 Dec. 1843, 1 March 1844.

[119] Home Office to Geo. Rice Trevor, 21 Aug. 1844, H.O. 41/18. A further sum of £35 10s. was spent in the maintenance of witnesses and in procuring information in the case of the Queen versus John Jones, alias Scybor Vawr.

[120] *Welshman,* 29 Dec. 1843, 5 Jan. 1844.

[121] Ibid., 12 Jan., 19 Jan. 1844; *Carmarthen Antiquary,* loc. cit., documents 48, 54, 56, 57, 58, 59.

[122] Sir Ben Bowen Thomas, *Baledi Morgannwg,* 1951, pp. 56–8, prints 'Cân Hiraethlon David Davies (Dai'r Cantwr)'.

[123] In the collection of Mr. D. Rhys Phillips, communicated to me through the courtesy of Mr. D. Myrddin Lloyd.

[124] *Welshman,* 9 Feb. 1844. The third convict was Henry Lewis (ten years' transportation); *Drysorfa Gynnulleidfaol,* Mawrth 1844. I cannot find that he had any association with Rebecca.

[125] *Welshman,* 8 Sept. 1843.

[126] The two gates were Fishguard West and Parcymorfa. Tenby MS. gives the number on Monday night, 11 Sept. 1843, as four hundred to five hundred increasing to one thousand to two thousand; Tobit Evans, op. cit., p. 173, gives two thousand to three thousand. Thomas Richards to Home Office, 13 Sept. 1843, Hugh Owen to Home Office, 20 Sept., 5 Nov. 1843, all in H.O.

45/454; same to same, 14 May 1844, H.O. 45/642; Home Office to Hugh Owen, 14 Sept., 21 Sept., 26 Sept. 1843, 4 June 1844, Home Office to Col. Love, 10 Nov. 1843, Home Office to Thomas Williams, 10 June 1844, all in H.O. 41/18; *Welshman*, 17 Nov. 1843. There is a letter from Home Office in answer to a request for money from a Thomas Williams, Castle Back, Aberystwyth, 11 July 1844, H.O. 41/18, who is probably the informer; if so, he had moved to Aberystwyth.

[127] Waunystradfeiris, Pontarllechau, Carregsawdde, *Welshman*, 15 Sept. 1843. Tenby MS. and Tobit Evans, op. cit., p. 177, give a fourth gate, Pontprenareth.

[128] Not to be confused with Porth-y-rhyd, the home of the 'Lion'.

[129] Tobit Evans, loc. cit., confuses Cil-y-cwm with Cilgerran. *Welshman*, 22 Sept., 13 Oct., 29 Dec. 1843, 22 March 1844; Col. Love to Home Office, 19 Sept., 3 Oct. 1843, H.O. 45/453; Geo. Rice Trevor to Home Office, 3 Oct. 1843, H.O. 45/454; Assizes 71/7.

[130] Handbill, Brecon, 7 Oct. 1843, Thos. Wood, Brecon, to magistrates of the hundred of Builth, 12 Oct. 1843, both in H.O. 45/454; Home Office to magistrates of hundred of Builth, 12 Oct. 1843, H.O. 41/18; *Welshman*, 20 Oct. 1843; *Commission of Inquiry for South Wales, Evidence*, p. 329, states this was the only gate destroyed in Brecknockshire; this is inaccurate, for the gate at Tair Dderwen was destroyed on 19 August 1843.

[131] *Welshman*, 8 Dec. 1843; Assizes 71/7. The only man sentenced was also accused of sending a letter to Evan Powell, Caecryn Mill, Llanfair-ar-y-bryn, threatening to burn down his dwellinghouse.

[132] *Welshman*, 22 Sept., 1 Dec. 1843; W. E. Powell to Home Office, 30 Nov.; A. L. Gwynne to Home Office, 3 Dec. 1843, both in H.O. 45/454; Home Office to W. E. Powell, 2 Dec., 8 Dec. 1843; Home Office to A. L. Gwynne, 4 Dec., 6 Dec. 1843, 13 March, 23 March, 4 April 1844, H.O. 41/18.

[133] Sir John Walsh to Home Office, 26 Sept., Chief Constable of Montgomeryshire to Home Office, 26 Sept. 1843, H.O. 45/454; replies 28 and 30 Sept., H.O. 41/18.

[134] Sir John Walsh to Home Office, 29 Sept., 5 Oct., 7 Oct. 1843, H.O. 45/454; replies 3 Oct., 10 Oct., 11 Oct. 1843, H.O. 41/18. *Welshman*, 6 Oct., 8 Dec. 1843 (reproducing *Times* articles giving a vivid description of Rhayader); *Commission of Inquiry for South Wales, Evidence*, p. 313.

[135] Wm. Chambers to Home Office, 2 Oct. 1843, H.O. 45/454; Col. Love to Home Office, 3 Oct. 1843, H.O. 45/453; Home Office to Wm. Chambers, 4 Oct. 1843, H.O. 41/18, and *Carmarthen Antiquary*, loc. cit., document 41.

[136] *Commission of Inquiry for South Wales, Evidence*, p. 54.

[137] I have been unable to date the sheep stealing and do not know if it occurred before or after the fire.

[138] James Evans was also charged with threatening Thomas Evans, Tyn-y-ffordd, on the same night with fire if he did not give up a farm he had taken. James Evans told him: 'If you transport me for seven years, I'll give you a coat when I come back'. This may sound mysterious to English readers, but 'rhoi cot' in colloquial Welsh is 'to give a thrashing'.

[139] Thomas Thomas's grand-daughter, aged eleven, lived at Pantycerrig during these incidents. She was the grand-mother of Emeritus Professor E. D. T. Jenkins.

¹⁴⁰ *Welshman*, 13 Oct., 20 Oct., 22 Dec. 1843, 5 Jan. 1844; Col. Love to Home Office, 20 Dec., 26 Dec. 1843, H.O. 45/453, 11 Dec. 1844, H.O. 45/642, 22 March 1845, H.O. 45/1126; Geo. Rice Trevor to Home Office, 2 Jan. 1844, H.O. 45/642, 7 June 1845, H.O. 45/1128; Home Office to Col. Love, 30 Dec. 1843, Home Office to Geo. Rice Trevor, 10 June, 12 July, 26 July 1845, all in H.O. 41/18; Assizes 71/7.

NOTES TO CHAPTER X

¹ Lytton Strachey and Roger Fulford (eds.), *The Greville Memoirs*, 1938, V, 135, 138.

² Proclamation, dated 20 Oct. 1843, in Welsh and English in N.L.W.; English version in Tobit Evans, op. cit., pp. 184–5; Home Office to Geo. Rice Trevor, 3 Oct. 1843, and to Sir John Walsh, 7 Oct. 1843, H.O. 41/18; *Welshman*, 6 Oct. 1843.

³ *Welshman*, 29 Sept. 1843, quoting *Times* and *Globe*; Lloyd Hall to Home Office, 30 Sept. 1843, H.O. 45/454.

⁴ Home Office to Geo. Rice Trevor, 18 Sept. 1843, H.O. 41/18.

⁵ Sir Hugh Owen to Home Office, 4 Oct., 7 Oct. 1843, Geo. Rice Trevor to Home Office, 5 Oct. 1843, Sir John Walsh to Home Office, 7 Oct., 8 Oct. 1843, Col. Powell to Home Office, 7 Oct. 1843, all in H.O. 45/454; Home Office to Col. Owen, 6 Oct. 1843, Home Office to duke of Wellington, 6 Oct. 1843, in H.O. 41/18.

⁶ Home Office to lords-lieutenant, Carms., Cards., Pembs., 3 Oct. 1843, H.O. 41/18.

⁷ Ibid., same to same, 16 Oct. 1843; ibid., Home Office to Col. Hankey, 26 Oct. 1843; Pembrokeshire Quarter Sessions Records, 1 Nov. 1843 (Hankey's qualification as magistrate). Treasury to Home Office, 28 Nov. 1843, H.O. 45/454, shows that Hankey was paid 30s. a day.

⁸ Home Office to Geo. Rice Trevor, 28 Sept. 1843, H.O. 41/18.

⁹ *Welshman*, 20 Oct., 10 Nov. 1843.

¹⁰ Home Office to Geo. Rice Trevor, 25 Sept. 1843, H.O. 41/18; Geo. Rice Trevor to William Chambers, 26 Oct. 1843, *Carm. Antiq. Soc. Trans.*, loc. cit., letter 24.

¹¹ Geo. Rice Trevor to Home Office, 13 Nov. 1843, H.O. 45/454; *Welshman*, 17 Nov. 1843. (Home Office to Rev. C. A. Prichard, 29 Sept. 1843, H.O. 41/18, mentions special constables who had come forward voluntarily in the Newcastle Emlyn area.)

¹² Sir James Graham to Sir Robert Peel, 17 Sept. 1843, Peel Papers (B.M.), MS. 40,449, folio 37.

¹³ Ibid., folio 43, same to same, 21 Sept. 1843.

¹⁴ 'These d——d colonels don't curse enough', he told Russell. 'They will never be any good at all till they curse. The brigadiers must curse them and they must curse their captains.'

¹⁵ Peel Papers, folio 69, Graham to Peel, 3 Oct. 1843; Home Office to lords-lieutenant, Carms., Cards., Pembs., 4 Oct., Home Office to Geo. Rice Trevor, 5 Oct., Home Office to General Brown, 9 Oct. 1843, all in H.O.

41/18; Geo. Rice Trevor to Home Office, 7 Oct., 13 Nov. 1843, H.O. 45/454; Col. Love to Home Office, 11 Nov. 1843, H.O. 45/453; *Welshman*, 13 Oct. 1843. (War Office to Home Office, 14 Dec., Treasury to War Office, 23 Dec. 1843, H.O. 45/454, and Home Office to War Office, 26 Dec. 1843, H.O. 41/18, show that Brown was allowed 15s. a day for his special service in South Wales.)

¹⁶ Col. Love to Home Office, 6 Sept. 1843, H.O. 45/453; Admiralty to Home Office, 11 Sept. 1843, H.O. 45/454.

¹⁷ *Welshman*, 20 Oct. 1843 and 16 Feb. 1844, quoting *United Services Gazette*. (It may well be that these units were continually changing.)

¹⁸ Geo. Rice Trevor to Home Office, 6 Sept. 1843, H.O. 45/454; Col. Love to Home Office, 7 Sept., 17 Nov. 1843, H.O. 45/453; Home Office to Col. Love, 8 Sept., 30 Sept. 1843, H.O. 41/18.

¹⁹ *Commission of Inquiry for South Wales, Report*, p. 15.

²⁰ Ibid., *Evidence*, p. 329, lists these nine gates which were removed on 13 Sept.; ibid., *Report*, p. 1, gives the number as seven. See handbill for public meeting at Llangammarch, 18 Oct. 1843, in H.O. 45/454; also *Welshman*, 27 Oct. 1843.

²¹ Col. Love to Home Office, 12 Dec. 1843, H.O. 45/453.

²² *Commission of Inquiry for South Wales, Evidence*, p. 371.

²³ *Welshman*, 21 July 1843.

²⁴ J. Homfray, high sheriff of Glamorgan, to Home Office, 9, 10 and 11 Oct. 1843, H.O. 45/454; *Commission of Inquiry for South Wales, Evidence*, p. 417.

²⁵ Thos. Newcombe, chief constable of Montgomeryshire to Home Office, 11 Oct. 1843; Lord Powis to Home Office, 13 Oct. 1843; J. E. Marsh to Home Office, 16 Oct. 1843, all in H.O. 45/454; Home Office to magistrates acting at Llangurig, 13 Oct. 1843; Home Office to Lord Powis, 14 Oct. 1843, both in H.O. 41/18.

²⁶ On the night of 27 Oct. Thos. Newcombe to Home Office, 19 Oct. 1843; Sir John Walsh to Home Office, 30 and 31 Oct. 1843, all in H.O. 45/454; Home Office to Sir John Walsh, 31 Oct. 1843, H.O. 41/18.

²⁷ Sir John Walsh to Home Office, 3 Nov., 4 Nov. 1843; Richards Banks to Home Office, 9 Nov. 1843, all in H.O. 45/454; Col. Love to Home Office, 11 Nov. 1843, H.O. 45/453; same to same, 8 Aug. 1845, H.O. 45/1126; *Welshman*, 1 Dec., 8 Dec. 1843, 23 Feb. 1844; *Commission of Enquiry for South Wales, Evidence*, p. 313; Tobit Evans, op. cit., pp. 201–5, has the same account as Tenby MS., but with several errors of transcription.

²⁸ Sir John Walsh to Home Office, 31 Dec. 1843, H.O. 45/454; Home Office to Sir John Walsh, 3 Jan. 1844, H.O. 41/18; *Welshman*, 29 Dec. 1843.

²⁹ The gate was destroyed on the night of 23 Jan. 1844. Thos. Newcombe to Home Office, 26 Jan. 1844; Col. Love to Home Office, 27 Jan. 1844; reports of petty sessions at Rhayader, 7 Feb., with correspondence between magistrates and Lord Powis, all in H.O. 45/642; Home Office to Col. Love, 30 Jan. 1844; Home Office to Lord Powis, 7 March 1844, both in H.O. 41/18.

³⁰ Col. Love to Home Office, 8 May 1844, H.O. 45/642; Home Office to Col. Love, 8 May 1844, H.O. 41/18.

³¹ On 12 and 13 Sept., respectively. Col. Love to Home Office, 23 Sept. 1844, H.O. 45/642.

[32] Waunystradferis. My only authorities for this incident are an identical account in Tenby MS. and Tobit Evans, op. cit., p. 215.

[33] The bar was at Plas-bach, near Gwarallt, two miles on the Lampeter side of New Inn. Geo. Rice Trevor to Home Office, 26 Feb. 1844, Col. Love to Home Office, 27 Feb. 1844, both in H.O. 45/642; Home Office to Geo. Rice Trevor, 27 Feb., 2 March 1844; Home Office to Col. Love, 1 March 1844, all in H.O. 41/18; *Welshman*, 1 March 1844.

[34] D. Jenkins to Home Office, 27 March 1844, with depositions of witnesses; Police Inspector Partridge to Col. Love, 29 March 1844; Col. Love to Home Office, 28 March, 30 March 1844; Evidence of J. Daniel, 29 March 1844; Col. Powell to Home Office, 10 May 1844, all in H.O. 45/642; Home Office to D. Jenkins, 29 March 1844; to Col. Love, 1 April, 2 April, 3 April 1844; to mayor of Cardigan, 6 April 1844; to Col. Powell, 1 May, 13 May 1844, all in H.O. 41/18; *Welshman*, 19 March 1844.

[35] Pembrokeshire Summer Assizes, 71/8, trial of John Llewellin, who pleaded guilty but was discharged on his own recognisances to appear when called upon; *Welshman*, 26 July 1844.

[36] Lloyd Hall to Home Office, 19 Aug., 20 Aug., 21 Sept., 6 Oct. 1843, H.O. 45/454.

[37] *Welshman*, 29 Dec. 1843, fines *re* Prendergast Gate.

[38] Geo. Rice Trevor to Home Office, 24 Oct. 1843, H.O. 45/454.

[39] Col. Love to Home Office, 20 Dec. 1843, H.O. 45/453; Col. Hankey to Home Office, 19 Dec. 1843; Col. Hankey to Col. Owen, 20 Dec. 1843; Col. Owen to Home Office, 21 Dec. 1843, all in H.O. 45/454; Col. Owen to Home Office, 5 May 1844; Col. Love to Home Office, 4 July 1844, both in H.O. 45/642; Home Office to Col. Hankey, 21 Dec. 1843, to Col. Owen, 23 Dec. 1843, to Col. Love, 26 Dec. 1843, to Col. Owen, 18 May 1844, all in H.O. 41/18; Graham to Peel, 21 Dec. 1843, B.M., MSS. 40,449, folio 273; *Welshman*, 22 Dec. 1843. The vicar was the Rev. J. W. James; he resigned his seat on the bench because of the outrage.

[40] Home Office to Geo. Rice Trevor, 2 Jan. 1844, H.O. 41/18; Trevor to Home Office, 7 Jan. 1844, H.O. 45/642; Trevor to Wm. Chambers, 10 Jan. 1844, *Carm. Antiq. Soc. Trans.*, LVI (1932), letter 32.

[41] Geo. Rice Trevor to Home Office, 22 Aug. 1843, H.O. 45/454; Geo. Rice Trevor to Wm. Chambers, junior, 22 Aug. 1843, *Carm. Antiq. Soc. Trans.*, loc. cit., letter 9.

[42] The six parishes were Llanarthney, Llandybie, Llangunnor, Llanfihangel-Aberbythych, Bettws and Llanedy. The chairman was John Morgan of Glan-yr-ynys in the parish of Llanddarog, a considerable farmer. (I am indebted for information about him to Mr. Michael Owen of Coventry.) Col. Love to Home Office, 15 Sept. 1843, H.O. 45/453; *Welshman*, 15 Sept. 1843; *Carmarthen Antiquary*, document 34 (William Chambers, junior's, letter to Hugh Williams, to be read at the meeting); Tenby MS.; Tobit Evans, op. cit., pp. 174–5.

[43] *Welshman*, 15 Sept. 1843.

[44] Ibid., 29 Sept. 1843. The parishes which sponsored the petition were Llanguicke, Llangadog, Llandeilo and Bettws. The meeting thanked the *Times* for its reports.

[45] The parishes represented were Tre-lech, Aber-nant, Cilrhedyn and Llanwinnio. The petition was explained in Welsh by 'Mr. Anthony of Carmarthen, a working man', possibly 'Anthony the Socialist' of an earlier chapter. The case of a squatter, who had had his habitation on Clawdd-coch Common destroyed within a few days of erecting it, was discussed. This is the only instance of sympathy for a squatter which I have found. *Welshman*, 29 Sept. 1843; *Bulletin of the Board of Celtic Studies*, XI (1944), 166.

[46] The parishes petitioning were Llandyfaelog, St. Ishmael, Llanstephan, Llan-gain, Pembrey and the borough of Kidwelly. Anthony addressed this meeting also. *Welshman*, 29 Sept. 1843; Col. Love to Home Office, 29 Sept. 1843, H.O. 45/453.

[47] *Welshman*, 6 Oct., 17 Nov. 1843.

[48] Ibid., 6 Oct. 1843. The Chairman was William Lewis of Clynfyw.

[49] Ibid., loc. cit.

[50] *Commission of Inquiry for South Wales, Evidence*, p. 133.

[51] Thos. Jenkins to Home Office, 10 Oct. 1843, Lloyd Hall to Home Office, 10 Oct. 1843, both in H.O. 45/454; handbill of public meeting to be held at Llechryd, 9 Oct. 1843, in H.O. 45/642; Home Office to Thos. Jenkins, 13 Oct. 1843, H.O. 41/18; *Welshman*, 13 Oct. 1843.

[52] *Welshman*, 14 Oct. 1843 (four and a half columns).

[53] Ibid., 20 Oct. 1843. I have not been able to ascertain the precise date of this meeting. Mynydd Pysgodlyn is some four to five miles up the river Dulais from Pontarddulais.

[54] Ibid., 3 Nov. 1843; ibid., 16 Feb. 1844, has a letter from Thomas Duncombe, M.P., to Thomas Emlyn Thomas, enclosing a letter from the Home Office to the effect that Sir James Graham had laid the petition before the queen. See *Commission of Inquiry for South Wales, Evidence*, p. 44, and especially pp. 53–60, the evidence of John Rees, Pantstod, Llanarth.

[55] Carmarthen County Hall, Main Trust, Miscellaneous MSS.; Main Trust Order Book, 18 Sept., 6 Oct. 1843; *Welshman*, 8 Sept., 6 Oct., 13 Oct. 1843.

[56] Ibid., 11 Aug., 29 Sept. 1843; *Carmarthen Antiquary*, loc. cit., document 39.

[57] Ibid., document 1; *Welshman*, 11 Aug. 1843.

[58] Ibid., 27 Oct. 1843.

[59] *Welshman*, 7 July, 11 Aug., 1 Sept., 15 Sept., 22 Sept. 1843; Aberystwyth Turnpike Trust Order Book, 1827–45 (N.L.W.), 26 Aug. 1843; Handbill for meeting of 26 Aug. 1843, in H.O. 45/454; ibid., Lloyd Hall to Home Office, 13 Sept. 1843 and Col. Powell to Home Office, 21 Sept. 1843.

[60] *Welshman*, 22 Sept. 1843, reproducing *Times* article.

[61] Geo. Rice Trevor to Home Office, 29 Aug. 1843, H.O. 45/454.

[62] Ibid., same to same, 4 Sept. 1843.

[63] Sir Robert Peel to Sir James Graham, 1 Sept. 1843, B.M. Add. MS. 40,449, folio 11.

[64] Ibid., folio 19, Sir James Graham to Sir Robert Peel, 4 Sept. 1843.

[65] Home Office to lords-lieutenant of Carms., Cards., and Pembs., 15 Sept. 1843, H.O. 41/18. I have entirely failed to trace Hall's report. I have searched through the Peel Papers in the British Museum as well as the Home Office papers and the Treasury Solicitors' papers in the Public Record Office.

[66] Geo. Rice Trevor to Home Office, 19 Sept. 1843, H.O. 45/454.

[67] Geo. H. Ellis to Home Office, 2 Nov. 1843, H.O. 45/454, a document of forty-nine pages. It is endorsed 'Copy sent confidentially to the Rt. Hon. Frankland Lewis'. This copy is now in N.L.W. See my 'A Report on the Turnpike Trusts', *National Library of Wales Journal*, VIII (1953), 171–5; also H.O. 74/1.

[68] *Welshman*, 13 Oct. 1843.

[69] The senior memoer of his family at the present day is his great-great-grandson, the earl of Plymouth.

[70] Lewis at first objected to him for some reason. Graham to Peel, 16 Sept. 1843, B.M. Add. MS. 40,449, folio 35.

[71] Ibid., folio 19, same to same, 4 Sept. 1843.

[72] They were allowed two guineas a day for personal expenses, in addition to conveyance and the salary of a clerk. Home Office to Lewis, Clive, Cripps, 13 Oct. 1843, all in H.O. 74/1.

[73] Various letters, Home Office to Rickards in H.O. 74/1. He was paid £700 for his own and his clerk's salary and to pay certain bills, and also £100 for his services after return to London.

[74] H.O. to Lewis, Clive, Cripps, 11 Oct. 1843, H.O. 74/1; draft in H.O. 45/454; *Commission of Inquiry for South Wales, Report*, p. iii.

[75] Ibid., *Evidence*, pp. 136, 226, 261.

[76] *Welshman*, 3 Nov. 1843.

[77] Ibid., 1 Dec. 1843.

[78] *Commission of Inquiry for South Wales, Evidence*, pp. 111–2; Tobit Evans, op. cit., pp. 208–12, with the usual number of errors in transcription.

[79] *Welshman*, 3 Nov. 1843; *Evidence*, pp. 73–8, the evidence of Capt. Lewis Evans.

[80] Ibid., pp. 162, 184–5.

[81] Ibid., p. 201; *Welshman*, 10 Nov. 1843.

[82] Ibid., 24 Nov. 1843; *Evidence*, p. 213; Haverfordwest (Williams and Williams) MS. 26,952, gives a list of grievances.

[83] *Welshman*, 17 Nov. 1843.

[84] Ibid., loc. cit. The parishes were Eglwyswrw, Llantood, Meline, Llanfair Nant-gwyn, Bridell and Whitechurch.

[85] Ibid., 24 Nov. 1843. The parishes were Llannarth, Llandisilio Gogo, Llanllwchaiarn, Llandysul, Dihewyd, Ciliau Aeron, Llanina, Llannerch-aeron, Llanddewi, Henfynyw.

[86] *Evidence*, pp. 270–1.

[87] Ibid., p. 295.

[88] Ibid., pp. 351–2.

[89] Ibid., p. 355.

[90] *Welshman*, 22 Dec. 1843, reproducing *Times* article.

[91] *Evidence*, p. 351.

[92] His evidence is given in *Evidence*, pp. 85–6.

[93] *Report of the Commission of Inquiry for South Wales*, 1844, *Evidence*, pp. 1–440, with twenty-eight pages of appendices. Unfortunately the *Report* and the *Evidence* are separately paged, making reference to them somewhat cumbersome.

[94] Col. Love to Home Office, 30 March 1844, H.O. 45/642.

[95] *Welshman*, 22 March 1844.

24

⁹⁶ Three manuscripts, which are the drafts of the sections on the poor law, clerks' fees, and the county rate, and which are in the hand of William Cripps, were deposited by his grandson, Sir Frederick Cripps, in the National Library of Wales, 24 November 1941.

⁹⁷ *Welshman*, 29 March 1844, reproducing *Times* article.

⁹⁸ Ibid., 17 May 1844. Col. Wood (M.P. for Brecknockshire) had, on 26 March, introduced a bill to exempt lime from toll which he now withdrew.

⁹⁹ *Commons Journal*, XCIX (1844), 489. There were also petitions from Boughrood Bridge Co., the magistrates of Brecon and of Llandeilo, the clerks to certain trusts, and the creditors of the Llandovery Suspension Bridge, but no information was submitted in respect of any of these petitions, ibid., pp. 525, 536. There is lengthy correspondence between Thomas Frankland Lewis and Penry Williams relating to the administration of the roads of Brecknockshire in Penpont MS. 2553 (N.L.W.).

¹⁰⁰ *Welshman*, 2 Aug. 1844.

¹⁰¹ *Archaeologia Cambrensis*, 1861, pp. 80–1 (obituary of Lord Cawdor); *Report of Commissioners on Municipal Corporations*, 1880, II, 690.

¹⁰² *Welshman*, loc. cit.

¹⁰³ See *Commons Journal*, XCIX (1844), 512, for the advance of £225,000.

¹⁰⁴ Not fifty years as recommended in the *Report*.

¹⁰⁵ There was a suggestion that these boards should be popularly elected. Geo. Rice Trevor to W. Chambers, 13 July 1844, *Carm. Antiq. Soc. Trans.*, loc. cit., letter 41.

¹⁰⁶ 7–8 Vict. c. xci. Amending acts were passed: 8–9 Vict. c. lxi (1845); 10–11 Vict. c. lxii (1847); 14–15 Vict. c. xvi (1851); 23–24 Vict. c. lxviii (1860); 38–39 Vict. c. xxv (1875); 41–42 Vict. c. xxiv (1878); 44 Vict. c. xiv (1881).

¹⁰⁷ Graham to Peel, 5 Aug. 1844, B.M., MS. 40,450, folio 87.

¹⁰⁸ T. F. Lewis to Home Office, 12 Sept. 1844, H.O. 45/454.

¹⁰⁹ Treasury to Home Office, 12 Sept. 1844, H.O. 45/454.

¹¹⁰ The Llangurig trustees appealed against the inadequacy of their award: Memorial to Home Office, 30 April 1845, H.O. 45/454. There was also an appeal in respect of the New Mill Trust in Glamorgan: Arthur E. Somerset to Home Office, 31 May 1845, H.O. 45/454. The umpire in the first case was was J. S. Pakington, M.P., and in the latter, Nassau Senior. In both cases the umpire confirmed the award.

¹¹¹ Form of Award in the Matter of the Turnpike Trusts, 13 Jan. 1845, H.O. 45/454B. For this see Chapter VI above. The report (without the award) is printed as 'Final Report of the Commissioners for the Consolidation of the Turnpike Trusts in South Wales, 29 Sept. 1845', in *Parliamentary Papers*, 1849 (105), LXVI, 355, a report of four pages. Supplementary awards were made on 26 March and 6 Sept. 1845; see also letter from the three commissioners to Home Office, 7 Oct. 1845, all in H.O. 45/454B. For precise sums in respect of every trust, see also Pembrokeshire County Roads Board Guard Book (a volume of MS. letters, resolutions, printed handbills, etc., in Pembrokeshire County Library, Haverfordwest; information conveyed to me by courtesy of the County Librarian, Mr. G. A. Dickman).

[112] For the work of the roads boards see Guard Book referred to in the previous note; also Cardiganshire County Roads Board Minute Book in N.L.W., and MS. in County Hall, Carmarthen. See Regina *v* Wiston (1845) relating to the repair of a road, Haverfordwest (Williams and Williams) Deeds and Documents (N.L.W.), 19476, forty-six papers. There are various documents for 1847 and 1848 relating to the interpretation and administration of the act of 1844 in H.O. 45/1809.

[113] Treasury to Home Office, 17 Dec. 1844, H.O. 45/454. He was given a salary of £500 a year in addition to his pay as officer in the Engineers. See Col. Love to Home Office, 2 Dec. 1846, H.O. 45/1431, for working of roads boards and the services of Capt. Harness.

[114] He gets two columns in *D.N.B.*

[115] For the finances of the board see printed 'Statement of Receipt and Expenditures on the Turnpike Roads of South Wales', in *Parliamentary Accounts and Papers*, annually.

[116] Petition, 13 Dec. 1843 (seventy-two signatories) and correspondence relating to it, in H.O. 45/453.

[117] Several letters in H.O. 45/454 and 45/642.

[118] Geo. Rice Trevor to Home Office, 26 Aug. 1843, H.O. 45/454; Col. Love to Home Office, 7 Sept. 1843, H.O. 45/453.

[119] There are numerous letters on this subject in H.O. 45/453, 45/454 and 41/18.

[120] Geo. Rice Trevor to Home Office, 12 April 1844, H.O. 45/642; Home Office to Col. Owen, 8 July 1844, H.O. 41/18.

[121] Home Office to Col. Love, 24 Oct. 1844, H.O. 41/18.

[122] This is made clear in a ruling given in Home Office to Col. Considine, 20 Jan. 1840, H.O. 41/15.

[123] *Welshman*, 18 Aug. 1843.

[124] *Commission of Inquiry for South Wales, Evidence*, p. 347.

[125] *Welshman*, 8 March 1844, gives itemised expenditure in respect of twenty-three toll-houses; ibid., 15 March 1844, gives total of this expenditure for three months as £524. Pembrokeshire Quarter Sessions Minute Book (N.L.W.), 2 Jan. 1844, authorises payment of £151 4s. 8d. in respect of the Fishguard gates and toll-houses.

[126] Geo. Rice Trevor to Home Office, 19 Oct. 1843, H.O. 45/454, including resolution and estimate of Carmarthenshire Quarter Sessions of that date.

[127] Home Office to Col. Love, 21 Nov. 1843, H.O. 41/18.

[128] Col. Love to Home Office, 18 Nov. 1843, H.O. 45/453.

[129] Geo. Rice Trevor to William Chambers, 23 Feb. 1844, *Carmarthen Antiquary*, loc. cit., letter 66; Home Office to Geo. Rice Trevor, 12 Feb., 6 March, 14 March 1844, H.O. 41/18; Treasury Solicitor to Geo. Rice Trevor, 27 Jan., 19 April, 22 July 1844, T 2/44.

[130] Geo. Rice Trevor to Home Office, 7 June 1845, H.O. 45/1128, deals with these matters in detail. See also Home Office to Geo. Rice Trevor, 10 June, 12 July, 26 July 1845, H.O. 41/18. Rewards in respect of Pantycerrig were: Margaret Bowen, £25; Margaret Thomas, £15; John Rowlands, £5; Geo. Thomas, £5; but Margaret Bowen (the servant girl) was given an additional gratuity of £25, making £50 in all. In respect of the convict's arrest, the following awards were made: Thomas Evans, £30; Daniel Howells, £30;

Geo. Thomas, £17 10s.; — Davies, £17 10s.; Thomas Lewis, £5. This correspondence also gives rewards in respect of Henry Evans, convicted of riot at Llanegwad: John Davies (prosecutor), £30; Susan Davies, his wife, £10; Methusalem Jones, police officer, £5; Evan Davies, police officer, £5.

131 Home Office to Col. Owen, 4 June 1844, H.O. 41/18.

132 Home Office to Swansea magistrates, 10 July 1844, H.O. 41/18; see ibid., same to same, 30 July 1844, for refusal of rewards to Glamorgan county police in respect of Pontarddulais.

133 *Welshman*, 8 March 1844; *Drysorfa Gynnulleidfaol*, Ebrill 1844. *Welshman*, loc. cit., states that he had himself been tried for obtaining money by false pretences, but had escaped because of a flaw in the indictment.

Since the completion of this book an article has appeared by Mr. J. F. Jones, curator of the County Museum, Carmarthen, entitled 'The Passing of Rebecca', *Welshman*, 7 Jan. 1955. This gives a digest of five letters from claimants for awards, namely William Francis (who arrested Shoni); James Banning, of the New Barley Mow, Llanelly (who had assisted in the arrest); a letter in respect of Griffith Jones, who had supplied information with regard to an attack on Pontarllechau; Daniel Lloyd, who identified one of the rioters at Llandeilo Rwnws on 7 July 1843; and Inspector Tierney on his own behalf and on behalf of the metropolitan policemen. Mr. Jones states that the schedule of awards indicates that a total of £1,400 was distributed, of which £335 went to the police and the remainder to civilian informers and assistants, among them £150 to William Francis and his workmen, and £30 to Daniel Lloyd.

134 *Welshman*, 10 Nov. 1843, 19 Jan., 26 Jan., 2 Feb. 1844.

135 Ibid., 2 Feb., 9 Feb. 1844.

136 James Brown, of Cwm Celyn and Blaina Ironworks, Abergavenny, to William Chambers, junior, Jan. 1844, *Carmarthen Antiquary*, loc. cit., document 63.

137 The details which follow, except where otherwise stated, are drawn from police records, kindly communicated to me by R. C. Sharman, Esq., archivist, State Library of Tasmania, Hobart.

138 This, together with the photograph of John Hughes in Tasmania, are in the possession of Mrs. Hughes, Tŷ-isha, Llan-non, and were communicated to me through the courtesy of the Rev. J. S. Williams. I am indebted to Mrs. Hughes for permission to reproduce the photograph.

139 *Launceston Examiner*, 19 Oct. 1867.

140 *Western Mail*, 24 Dec. 1921.

141 Capt. Scott to R. J. Nevill, 26 April, 30 April 1848, Nevill MSS. (N.L.W.), 1165–6.

142 A ballad 'Yn ngwlad y Negro Du' is attributed to him, but would anyone living in Tasmania call it 'The land of the black negro'? There is a 'Can Cwynfanus' and a 'Trydedd Gân', said to be by Dai'r Cantwr, in Gaianydd Williams Collection (Cardiff Public Library), II, 69, 107. Another is said to have been published in *Merthyr Guardian*, 1853. See *Western Mail*, 30 Dec. 1921; D. Rhys Phillips, *Journal of the Welsh Bibliographical Society*, 1941, p. 264; Sir Ben Bowen Thomas, *Baledi Morgannwg*, 1951, p. 117.

143 Superintendent of police, Ross, to Beili Glas (D. Rhys Phillips), 13 Oct. 1897, Beili Glas in 'Echo of the Rebecca Riots', *Western Mail*, 22 Dec. 1921.

[144] See digest of various letters in W. Lloyd Davies, 'Notes on Hugh Williams and the Rebecca Riots', *Bulletin of the Board of Celtic Studies*, XI (1944), 163–5, for this paragraph.

[145] For this correspondence, see Chapter II above. It constitutes H.O. 45/1811. See also Col. Love to Home Office, 6 Jan. 1846 (an error for 1847), H.O. 45/1431.

[146] Col. Love, loc. cit.; see Chapter V, note 183, above.

[147] Cobden papers (unscheduled) in British Museum.

[148] P. W. Gates, *The Illinois Central Railroad and its Colonisation Work*, Harvard, 1934.

[149] E. H. Cawley, *The American Diaries of Richard Cobden*, Princeton, 1952, p. 195. Hugh Williams arrived in New York on 23 May 1859.

[150] Hugh Williams, from Astor House, New York, to Samuel Roberts in Tennessee, 25 May 1859, N.L.W., MS. 13,197C. Williams states in this letter that he was returning to Wales in Sept. 1859. See also Samuel Roberts, from Conway, to James Nicholas, Gomer, Ohio, Jan. 1879. I have to thank Professor Wilbur S. Shepperson for drawing my attention to these letters.

[151] Gildas, *St. Clears Past and Present*, 1888, p. 10.

[152] T. I. Jeffreys Jones, 'The Court Leet Presentments of St. Clears', *Bulletin of the Board of Celtic Studies*, XIII (1948), 35.

[153] Death certificate of Anne Williams, 9 August 1861. Sub-district of St. Clears.

[154] Marriage certificate of Hugh Williams and Elizabeth Anthony, 9 Oct. 1861. District of Clifton.

[155] Tombstone in St. Ishmaels' Church gives her age as seventy-five when she died, 25 Feb. 1909.

[156] Hugh Peter Marcus, died 30 July 1862, aged six weeks; Hugh Peter Dafydd, died 2 June 1863, aged four weeks; Hugh Dafydd Anthony, born 28 May 1869, died in London, 15 May 1905 (his son is Hugh Williams, the celebrated West End actor); William Arthur Glanmor, born 19 Sept. 1873, educated at Clifton and Sandhurst, commissioned in the South Wales Borderers, awarded D.S.O. for service in West Africa, killed in action in Bothaville, South Africa, 8 Nov. 1900 (for his obituary, see *Welsh Gazette*, 15 Nov. 1900).

[157] The Garthe Estate. Particulars of Sale, 13 Oct. 1869. I have to thank Mr. Caleb Rees for giving me a copy of this document and also for the portrait of Hugh Williams here reproduced.

[158] Elwyn Evans, 'Nassau Senior in Wales', *National Library of Wales Journal*, VII (1951), 76.

INDEX

Aberaeron, 115, 215, 229, 235, 267.
Aberafon, 229.
Abergwili, 140, 155, 177, 198.
Aber-nant, 135, 142, 202, 204, 206.
Aber-porth, 236.
Aberystwyth, 5, 21, 43, 44, 88, 99, 100, 115, 130, 153, 164, 167, 211, 262, 269, 278, 283, see Workhouses.
Acreage returns (1801) 72, 73, 104.
Acts,
    Civil Registration (1836) 126; Corporation (repeal of, 1828) 126; Dissenters' Marriage (1836) 126; General Turnpike (1822) 178; Highways (1555) 159; Highways (1835) 159, 173, 180; Municipal Corporations (1835) 44, 45, 46, 100, 183; Poor Law Amendment (1834) 38, 136, 137, 138, 141, 144, 180, 210; Reform (1832) 16, 21, 22, 24, 26, 30, 44, 66, 126, 138, 149; Test (repeal of, 1828) 126; Tithe Commutation (1836) 132, 136; Turnpike Trusts, South Wales (1844) 281, 291; Union of England and Wales (1536) 12, 19.
Adams, Edward (Abadam) 237.
Address to the Inhabitants of Conwil Gaio, 120, 242.
Adpar, 14, 21, 22, 44, 183.
Advowsons, 6.
Agents, land, 31, 42, 68, 226, 235.
Agrarian movement, 106, 190, 244.
Agricultural implements, 67, 74–5.
Agricultural labourers, 74–5, 107, 108, 109, 172, 243; wages, 103, 108, 109–10.
Agricultural Revolution, 15, 69.
Agricultural societies, 15, 70–1, 85.
Agriculture, 68–77, 85, 90, 96, 104, 107.
Agriculture, Board of (1793) 64; Reports: Cardiganshire, 14, 64; Carmarthenshire, 64, 70, 71; Pembrokeshire, 64, 70, 132; South Wales, 66, 74.
Albany Chapel, 171.
Allt Cunedda, 273, 290.
Alltyrodyn, 65, 199.

Amman river, 165.
Amserau, Yr, 154.
Andover, 146.
Anglicisation of the gentry, see Gentry.
Anthony, Walter, 156.
Arches, Court of, 128.
Artillery, 214.
Assizes,
    Brecknockshire, 30; Cardiff (Special Commission) 152, 223, 251; Cardiganshire, Summer 1843, 227; Carmarthenshire, Summer 1843, 208, Winter 1843, 215, 230, 232, 240, 257, 259, 264, Spring 1844, 204, 208, 241, 255, 259, Summer 1844, 199, 224; Glamorganshire, Spring 1844, 223, 230; Pembrokeshire, Spring 1840, 188, Summer 1843, 57, Winter 1843, 238, 271, Spring 1844, 41, 233, 259.
Atlas, The, 222.
Aubrey, John, 72.
Auctions, mock, 55.

Bacon, Anthony, 4.
Bailiffs, 238, 254.
Bala magistrates, strike of, 34–5.
Ballot, 15, 31, 125, 149, 217, 279.
Bangor Teify, 241.
Banks, 18, 111, 113–14, 133; Aberystwyth and Tregaron (Y Ddafad Ddu) 113; Aberystwyth (Y Llong) 113; Carmarthen, Messrs. Morris, 27; Carmarthen, Waters, Jones and Co., 113; Haverfordwest, Nathaniel Phillips, 113, 173; Haverfordwest, Union, 113.
Baptist (denomination) 125–6, 247.
Bastardy, see Illegitimacy.
Beaufort, duke of, 48.
Begelly, 81, 278.
Bidding, 94, 140.
Birth rate, 93.
Black Mountain, 1, 52, 76, 165, 230, 270, 272.
Blackpool, 225.
Blackwood's Magazine, 155.
Blaen-y-coed, 202, 203, 206.

Foster, Thomas Campbell,
sent to South Wales, 40, 210; on
rents, 105; on tithe, 133–4; on
poor law, 144; on Nonconformity,
155, 211; on turnpike trusts, 183,
275; on Pontarddulais riot, 251;
attends secret meetings, 226–7,
242, 244; attends demonstrations,
244, 245; accompanies Commission of Inquiry, 278, 279;
presentation to, 211; in Ireland,
211; see *Times, The.*
Freehold, see Tenure, land.
Freeman, Captain (Cardiganshire
police) 61.
Freemasonry, 156.
French invasion (1797) 5, 7, 188.
Friendly societies, 156–7.
Furnace (Llanelly) 229.

Game, 18;
gamekeepers, 42, 235, 238, 239;
game-laws, 42–3.
Garreg, 194, 196.
Gate-keepers, 120, 176, 188, 198,
253, 260.
Gates,
Aberaeron, 229; Aberafon, 229;
Abergwili, 177; Adpar (see Newcastle Emlyn); Bolgoed, 221, 223;
Botalog, 269; Bronfelen, 223;
Builth, 270; Burton, 230; Bwlch-
y-clawdd, 196, 199, 200, 231;
Bwlch-y-domen, 196; Canaston
Bridge, 223; Cardigan, 183, 215,
223, 270; Carmarthen, 183, 198,
200, 202, 204, 224, 231; Carreg
Sawdde (see Llangadog); Castell
Rhingyll, 214; Cefn Llanddewi,
259; Cenarth, 224; Croes-faen,
269; Croeslwyd (see Carmarthen); Dolauhirion, 259; Dryslwyn, 214; Efail-wen, 55, 76, 116,
149, 167, 180, 187, 188–9, 191;
Felindre Siencyn, 198; Fishguard,
196, 215, 233, 258; Foelycastell,
231; Furnace (see Llanelly);
Garreg, 194, 196, 221; Glangwili,
231–2; Glasbury, 270; Gwarallt,
223, 270; Haverfordwest, 183,
193, 196, 232–3, 258; Hendy,
249, 253; Kidwelly, 221; Lampeter, 228, 233; Llanddarog, 196,
214, 224; Llandeilo, 230, 243–4;
Llandeilo Rwnws, 198, 223;
Llanelly, 178, 229, 262; Llan-

Gates *(continued)*
fihangel-ar-arth, 199; Llangadog,
215, 224, 259, 270; Llangurig,
262, 270; Llanidloes, 270; Llan-
non (Cards.) 260; Llantrisant,
269; Maes-gwyn, 116, 187;
Meinciau, 221, 224; Mermaid
(see St. Clears); Nant-y-clawdd,
196; Narberth, 195, 224; Newbridge-on-Wye, 269; Newcastle
Emlyn, 198, 199, 214, 224; New
Inn, 229; Parcymorfa (see Fishguard); Penllwyni, 198; Pentre-
bach, 260; Pen-y-garn, 215, 224,
231; Plaindealings (see Narberth); Pontarddulais, 249; Pontarllechau, 230; Pont-tyweli, 196,
199, 223; Pontyates, 221; Porth-
y-rhyd, 224, 225, 230, 248;
Porth-y-rhyd (near Llandovery)
259; Poundffald, 224; Prendergast (see Haverfordwest); Pumsaint, 223; Pwll-trap, 190–1, 195;
Redstone (see Narberth);
Rhayader, 178, 262, 269–70;
Rhydypandy, 221, 223; Robeston
Wathan, 195; St. Clears, 190–1,
196; St. Harmons (see
Rhayader); Sandy (see Llanelly); Scleddy (see Fishguard);
Spudders Bridge, 254, 257; Steynton, 270; Tair Derwen, 231; Tir-
f:an (see Llanelly); Tonyrefail,
268; Tŷ-coch, 230; Tŷ-gwyn (see
Carmarthen); Trevaughan, 191,
193, 194, 196, 231; Troedrhiwgribyn, 196; Tumble, 226; Walk
(see Llandeilo); Water Street
(see Carmarthen); Ystradfeiric
(see Llangadog).
Gelligylwnog, 255, 257.
Gelliwernen, 239, 244, 245.
Gentry,
anglicisation, 17, 34, 68, 124;
non-residence, 17, 34, 36, 68, 70.
Geographical limits of rioting, 174,
260, 268–9.
Glamorgan, 1, 92, 116, 158, 181,
214, 219, 221, 222, 229, 258, 269,
280;
Vale of, 160, 248.
Glangwili, 231–2.
Glanmedenny, 240.
Glasbury, 270.
Gloucester, 87, 160, 181.

Index

25